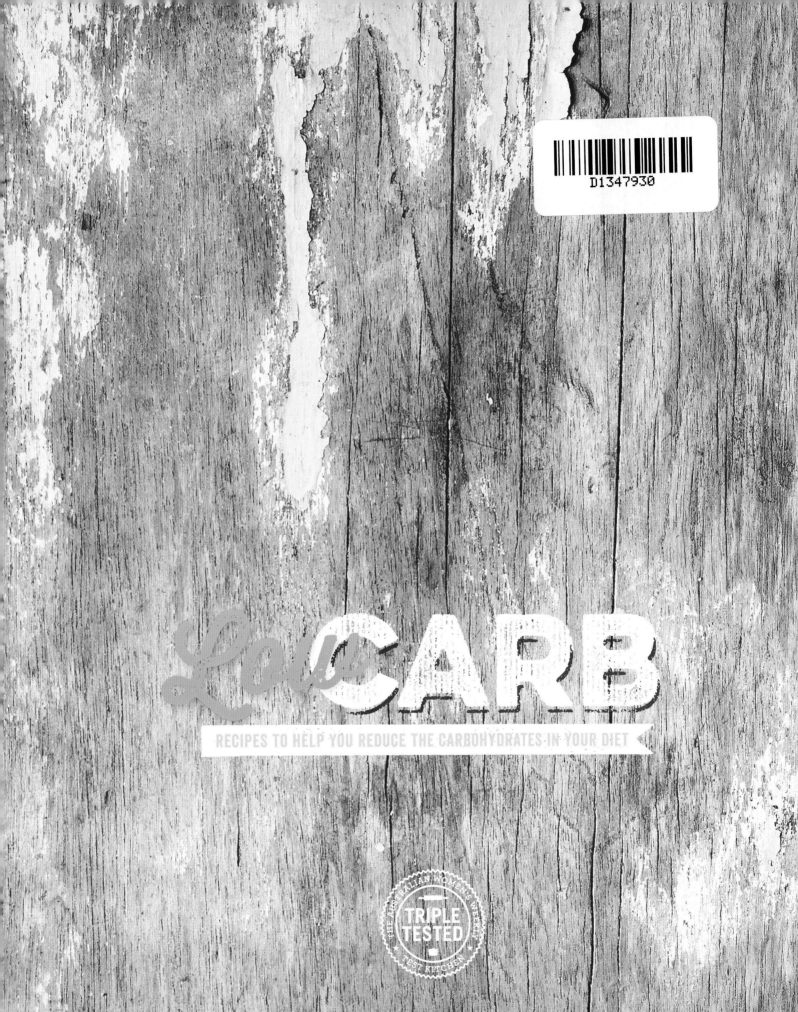

Low CARB

RECIPES TO HELP YOU REDUCE THE CARBOHYDRATES IN YOUR DIET

BAUER
MEDIA GROUP

First published in 2016 by Bounty Books based on materials licensed to it by Bauer Media Books, Australia. Reprinted in 2016.

Bauer Media Books are published by
Bauer Media Pty Limited
54 Park St, Sydney; GPO Box 4088,
Sydney, NSW 2001 Australia
phone +61 2 9282 8618; fax +61 2 9126 3702
www.awwcookbooks.com.au

Publisher Jo Runciman
Editorial & food director Pamela Clark
Director of sales, marketing & rights Brian Cearnes
Art director & designer Hannah Blackmore
Senior editor Stephanie Kistner
Food editors Rebecca Meli, Louise Patniotis
Operations manager David Scotto

Printed by Leo Paper Products Ltd in China.

Published and distributed in the
United Kingdom by Bounty Books,
a division of Octopus Publishing Group Ltd
Carmelite House
50 Victoria Embankment
London, EC4Y 0DZ
United Kingdom
info@octopus-publishing.co.uk;
www.octopusbooks.co.uk

International foreign language rights,
Brian Cearnes, Bauer Media Books
bcearnes@bauer-media.com.au

A catalogue record for this book is
available from the British Library.
ISBN: 978-0-75373-072-0
© Bauer Media Pty Ltd 2016
ABN 18 053 273 546

THE AUSTRALIAN
Women's Weekly

Low CARB

RECIPES TO HELP YOU REDUCE THE CARBOHYDRATES IN YOUR DIET

ℬℬ **Bounty**
Books

CONTENTS

Low CARB LIVING

If you've been struggling to control your weight take some comfort in knowing that you are not alone. The truth is that in Australia, along with the most of the developed world, it is now more common to be overweight than it is to be a healthy weight.

This is a relatively new phenomena, it only really happened in the last fifty or so years. If we look back just a couple of generations, being very overweight was far less common and the vast majority of people did not have to think about what sort of a diet they should be following. People ate according to the availability of foods, their culture and the style of eating they had been brought up with. Comparing the diets and the lifestyles of our grandparents and beyond gives us some insight into what might be going wrong for us today. What is it that is making it so hard for us to keep our waistlines under control?

One of the major changes is how we buy and prepare food. In past generations they had to buy raw ingredients that were then prepared and cooked into a meal at home, principally by women. As food companies grew and technologies developed to allow for an explosion in pre-prepared and packaged foods, there was a dramatic shift in how people ate. This liberated women from the home of course and so there were many benefits, but it did alter the nutrition of our food supply.

Today we eat out or grab takeaway much more often. We can buy partially or fully prepared meals at the supermarket to quickly throw together or heat up at home. Food is available pretty much 24/7 and we need never be hungry for very long. Vending machines tempt us with soft drinks, fruit juices, confectionery bars and salty chips or snacks. Lollies in brightly coloured packets grab

being high in refined carbohydrates and low on nutrients. This means that we need to eat more of them to meet our nutritional requirements. Many are not doing that and ending up in a state of being overfed but malnourished.

LOW FAT VS LOW CARB

For decades there has been a debate over the best type of diet for weight control. Back in the 1960s researchers were principally in two camps – those that favoured a low fat diet and those that favoured a low carbohydrate diet. The low fat approach won out and was the dominant style of diet advice for the next few decades.

Today we eat out or grab takeaway much more often. We can buy partially or fully prepared meals at our supermarket to quickly throw together or heat up at home.

our attention and test our resolve to ignore them at the checkout – even at the petrol station.

In a nutshell this has made it all too easy to overeat. Such foods are packed with kilojoules making them very energy dense, while also

The theory was simple. Fat has more than double the kilojoules per gram of either carbohydrate or protein (37kJ compared to 17kJ for carbohydrate and 16kJ for protein). Fat is energy dense stuff and therefore for the same kilojoules you can eat a far larger volume of carb-rich or protein-rich food. We also know that when you eat fat it can readily be stored as fat on your body if surplus to your needs. In contrast it is energetically unfavourable for your body to convert carbohydrates to body fat as it takes energy to do it and it can't be converted back into glucose – a gold fuel for the brain and many other cells.

SO WHAT WENT WRONG?

The food industry responded to the demand for low fat and fat free foods. They produced them in abundance. Walk down the aisles of

and since lollies are fat free, they were almost thought a good treat! The result was a dramatic increase in the amount of refined carbohydrate. This was not a naturally low fat diet such as traditionally followed by the Japanese for example, this was a modern, highly processed low fat diet. And it didn't work. People kept getting fatter.

Low carbohydrate diets have always been there in the background but today they are once again in the spotlight and have centre stage. There is also some good evidence to support their use. Several studies have compared them to a low

The food industry responded to the demand for low fat and fat free foods… The result was a dramatic increase in the amount of refined carbohydrate. This was not a naturally low fat diet… this was a modern, highly processed low fat diet. And it didn't work. People kept getting fatter.

any supermarket and you could load your trolley with low fat cheese, milk and yoghurt, low fat sausages and reduced fat pies, low fat snack bars, low fat biscuits, reduced fat cakes

fat approach and found them to produce better weight and body fat loss, at least in the short term. Over the course of a year or longer there are far fewer studies, but those that have followed participants for this long have found that the biggest factor contributing to the success of the diet is the person's ability to stick

Concentrating on lowering the carbohydrate in your diet has another major benefit. It ensures you cut out those aforementioned foods that

> *Concentrating on lowering the carbohydrate in your diet has another major benefit. It ensures you cut out those aforementioned foods that offer us little nutrition including chips, lollies, cakes, biscuits and soft drinks.*

to it. In other words, if you like your chosen diet and find it relatively easy to stick to, you'll get the best results.

BENEFITS OF REDUCING CARBS

The theory of a low carbohydrate diet is that by lowering the availability of carbohydrate to your body, it is forced to burn more fat. Secondly, that fat slows down digestion – food stays longer in your stomach and takes longer to be broken down and absorbed. This can help you to feel less hungry – something that can certainly be a problem on a low fat diet. Protein is also highly satiating and so ensuring a good source of protein in each meal can help you to eat less.

offer us little nutrition including chips, lollies, cakes, biscuits and soft drinks. It diverts you away from highly processed, sugary cereals for breakfast and away from a vast array of snack foods. If done in the right way it can divert you towards healthier, more nutritious and wholesome foods, while helping you to keep your blood glucose levels under control and reduce the amount of insulin your body needs to produce.

HEALTHY CHOICES

A word of caution however: Let's learn from the mistakes of the low fat era and ensure we don't make them with the low carb approach. A highly processed low carb snack bar is not a healthy choice. A low carb cake is still a kilojoule dense cake. In other words don't be fooled into thinking a low carb label is a license to eat.

Embrace a foundation of wholesome, minimally processed food, including plenty of plant food. Ensure you opt for healthy fats including extra virgin olive oil, avocado, nuts and seeds and be mindful of eating a broad array of vegies and a little fruit (our tables will guide you towards the carb content). Enjoy a variety of naturally protein-rich foods rather than processed protein bars and shakes. Put together in this way, a low carb eating plan can indeed be healthy, nutritious and a means to better weight control.

Dr Joanna McMillan
Accredited Practising Dietitian & Nutritionist
www.drjoanna.com.au | www.getlean.com.au

TIPS FOR EATING THE LOW-CARB WAY

- Cook from raw ingredients as much as possible.

- **Reduce the amount of pre-packaged, processed foods.**

- Choose from healthy fats including extra virgin olive oil, avocado, nuts and seeds.

- **Eat from a broad range of vegetables and some fruits.**

- Enjoy a variety of naturally protein-rich foods rather than processed protein bars and shakes.

- **Eating a good source of protein in each meal will keep you full for longer, reducing your craving to snack.**

- Junk food is very high in carbs and contains no nutritional benefits.

- **Re-think the way you snack – have some berries or cherry tomatoes on hand to fill the gap.**

- Cook low carb recipes that you like to eat. If you enjoy the food, chances are you will find it easier to stick to your chosen diet.

HOW MANY CARBS IN FRUIT & VEG?

CARBS IN FRESH VEGIES

VERY LOW CARB
(<5g/100g raw weight)
Grams carbohydrate per 100g raw weight

Asparagus	1.4
Bamboo shoots (canned)	1.6
Bean sprouts	1.4
Buk choy	0.9
Broad beans	2.2
Broccoli	0.4
Broccolini	0.4
Brussels sprouts	2.1
Cabbage	3.4
Capsicum	3.5
Cauliflower	1.9
Celery	2.3
Cos lettuce	0.7
Cucumber	2.1
Daikon	2.9
Eggplant	2.4
Fennel	3.3
Green beans	2.4
Iceberg lettuce	0.4
Kale	2.3
Kohlrabi	4.2
Leek	3.3
Mushroom	1.4
Okra	2.4
Radicchio	0.7
Red radish	1.9
Rocket	2.2
Snow pea	4.5
Spinach	0.7
Spring onion	4.6
Sugar snap pea	2.7
Tomato	2.4
Watercress	1.3
Zucchini	1.6

LOW CARB
(5-10g/100g raw weight)

Beetroot	8.4
Carrot	5.0
Celeriac	5.0
Onion	5.1
Peas	9.7
Pumpkin	8.1

MODERATE CARB
(10-15g/100g raw weight)

Corn, fresh on cob	12.5
Garlic	10.2
Potato	12.3

HIGHER CARB
(≥15g/100g raw weight)

Sweet potato (kumara & purple varieties)	19.3

CARBS IN FRESH FRUIT

VERY LOW CARB
(<5g/100g raw weight)
Grams carbohydrate per 100g raw weight

Avocado	0.5
Grapefruit	4.8
Lemon	1.8
Lime	1.2
Rhubarb (although sugar is usually added during stewing)	1.8
Strawberries	2.7

LOW CARB
(5-10g/100g raw weight)

Apricot	7.7
Blackberries	7.5
Figs	8.1
Kiwi fruit, peeled	9.8
Nectarine	7.7
Oranges	8.1
Papaya & pawpaw	6.9
Passionfruit	5.7
Peach	6.4
Pineapple	8.0
Plum	7.1
Raspberries	7.4
Rockmelon	5.7
Watermelon	5.0

MODERATE CARB
(10-15g/100g raw weight)

Apple	10.8
Blueberries	11.3
Brown pear	14.3
Cherries	11.9
Mango	11.6
Nashi pear	11.1
Packham pear	10.8
Pomegranate	13.5

HIGHER CARB
(≥15g/100g raw weight)

Banana	19.9
Black grapes	15.7
Custard apple	15.8
Green grapes	15.0
Lychee	16.2
Persimmon	16.1

CARBS IN LEGUMES

ALL CANNED & DRAINED
Grams carbohydrate per 100g cooked

Borlotti beans	18
Red kidney beans	14
Cannellini beans	12
Chickpeas	14
Lentils	7
Soy beans	3
Green peas	6

Low CARB LUNCH

When you're reducing your carb intake it's time to think outside the lunchbox. With a little preparation the night before, salads, soups and burgers without buns, can easily be packaged and made portable.

BROAD BEAN & BRUSSELS SPROUT SALAD WITH POACHED EGGS

2 TABLESPOONS WHITE VINEGAR

4 EGGS

200G (6½ OUNCES) FROZEN BROAD (FAVA) BEANS, THAWED, PEELED

400G (12½ OUNCES) BRUSSELS SPROUTS, OUTER LEAVES SEPARATED, REMAINING SHREDDED

½ CUP (50G) WALNUTS, ROASTED

½ CUP LIGHTLY PACKED FRESH DILL LEAVES

⅓ CUP (25G) SHAVED PARMESAN

2 TABLESPOONS EXTRA VIRGIN OLIVE OIL

2 TABLESPOONS WHITE VINEGAR, EXTRA

1 Add vinegar to a deep frying pan of simmering water. Break eggs, one at a time, into a cup; slide each egg into the water. Gently poach eggs for 3 minutes or until whites are set. Remove from pan with a slotted spoon; drain on paper towel.

2 Meanwhile, add broad beans to a medium saucepan of boiling water; boil for 30 seconds. Add shredded sprouts and outer leaves; boil a further 5 seconds. Drain. Place beans and sprouts in a large bowl of iced water; stand until cold. Drain well.

3 Place beans and sprouts in a medium bowl with walnuts, half the dill and half the parmesan; season to taste, toss gently to combine.

4 Serve salad topped with eggs, remaining dill and remaining parmesan. Drizzle with combined oil and extra vinegar. Season.

nutritional count per serving 24.7g total fat (4.8g saturated fat); 1346kJ (321 cal); 3.4g carbohydrate; 17g protein; 6g fibre

PREP + COOK TIME
30 MINUTES
SERVES
4

PREP + COOK TIME

35 MINUTES

SERVES

4

TURKISH HALOUMI
& POMEGRANATE SALAD

1 TABLESPOON LEMON JUICE

2 TABLESPOONS LIGHT OLIVE OIL

1 MEDIUM BULB FENNEL (300G), TRIMMED, SLICED VERY THINLY

500G (1 POUND) BABY TARGET BEETROOT, SLICED VERY THINLY

4 RED RADISHES (140G), TRIMMED, SLICED VERY THINLY

2 GREEN ONIONS (SCALLIONS), SLICED THINLY

⅓ CUP (80ML) POMEGRANATE SEEDS

¼ CUP FIRMLY PACKED FRESH MINT LEAVES

125G (4 OUNCES) MIZUNA

¾ CUP (120G) WHOLE DRY ROASTED ALMONDS

360G (11½ OUNCES) HALOUMI CHEESE, SLICED THICKLY

1 Combine juice and oil in a large bowl. Add fennel, beetroot, radish, green onions, pomegranate, mint, mizuna and almonds; toss gently to combine.

2 Cook haloumi in a large oiled frying pan until browned on both sides.

3 Serve salad topped with haloumi.

nutritional count per serving 41.3g total fat (12.5g saturated fat); 2382kJ (569 cal); 16.7g carbohydrate; 28.5g protein; 6.9g fibre

tips Use a mandoline or V-slicer to cut the fennel, radishes and beetroot into very thin slices. If target beetroot are not available, you can use golden or red beetroot instead.

GRILLED VEGETABLE & RICOTTA STACK

2 BABY EGGPLANTS (120G), SLICED THICKLY LENGTHWAYS

1 MEDIUM GREEN CAPSICUM (BELL PEPPER) (200G), SLICED THICKLY LENGTHWAYS

1 MEDIUM RED CAPSICUM (BELL PEPPER) (200G), SLICED THICKLY LENGTHWAYS

2 LARGE ZUCCHINI (300G), SLICED THICKLY LENGTHWAYS

4 X 175G (5½-OUNCE) FLAT MUSHROOMS

2 CUPS (400G) FIRM RICOTTA

2 CLOVES GARLIC, CRUSHED

½ CUP FINELY CHOPPED FRESH BASIL

1 TABLESPOON FINELY CHOPPED FRESH FLAT-LEAF PARSLEY

1 TABLESPOON FINELY GRATED LEMON RIND

2 TABLESPOONS TOASTED PINE NUTS

2 TABLESPOONS FRESH FLAT-LEAF PARSLEY LEAVES, EXTRA

2 TABLESPOONS SMALL FRESH BASIL LEAVES, EXTRA

TOMATO PESTO

½ CUP (70G) DRAINED SEMI-DRIED TOMATOES

¼ CUP LOOSELY PACKED FRESH BASIL LEAVES

2 TABLESPOONS BALSAMIC VINEGAR

1 SMALL CLOVE GARLIC, CRUSHED

2 TABLESPOONS WATER

1 Cook eggplant, capsicums, zucchini and mushrooms, in batches, on a heated oiled grill plate (or grill or barbecue) over medium-high heat until vegetables are browned and tender.

2 Meanwhile, combine ricotta, garlic, basil, parsley and rind in a medium bowl; season to taste.

3 Make tomato pesto.

4 Divide mushrooms, stem-side up, among serving plates; top with layers of ricotta mixture, eggplant, zucchini and capsicum. Drizzle stack with pesto; sprinkle with pine nuts, extra parsley and extra basil.

tomato pesto Place ingredients in a food processor or blender; pulse until just combined. Season to taste.

nutritional count per serving 15.9g total fat (5.5g saturated fat); 1271kJ (304 cal); 15.6g carbohydrate; 19.3g protein; 9.3g fibre

PREP + COOK TIME

50 MINUTES

SERVES

4

FISH PROVENÇALE WITH HERBED TOMATOES

We used blue-eye trevalla in this recipe, but you can use any firm white fish such as perch or ling.

300G (9½ OUNCES) BRUSSELS SPROUTS, TRIMMED, HALVED

⅓ CUP (80ML) OLIVE OIL

4 X 150G (4½-OUNCE) WHITE FISH FILLETS

2 MEDIUM ZUCCHINI (240G), SLICED THINLY LENGTHWAYS

250G (8 OUNCES) CHERRY TOMATOES

1 TABLESPOON COARSELY CHOPPED FRESH FLAT-LEAF PARSLEY

1 TABLESPOON COARSELY CHOPPED FRESH TARRAGON

1 TABLESPOON COARSELY CHOPPED FRESH DILL

1 Boil, steam or microwave brussels sprouts until just tender; drain.

2 Heat 1 tablespoon of the oil in a large non-stick frying pan over high heat. Season fish. Cook fish for 5 minutes each side or until browned and cooked through. Remove from pan; cover to keep warm.

3 Heat 2 tablespoons of the remaining oil in same cleaned pan over medium-high heat; cook zucchini and brussels sprouts, turning, for 3 minutes or until lightly browned. Season to taste.

4 Meanwhile, heat remaining oil in a medium frying pan over medium heat. Add tomatoes; cook, covered, for 8 minutes, stirring occasionally, or until tomatoes start to break down. Remove pan from heat. Add half the herbs; season to taste.

5 Serve fish and herbed tomatoes with vegetables; sprinkle with remaining herbs.

nutritional count per serving 19.5g total fat (3.1g saturated fat); 1408kJ (336 cal); 4g carbohydrate; 33.5g protein; 5g fibre

PORK LARB

Larb is a classic Thai salad that can be made with beef, chicken or pork mince, or vegetables.

1 TABLESPOON PEANUT OIL

2 TABLESPOONS FINELY CHOPPED
FRESH LEMON GRASS

1 FRESH SMALL RED CHILLI, CHOPPED FINELY,
PLUS EXTRA, SLICED, TO SERVE

2 CLOVES GARLIC, CRUSHED

40G (1½-OUNCE) PIECE FRESH GINGER,
GRATED FINELY

1.4KG (2¾ POUNDS) LEAN MINCED (GROUND) PORK

2 TABLESPOONS FISH SAUCE

⅔ CUP (160ML) LIME JUICE

5 FRESH KAFFIR LIME LEAVES, SHREDDED FINELY

⅔ CUP LOOSELY PACKED FRESH MINT LEAVES

½ CUP LOOSELY PACKED FRESH CORIANDER
(CILANTRO) LEAVES

4 GREEN ONIONS (SCALLIONS), SLICED THINLY

4 SHALLOTS (100G), SLICED THINLY

8 ICEBERG LETTUCE LEAVES, TRIMMED

1 MEDIUM CARROT (120G), CUT INTO LONG STRIPS

1 LEBANESE CUCUMBER (130G), CUT INTO
LONG THIN STRIPS

2 TABLESPOONS COARSELY CHOPPED
UNSALTED PEANUTS

LIME HALVES, TO SERVE

1 Heat oil in a wok or large frying pan over medium heat; cook lemon grass, chopped chilli, garlic and ginger, stirring, for 2 minutes or until fragrant. Increase heat to high, then add pork; cook, stirring, for 10 minutes or until pork is browned. Add fish sauce and half the juice; cook, stirring, for 5 minutes. Remove wok from heat; stir in lime leaves, herbs, green onion, shallots and remaining juice.

2 Spoon larb mixture into lettuce leaves; top with carrot, cucumber, extra chilli and peanuts. Serve with lime.

nutritional count per serving 25g total fat (8g saturated fat); 2420kJ (578 cal); 6.2g carbohydrate; 78.9g protein; 4.6g fibre

tips You will need about 10 limes for this recipe. To easily separate the lettuce leaves, remove core from lettuce, then place lettuce, core-side up under cold running water. The water will run between the leaves, loosening them for easy separation. Use a julienne peeler to cut the carrot and cucumber into long thin strips. Julienne peelers are available from kitchenware stores and Asian food stores.

PREP +
COOK TIME
30 MINUTES
SERVES
4

**PREP +
COOK TIME**
30 MINUTES
SERVES
4

CHICKEN WITH ZUCCHINI & SALSA VERDE

4 CHICKEN BREAST FILLETS (680G), HALVED LENGTHWAYS

1 TABLESPOON OLIVE OIL

5 MEDIUM ZUCCHINI (500G)

⅓ CUP (25G) FLAKED ALMONDS, TOASTED

100G (3 OUNCES) GOAT'S FETTA, CRUMBLED

¼ CUP FRESH FLAT-LEAF PARSLEY LEAVES

SALSA VERDE

½ CUP COARSELY CHOPPED FRESH FLAT-LEAF PARSLEY

¼ CUP COARSELY CHOPPED FRESH BASIL

1 CLOVE GARLIC, CRUSHED

2 TEASPOONS DRAINED BABY CAPERS, RINSED

1 TEASPOON DIJON MUSTARD

¼ CUP (60ML) OLIVE OIL

2 TEASPOONS RED WINE VINEGAR

1 Season chicken. Heat oil in a large frying pan over medium-high heat; cook chicken, in batches, for 4 minutes each side or until browned and cooked through. Remove from pan; cover to keep warm.

2 Using a vegetable spiralizer, cut zucchini into spirals.

3 Make salsa verde.

4 Serve chicken with zucchini topped with salsa verde, almonds, fetta and parsley.

salsa verde Combine herbs, garlic and capers in a small bowl; whisk in mustard, oil and vinegar until thickened.

nutritional count per serving 31.8g total fat (8.6g saturated fat); 2030kJ (485 cal); 2.7g carbohydrate; 45.6g protein; 3.7g fibre

tip A spiralizer is a kitchen gadget that cuts vegetables into long thin spirals. If you don't have one, you can use a mandoline or V-slicer.

PEA & PRAWN PATTIES WITH WATERCRESS SALAD

1½ CUPS (180G) FROZEN PEAS

1 CLOVE GARLIC, PEELED

250G (4 OUNCES) PEELED UNCOOKED MEDIUM KING PRAWNS (SHRIMP), CHOPPED COARSELY

1 TABLESPOON FRESH TARRAGON LEAVES, CHOPPED COARSELY

½ TEASPOON FINELY GRATED LEMON RIND

1 TABLESPOON GROUND ALMONDS

2 CUPS (235G) FIRMLY PACKED TRIMMED WATERCRESS

1 MEDIUM FENNEL BULB (300G), SLICED THINLY

1 STALK CELERY (150G), TRIMMED, SLICED THINLY ON THE DIAGONAL

¼ CUP (40G) ROASTED WHOLE BLANCHED ALMONDS, CHOPPED COARSELY

1 TABLESPOON FRESH TARRAGON LEAVES, EXTRA

2 TABLESPOONS DILL SPRIGS

2 TABLESPOONS OLIVE OIL

MUSTARD & LEMON DRESSING

1½ TABLESPOONS DIJON MUSTARD

1 TABLESPOON LEMON JUICE

2 TABLESPOONS OLIVE OIL

1 Boil, steam or microwave peas and garlic together until peas are tender; drain.

2 Blend or process garlic and 1 cup of the peas with prawns, chopped tarragon, rind and ground almonds until combined; season. Using oiled hands, roll level tablespoons of mixture into 16 balls; flatten slightly. Cover; refrigerate for 1 hour. (The patties are quite sticky, however they will not fall apart during cooking.)

3 Meanwhile, make mustard and lemon dressing.

4 Place watercress, fennel, celery, blanched almonds, extra tarragon, dill and remaining peas in a large bowl with half the dressing; toss to combine.

5 Heat oil in a large non-stick frying pan over medium heat; cook patties, in batches, for 2 minutes each side or until golden and cooked through. Remove from pan; cover to keep warm.

6 Serve patties with watercress salad, drizzled with remaining dressing.

mustard & lemon dressing Whisk ingredients in a small bowl until combined; season to taste.

nutritional count per serving 25.4g total fat (3.5g saturated fat); 1507kJ (360 cal); 10g carbohydrate; 20.9g protein; 6.7g fibre

tips Patties can be made up to 1 day ahead; store in an airtight container in the fridge. Use a mandoline or V-slicer to slice the fennel very thinly.

**PREP +
COOK TIME**

45 MINUTES
(+ REFRIGERATION)

SERVES

4

SPICED CARROT SOUP WITH SMOKED ALMONDS

2 TABLESPOONS EXTRA VIRGIN OLIVE OIL

2 MEDIUM BROWN ONIONS (300G), CHOPPED COARSELY

20G (¾-OUNCE) PIECE FRESH GINGER, GRATED FINELY

2 TEASPOONS GROUND CUMIN

1 TEASPOON GROUND CORIANDER

½ CINNAMON STICK

1KG (2 POUNDS) CARROTS, CUT INTO 1CM (½-INCH) ROUNDS

2 CUPS (500ML) VEGETABLE STOCK

3 CUPS (750ML) WATER

¾ CUP (200G) GREEK-STYLE YOGHURT

2 CLOVES GARLIC, CRUSHED

½ SMALL RED ONION (50G), SLICED THINLY

¼ CUP (40G) CHOPPED SMOKED ALMONDS

8 SPRIGS FRESH CORIANDER (CILANTRO)

1 Heat oil in a large saucepan over medium heat; cook brown onion, stirring, until soft.

2 Add ginger, cumin, ground coriander and cinnamon to the pan; cook, stirring, until fragrant. Add carrot, stock and the water; bring to the boil. Reduce heat; simmer, covered, for 20 minutes or until carrot is soft. Remove cinnamon stick. Stand soup for 10 minutes.

3 Meanwhile, combine yoghurt and garlic in a small bowl.

4 Blend soup in batches until smooth (or use a stick blender). Return soup to same pan; stir over medium heat until hot. Season.

5 Ladle soup into serving bowls; top with yoghurt mixture, red onion, almonds and coriander. Sprinkle with pepper.

nutritional count per serving 19.2g total fat (4g saturated fat); 1404kJ (335 cal); 25.6g carbohydrate; 9.2g protein; 13g fibre

SPICED CHICKPEA & BROAD BEAN SOUP

1 TABLESPOON EXTRA VIRGIN OLIVE OIL

1 MEDIUM BROWN ONION (150G), CHOPPED COARSELY

2 MEDIUM CARROTS (240G), CHOPPED COARSELY

2 TRIMMED CELERY STALKS (200G), CHOPPED COARSELY

2 CLOVES GARLIC, CHOPPED

2 TEASPOONS GROUND CUMIN

2 TEASPOONS GROUND CORIANDER

2 TEASPOONS PAPRIKA

½ TEASPOON GROUND CINNAMON

400G (12½ OUNCES) CANNED DICED TOMATOES

1.5 LITRES (6 CUPS) VEGETABLE STOCK

½ CUP (100G) FRENCH-STYLE GREEN LENTILS, RINSED

400G (12½ OUNCES) CANNED CHICKPEAS (GARBANZO BEANS), DRAINED, RINSED

2 CUPS (320G) FROZEN BROAD (FAVA) BEANS

¼ CUP COARSELY CHOPPED FRESH FLAT-LEAF PARSLEY

¼ CUP COARSELY CHOPPED FRESH CORIANDER (CILANTRO)

6 EGGS

¼ TEASPOON GROUND CUMIN, EXTRA

½ TEASPOON SEA SALT FLAKES

1 Heat oil in a large saucepan over medium heat; cook onion, carrot, celery and garlic, stirring, for 5 minutes or until softened. Add spices; cook, stirring, until fragrant.

2 Add tomatoes and stock; bring to the boil. Add lentils and chickpeas; simmer, uncovered, for 10 minutes.

3 Meanwhile, pour boiling water over broad beans in a heatproof bowl; stand 2 minutes. Drain. Peel broad beans.

4 Add broad beans to the pan; simmer, uncovered, for a further 5 minutes or until lentils are tender. Stir in half the herbs; season to taste.

5 Meanwhile, half-fill a large frying pan with water; bring to the boil. Break an egg into a cup, then slide into pan; repeat with remaining eggs. When all eggs are in pan, return water to the boil. Cover pan, turn off heat; stand for 4 minutes or until a light film of egg white sets over yolks. Remove eggs one at a time, using slotted spoon.

6 Ladle soup into serving bowls; top with an egg, remaining herbs and combined extra cumin and salt. Serve sprinkled with pepper.

nutritional count per serving 10.7g total fat (2.6g saturated fat); 1166kJ (278 cal); 21.6g carbohydrate; 19.4g protein; 8.4g fibre

tip This soup can be prepared to the end of step 3, up to 6 hours ahead.

PREP +
COOK TIME
35 MINUTES
SERVES
6

QUINOA, ZUCCHINI & FETTA SALAD

Use a julienne peeler, mandoline or V-slicer to cut the zucchini into long thin strips, or coarsely grate it instead, if you prefer.

¾ CUP (150G) WHITE QUINOA

1½ CUPS (375ML) WATER

½ CUP (70G) HAZELNUTS

2 MEDIUM ZUCCHINI (240G), CUT INTO LONG THIN STRIPS

250G (8 OUNCES) HEIRLOOM OR MIXED CHERRY TOMATOES, HALVED

½ SMALL RED ONION (50G), SLICED THINLY

100G (3 OUNCES) FETTA, CRUMBLED

1 CUP LOOSELY PACKED FRESH SMALL BASIL LEAVES

2 TABLESPOONS EXTRA VIRGIN OLIVE OIL

1 TABLESPOON RED WINE VINEGAR

1 Rinse quinoa under cold water; drain well. Place in a medium saucepan with the water; bring to the boil. Reduce heat; simmer, covered, for 15 minutes or until water is absorbed and quinoa is tender. Transfer to a large serving bowl to cool.

2 Meanwhile, roast hazelnuts in a medium frying pan over medium heat for 4 minutes or until golden. Rub hot hazelnuts in a clean tea towel to remove most of the skin; discard skin. Coarsely chop nuts.

3 Add nuts to quinoa in bowl with zucchini, tomatoes, onion, half the fetta and half the basil. Drizzle with combined oil and vinegar; toss gently to combine. Season to taste. Serve topped with remaining fetta and remaining basil, sprinkled with pepper.

nutritional count per serving 28g total fat (5.9g saturated fat); 1791kJ (428 cal); 27.6g carbohydrate; 13.2g protein; 6g fibre

serving suggestion Serve with steamed asparagus and crusty bread.

ZA'ATAR CHICKPEAS & VEGETABLE SALAD

When roasting the vegetables, ensure they are placed in a single layer so they roast quickly without steaming. If necessary, divide the vegetables between two trays.

400G (12½ OUNCES) BUTTERNUT PUMPKIN, UNPEELED

1 LARGE RED ONION (300G), CUT INTO THIN WEDGES

1 MEDIUM RED CAPSICUM (BELL PEPPER) (200G), SLICED THICKLY

1 MEDIUM YELLOW CAPSICUM (BELL PEPPER) (200G), SLICED THICKLY

400G (12½ OUNCES) RAINBOW BABY (DUTCH) CARROTS, TRIMMED

2 TABLESPOONS OLIVE OIL

400G (12½ OUNCES) CANNED CHICKPEAS (GARBANZO BEANS), DRAINED, RINSED

2 TABLESPOONS ZA'ATAR

¼ CUP (60ML) RED WINE VINEGAR

¼ CUP (60ML) OLIVE OIL, EXTRA

60G (2 OUNCES) RED VEINED SORREL OR BABY SPINACH LEAVES

100G (3 OUNCES) PERSIAN FETTA, CRUMBLED

⅓ CUP LIGHTLY PACKED SMALL FRESH MINT LEAVES

1 Preheat oven to 220°C/425°F. Line a large oven tray with baking paper.

2 Cut unpeeled pumpkin into thin wedges; halve crossways. Place pumpkin, onion, capsicum and carrots, in a single layer, on oven tray; drizzle with half the oil, then season. Bake for 25 minutes or until tender.

3 Meanwhile, place chickpeas on another baking-paper-lined oven tray. Drizzle with remaining oil, sprinkle with za'atar; toss gently to coat. Bake for 25 minutes or until golden and crisp.

4 Whisk vinegar and extra oil in a small bowl; season.

5 Pour dressing into two 2-cup (500ml) jars. Layer all ingredients in jars finishing with fetta and chickpeas.

nutritional count per serving 31.7g total fat (5.8g saturated fat); 1933kJ (462 cal); 29g carbohydrate; 13.3g protein; 12.6g fibre

tips Rainbow baby carrots are also sold as heirloom carrots; they are available from most supermarkets and greengrocers. This salad makes a great portable lunch, simply secure the lid to seal the jar and off you go. When you're ready to serve, turn the lidded jars upside down to disperse the dressing.

serving suggestion Serve with grilled flatbread.

**PREP +
COOK TIME**
45 MINUTES
SERVES
4

**PREP +
COOK TIME**

1¼ HOURS

SERVES

4

GREEK-STYLE BAKED EGGPLANT

4 SMALL EGGPLANT (1KG), HALVED LENGTHWAYS

2 TABLESPOONS OLIVE OIL

1 MEDIUM RED ONION (170G), CHOPPED FINELY

2 STALKS CELERY (300G), TRIMMED, CHOPPED FINELY

1 CLOVE GARLIC, CRUSHED

2 TEASPOONS FINELY CHOPPED FRESH OREGANO

1 LARGE RED CAPSICUM (BELL PEPPER) (350G), CHOPPED FINELY

2 MEDIUM ROMA (EGG) TOMATOES (150G), CHOPPED FINELY

1 TEASPOON FINELY GRATED LEMON RIND

1 TEASPOON LEMON JUICE

100G (3 OUNCES) FETTA, CRUMBLED

⅔ CUP (100G) PITTED BLACK OLIVES, CHOPPED FINELY

¾ CUP (55G) PANKO (JAPANESE) BREADCRUMBS

¾ CUP (60G) FINELY GRATED PARMESAN

1 TABLESPOON COARSELY CHOPPED FRESH FLAT-LEAF PARSLEY

1 LEBANESE CUCUMBER (130G), GRATED COARSLEY

1 CUP (280G) GREEK-STYLE YOGHURT

¼ CUP FRESH FLAT-LEAF PARSLEY LEAVES, EXTRA

1 Preheat oven to 220°C/425°F. Line two oven trays with baking paper.

2 Using a small knife, cut a 1cm (½-inch) border inside each eggplant half; scoop out the flesh without breaking the skin. Reserve flesh for another use. Place eggplant shells, cut-side-up on oven trays; cover with foil. Bake for 25 minutes.

3 Meanwhile, heat half the oil in a large frying pan over medium heat; cook onion, celery, garlic and oregano, stirring, for 3 minutes or until soft. Add capsicum; cook, stirring, for 3 minutes or until soft. Stir in tomato, rind and juice; remove from heat. Stir in fetta and olives; season to taste.

4 Combine breadcrumbs, parmesan and parsley in a small bowl; season.

5 Reduce oven to 200°C/400°F.

6 Spoon capsicum mixture into eggplant shells; top with breadcrumb mixture. Bake for 25 minutes or until eggplant is tender.

7 Meanwhile, combine cucumber and yoghurt in a small bowl; season to taste.

8 Serve eggplant drizzled with remaining oil and topped with yoghurt mixture, extra parsley and pepper.

nutritional count per serving 30.4g total fat (11.8g saturated fat); 2154kJ (514 cal); 32.5g carbohydrate; 21.3g protein; 11.3g fibre

serving suggestion Serve with a green leaf salad.

SALSAS

CAPSICUM & FETTA

prep + cook time 30 minutes **serves** 4 (makes 2 cups)
Quarter 1 medium (200g) red and 1 medium (200g)
yellow capsicum; discard seeds and membranes.
Roast under hot grill, skin-side up, until skin blisters
and blackens. Place in a heatproof bowl, cover with
plastic wrap; stand 5 minutes. Peel away skin, then cut
into strips. Combine capsicum, 1 tablespoon white
wine vinegar and 1 cup loosely packed torn fresh
flat-leaf parsley leaves in a bowl; season. Top with
25g (¾oz) crumbled goat's cheese fetta; drizzle
with 1 tablespoon olive oil. Season with pepper.
nutritional count per serving 6.5g total fat (1.8g
saturated fat); 375kJ (89 cal); 2.9g carbohydrate;
3g protein; 3.3g fibre

EGGPLANT & CHILLI

prep + cook time 50 minutes **serves 4** (makes 2 cups)
Preheat oven to 200°C/400°F. Pierce 1 large (500g)
eggplant with a fork; place on an oven tray. Bake for
30 minutes or until just tender. Stand 10 minutes.
When cool enough to handle, peel and coarsely chop
eggplant; place in a bowl with ½ small (40g) finely
chopped red onion, 1 thinly sliced fresh long red chilli
and 1 tablespoon lemon thyme leaves. Season. Whisk
1 tablespoon extra virgin olive oil, 1 tablespoon lemon
juice and 1 teaspoon ground sumac in a small jug;
pour over eggplant mixture, toss to combine.
nutritional count per serving 5g total fat (0.7g
saturated fat); 317kJ (76 cal); 4g carbohydrate;
1.6g protein; 3.8g fibre

AVOCADO & BACON

prep + cook time 20 minutes **serves** 4 (makes 1½ cups)
Cook 2 finely chopped shortcut bacon slices in a
non-stick frying pan over medium-high heat until
browned and crisp; drain. Place 1 large coarsely
chopped avocado, 1 thinly sliced green onion and
half the bacon in a small bowl. Whisk 1 tablespoon
olive oil and 1 tablespoon lemon juice in a small jug;
season. Pour dressing over salsa; toss to combine.
Top with remaining bacon.

nutritional count per serving 20.4g total fat (4.7g
saturated fat); 879kJ (210 cal); 0.7g carbohydrate;
5.5g protein; 1.7g fibre

BEAN & TOMATO

prep + cook time 20 minutes **serves** 4 (makes 2 cups)
Cut 250g (8oz) green beans into 1cm (¾in) pieces.
Boil, steam or microwave beans until just tender.
Refresh under cold water to cool; drain well. Place
beans, 2 teaspoons balsamic vinegar, 100g (3oz)
quartered grape tomatoes and 2 tablespoons toasted
pine nuts in a small bowl; toss to combine. Sprinkle
with 1 teaspoon pistachio dukkah.

nutritional count per serving 5.3g total fat (0.3g
saturated fat); 311kJ (74 cal); 2.8g carbohydrate;
2.6g protein; 2.3g fibre

BAKED PUMPKIN
& RICOTTA

500G (1 POUND) JAP PUMPKIN, CUT INTO WEDGES

1 SMALL RED ONION (80G), CUT INTO
THIN WEDGES

1 FRESH LONG RED CHILLI, SEEDED, SLICED

½ TEASPOON GROUND CINNAMON

2 TABLESPOONS OLIVE OIL

1 CUP (240G) FRESH RICOTTA

⅓ CUP (50G) PINE NUTS

½ CUP (35G) PANKO (JAPANESE) BREADCRUMBS

½ CUP (40G) FINELY GRATED PARMESAN

1 TEASPOON FINELY GRATED LEMON RIND

2 TABLESPOONS OLIVE OIL, EXTRA

400G (12½ OUNCES) CANNED BUTTER BEANS,
DRAINED, RINSED

175G (5½ OUNCES) BROCCOLINI,
HALVED LENGTHWAYS

½ CUP LOOSELY PACKED FRESH FLAT-LEAF
PARSLEY LEAVES, CHOPPED COARSELY

1 MEDIUM LEMON (140G), RIND CUT INTO
THIN STRIPS (SEE TIP)

1 Preheat oven to 220°C/425°F.

2 Place pumpkin in four shallow 2-cup (500ml) ovenproof dishes with onion, chilli and cinnamon; drizzle with oil. Season; toss to combine. Drop spoonfuls of ricotta onto pumpkin. Roast for 25 minutes or until pumpkin is just tender.

3 Meanwhile, place pine nuts on an oven tray; place in oven for 3 minutes or until browned lightly. Cool.

4 Combine breadcrumbs, parmesan, grated rind and extra oil in a small bowl; season.

5 Sprinkle beans over pumpkin; arrange broccolini on top, then sprinkle with pine nuts and breadcrumb mixture. Return to oven for a further 10 minutes or until breadcrumbs are browned.

6 Serve sprinkled with parsley and strips of rind.

nutritional count per serving 35.8g total fat (8.6g saturated fat); 2057kJ (491 cal); 21.4g carbohydrate; 17.6g protein; 8.9g fibre

tip If you have one, use a zester to create the strips of lemon rind. If you don't have one, use a vegetable peeler to remove the rind, avoiding the white pith, then cut it into long thin strips.

PREP +
COOK TIME

I HOUR

SERVES

4

PREP +
COOK TIME
35 MINUTES
SERVES
4

LAMB FILLET SALAD WITH SPINACH PESTO DRESSING

The oil from the marinated goat's cheese adds an extra depth of flavour to this dish. The cheese we used was marinated in a mixture of olive oil, garlic, thyme and chilli.

8 LAMB FILLETS (550G)

1 CLOVE GARLIC, CRUSHED

1 TABLESPOON OLIVE OIL

4 LARGE FLAT MUSHROOMS (320G)

1 SMALL RED ONION (100G), CUT INTO THIN WEDGES

3 MEDIUM HEIRLOOM TOMATOES (450G), QUARTERED

1 MEDIUM RADICCHIO (200G), LEAVES SEPARATED

25G (¾ OUNCE) BABY ROCKET (ARUGULA) LEAVES

½ CUP (100G) SOFT MARINATED GOAT'S CHEESE, RESERVE 2 TABLESPOONS OF THE MARINATING OIL (SEE NOTE ABOVE)

¼ CUP FRESH MICRO CRESS

SPINACH PESTO DRESSING

½ CUP (130G) BABY SPINACH PESTO

¼ CUP (60ML) OLIVE OIL

1 Combine lamb, garlic and oil in a medium bowl; season.

2 Cook mushrooms and onion on a heated oiled grill plate (or grill or barbecue) until browned and just tender; season. Remove from heat; cover to keep warm.

3 Cook lamb on heated oiled grill plate for 10 minutes or until cooked as desired. Remove from heat; rest, covered, for 5 minutes before slicing.

4 Meanwhile, make spinach pesto dressing.

5 Place mushrooms and onion in a large bowl with tomatoes, radicchio, rocket and reserved marinating oil; toss gently to combine. Season to taste.

6 Add lamb to salad; toss to combine. Arrange salad on a large serving platter. Top with crumbled cheese; drizzle with dressing and sprinkle with micro cress.

spinach pesto dressing Place ingredients in a small screw-top jar; shake well to combine.

nutritional count per serving 44g total fat (11g saturated fat); 2513kJ (600 cal); 8g carbohydrate; 41.3g protein; 5.3g fibre

ROASTED TOMATO & WHITE BEAN SOUP

Tomatoes contain the carotenoid lycopene, an antioxidant that gives them their red colour, and may be useful in reducing the risk of some cancers and heart disease. While cooking does slightly reduce the vitamin C content in tomatoes, it actually increases the lycopene content.

1KG (2 POUNDS) RIPE ROMA (EGG) TOMATOES, QUARTERED

1 MEDIUM RED ONION (170G), CUT INTO WEDGES

6 CLOVES GARLIC, UNPEELED

1 TABLESPOON MAPLE SYRUP

½ CUP (125ML) EXTRA VIRGIN OLIVE OIL

⅓ CUP LOOSELY PACKED SAGE LEAVES

400G (12½ OUNCES) CANNED CANNELLINI BEANS, DRAINED, RINSED

2 CUPS (500ML) WATER

1 Preheat oven to 200°C/400°F.

2 Place tomatoes, onion and garlic in a roasting pan. Combine maple syrup and half the oil in a bowl, season to taste; pour over vegetables, then toss to coat. Roast for 45 minutes or until tomatoes are very soft and coloured at the edges.

3 Meanwhile, heat remaining oil in a small frying pan over medium heat; fry sage leaves, stirring for 1 minute or until crisp. Remove with a slotted spoon; drain on paper towel. Reserve sage oil.

4 Peel roasted garlic. Blend garlic, onion, two-thirds of the tomatoes and two-thirds of the beans until smooth. Pour mixture into a large saucepan with the water and remaining beans; cook over medium heat, stirring occasionally until warmed through. Season to taste.

5 Ladle soup into bowls. Top with remaining tomatoes and crisp sage leaves; drizzle with reserved sage oil.

nutritional count per serving 29g total fat (4.5g saturated fat); 1512kJ (361 cal); 19g carbohydrate; 5.7g protein; 2.1g fibre

PREP +
COOK TIME

20 MINUTES

SERVES

2

VEGETABLE CURRY OMELETTES

You can also cut the carrot into thin strips using a julienne peeler, available from kitchenware and Asian food stores.

1 TABLESPOON VEGETABLE OIL

¼ CUP (75G) MASSAMAN CURRY PASTE

400ML CANNED LIGHT COCONUT MILK

2 TEASPOONS SESAME OIL

1 MEDIUM CARROT (120G), GRATED COARSELY

1 MEDIUM RED CAPSICUM (BELL PEPPER) (200G), CUT INTO MATCHSTICKS

230G (7 OUNCES) BABY CORN, HALVED LENGTHWAYS

3 EGGS

1 TABLESPOON WATER

½ CUP (40G) BEAN SPROUTS

¼ CUP LIGHTLY PACKED FRESH MINT LEAVES

¼ CUP LIGHTLY PACKED FRESH THAI BASIL LEAVES

1 Heat half the vegetable oil in a medium saucepan over medium heat; cook curry paste for 2 minutes or until fragrant. Stir in coconut milk and sesame oil; bring to a simmer. Add carrot, capsicum and corn; simmer, uncovered, for 3 minutes or until tender. Season to taste.

2 Meanwhile, heat 1 teaspoon of the remaining vegetable oil in a small 20cm (8-inch) (base measurement) non-stick frying pan over medium heat. Whisk eggs and the water. Pour half the egg mixture into pan, swirl to coat the base; cook for 1 minute or until golden underneath. Turn or flip omelette, cook for a further 30 seconds; transfer to a warmed plate. Repeat with remaining vegetable oil and egg mixture.

3 Divide vegetable curry mixture and sprouts between omelettes; fold omelette over. Serve topped with herbs.

nutritional count per serving 38.1g total fat (18g saturated fat); 2039kJ (488 cal); 17g carbohydrate; 15.9g protein; 8.6g fibre

LAMB KOFTA
WITH SPICED YOGHURT

2 TABLESPOONS BURGHUL (CRACKED WHEAT)

250G (8 OUNCES) MINCED (GROUND) LAMB

1 EGG, BEATEN LIGHTLY

1 SMALL BROWN ONION (80G), CHOPPED FINELY

2 TABLESPOONS PINE NUTS, CHOPPED FINELY

1 TABLESPOON FINELY CHOPPED FRESH MINT

**1 TABLESPOON FINELY CHOPPED
FRESH FLAT-LEAF PARSLEY**

VEGETABLE OIL, FOR SHALLOW-FRYING

200G (6½ OUNCES) BABY SPINACH LEAVES

1 SMALL RED ONION (100G), CUT INTO THIN WEDGES

125G (4 OUNCES) CHERRY TOMATOES, HALVED

**125G (4 OUNCES) BABY ROMA (EGG) TOMATOES,
HALVED**

**⅓ CUP LOOSELY PACKED FRESH
FLAT-LEAF PARSLEY LEAVES**

¼ CUP FRESH MINT LEAVES

2 TABLESPOONS POMEGRANATE SEEDS (SEE TIPS)

SPICED YOGHURT

1 CUP (280G) GREEK-STYLE YOGHURT

**2 FRESH SMALL RED CHILLIES, SEEDED,
CHOPPED FINELY**

1 TABLESPOON FINELY CHOPPED FRESH MINT

**1 TABLESPOON FINELY CHOPPED
FRESH FLAT-LEAF PARSLEY**

**1 TABLESPOON FINELY CHOPPED
FRESH CORIANDER (CILANTRO)**

1 CLOVE GARLIC, CRUSHED

½ TEASPOON GROUND CUMIN

1 Cover burghul with cold water in a small bowl; stand 10 minutes. Drain; pat dry with paper towel to remove as much water as possible.

2 Place burghul in a large bowl with lamb, egg, onion, pine nuts and finely chopped herbs; season. Use your hands to combine the mixture. Roll rounded tablespoons of mixture into balls. Place balls on a tray, cover; refrigerate for 30 minutes.

3 Meanwhile, make spiced yoghurt.

4 Heat oil in a large frying pan over medium-high heat; shallow-fry kofta, in batches, for 10 minutes or until browned and cooked through. Drain on paper towel.

5 Serve kofta with remaining ingredients, topped with spiced yoghurt and pepper.

spiced yoghurt Combine ingredients in a medium bowl.

nutritional count per serving 19.5g total fat (6.8g saturated fat); 1444kJ (345 cal); 16.5g carbohydrate; 23.5g protein; 4.3g fibre

tips Fresh pomegranate seeds can sometimes be found in the fridge section of supermarkets or good greengrocers. If they're not available, cut a whole pomegranate in half crossways; hold it, cut-side down, in the palm of your hand over a bowl, then hit the outside firmly with a wooden spoon. The seeds should fall out easily; discard any white pith that falls out with them. Pomegranate seeds will keep in the fridge for up to a week. This recipe is easily transportable; store the spiced yoghurt in a separate container until ready to serve.

**PREP +
COOK TIME**
30 MINUTES
SERVES
4

ROAST BEEF & WATERCRESS SALAD

We used fresh horseradish in this recipe. If it's not available, you can use bottled prepared horseradish instead.

1 TABLESPOON OLIVE OIL

600G (1¼-POUND) PIECE BEEF EYE-FILLET

1 LEBANESE CUCUMBER (130G), PEELED INTO RIBBONS

125G (4 OUNCES) TRUSS CHERRY TOMATOES, HALVED

125G (4 OUNCES) BABY ROMA (EGG) TOMATOES, HALVED

100G (3 OUNCES) WATERCRESS

1 SMALL RED ONION (100G), SLICED THINLY

HORSERADISH BUTTERMILK DRESSING

½ CUP (125ML) BUTTERMILK

⅓ CUP (100G) MAYONNAISE

1 TABLESPOON FINELY GRATED FRESH HORSERADISH (SEE NOTE ABOVE)

1 CLOVE GARLIC, CRUSHED

1 TEASPOON FRESHLY GROUND BLACK PEPPER

1 Preheat oven to 200°C/400°F.

2 Heat oil in a medium flameproof baking dish over medium-high heat; cook beef, turning, until browned. Roast in oven, uncovered, for 15 minutes or until cooked as desired. Remove from oven; rest, covered, for 5 minutes before slicing thinly.

3 Meanwhile, make horseradish buttermilk dressing.

4 Place beef in a large bowl with cucumber, tomatoes, watercress and onion; toss gently to combine. Serve salad with dessing.

horseradish buttermilk dressing Place buttermilk, mayonnaise, horseradish and garlic in a screw-top jar; shake well. Season with salt; sprinkle with pepper.

nutritional count per serving 32g total fat (9.7g saturated fat); 2036kJ (486 cal); 11.8g carbohydrate; 36.6g protein; 2.8g fibre

tip The beef can be cooked up to 2 hours ahead; cover, refrigerate until required.

KUMARA TURKEY BURGER

The kumara needs to be about 12cm (4¾ inches) in diameter, as it will serve as the 'bun' for the burgers.

1 LARGE KUMARA (ORANGE SWEET POTATO) (500G), UNPEELED

COOKING-OIL SPRAY

⅓ CUP (25G) QUINOA FLAKES

¼ CUP (60ML) MILK

1 SMALL ZUCCHINI (90G), GRATED COARSELY

1 SMALL PURPLE CARROT (70G), GRATED COARSELY

1 SMALL RED ONION (100G), GRATED COARSELY

400G (12½ OUNCES) MINCED (GROUND) FREE-RANGE TURKEY OR CHICKEN

1 TABLESPOON FINELY CHOPPED FRESH FLAT-LEAF PARSLEY

2 TABLESPOONS OLIVE OIL

1 LARGE TOMATO (220G), SLICED THINLY

100G (3 OUNCES) TRIMMED WATERCRESS

1 SMALL RED ONION (100G), EXTRA, SLICED THINLY

1 TABLESPOON SESAME SEEDS, TOASTED

GREEN TAHINI

¼ CUP (70G) TAHINI

2 TABLESPOONS FRESH FLAT-LEAF PARSLEY LEAVES

2 TABLESPOONS LEMON JUICE

1 TABLESPOON OLIVE OIL

1 SMALL CLOVE GARLIC, CRUSHED

1 Preheat oven to 200°C/400°F. Oil and line two large oven trays with baking paper.

2 Cut kumara into 12 x 1.5cm (¾-inch) thick rounds; discard tapered ends. Place kumara slices, in a single layer, on oven trays; spray with cooking oil. Roast for 20 minutes or until tender. Cover to keep warm.

3 Meanwhile, make green tahini.

4 Combine quinoa flakes and milk in a small bowl; stand for 10 minutes.

5 Combine zucchini, carrot, onion, turkey, parsley and quinoa mixture in a medium bowl; season to taste. Using damp hands, shape turkey mixture into six 8cm (3¼-inch) patties. Cover, refrigerate for 30 minutes.

6 Heat oil in a large non-stick frying pan over medium heat; cook patties for 4 minutes on each side or until golden and cooked through.

7 Place patties on six kumara rounds; top with tomato, green tahini, watercress, extra onion and remaining kumara rounds. Sprinkle with sesame seeds.

green tahini Process ingredients until smooth; season to taste.

nutritional count per burger 21g total fat (3.4g saturated fat); 1605kJ (383 cal); 23.6g carbohydrate; 22g protein; 6.3g fibre

PREP +
COOK TIME
30 MINUTES
SERVES
4

SALADE NIÇOISE

4 EGGS

200G (6½ OUNCES) BABY GREEN BEANS,
TRIMMED, HALVED LENGTHWAYS

¼ CUP (60ML) OLIVE OIL

600G (1¼ POUNDS) SASHIMI GRADE TUNA STEAKS

1 TABLESPOON LEMON JUICE

2 TABLESPOONS WHITE WINE VINEGAR

3 MEDIUM HEIRLOOM TOMATOES (450G),
CUT INTO WEDGES

1 MEDIUM AVOCADO (250G), HALVED, SLICED

2 TABLESPOONS DRAINED CAPERS, RINSED

¼ CUP FIRMLY PACKED FRESH FLAT-LEAF
PARSLEY LEAVES

1 MEDIUM RADICCHIO (200G), LEAVES SEPARATED

1 Cover eggs with cold water in a small saucepan; bring to the boil. Boil, uncovered, for 5 minutes. Drain; rinse eggs under cold water until cool enough to handle. Peel. Cut eggs in half or quarters.

2 Meanwhile, boil, steam or microwave beans until just tender; drain. Rinse under cold water; drain.

3 Rub 1 tablespoon of the oil all over tuna; season. Cook tuna on a heated oiled grill plate (or grill or barbecue) for 1 minute each side or until seared. Remove from heat; rest, covered, for 5 minutes before slicing.

4 Whisk remaining oil with juice and vinegar in a large bowl. Add beans, tuna, boiled eggs and remaining ingredients; toss gently to combine. Serve sprinkled with pepper.

nutritional count per serving 34.7g total fat (7.2g saturated fat); 2325kJ (555 cal); 5.6g carbohydrate; 52g protein; 5.7g fibre

FISH CAKES
WITH HERB SALAD

500G (1 POUND) REDFISH FILLETS, SKIN AND BONES REMOVED

2 TABLESPOONS RED CURRY PASTE

2 FRESH KAFFIR LIME LEAVES, TORN INTO PIECES

2 GREEN ONIONS (SCALLIONS), SLICED

1 TABLESPOON FISH SAUCE

¼ CUP (60ML) LIME JUICE

3 SNAKE BEANS (30G), CHOPPED FINELY

2 TABLESPOONS FINELY CHOPPED FRESH CORIANDER (CILANTRO)

COOKING-OIL SPRAY

1 CUP (80G) BEAN SPROUTS

1 CUP LOOSELY PACKED FRESH BASIL LEAVES

1 CUP LOOSELY PACKED FRESH CORIANDER (CILANTRO) LEAVES, EXTRA

2 FRESH LONG RED CHILLIES, CUT INTO STRIPS

LEMON GRASS & CHILLI DIPPING SAUCE

10CM (4-INCH) STALK FRESH LEMON GRASS (20G), WHITE PART ONLY, CHOPPED FINELY

1 SMALL RED CHILLI, SEEDED, CHOPPED FINELY

⅓ CUP (80ML) LIME JUICE

¼ CUP (60ML) FISH SAUCE

¼ CUP (60ML) PEANUT OIL

1 TABLESPOON COCONUT SUGAR

1 SMALL CLOVE GARLIC, CRUSHED

1 Make lemon grass and chilli dipping sauce.

2 Cut fish into small pieces. Blend or process fish with curry paste, lime leaves, green onion, fish sauce and 1 tablespoon of the juice until mixture forms a smooth paste. Transfer fish mixture to a medium bowl; stir in beans and chopped coriander. Season.

3 Shape ¼ cup measures of the fish mixture into patties; you need 12 fish cakes in total. Spray fish cakes with oil.

4 Cook fish cakes, on a heated oiled grill plate (or grill or barbecue) over high heat for 2 minutes each side or until cooked through.

5 Place sprouts, basil, extra coriander leaves, chilli and remaining juice in a medium bowl; toss to combine.

6 Serve fish cakes with salad and dipping sauce.

lemon grass & chilli dipping sauce Place ingredients in a screw-top jar; shake well.

nutritional count per serving 17.2g total fat (3.3g saturated fat); 1302kJ (311 cal); 7.6g carbohydrate; 29.7g protein; 2.8g fibre

tip To avoid fish cakes sticking to the grill plate, line the grill plate first with a sheet of baking paper.

**PREP +
COOK TIME**

35 MINUTES

SERVES

4

CRACKERS

BASIC CRACKERS

prep + cook time 45 minutes (+ refrigeration & cooling)
makes 12

Preheat oven to 180°C/350°F. Pulse 1½ cups natural ground almonds, 1 egg, 30g (1oz) chopped cold butter and ½ teaspoon salt in a food processor until mixture comes together. Knead lightly until smooth. Roll dough between baking paper into a 20cm x 30cm (8-in x 12-in) rectangle. Refrigerate 30 minutes. Remove top sheet baking paper; cut dough into 12 rectangles. Lift dough on paper onto an oven tray. Using the back of a knife, make an indent at centre of each rectangle; prick all over with a fork. Bake 20 minutes or until golden. Leave on tray for 5 minutes; cool on wire rack.

nutritional count per cracker 9.8g total fat (1.8g saturated fat); 440kJ (105 cal); 0.5g carbohydrate; 3.3g protein; 1.1g fibre

TRIO OF SEEDS

prep + cook time 45 minutes (+ refrigeration & cooling)
makes 12

Preheat oven to 180°C/350°F. Place ingredients for basic crackers in a food processor with 1 tablespoon each of linseeds, sunflower seeds and pepitas; pulse until mixture comes together. Knead lightly until smooth. Roll dough between baking paper into a 25cm x 40cm (10-in x 16-in) rectangle. Refrigerate 30 minutes. Remove top sheet baking paper. Lift dough on paper onto an oven tray. Bake 20 minutes or until golden. Leave on tray for 5 minutes; cool on a wire rack. Break into 12 pieces.

nutritional count per cracker 11g total fat (2g saturated fat); 501kJ (120 cal); 0.6g carbohydrate; 4g protein; 1.3g fibre

FENNEL & POPPY SEEDS

prep + cook time 45 minutes (+ refrigeration & cooling)
makes 24

Preheat oven to 180°C/350°F. Place ingredients for basic crackers in a food processor with 2 teaspoons each of fennel seeds and poppy seeds; pulse until mixture comes together. Knead lightly until smooth. Roll dough between baking paper into a 20cm x 30cm (8-in x 12-in) rectangle. Refrigerate 30 minutes. Remove top sheet baking paper. Cut dough into 12 x 10cm (4-in) squares; cut squares diagonally into triangles. Lift dough on paper onto an oven tray. Brush with water, sprinkle with ¼ teaspoon sea salt flakes. Bake 20 minutes or until golden. Leave on tray 5 minutes; cool on wire rack.

nutritional count per cracker 5g total fat (0.9g saturated fat); 227kJ (54 cal); 0.3g carbohydrate; 1.7g protein; 0.6g fibre

ROSEMARY & PARMESAN

prep + cook time 45 minutes (+ refrigeration & cooling)
makes 15

Preheat oven to 180°C/350°F. Place ingredients for basic crackers in a food processor with ¼ cup finely grated parmesan and 2 tablespoons finely chopped fresh rosemary; pulse until mixture comes together. Knead lightly until smooth. Roll dough between baking paper into a 25cm x 40cm (10-in x 16-in) rectangle. Refrigerate 30 minutes. Remove top sheet baking paper. Lift dough on paper onto an oven tray. Bake 20 minutes or until golden. Leave on tray 5 minutes; cool on a wire rack. Break into 15 pieces.

nutritional count per cracker 7.8g total fat (1.5g saturated fat); 352kJ (81 cal); 0.4g carbohydrate; 2.6g protein; 0.9g fibre

TEX MEX PORK

500G (1 POUND) PORK FILLET

2 TEASPOONS OLIVE OIL

2 TEASPOONS CAJUN SEASONING MIX

½ TEASPOON MEXICAN CHILLI POWDER

1 SMALL AVOCADO (200G), QUARTERED, SLICED

250G (8 OUNCES) HEIRLOOM CHERRY TOMATOES, HALVED

2 SHALLOTS (50G), SLICED THINLY

1 LEBANESE CUCUMBER (130G), CHOPPED FINELY

⅓ CUP FRESH CORIANDER (CILANTRO) LEAVES

2 TABLESPOONS EXTRA VIRGIN OLIVE OIL

1 TABLESPOON LIME JUICE

1 RED OAKLEAF LETTUCE, LEAVES SEPARATED

1 Brush pork with olive oil; rub all over with combined seasoning mix and chilli powder. Cover; refrigerate for 3 hours.

2 Cook pork, on a heated oiled grill plate (or grill or barbecue) over medium-high heat for 4 minutes or until browned all over. Reduce heat; cook a further 10 minutes or until cooked. Remove from heat; rest, covered, for 5 minutes.

3 Meanwhile, combine avocado, tomatoes, shallots, cucumber and coriander in a medium bowl. Whisk extra virgin olive oil and juice in a jug; season. Pour dressing over avocado mixture; toss gently to coat.

4 Thinly slice pork. Serve pork on lettuce with avocado mixture, drizzle with any pork resting juices. Sprinkle with pepper.

nutritional count per serving 22g total fat (4.5g saturated fat); 1412kJ (337 cal); 3.4g carbohydrate; 29.7g protein; 3g fibre

CAULIFLOWER BURGERS

350G (11 OUNCES) BEETROOT (BEETS), PEELED, GRATED COARSELY

1 SMALL RED ONION (100G), SLICED THINLY

1 TEASPOON SALT FLAKES

¼ CUP (60ML) RED WINE VINEGAR

1 TABLESPOON LIGHT BROWN SUGAR

2 TABLESPOONS CHOPPED FRESH THYME

250G (8 OUNCES) CAULIFLOWER, CHOPPED COARSELY

140G (4½-OUNCE) PIECE CHEDDAR

½ CUP (100G) CANNED CANNELLINI BEANS, DRAINED, RINSED

1 CUP (70G) FRESH BREADCRUMBS

2 TABLESPOONS CHOPPED FRESH FLAT-LEAF PARSLEY

2 TEASPOONS FINELY GRATED LEMON RIND

2 TABLESPOONS SKINLESS CHOPPED HAZELNUTS, TOASTED

1 EGG WHITE, BEATEN LIGHTLY

2 TABLESPOONS VEGETABLE OIL

8 LARGE BUTTER (BOSTON) LETTUCE LEAVES

125G (4 OUNCES) CHERRY HEIRLOOM TOMATOES, HALVED

LEMON MAYONNAISE

⅓ CUP (100G) MAYONNAISE

2 TEASPOONS FINELY GRATED LEMON RIND

2 TEASPOONS LEMON JUICE

1 Place beetroot, onion, salt, vinegar, sugar and thyme in medium saucepan; bring to the boil. Reduce heat; simmer, uncovered, stirring occasionally, for 20 minutes or until beetroot is tender and slightly sticky. Cool.

2 Meanwhile, boil, steam or microwave cauliflower until tender. Drain; cool. Thinly slice 90g (3 ounces) of the cheddar; grate remaining cheddar.

3 Place cauliflower and beans in a food processor, pulse until coarsely chopped (do not over process). Transfer to a large bowl. Add ¼ cup (15g) of the breadcrumbs, the grated cheddar, parsley, rind and nuts; season, stir to combine. Shape cauliflower mixture into four patties. Refrigerate for 30 minutes.

4 Make lemon mayonnaise.

5 Dip patties in egg white; coat patties in remaining breadcrumbs.

6 Heat oil in a large frying pan over medium-high heat; cook patties for 4 minutes each side or until browned and crisp. Drain on paper towel. Immediately top with sliced cheese for cheese to melt.

7 Place each patty in a lettuce leaf; top with tomato and a generous spoonful of the beetroot mixture (you will only use half the mixture, see tips). Drizzle with lemon mayonnaise; top with remaining lettuce leaf.

lemon mayonnaise Whisk ingredients in a small bowl until combined; season to taste.

nutritional count per burger 35g total fat (10.8g saturated fat); 2297kJ (548 cal); 35.3g carbohydrate; 19.7g protein; 7.3g fibre

tip Refrigerate leftover beetroot mixture in an airtight container for up to 1 week.

**PREP +
COOK TIME**

40 MINUTES
(+ REFRIGERATION)

MAKES

4

PREP TIME
30 MINUTES
SERVES
4

VIETNAMESE PRAWN SALAD

2 TABLESPOONS FISH SAUCE

1 TABLESPOON COCONUT SUGAR

1 FRESH LONG RED CHILLI, SLICED THINLY

1 TABLESPOON FINELY GRATED FRESH GINGER

1 CLOVE GARLIC, CRUSHED

¼ CUP (60ML) LIME JUICE

2 TABLESPOONS PEANUT OIL

1 LARGE CARROT (180G), CUT INTO RIBBONS

120G (4 OUNCES) DAIKON, CUT INTO MATCHSTICKS

50G (1½ OUNCES) TRIMMED WATERCRESS

2 GREEN ONIONS (SCALLIONS), CUT INTO STRIPS

1 STALK CELERY (150G), TRIMMED, CUT INTO MATCHSTICKS

200G (6½ OUNCES) YELLOW GRAPE TOMATOES, SQUASHED

½ CUP FRESH MINT LEAVES

½ CUP FRESH CORIANDER (CILANTRO) LEAVES

½ CUP FRESH THAI BASIL LEAVES

16 COOKED KING PRAWNS (SHRIMP) (800G), PEELED, TAILS INTACT

LIME WEDGES, TO SERVE

1 Place fish sauce, coconut sugar, chilli, ginger, garlic, juice and oil in a screw-top jar; shake well.

2 Place carrot, daikon, watercress, green onion, celery, tomatoes, herbs and prawns in a large bowl with half the dressing; toss gently to combine.

3 Serve salad with lime wedges and remaining dressing.

nutritional count per serving 10g total fat (1.8g saturated fat); 1026kJ (245 cal); 12g carbohydrate; 23.5g protein; 4.7g fibre

tip Salad and dressing can be made a day ahead, store separately. Add dressing to salad just before serving.

CHAR-GRILLED LAMB & VEGETABLES

2 SMALL EGGPLANT (460G), QUARTERED

4 MEDIUM YELLOW PATTY-PAN SQUASH (120G), HALVED

¼ CUP (60ML) OLIVE OIL

500G (1 POUND) LAMB BACK STRAP

⅔ CUP (190G) GREEK-STYLE YOGHURT

2 CLOVES GARLIC, CHOPPED FINELY

½ CUP COARSELY CHOPPED FRESH MINT

1 TABLESPOON LEMON JUICE

2 TABLESPOONS DRAINED BABY CAPERS, RINSED

1 MEDIUM RADICCHIO (200G), LEAVES SEPARATED

2 TABLESPOONS FRESH MINT LEAVES, EXTRA

1 Place eggplant, squash and 2 tablespoons of the oil in a medium bowl, season; toss to coat.

2 Cook vegetables, in batches, on a heated oiled grill plate (or grill or barbecue) over medium-high heat for 2 minutes each side or until lightly charred. Remove from heat; cover to keep warm.

3 Brush lamb with remaining oil; season. Cook lamb on a heated oiled grill plate (or grill or barbecue) over medium-high heat for 5 minutes or until cooked as desired. Remove from heat; rest, covered, for 5 minutes, before slicing.

4 Meanwhile, combine yoghurt, garlic, mint, juice and capers in a small bowl; season to taste.

5 Serve lamb with radicchio and grilled vegetables; drizzle with yoghurt sauce, top with extra mint and sprinkle with pepper.

nutritional count per serving 24.3g total fat (6.5g saturated fat); 1691kJ (404 cal); 11.7g carbohydrate; 32.3g protein; 4.9g fibre

tip Beef or chicken can be used instead of the lamb.

PREP +
COOK TIME
35 MINUTES
SERVES
4

Low CARB DINNER

When deciding what to have for dinner, it usually starts with a protein such as chicken or beef. But it's the potatoes, rice and pasta served with it that can send the carbs sky high. Make the most of low-carb vegies and legumes to fill your plate.

LAMB & RATATOUILLE WITH PESTO DRESSING

5 BABY EGGPLANT (300G), SLICED THICKLY LENGTHWAYS

1 MEDIUM ZUCCHINI (120G), SLICED THICKLY LENGTHWAYS

1 MEDIUM RED ONION (170G), CUT INTO WEDGES

1 MEDIUM RED CAPSICUM (BELL PEPPER) (200G), QUARTERED LENGTHWAYS, SEEDS REMOVED

1 MEDIUM YELLOW CAPSICUM (BELL PEPPER) (200G), QUARTERED LENGTHWAYS, SEEDS REMOVED

250G (8 OUNCES) TRUSS GRAPE TOMATOES

1 BULB GARLIC, HALVED CROSSWAYS

1 TABLESPOON OLIVE OIL

900G (1¾ POUNDS) LAMB BACKSTRAPS

120G (4 OUNCES) FIRM GOAT'S CHEESE

PESTO DRESSING

2 CLOVES GARLIC, CRUSHED

2 TABLESPOONS FINELY GRATED PARMESAN

1 TABLESPOON TOASTED PINE NUTS

1 TABLESPOON LEMON JUICE

½ CUP FIRMLY PACKED FRESH BASIL LEAVES

⅓ CUP (80ML) OLIVE OIL

1 Preheat oven to 200°C/400°F. Oil two large shallow baking trays.

2 Combine eggplant, zucchini, onion, capsicums, tomatoes, garlic and oil in a large bowl. Season. Divide vegetables between trays. Roast, uncovered, for 25 minutes or until vegetables are tender, turning occasionally.

3 Meanwhile, make pesto dressing.

4 Cook lamb in a heated large non-stick frying pan over medium-high heat for 5 minutes each side or until browned and cooked as desired. Remove from pan; rest, covered, for 5 minutes before slicing thickly.

5 Serve lamb, vegetables and cheese on a large platter; drizzle with dressing.

pesto dressing Blend or process ingredients until smooth. Season to taste.

nutritional count per serving 46.7g total fat (13.3g saturated fat); 2981kJ (713 cal); 10.2g carbohydrate; 60g protein; 7.3g fibre

PREP +
COOK TIME

1 HOUR

SERVES

4

KERALA SALMON WITH LIME PICKLE YOGHURT

Based on a recipe from the Indian coastal province of Kerala, this delicious grilled fish is even better with the tangy lime pickle yoghurt spooned over the top.

2 TEASPOONS CORIANDER SEEDS

1 TEASPOON CUMIN SEEDS

2 CARDAMOM PODS, BRUISED

1 CINNAMON STICK

1 TEASPOON GROUND TURMERIC

½ TEASPOON CHILLI POWDER

2 TABLESPOONS PEANUT OIL

2 CLOVES GARLIC, CRUSHED

4 X 200G (6½-OUNCE) SALMON CUTLETS

100G (3 OUNCES) BABY SPINACH LEAVES

LIME PICKLE YOGHURT

½ CUP (140G) LOW-FAT GREEK-STYLE YOGHURT

2 TABLESPOONS LIME PICKLE, CHOPPED FINELY

1 Dry-fry coriander, cumin, cardamom and cinnamon in a small heated frying pan, stirring, over medium heat until fragrant. Stir in turmeric and chilli powder. Remove from heat.

2 Crush spices, using a mortar and pestle, until ground finely. Transfer spices to a large bowl; stir in oil and garlic. Add fish; turn to coat in spice mixture. Cover; refrigerate 30 minutes.

3 Meanwhile, make lime pickle yoghurt.

4 Cook fish, on a heated oiled grill plate (or grill or barbecue) over medium-high heat for 3 minutes each side or until cooked to your liking.

5 Serve fish with spinach and lime pickle yoghurt; season to taste.

lime pickle yoghurt Place ingredients in a small bowl; swirl pickle through yoghurt.

nutritional count per serving 37.4g total fat (9g saturated fat); 2516kJ (602 cal); 5.4g carbohydrate; 60.6g protein; 0.8g fibre

tip Lime pickle is sold in jars and is available from most large supermarkets.

MINTED LAMB CUTLETS WITH BEETROOT SALAD

⅓ CUP (80ML) OLIVE OIL

2 CLOVES GARLIC, CRUSHED

½ CUP COARSELY CHOPPED FRESH MINT

8 FRENCH-TRIMMED LAMB CUTLETS (400G)

500G (1 POUND) BABY BEETROOT (BEETS), STEMS ATTACHED

500G (1 POUND) GOLDEN BABY BEETROOT (BEETS), STEMS ATTACHED

400G (12½ OUNCES) JAP PUMPKIN, UNPEELED, CUT INTO THICK WEDGES

250G (8 OUNCES) BABY BEETROOT (BEET) LEAVES

2 TABLESPOONS RASPBERRY VINEGAR

¼ CUP (20G) SHAVED PARMESAN

¼ CUP COARSELY CHOPPED FRESH MINT, EXTRA

1 Combine 1 tablespoon of the oil, garlic and mint in a large shallow dish, add lamb; toss lamb to coat. Cover; refrigerate for 3 hours or overnight.

2 Preheat oven to 200°C/400°F. Line a large oven tray with baking paper.

3 Trim beetroot, leaving 3cm (1¼ inches) of the stem attached; discard roots. Wrap beetroot in foil. Place beetroot and pumpkin on oven tray. Bake for 30 minutes or until tender. When cool enough to handle, remove skin from beetroot. Cover to keep warm.

4 Cook lamb on a heated grill plate (or grill or barbecue) for 3 minutes each side or until cooked to your liking. Remove from heat; stand, covered, for 5 minutes to rest.

5 Place beetroot and pumpkin in a medium bowl with beetroot leaves and combined vinegar and remaining oil; toss gently to combine. Season to taste. Top salad with lamb, parmesan and extra mint.

nutritional count per serving 31.5g total fat (9g saturated fat); 2089kJ (500 cal); 30.1g carbohydrate; 19.1g protein; 12.2g fibre

tips Refresh beetroot leaves in a bowl of iced water. You can use baby rocket leaves instead of beetroot, if you prefer.

**PREP +
COOK TIME**

1 ½ HOURS

SERVES

4

LEMON & THYME VEAL CUTLETS WITH BEETROOT SALAD

500G (1 POUND) BABY BEETROOT (BEETS), STEMS ATTACHED

4 X 200G (6½-OUNCE) VEAL CUTLETS

2 CLOVES GARLIC, CRUSHED

1 TABLESPOON FRESH THYME LEAVES

1 TABLESPOON LEMON JUICE

1 TABLESPOON OLIVE OIL

170G (5½ OUNCES) ASPARAGUS, TRIMMED, HALVED LENGTHWAYS

250G (8 OUNCES) FRISEE LEAVES, TRIMMED

½ CUP (50G) ROASTED WALNUTS

120G (4 OUNCES) GOAT'S CHEESE, CRUMBLED

LEMON DRESSING

1 MEDIUM LEMON (140G)

1 TABLESPOON OLIVE OIL

WHITE BEAN SAUCE

400G (12½ OUNCES) CANNED CANNELLINI BEANS, DRAINED, RINSED

½ CUP (125ML) SALT-REDUCED CHICKEN STOCK

1 SMALL CLOVE GARLIC, CRUSHED

½ TEASPOON FINELY GRATED LEMON RIND

1 Preheat oven to 200°C/400°F.

2 Trim beetroot, leaving 3cm (1¼ inches) of the stem attached; discard roots. Wrap beetroot in foil. Place beetroot on an oven tray. Roast for 50 minutes or until tender. When cool enough to handle; remove skin. Cut beetroot in half.

3 Combine veal, garlic, thyme, juice and oil in a large bowl; stand 10 minutes.

4 Cook veal on a heated oiled grill plate (or grill or barbecue) for 3 minutes each side or until browned and cooked as desired. Cover; stand 5 minutes.

5 Meanwhile, boil, steam or microwave asparagus until tender.

6 Make lemon dressing and white bean sauce.

7 Place beetroot and asparagus in a large bowl with frisee and dressing; toss gently to combine. Top with walnuts and cheese.

8 Serve veal with beetroot salad, topped with bean sauce.

lemon dressing Using a zester or small sharp knife, cut lemon rind into long thin strips. Squeeze juice from lemon; you need 2 tablespoons. Place ingredients in a screw-top jar; shake well.

white bean sauce Blend or process ingredients until combined; season. Transfer to a small saucepan over medium heat; stir for 3 minutes or until heated through.

nutritional count per serving 27.2g total fat (7.2g saturated fat); 2189kJ (523 cal); 26g carbohydrate; 40.3g protein; 7.3g fibre

LAMB SHANKS WITH WHITE BEAN PUREE

2 TABLESPOONS OLIVE OIL

8 FRENCH-TRIMMED LAMB SHANKS (1.6KG)

1½ CUPS (375ML) DRY RED WINE

2 CUPS (500ML) BEEF STOCK

3 CLOVES GARLIC, CRUSHED

2 SMALL PARSNIPS (240G), HALVED LENGTHWAYS

200G (6½ OUNCES) BABY CARROTS, TRIMMED

20G (¾ OUNCE) BUTTER

1 SMALL BROWN ONION (80G), CHOPPED FINELY

1 TRIMMED CELERY STALK (100G), CHOPPED FINELY

1 TABLESPOON PLAIN (ALL-PURPOSE) FLOUR

1 TABLESPOON TOMATO PASTE

4 SPRIGS FRESH ROSEMARY, CHOPPED COARSELY

WHITE BEAN PUREE

1½ X 400G (12½ OUNCES) CANNED CANNELLINI BEANS, DRAINED, RINSED

¾ CUP (180ML) CHICKEN STOCK

2 CLOVES GARLIC, QUARTERED

1 TABLESPOON LEMON JUICE

2 TABLESPOONS OLIVE OIL

CARAMELISED RED ONION

40G (1½ OUNCES) BUTTER

2 SMALL RED ONIONS (200G), SLICED THINLY

1 TABLESPOON BROWN SUGAR

¼ CUP (60ML) RASPBERRY OR RED WINE VINEGAR

1 Preheat oven to 150°C/300°F.

2 Heat half the oil in a large flameproof baking dish over medium-high heat; cook lamb until browned all over. Stir in wine, stock and garlic; bring to the boil. Cover dish; roast lamb for 4 hours, turning twice during cooking, or until tender. Remove from oven.

3 Increase oven to 200°C/400°F. Toss parsnips and carrots in remaining oil on an oven tray; season. Roast 20 minutes, turning halfway during cooking, or until tender.

4 Meanwhile, make white bean puree and caramelised red onion.

5 Remove lamb from dish; cover to keep warm. Skim off excess fat from pan juices; pour pan juices into a large heatproof jug, reserve. Return dish to medium heat, melt butter; cook onion and celery, stirring, 5 minutes or until celery is just tender. Stir in flour; cook, stirring, 2 minutes. Gradually add reserved pan juices, paste and rosemary; cook, stirring until mixture boils and thickens. Strain.

6 Spoon bean puree on a serving platter; top with vegetables, lamb and onion. Serve drizzled with sauce.

white bean puree Bring beans and stock to the boil in a medium saucepan. Reduce heat; simmer, covered, 15 minutes. Remove lid; simmer, stirring occasionally, for 10 minutes or until liquid is absorbed. Process beans, garlic and juice until almost smooth. With motor operating, gradually add oil until smooth. Season.

caramelised red onion Melt butter in a medium pan over medium-low heat; cook onion, stirring, for 15 minutes or until browned and soft. Stir in sugar and vinegar; cook, stirring, for 15 minutes or until onion is caramelised.

nutritional count per serving 43.2g total fat (16.4g saturated fat); 3381kJ (809 cal); 38.4g carbohydrate; 52.5g protein; 11.5g fibre

LOW-CARB DINNER

PREP +
COOK TIME

5 HOURS

SERVES

4

LAMB, BURGHUL & CUCUMBER SALAD

800G (1½ POUNDS) LAMB FILLETS, TRIMMED

2 TABLESPOONS OLIVE OIL

1 CLOVE GARLIC, CRUSHED

2 TABLESPOONS COARSELY CHOPPED FRESH MINT

1 TABLESPOON COARSELY CHOPPED FRESH SAGE

¾ CUP (120G) BURGHUL (CRACKED WHEAT)

2 TEASPOONS FINELY GRATED LEMON RIND

1 LEBANESE CUCUMBER (130G)

4 RED RADISHES (140G), TRIMMED

⅓ CUP (35G) WALNUTS

½ CUP FIRMLY PACKED FRESH MINT LEAVES, EXTRA

LEMON GARLIC DRESSING

2 TABLESPOONS LEMON JUICE

1 CLOVE GARLIC, CRUSHED

¼ CUP (60ML) OLIVE OIL

1 Place lamb in a large bowl with combined oil, garlic, chopped mint and sage. Cover; refrigerate 3 hours or overnight.

2 Make lemon garlic dressing.

3 Place burghul in a medium bowl; cover with cold water. Stand 10 minutes; drain. Using your hands, squeeze out as much excess water as possible. Spread burghul in a thin, even layer on a tray; stand a further 15 minutes. Return dry burghul to bowl with rind and half the dressing; toss gently to combine.

4 Season lamb. Heat an oiled grill plate (or grill or barbecue) to medium-high heat; cook lamb for 5 minutes each side or until cooked to your liking. Remove from heat; rest, covered, for 5 minutes before slicing thickly.

5 Meanwhile, using a sharp knife, mandoline or V-slicer, cut cucumber lengthways into ribbons and radishes into thin slices. Place cucumber and radishes in a medium bowl with walnuts, remaining dressing and half the extra mint; toss gently to combine.

6 Divide burghul mixture among serving plates; top with cucumber mixture, lamb and remaining extra mint.

lemon garlic dressing Place ingredients in a screw-top jar; shake well. Season to taste.

nutritional count per serving 42.2g total fat (8.3g saturated fat); 2565kJ (613 cal); 10g carbohydrate; 49g protein; 2.3g fibre

MINT LAMB SKEWERS WITH GARLIC BEANS

Run a teaspoon down the centre of the cucumber to remove the seeds. If you use bamboo skewers, soak them in water for at least 1 hour before use to prevent them splintering and scorching during cooking.

2 CLOVES GARLIC, QUARTERED

½ CUP LOOSELY PACKED FRESH MINT LEAVES

½ TEASPOON CRACKED BLACK PEPPER

½ TEASPOON SEA SALT FLAKES

1 TABLESPOON OLIVE OIL

8 LAMB FILLETS (550G)

GARLIC BEANS

400G (12½ OUNCES) GREEN BEANS, TRIMMED

2 TABLESPOONS OLIVE OIL

1 CLOVE GARLIC, SLICED THINLY

2 TABLESPOONS TOASTED PINE NUTS

TZATZIKI DRESSING

1 LEBANESE CUCUMBER (130G), HALVED LENGTHWAYS

2 TABLESPOONS LEMON JUICE

1 CLOVE GARLIC, CRUSHED

1 CUP (280G) GREEK-STYLE YOGHURT

1 Pound garlic, mint, pepper and salt in a mortar and pestle until mixture resembles a thick paste. Stir in oil.

2 Thread lamb onto eight 25cm (10-inch) metal skewers. Place lamb in a shallow baking dish, add mint mixture; turn skewers to coat in mixture.

3 Make garlic beans.

4 Make tzatziki dressing.

5 Cook lamb on a heated oiled grill plate (or grill or barbecue) for 10 minutes, turning occasionally, until cooked as desired. Remove lamb from heat.

6 Serve lamb with garlic beans and tzatziki dressing.

garlic beans Boil, steam or microwave beans until just tender; drain. Add beans to a large bowl of iced water; drain well. Halve lengthways; place in a large bowl. Heat oil and garlic in a small frying pan over low heat until garlic just changes colour. Add pine nuts; stir until heated through. Drizzle mixture over beans.

tzatziki dressing Remove and discard seeds from cucumber; coarsely grate flesh into a medium bowl. Stir in remaining ingredients until combined.

nutritional count per serving 28.3g total fat (7.5g saturated fat); 1927kJ (461 cal); 14g carbohydrate; 35.5g protein; 4.4g fibre

PREP + COOK TIME

45 MINUTES

SERVES

4

**PREP +
COOK TIME**

40 MINUTES

SERVES

4

JERK FISH WITH SLAW & AVOCADO CREAM

800G (1½ POUNDS) FIRM WHITE FISH FILLETS

1½ TABLESPOONS GARLIC POWDER

1½ TEASPOONS CAYENNE PEPPER

1 TEASPOON GROUND CINNAMON

1 TEASPOON GROUND ALLSPICE

½ TEASPOON DRIED THYME LEAVES

2 TABLESPOONS OLIVE OIL

1 CUP (280G) GREEK-STYLE YOGHURT

2 TABLESPOONS HARISSA SAUCE

2 RADICCHIO (400G), LEAVES SEPARATED

LIME WEDGES, TO SERVE

SLAW

350G (11 OUNCES) WHITE CABBAGE, SHREDDED

2 CUPS LOOSELY PACKED FRESH CORIANDER (CILANTRO) LEAVES

1 SMALL RED ONION (100G), HALVED, SLICED THINLY

2 TABLESPOONS SLICED PICKLED JALAPEÑO

¼ CUP (60ML) FRESHLY SQUEEZED ORANGE JUICE

1 CLOVE GARLIC, CRUSHED

AVOCADO CREAM

2 SMALL AVOCADOS (400G), HALVED

⅓ CUP (80G) SOUR CREAM

2 TABLESPOONS LIME JUICE

1 Cut fish fillets diagonally into 1.5cm (¾-inch) wide, 12cm (4¾-inch) long strips. Combine garlic powder, cayenne, cinnamon, allspice, thyme and oil in a medium bowl; season. Add fish; toss to coat well in mixture. Cover; refrigerate until required.

2 Make slaw, then avocado cream.

3 Combine yoghurt and harissa in a small bowl; season to taste.

4 Heat a large, non-stick frying pan over high heat; cook fish, in two batches, for 4 minutes or until just cooked.

5 Fill radicchio leaves with slaw and fish, top with avocado cream and harissa yoghurt (drizzle with a little extra harissa sauce if you like). Serve with lime wedges.

slaw Place ingredients in a large bowl; toss to combine. Season to taste.

avocado cream Combine ingredients in a small bowl; season to taste.

nutritional count per serving 38.3g total fat (12.7g saturated fat); 2745kJ (657 cal); 23.3g carbohydrate; 50.1g protein; 8.4g fibre

tips Fish can be prepared 4 hours ahead to the end of step 1. Avocado cream, harissa yoghurt and coleslaw (without the orange juice) can also be prepared 4 hours ahead; add juice to coleslaw just before serving.

Jerk is both the name for a Jamaican dry or wet spice seasoning, characterised by allspice and chillies, and the method of cooking over barbecue coals. Traditionally the seasoning is rubbed over chicken, pork and fish.

LAMB & EGGPLANT PIES

Cover fillo pastry sheets with a damp tea towel to prevent them from drying out while not using.

2 TEASPOONS VEGETABLE OIL

1 MEDIUM RED ONION (170G), CHOPPED FINELY

1 CLOVE GARLIC, CHOPPED FINELY

500G (1 POUND) LEAN MINCED (GROUND) LAMB

1 MEDIUM EGGPLANT (300G), CHOPPED COARSELY

2 TEASPOONS GROUND CUMIN

4 MEDIUM ROMA (EGG) TOMATOES (300G), CHOPPED COARSELY

1 TABLESPOON LEMON JUICE

¼ CUP (40G) PINE NUTS

100G (3 OUNCES) FETTA, CRUMBLED

2 SHEETS FILLO PASTRY

COOKING-OIL SPRAY

OAK LEAF & HERB SALAD

2 TABLESPOONS OLIVE OIL

2 TABLESPOONS WHITE WINE VINEGAR

1 TABLESPOON DIJON MUSTARD

2 TEASPOONS WHITE (GRANULATED) SUGAR

1 GREEN OAK LEAF LETTUCE, LEAVES SEPARATED

¼ CUP COARSELY CHOPPED FRESH CHIVES

½ CUP FIRMLY PACKED FRESH FLAT-LEAF PARSLEY

1 Preheat oven to 180°C/350°F. Oil four 10cm (4-inch), 1-cup (250ml) ovenproof dishes; place on an oven tray.

2 Heat oil in a large deep frying pan; cook onion and garlic, stirring, until soft. Add lamb; cook, stirring, until browned. Add eggplant and cumin; cook, covered, stirring occasionally, for 10 minutes or until eggplant is soft. Stir in tomato, juice and pine nuts; remove from heat. Spoon mixture into dishes; top with fetta.

3 Place one sheet of pastry on a clean, flat surface. Spray with oil; fold in half crossways, spray with oil. Cut in half to make 2 pieces. Repeat with remaining pastry, making 4 pieces of pastry in total. Place each piece of pastry over lamb mixture, lightly scrunching and tucking pastry around mixture.

4 Bake pies for 15 minutes or until pastry is golden.

5 Meanwhile, make oak leaf and herb salad.

6 Serve pies with salad.

oak leaf & herb salad Place oil, vinegar, mustard and sugar in a screw-top jar; shake well. Season to taste. Place lettuce and herbs in a medium bowl with dressing; toss gently to combine.

nutritional count per serving 34.5g total fat (9.9g saturated fat); 2170kJ (519 cal); 13.7g carbohydrate; 35.3g protein; 6.2g fibre

PREP +
COOK TIME

1 HOUR

SERVES

4

**PREP +
COOK TIME**

2 HOURS

SERVES

6

PINK PEPPERCORN LAMB WITH BALSAMIC ONIONS

2 CLOVES GARLIC, CRUSHED

8 SPRIGS FRESH LEMON THYME, CHOPPED

1 TABLESPOON PINK PEPPERCORNS, CRUSHED, PLUS EXTRA, TO SERVE

1.7KG (3½ POUNDS) BONED LEG OF LAMB

¼ CUP (60ML) EXTRA VIRGIN OLIVE OIL

800G (1½ POUNDS) RAINBOW BABY (DUTCH) CARROTS, TRIMMED

1 BULB GARLIC, HALVED CROSSWAYS

¾ CUP (90G) PITTED GREEN OLIVES, HALVED

BALSAMIC ONIONS

1 TABLESPOON BALSAMIC VINEGAR

1 TABLESPOON WHOLEGRAIN MUSTARD

2 TABLESPOONS VEGETABLE OIL

400G (12½ OUNCES) BABY ONIONS, HALVED

SALSA VERDE

1 CUP FIRMLY PACKED FRESH FLAT-LEAF PARSLEY

2 TEASPOONS FRESH LEMON THYME LEAVES

2 TEASPOONS DRAINED CAPERS, RINSED

1 SMALL CLOVE GARLIC, CRUSHED

¼ CUP (60ML) OLIVE OIL

1 TABLESPOON WHITE WINE VINEGAR

1 Preheat oven to 150°C/300°F.

2 Combine crushed garlic, thyme and peppercorns in a small bowl. Place lamb on a chopping board, cut-side up; cover with plastic wrap, pound with meat mallet. Rub garlic mixture on cut side of lamb. Roll lamb tightly; tie with kitchen string at 2cm (¾-inch) intervals. Place lamb in a large deep roasting pan; brush with 1 tablespoon of the oil.

3 Place carrots in another roasting pan; drizzle with 1 tablespoon of oil. Roast lamb and carrots, uncovered, for 1 hour 40 minutes or until lamb is cooked as desired. Add garlic to carrots, drizzle with remaining oil; roast alongside lamb, for last 20 minutes of cooking.

4 Meanwhile, make balsamic onions and salsa verde.

5 Remove lamb from oven; cover with foil. Increase oven to 200°C/400°F. Add olives to carrots; roast for 5 minutes or until heated.

6 Add balsamic onions to carrot mixture; toss to combine. Serve lamb with carrot mixture, salsa verde and extra peppercorns.

balsamic onions Bring vinegar and mustard to the boil in a small saucepan. Reduce heat; simmer, uncovered, for 5 minutes or until glaze thickens slightly. Heat oil in a large frying pan over medium heat; cook onions, stirring, 10 minutes or until soft, brushing frequently with glaze.

salsa verde Blend or process ingredients until well combined. Season to taste.

nutritional count per serving 37.7g total fat (9.8g saturated fat); 2512kJ (600 cal); 12.7g carbohydrate; 48.6g protein; 9g fibre

tip Rainbow baby carrots are also sold as heirloom carrots; they are available from most supermarkets and greengrocers.

EGGPLANT BOLOGNESE BAKE

2 MEDIUM EGGPLANT (600G)

200G (6½ OUNCES) BABY SPINACH LEAVES

¾ CUP (180G) FRESH RICOTTA

1 EGG WHITE

½ CUP (50G) COARSELY GRATED MOZZARELLA

⅓ CUP (25G) COARSELY GRATED PARMESAN

50G (1½ OUNCES) BABY ROCKET (ARUGULA) LEAVES

BOLOGNESE SAUCE

1 TABLESPOON OLIVE OIL

1 LARGE BROWN ONION (200G), CHOPPED

1 SMALL RED CAPSICUM (BELL PEPPER) (150G), CHOPPED COARSELY

1 SMALL GREEN CAPSICUM (BELL PEPPER) (150G), CHOPPED COARSELY

2 CLOVES GARLIC, CRUSHED

250G (8 OUNCES) MINCED (GROUND) BEEF

1 TABLESPOON TOMATO PASTE

½ CUP (125ML) DRY RED WINE

400G (12½ OUNCES) CANNED CHOPPED TOMATOES

2 TABLESPOONS COARSELY CHOPPED FRESH BASIL

1 Preheat oven to 180°C/350°F.

2 Make bolognese sauce.

3 Meanwhile, cut eggplant into 2mm (⅛-inch) thick slices; cook eggplant on a heated oiled grill plate (or grill or barbecue) until just tender.

4 Boil, steam or microwave spinach until wilted; drain. Squeeze as much liquid as possible from spinach; cool for 10 minutes. Combine spinach, ricotta and egg white in a medium bowl; season.

5 Spread 1 cup of the bolognese sauce over base of a shallow 2-litre (8-cup) ovenproof dish. Layer with half the eggplant, half the spinach mixture and another 1 cup of bolognese sauce. Repeat layering with remaining eggplant, spinach mixture and bolognese sauce. Top with mozzarella and parmesan.

6 Bake for 20 minutes or until cheeses are browned. Stand for 10 minutes. Serve with rocket

bolognese sauce Heat oil in a medium frying pan over medium heat; cook onion, capsicums and garlic, stirring, for 5 minutes or until onion softens. Remove from pan. Increase heat to high, add beef; cook, stirring, 5 minutes or until beef is browned all over. Return vegetables to pan with tomato paste; cook, stirring, 3 minutes. Add wine; cook, stirring, 2 minutes. Add tomatoes; bring to the boil. Reduce heat; simmer, uncovered, for 25 minutes or until mixture thickens slightly. Stir in basil; season.

nutritional count per serving 23.7g total fat (10.8g saturated fat); 1743kJ (416 cal); 10.8g carbohydrate; 32.5g protein; 8.1g fibre

**PREP +
COOK TIME**
30 MINUTES
SERVES
4

LAMB & BLACK BEAN
STIR-FRY

1 TABLESPOON PEANUT OIL

500G (1 POUND) LAMB BACKSTRAP (EYE OF LOIN), SLICED THINLY

300G (9½ OUNCES) BROCCOLINI, TRIMMED

300G (9½ OUNCES) GREEN BEANS, HALVED CROSSWAYS

300G (9½ OUNCES) SNOW PEAS

⅔ CUP (160ML) WATER

½ CUP (125ML) BLACK BEAN SAUCE

4 GREEN ONIONS (SCALLIONS), CUT INTO 5CM (2-INCH) LENGTHS

3 TEASPOONS SAMBAL OELEK

1 Heat half the oil in a wok over high heat; stir-fry lamb, in batches, until browned all over. Remove from wok.

2 Heat remaining oil in wok; stir-fry broccolini, beans, snow peas and half the water until tender. Remove from wok.

3 Return lamb to wok with black bean sauce and the remaining water; stir-fry until lamb is heated through.

4 Return vegetables to wok with green onions and sambal oelek; stir-fry to combine.

nutritional count per serving 13.4g total fat (3.5g saturated fat); 1429kJ (341 cal); 14.5g carbohydrate; 36.2g protein; 8.4g fibre

OSSO BUCO WITH SOFT POLENTA

1 TABLESPOON OLIVE OIL

8 PIECES VEAL OSSO BUCO (1.6KG) (SEE TIP)

1 MEDIUM BROWN ONION (150G), CHOPPED

2 CLOVES GARLIC, CRUSHED

1 TRIMMED STALK CELERY (100G), CHOPPED

1 LARGE CARROT (180G), CHOPPED COARSELY

2 TABLESPOONS TOMATO PASTE

400G (12½ OUNCES) CANNED CRUSHED TOMATOES

½ CUP (125ML) DRY WHITE WINE

1 CUP (250ML) BEEF STOCK

1 CUP (250ML) WATER

1 TEASPOON FRESH ROSEMARY LEAVES

1 MEDIUM EGGPLANT (300G), CHOPPED COARSELY

1 MEDIUM RED CAPSICUM (BELL PEPPER) (200G), CHOPPED COARSELY

GREMOLATA

2 TEASPOONS FINELY GRATED LEMON RIND

¼ CUP FINELY CHOPPED FRESH FLAT-LEAF PARSLEY

1 TABLESPOON FINELY CHOPPED FRESH ROSEMARY

1 CLOVE GARLIC, CHOPPED FINELY

SOFT POLENTA

1¼ CUPS (310ML) CHICKEN STOCK

¾ CUP (180ML) MILK

¾ CUP (125G) POLENTA

½ CUP (125ML) MILK, EXTRA

2 TABLESPOONS FINELY GRATED PARMESAN

1 Heat half the oil in a large saucepan over medium-high heat; cook veal, in batches, until browned all over. Remove from pan.

2 Heat remaining oil in same pan over medium heat; cook onion, garlic, celery and carrot, stirring, for 5 minutes or until vegetables soften. Stir in paste, tomatoes, wine, stock, the water and rosemary; bring to the boil.

3 Return veal to pan, fitting pieces upright and tightly together in a single layer; return to the boil. Reduce heat; simmer, covered, for 1½ hours. Add eggplant; simmer, uncovered, for 15 minutes. Add capsicum; cook for another 15 minutes or until vegetables are tender.

4 Meanwhile, make gremolata and soft polenta.

5 Remove veal and vegetables from dish; cover to keep warm. Bring sauce to the boil; boil, uncovered, 10 minutes or until sauce thickens slightly. Season to taste.

6 Divide polenta, veal and vegetables among serving plates; top with sauce and gremolata.

gremolata Combine ingredients in a small bowl.

soft polenta Bring stock and milk to the boil in a medium saucepan. Gradually add polenta, stirring constantly. Reduce heat; simmer, stirring for 10 minutes or until polenta thickens. Add extra milk and parmesan; stir to combine. Season to taste.

nutritional count per serving 17.5g total fat (5.9g saturated fat); 3379kJ (808 cal); 39.9g carbohydrate; 112.9g protein; 9.3g fibre

tip Ask your butcher to cut the veal shin into fairly thick pieces (about 3cm/1¼ inches) for you.

PREP + COOK TIME

3 HOURS

SERVES

4

PREP +
COOK TIME
35 MINUTES
(+ REFRIGERATION)

SERVES
4

HOISIN BEEF STIR-FRY

1 TEASPOON SESAME OIL

1 FRESH SMALL RED CHILLI, CHOPPED FINELY

2 CLOVES GARLIC, CRUSHED

1 TEASPOON FINELY GRATED FRESH GINGER

⅓ CUP (80ML) CHINESE RICE WINE

⅓ CUP (80ML) SOY SAUCE

800G (1½ POUNDS) BEEF STRIPS

1 TABLESPOON PEANUT OIL

100G (3 OUNCES) FRESH SHIITAKE MUSHROOMS, TRIMMED, SLICED THINLY

500G (1 POUND) CHOY SUM, HALVED

4 GREEN ONIONS (SCALLIONS), HALVED LENGTHWAYS

¼ CUP (60ML) WATER

¼ CUP (60ML) HOISIN SAUCE

1 FRESH LONG RED CHILLI, SLICED THINLY ON THE DIAGONAL, EXTRA

1 Combine sesame oil, chilli, garlic, ginger, half the rice wine and half the soy sauce in a large bowl. Add beef; toss to coat in mixture. Cover; refrigerate for 3 hours or overnight.

2 Heat half the peanut oil in a wok or large frying pan; stir-fry undrained beef mixture, in batches, until beef is browned all over and just cooked through. Remove from wok.

3 Heat remaining peanut oil in wok; stir-fry mushrooms, choy sum stalks, green onion and the water. Cover; cook for 5 minutes or until vegetables are tender.

4 Return beef to wok with hoisin, choy sum leaves, remaining rice wine and remaining soy sauce; stir-fry until choy sum leaves just wilt. Serve stir-fry topped with extra chilli.

nutritional count per serving 11.3g total fat (2.7g saturated fat); 1623kJ (388 cal); 9.4g carbohydrate; 54g protein; 6.3g fibre

tip Remove seeds from chilli if you prefer less heat.

SEAFOOD STEW

4 CLEANED BABY SQUID HOODS (480G)

2 BABY FENNEL BULBS (260G)

2 TABLESPOONS LEMON JUICE

1 TABLESPOON OLIVE OIL

2 MEDIUM BROWN ONIONS (300G), CHOPPED FINELY

4 CLOVES GARLIC, CRUSHED

3 X 5CM (2¼-INCH) STRIPS THINLY SLICED ORANGE RIND, PLUS EXTRA TO SERVE

1 FRESH LONG RED CHILLI, CHOPPED FINELY

PINCH SAFFRON THREADS

⅓ CUP (80ML) DRY WHITE WINE

800G (1½ POUNDS) CANNED DICED TOMATOES

1 LITRE (4 CUPS) FISH STOCK

1KG (2 POUNDS) LARGE UNCOOKED PRAWNS, PEELED, DEVEINED, WITH TAILS INTACT

200G (6½ OUNCES) PIPIS, SCRUBBED

250G (8 OUNCES) SMALL BLACK MUSSELS, SCRUBBED, BEARD REMOVED

200G (6½ OUNCES) BABY OCTOPUS, CLEANED

1 Insert a large knife into a squid hood. Using a small sharp knife, cut 1cm (½-inch) thick slices on one side of squid. Repeat with remaining squid.

2 Trim fennel; reserve fronds. Using a mandoline or V-slicer, slice fennel as thinly as possible. Combine fennel and juice in a small bowl.

3 Heat oil in a large saucepan; cook onion, stirring, until soft. Add garlic; cook, stirring, for 1 minute.

4 Stir rind, chilli, saffron and wine into onion mixture; cook, stirring, for 2 minutes. Add tomatoes; simmer, uncovered, for 10 minutes or until mixture thickens slightly. Add stock; simmer, uncovered, for 20 minutes or until liquid is reduced by about a quarter.

5 Add squid, prawns, pipis, mussels and octopus to pan. Cover; simmer, stirring occasionally, for 5 minutes or until seafood is cooked.

6 Serve stew with fennel mixture; sprinkle with reserved fronds and extra rind.

nutritional count per serving 9.4g total fat (2.3g saturated fat); 1806kJ (431 cal); 15g carbohydrate; 66g protein; 5.4g fibre

tip Some mussels might not open – these may need to be opened with a knife, or might not have cooked as quickly as the others. Farmed mussels will not all open up during cooking, and some will not open after excessive cooking – you do not have to discard these, just open with a knife and cook a little more, if you wish.

**PREP +
COOK TIME**
45 MINUTES
SERVES
4

BEEF STEAK WITH CAPSICUM RELISH

You can make the capsicum relish the day before; store, covered, in the fridge. Reheat just before serving.

3 MEDIUM RED CAPSICUMS (BELL PEPPERS) (600G)

1 TEASPOON OLIVE OIL

1 LARGE BROWN ONION (200G), SLICED THINLY

2 CLOVES GARLIC, SLICED THINLY

1½ TABLESPOONS BROWN SUGAR

2 TABLESPOONS SHERRY VINEGAR

3 FRESH SMALL RED CHILLIES, SEEDED, CHOPPED FINELY

2 X 450G (14½-OUNCE) NEW YORK CUT BEEF SIRLOIN STEAKS

⅓ CUP (80ML) OLIVE OIL, EXTRA

750G (1½ POUNDS) SMALL KUMARA (ORANGE SWEET POTATO), CUT INTO WEDGES

2 TABLESPOONS SMALL FRESH FLAT-LEAF PARSLEY LEAVES

1 Quarter capsicums; discard seeds and membranes. Roast under hot grill (or in a 240°C/475°F oven), skin-side up, until skin blisters and blackens. Place in a heatproof bowl, cover with plastic wrap; stand for 5 minutes. Peel away skin, then slice thinly.

2 Heat oil in a medium frying pan over medium heat; cook onion and garlic, stirring, for 5 minutes or until onion softens. Add sugar, vinegar, chilli and capsicum; cook, stirring, for 5 minutes.

3 Coat beef with half the extra oil; season. Cook beef on a heated oiled grill plate (or grill or barbecue), over medium-high heat, for 4 minutes each side or until browned and cooked as desired. Remove from heat; rest, covered, for 5 minutes.

4 Boil, steam or microwave kumara until just tender; drain. Heat remaining extra oil in a large frying pan over high heat; cook kumara, in two batches, for 1 minute each side or until browned. Season to taste.

5 Serve sliced steaks with capsicum relish and kumara; top with parsley.

nutritional count per serving 33.9g total fat (9.2g saturated fat); 3033kJ (726 cal); 47.4g carbohydrate; 53.6g protein; 8.8g fibre

CHILLI CON CARNE WITH AVOCADO SALAD

1 TABLESPOON OLIVE OIL

1 MEDIUM BROWN ONION (150G), CHOPPED FINELY

1 CLOVE GARLIC, CRUSHED

500G (1 POUND) MINCED (GROUND) BEEF

60G (1-OUNCE) SACHET TACO SEASONING

1 CUP (250ML) BEEF STOCK

2 TABLESPOONS TOMATO PASTE

800G (1½-POUND) CANNED CRUSHED TOMATOES

1 TABLESPOON FINELY CHOPPED FRESH OREGANO

400G (12½-OUNCE) CANNED KIDNEY BEANS, DRAINED, RINSED

LIME CHEEKS, TO SERVE

AVOCADO SALAD

1 LARGE AVOCADO (320G), HALVED, SLICED

125G (4 OUNCES) YELLOW GRAPE TOMATOES, HALVED

½ SMALL RED ONION (50G), SLICED THINLY

1 FRESH LONG RED CHILLI, CHOPPED FINELY

¼ CUP LOOSELY PACKED FRESH CORIANDER (CILANTRO)

1 Heat oil in a medium saucepan; cook onion and garlic, stirring, until onion softens. Add beef and taco seasoning; stir until beef is browned. Stir in stock, paste, tomatoes and oregano; bring to the boil. Reduce heat; simmer, covered, for 30 minutes.

2 Stir beans into beef mixture; simmer, uncovered, for a further 30 minutes or until thickened slightly. Season to taste.

3 Meanwhile, make avocado salad.

4 Serve chilli con carne with salad and lime cheeks.

avocado salad Place ingredients in a medium bowl; toss gently to combine.

nutritional count per serving 35.4g total fat (11.2g saturated fat); 2527kJ (604 cal); 25g carbohydrate; 41g protein; 10.3g fibre

tips You can use 2 teaspoons dried oregano instead of the fresh if you prefer or if fresh is unavailable. Store chilli con carne mixture, covered, in the fridge for up to 3 days or freeze for up to 3 months.

PREP +
COOK TIME

1¼ HOURS

SERVES

4

280g polenta
85g plain
2 tbs Bog S.   1400C
1 egg   425
150 min b milk
2 chillies

CHICKEN SATAY SKEWERS WITH CRUNCHY SALAD

1KG (2 POUNDS) CHICKEN THIGH FILLETS, CHOPPED COARSELY

100G (3 OUNCES) WHITE CABBAGE, SHREDDED FINELY

2 GREEN ONIONS (SCALLIONS), SLICED THINLY

1 STALK CELERY (150G), TRIMMED, SLICED THINLY

100G (3 OUNCES) DAIKON, CUT INTO THICK MATCHSTICKS

180G (5½ OUNCES) BABY SALAD MIX

1 CUP (80G) BEAN SPROUTS

¼ CUP (35G) ROASTED PEANUTS, CHOPPED COARSELY

¼ CUP LOOSELY PACKED FRESH CORIANDER (CILANTRO) LEAVES

LIME CHEEKS, TO SERVE

SATAY SAUCE

½ CUP (75G) ROASTED PEANUTS, CHOPPED COARSELY

1 TABLESPOON LIGHT BROWN SUGAR

1 CUP (250ML) COCONUT MILK

1 TEASPOON FISH SAUCE

¼ CUP (60ML) SOY SAUCE

1 TEASPOON CHILLI FLAKES

1 TABLESPOON PEANUT BUTTER

CHILLI LIME DRESSING

1 FRESH SMALL RED CHILLI, SLICED THINLY

¼ CUP (60ML) LIME JUICE

1 TABLESPOON SOY SAUCE

1 TABLESPOON PEANUT OIL

1 Make satay sauce.

2 Thread chicken onto eight 23cm (9¼-inch) metal skewers, coat with half the satay sauce.

3 Cook skewers on a heated oiled grill plate (or grill or barbecue) for 10 minutes, brushing occasionally with remaining satay sauce, or until chicken is cooked through.

4 Make chilli lime dressing.

5 Place cabbage, green onion, celery, daikon, salad mix, sprouts, peanuts and coriander in a large bowl; toss gently to combine.

6 Serve skewers with salad, dressing and lime cheeks.

satay sauce Stir ingredients in a medium bowl until combined.

chilli lime dressing Place ingredients in a screw-top jar; shake well to combine.

nutritional count per serving 33.9g total fat (14.2g saturated fat); 1763kJ (421 cal); 12.7g carbohydrate; 13.4g protein; 7.2g fibre

tip If you use bamboo skewers, soak them in water for at least 1 hour before use to prevent them splintering and scorching during cooking.

KUMARA CANNELLONI

3 MEDIUM KUMARA (ORANGE SWEET POTATO) (1.2KG), UNPEELED

500G (1 POUND) FRESH RICOTTA

1 EGG, BEATEN LIGHTLY

2 GREEN ONIONS (SCALLIONS), SLICED THINLY

¼ CUP FINELY CHOPPED FRESH FLAT-LEAF PARSLEY

¼ CUP FINELY CHOPPED FRESH CHIVES

2 TABLESPOONS FINELY CHOPPED FRESH THYME

1 CUP (80G) FINELY GRATED PARMESAN

1 CUP (80G) FINELY GRATED PECORINO CHEESE

100G (3 OUNCES) SOURDOUGH, CRUST REMOVED, TORN INTO SMALL PIECES

¼ CUP (40G) PINE NUTS

½ TEASPOON GROUND NUTMEG

1½ TABLESPOONS OLIVE OIL

⅓ CUP (25G) FLAKED PARMESAN, EXTRA

2 TABLESPOONS FRESH THYME SPRIGS, EXTRA

CHEESE SAUCE

1 CUP (250ML) THICKENED (HEAVY) CREAM

¾ CUP (90G) COARSELY GRATED CHEDDAR

1 Preheat oven to 200°C/400°F. Place one of the kumara on an oven tray. Bake for 30 minutes or until tender; cool. Reduce oven to 160°C/325°F.

2 Meanwhile, peel remaining kumara. Using a mandoline or V-slicer, cut kumara lengthways into 3mm (⅛-inch) thin slices. Trim slices to 5.5cm x 12cm (2¼-inch x 4¾-inch) rectangles; you will need 36 rectangles (see tips).

3 Bring a large saucepan of water to the boil. Season. Add half the kumara slices; boil for 1½ minutes or until softened. Remove from pan with a slotted spoon; place on a tray to cool. Repeat with remaining kumara slices.

4 When cool enough to handle, remove skin from baked kumara. Add baked kumara to a processor with ricotta; process until smooth. Transfer to a large bowl. Stir in egg, green onion, herbs and half the cheeses. Season.

5 Oil a 22cm x 26cm (8¾-inch x 10½-inch) roasting pan. Place 1 heaped tablespoon of filling at the short end of a kumara slice; roll to enclose filling. Place, seam-side down, in pan. Repeat with remaining kumara slices and filling, until pan is filled, in a single layer.

6 Combine sourdough, pine nuts and nutmeg in a medium bowl with 1 tablespoon of the oil and remaining cheeses. Sprinkle over kumara cannelloni.

7 Bake for 15 minutes or until top is golden and crunchy.

8 Meanwhile, make cheese sauce.

9 Serve kumara cannelloni topped with cheese sauce, extra flaked parmesan and extra thyme; drizzle with remaining oil.

cheese sauce Stir ingredients in a small saucepan over medium heat, without boiling, for 4 minutes or until cheddar melts and sauce thickens slightly. Season.

nutritional count per serving 46.8g total fat (24.7g saturated fat); 2925kJ (698 cal); 38.8g carbohydrate; 29.2g protein; 5.4g fibre

tips There will be some wastage from slicing the kumara. Leftover kumara can be chopped and cooked in soups, purees and mashes. You could layer the kumara slices and filling mixture instead of rolling them, if you like.

PREP +
COOK TIME
50 MINUTES
SERVES
4

SPANISH CHICKEN & CHORIZO STEW

Chorizo is a sausage made of coarsely ground pork and highly seasoned with garlic and chilli. It is available both smoked and dry-cured, or fresh (raw). It's widely used in Spanish, Portuguese and Mexican cookery, although each country has its own variation.

1 CUP (250ML) CHICKEN STOCK

PINCH SAFFRON THREADS

340G (11 OUNCES) CURED CHORIZO SAUSAGE, SLICED THICKLY

4 CHICKEN MARYLANDS (1.6KG), SEPARATED AT JOINT INTO LEG AND THIGH PORTIONS

2 TEASPOONS OLIVE OIL

1 MEDIUM BROWN ONION (150G), SLICED THICKLY

1 MEDIUM RED CAPSICUM (BELL PEPPER) (200G), SLICED THICKLY

2 TEASPOONS SMOKED PAPRIKA

800G (1½ POUNDS) CANNED CRUSHED TOMATOES

½ CUP (75G) SEEDED BLACK OLIVES

½ CUP FRESH FLAT-LEAF PARSLEY SPRIGS

1 Combine stock and saffron in a small bowl. Set aside until required.

2 Cook chorizo in a large saucepan, over medium heat, until browned. Drain on paper towel.

3 Cook chicken in same pan, in batches, until browned all over. Remove from pan.

4 Heat oil in same pan, add onion and capsicum; cook, stirring, for 2 minutes or until onion softens. Add paprika; cook, stirring, until fragrant.

5 Return chorizo and chicken to pan with stock mixture and tomatoes, cover; bring to the boil. Reduce heat; simmer, covered, for 20 minutes or until chicken is cooked through. Stir in olives.

6 Serve stew topped with parsley.

nutritional count per serving 31.4g total fat (9.6g saturated fat); 2605kJ (622 cal); 11.5g carbohydrate; 69.9g protein; 6.2g fibre

tip Chorizo is available from the delicatessen section of some supermarkets, as well as Spanish delicatessens and some specialty butcher shops.

MOROCCAN CHICKEN & CHICKPEA CASSEROLE

1.3KG (2¾ POUNDS) CHICKEN THIGH FILLETS

1 TABLESPOON MOROCCAN SPICE MIX

2 TABLESPOONS OLIVE OIL

400G (12½ OUNCES) CANNED CHICKPEAS (GARBANZO BEANS), DRAINED, RINSED

½ CUP (75G) DRIED APRICOTS

1 LARGE BROWN ONION (200G), SLICED THINLY

800G (1½ POUNDS) CANNED CRUSHED TOMATOES

½ CUP (125ML) CHICKEN STOCK

¾ CUP (150G) TRI-COLOURED QUINOA

⅓ CUP FRESH FLAT-LEAF PARSLEY SPRIGS

1 Preheat oven to 200°C/400°F.

2 Place chicken and spice mix in a large bowl; rub to coat.

3 Heat half the oil in a large frying pan; cook chicken, in batches, until browned both sides. Transfer chicken to a 4-litre (16-cup) ovenproof dish. Add chickpeas and apricots; stir to combine.

4 Heat remaining oil in same frying pan; cook onion, stirring, until softened. Add tomatoes and stock; bring to the boil. Carefully pour tomato mixture over chicken mixture; cover. Transfer to oven; roast for 15 minutes or until chicken is cooked through. Season to taste.

5 Meanwhile, cook quinoa in a large saucepan of boiling water for 12 minutes or until tender; drain.

6 Top casserole with parsley, serve with quinoa.

nutritional count per serving 36.9g total fat (9.1g saturated fat); 3511kJ (840 cal); 49g carbohydrate; 72.8g protein; 11.1g fibre

PREP +
COOK TIME

40 MINUTES

SERVES

4

MARINADES & RUBS

THESE RECIPES ARE ENOUGH TO COVER ABOUT 800G (1½LB) MEAT AND WILL SERVE 4.

LEMON HERB MARINADE

prep time 10 minutes **makes** ½ cup

Combine the finely grated rind and juice of 1 lemon with 1 tablespoon chopped fresh flat-leaf parsley, 1 tablespoon chopped fresh basil, 1 tablespoon chopped fresh oregano, 1 crushed clove garlic and 2 tablespoons olive oil. Season.

nutritional count per tablespoon 6.1g total fat (1g saturated fat); 238kJ (57 cal); 0.4g carbohydrate; 0.1g protein; 0.3g fibre

tip Use half the mixture to marinate the food, then drizzle remaning over cooked food before serving.

goes with Lamb, chicken and prawns.

FIVE-SPICE MARINADE

prep time 5 minutes **makes** ⅓ cup

Combine 2 tablespoons oyster sauce, 1 tablespoon hoisin sauce, 1 tablespoon dry sherry, 1 teaspoon chinese five-spice and 1 crushed clove garlic in a small bowl.

nutritional count per tablespoon 0.5g total fat (0.1g saturated fat); 146kJ (35 cal); 5.2g carbohydrate; 0.6g protein; 0.8g fibre

tip To avoid burning, cook the marinated food in the oven rather than on a grill plate (or barbecue).

goes with Chicken and pork.

SMOKY PEPPER SALT

prep time 5 minutes **makes** ¼ cup

Combine 1 teaspoon mustard powder, 1 tablespoon light brown sugar, 1 teaspoon cracked black pepper, 1 tablespoon smoked paprika, ½ teaspoon cayenne pepper and 2 teaspoons sea salt in a small bowl.

nutritional count per tablespoon 1.2g total fat (0.1g saturated fat); 158kJ (38 cal); 5.4g carbohydrate; 1g protein; 0.9g fibre

goes with Beef, chicken, lamb and pork.

SWEET PAPRIKA RUB

prep time 5 minutes **makes** ¼ cup

Combine 2 teaspoons sweet paprika, 1 tablespoon ground cumin, 1 tablespoon ground coriander, 1 teaspoon garlic powder and 2 tablespoons olive oil in a small bowl.

nutritional count per tablespoon 13.7g total fat (2.1g saturated fat); 588kJ (141 cal); 2.4g carbohydrate; 1.3g protein; 0.8g fibre

goes with Fish, pork and beef.

MOROCCAN CHICKEN WITH CAULIFLOWER PILAF

The warm colours and flavours of Moroccan food start with an assortment of wonderful spices. Harissa, paprika, ras el hanout, ginger, cumin, cinnamon and saffron, the spices are balanced to enhance the flavour of the food, while the aroma readies the appetite for what is to come. Ensure you use fresh spices that retain their fragrant flavour and aroma.

8 CHICKEN DRUMSTICKS (1.2KG)

2 TABLESPOONS MOROCCAN SPICE MIX

2 TABLESPOONS OLIVE OIL

2 MEDIUM RED ONIONS (340G), CUT INTO WEDGES

4 WEDGES PRESERVED LEMON, FLESH REMOVED, ONE THINLY SLICED

½ CUP LOOSELY PACKED FRESH FLAT-LEAF PARSLEY LEAVES

CAULIFLOWER PILAF

2 TABLESPOONS OLIVE OIL

400G (12½ OUNCES) CANNED CHICKPEAS (GARBANZO BEANS), DRAINED, RINSED

1 MEDIUM CAULIFLOWER (1KG), STEMS CHOPPED FINELY, FLORETS CHOPPED COARSELY

⅓ CUP (45G) PISTACHIOS

¼ CUP COARSELY CHOPPED FRESH FLAT-LEAF PARSLEY

1 Preheat oven to 200°C/400°F. Oil two large shallow oven trays; line with baking paper.

2 Place chicken, spice mix and half the oil in a large bowl; toss to coat chicken in spice mix. Season.

3 Heat half the remaining oil in a large deep frying pan over high heat; cook chicken, in batches, for 3 minutes or until browned. Transfer to one of the trays.

4 Heat remaining oil in same pan; cook onion, stirring occasionally for 2 minutes, or until softened slightly. Transfer onion to remaining oven tray. Roast onion for 15 minutes and chicken for 25 minutes or until cooked.

5 Meanwhile, make cauliflower pilaf.

6 Serve pilaf topped with chicken and onions, sprinkled with preserved lemons and parsley.

cauliflower pilaf Heat oil in a large frying pan over high heat; cook chickpeas, stirring occasionally, for 4 minutes or until they start to make a popping sound. Meanwhile, process cauliflower, in batches, until finely chopped. Add to frying pan; cook, stirring occasionally, for 12 minutes or until cauliflower is just tender. Stir in remaining ingredients; season to taste.

nutritional count per serving 42.2g total fat (8.5g saturated fat); 2711kJ (649 cal); 19.2g carbohydrate; 42.3g protein; 13.3g fibre

tips Chicken thigh fillets would also work well in this recipe. Preserved lemon is a North African specialty. Only the rind is used; remove and discard the flesh from the rind. Rinse the rind well under cold water before use.

BROCCOLI 'PIZZA' WITH ZUCCHINI

Passata is sieved tomato puree sold alongside other bottled pasta sauces in most supermarkets. You can use your favourite pasta sauce instead, if you like.

1KG (2 POUNDS) BROCCOLI, TRIMMED, CUT INTO FLORETS

¼ CUP (30G) COARSELY GRATED CHEDDAR

1 EGG, BEATEN LIGHTLY

¾ CUP (60G) COARSELY GRATED PARMESAN

½ CUP (130G) TOMATO PASSATA

2 SMALL ZUCCHINI (180G), SLICED THINLY INTO RIBBONS

1 CUP FRESH BASIL LEAVES

1 FRESH SMALL RED (SERRANO) CHILLI, SLICED THINLY

100G (3 OUNCES) BUFFALO MOZZARELLA, TORN ROUGHLY

1 TABLESPOON OLIVE OIL

1 TABLESPOON FINELY GRATED LEMON RIND OR THIN STRIPS (SEE TIP)

1 TABLESPOON LEMON JUICE

1 Preheat oven to 200°C/400°F. Line two oven trays with baking paper; mark a 22cm (8¾-inch) round on each sheet of paper, turn paper over.

2 Process broccoli until finely chopped. Transfer to a microwave-safe bowl, cover with plastic wrap; microwave on HIGH (100%) for 12 minutes or until tender (you can steam the broccoli instead, but do not boil it as this will make the crust too soggy). Drain. When cool enough to handle, place broccoli in the centre of a clean tea towel; gather the ends together, then squeeze out as much excess moisture as possible.

3 Place broccoli in a large bowl with cheddar, egg and ¼ cup of the parmesan; stir to combine. Season. Divide broccoli mixture between trays; spread mixture inside the marked rounds, smooth the surface. Bake bases for 25 minutes or until golden.

4 Spread bases with passata, top with half the zucchini and half the basil, the chilli, mozzarella and remaining parmesan. Bake for 20 minutes or until golden and crisp.

5 Meanwhile, combine oil, rind, juice, remaining zucchini and remaining basil in a medium bowl; season.

6 Serve pizzas topped with zucchini salad.

nutritional count per serving 26.5g total fat (8.1g saturated fat); 1280kJ (306 cal); 3.3g carbohydrate; 13.2g protein; 1.3g fibre

tip If you have one, use a zester to create strips of lemon rind. If you don't have one, peel two long, wide strips of rind from the lemon, without the white pith, then cut them lengthways into thin strips.

PREP +
COOK TIME
I HOUR
SERVES
4

CHICKEN WINGS WITH BROCCOLI RICE

2 TABLESPOONS SALT-REDUCED SOY SAUCE

3 CLOVES GARLIC, CRUSHED

2 TABLESPOONS FINELY CHOPPED FRESH LEMON GRASS

1 TEASPOON CASTER (SUPERFINE) SUGAR

1 TABLESPOON PEANUT OIL

2KG (4 POUNDS) CHICKEN WINGS, TIPS REMOVED

20G (¾-OUNCE) PIECE FRESH GINGER, CUT INTO THIN MATCHSTICKS

500G (1 POUND) BROCCOLI, CHOPPED FINELY

⅓ CUP LOOSELY PACKED FRESH CORIANDER (CILANTRO) SPRIGS

GINGER DIPPING SAUCE

20G (¾-OUNCE) PIECE FRESH GINGER, CUT INTO THIN MATCHSTICKS

1 SMALL CLOVE GARLIC, CRUSHED

1½ CUPS (375ML) SALT-REDUCED CHICKEN STOCK

1 TABLESPOON SALT-REDUCED SOY SAUCE

GREEN ONION BROTH

2 CUPS (500ML) SALT-REDUCED CHICKEN STOCK (SEE TIP)

2 GREEN ONIONS (SCALLIONS), SLICED THINLY ON THE DIAGONAL

1 Preheat oven to 200°C/400°F. Oil two large shallow oven trays; line with baking paper.

2 Combine soy sauce, garlic, lemon grass, sugar and oil in a medium bowl, add chicken; toss to coat chicken in mixture. Divide chicken, in a single layer, between oven trays; top with ginger. Roast for 40 minutes, basting with cooking juices twice during cooking, or until chicken is browned and cooked through.

3 Meanwhile, make ginger dipping sauce, then green onion broth.

4 Process broccoli, in batches, until finely chopped and resembles rice grains. Blanch in a medium saucepan of boiling water for 20 seconds; drain. Spread on paper towel to dry; season to taste.

5 Pour warm broth into serving cups. Serve broccoli rice topped with chicken, coriander and dipping sauce.

ginger dipping sauce Combine ingredients in a medium bowl.

green onion broth Heat stock in a small saucepan until warm; stir in green onions.

nutritional count per serving 49.5g total fat (14.3g saturated fat); 2774kJ (664 cal); 4.7g carbohydrate; 48g protein; 5.6g fibre

tips You can make your own stock for the green onion broth using the wing tips, ginger and onion offcuts. Place in a medium saucepan with 1 litre (4 cups) water; simmer for 15 minutes, skim surface. Drain. Eat chicken with a little bit of everything in each mouthful for a good balance of flavours.

RED CHICKEN SALAD

⅔ CUP (160ML) TARRAGON VINEGAR

¼ CUP (55G) CASTER (SUPERFINE) SUGAR

1 MEDIUM RED ONION (170G), HALVED, SLICED THINLY

½ MEDIUM RED CABBAGE (750G), SHREDDED FINELY

¼ CUP (20G) FLAKED ALMONDS

450G (14½ OUNCES) CANNED BABY BEETROOT (BEETS), DRAINED

3 CUPS (900G) SHREDDED COOKED CHICKEN (SEE TIP)

¼ CUP FRESH CHIVES, CUT INTO LENGTHS

2 SMALL RADICCHIOS (300G), LEAVES SEPARATED

150G (4½ OUNCES) GOAT'S CHEESE, CRUMBLED

1 TABLESPOON EXTRA VIRGIN OLIVE OIL

1 Whisk vinegar and sugar in a large bowl until sugar is dissolved. Add onion and cabbage; toss gently to coat. Stand 30 minutes to pickle slightly. Drain in a colander; discard excess dressing. Season to taste.

2 Meanwhile, stir almonds in a small frying pan over medium heat until lightly toasted.

3 Cut larger pieces of beetroot into irregular shapes. Add beetroot to cabbage mixture with chicken and half the chives; toss gently to combine.

4 Arrange radicchio on a serving platter; top with cabbage mixture, goat's cheese, almonds and remaining chives. Drizzle with oil.

nutritional count per serving 25g total fat (8.9g saturated fat); 2294kJ (548 cal); 28.4g carbohydrate; 46g protein; 11.3g fibre

tip You will need to buy a large barbecued chicken weighing about 900g (1¾ pounds) for this recipe.

PREP TIME

20 MINUTES
(+ STANDING)

SERVES

4

PREP +
COOK TIME
50 MINUTES
SERVES
4

CHICKEN TIKKA WITH CAULIFLOWER RICE

1 TABLESPOON PEANUT OIL

800G (1½ POUNDS) CHICKEN THIGH FILLETS, SLICED THICKLY

1 MEDIUM BROWN ONION (150G), CUT INTO WEDGES

1 LARGE RED CAPSICUM (BELL PEPPER) (350G), CHOPPED COARSELY

250G (8 OUNCES) TRUSS CHERRY TOMATOES

⅓ CUP (100G) TIKKA CURRY PASTE

2 FRESH LONG GREEN CHILLIES, SLICED THINLY

300ML LIGHT COOKING CREAM

1 SMALL CAULIFLOWER (1KG), STEMS FINELY CHOPPED, FLORETS COARSELY CHOPPED

¾ CUP LOOSELY PACKED FRESH CORIANDER (CILANTRO) LEAVES

RAITA

¾ CUP (200G) GREEK-STYLE YOGHURT

1 LEBANESE CUCUMBER (130G), SEEDED, CHOPPED FINELY

1 TABLESPOON FINELY CHOPPED FRESH MINT

1 Heat oil in a large deep frying pan over medium-high heat; cook chicken, in batches, until browned all over. Remove from pan.

2 Add onion, capsicum and tomatoes to same pan, reduce heat to medium; cook, stirring, for 5 minutes or until onion softens. Remove tomatoes from pan; cover to keep warm. Add paste and half the chilli to pan; cook, stirring, for 2 minutes or until fragrant. Return chicken to pan with cooking cream; bring to the boil. Reduce heat; simmer, uncovered, for 10 minutes or until chicken is cooked through. Remove from heat; return tomatoes to mixture.

3 Meanwhile, process cauliflower until finely chopped and resembles rice. Place cauliflower in a large frying pan over medium heat; cook, stirring occasionally, for 10 minutes or until just tender. Season to taste.

4 Make raita.

5 Top chicken with coriander and remaining chilli. Serve with cauliflower rice and raita.

raita Combine ingredients in a small bowl; season.

nutritional count per serving 39.9g total fat (16.2g saturated fat); 2818kJ (674 cal); 20.4g carbohydrate; 50.6g protein; 10g fibre

BARBECUED CHERMOULLA CHICKEN WITH PEA PUREE

2 CLOVES GARLIC

2 SHALLOTS (50G)

1 FRESH SMALL RED THAI CHILLI

1 SPRIG FRESH CORIANDER (CILANTRO), STEM AND ROOT ATTACHED

2 TEASPOONS GROUND CUMIN

1 TEASPOON SMOKED PAPRIKA

1½ TABLESPOONS EXTRA VIRGIN OLIVE OIL

8 X 125G (4-OUNCE) CHICKEN THIGH FILLETS

100G (3 OUNCES) SNOW PEA TENDRILS

PEA PUREE

500G (1 POUND) FROZEN BABY PEAS, THAWED

25G (¾ OUNCE) BUTTER

¾ CUP (180G) SOUR CREAM

1 Blend or process garlic, shallots, chilli, coriander, cumin, paprika and half the oil until almost smooth. Transfer mixture to a large bowl; add chicken, rub mixture all over chicken. Season.

2 Cook chicken on a heated, oiled grill plate (or grill or barbecue), until chicken is browned both sides and cooked through.

3 Meanwhile, make pea puree.

4 Serve chicken with pea puree and snow pea tendrils; drizzle with remaining oil, sprinkle with pepper.

pea puree Stir peas and butter in a medium saucepan, over medium heat, for 5 minutes or until peas are tender and butter is melted. Blend or process pea mixture with sour cream until smooth.

nutritional count per serving 39.9g total fat (16g saturated fat); 2709kJ (648 cal); 10.9g carbohydrate; 57g protein; 11g fibre

PREP +
COOK TIME

35 MINUTES

SERVES

4

TOFU & VEGETABLE
RED CURRY

1 TABLESPOON VEGETABLE OIL

1 MEDIUM RED ONION (170G), SLICED THINLY

⅓ CUP (100G) RED CURRY PASTE

1 CUP (250ML) COCONUT MILK

½ CUP (125ML) WATER

400G (12½ OUNCES) BABY (DUTCH) CARROTS, TRIMMED

5 KAFFIR LIME LEAVES, SHREDDED

175G (5½ OUNCES) BROCCOLINI, TRIMMED

200G (6½ OUNCES) FRIED TOFU PUFFS, HALVED

100G (3 OUNCES) SNOW PEAS, TRIMMED

1 Heat oil in a medium saucepan over medium heat; cook onion, stirring, for 3 minutes until softened slightly.

2 Add curry paste, coconut milk, the water, carrots and half the lime leaves to pan, bring to a simmer; cook, stirring, for 4 minutes. Add broccolini and tofu puffs; cook for 2 minutes. Add snow peas; simmer, for 1 minute or until just tender. Season to taste.

3 Serve curry topped with remaining lime leaves.

nutritional count per serving 23g total fat (13g saturated fat); 1477kJ (353 cal); 20g carbohydrate; 17.2g protein; 8g fibre

serving suggestion Serve with steamed jasmine rice.

PORTUGUESE-STYLE CHICKEN THIGHS

2 TEASPOONS CRACKED BLACK PEPPER

2 FRESH SMALL RED CHILLIES, SEEDED, CHOPPED FINELY

½ TEASPOON HOT PAPRIKA

1 CLOVE GARLIC, CRUSHED

1 TEASPOON FINELY GRATED ORANGE RIND

¼ CUP (60ML) FRESHLY SQUEEZED ORANGE JUICE

2 TABLESPOONS RED WINE VINEGAR

2 TABLESPOONS OLIVE OIL

6 CHICKEN THIGH FILLETS (660G), HALVED

1 TABLESPOON OLIVE OIL, EXTRA

2 MEDIUM CORN COBS (800G), HUSK AND SILKS REMOVED

3 MEDIUM ORANGES (720G), PEELED, SLICED

300G (9½ OUNCES) BABY SPINACH LEAVES

1 MEDIUM RED ONION (170G), SLICED THINLY

1 Combine pepper, chilli, paprika, garlic, rind, juice, vinegar and oil in a medium bowl. Reserve about a quarter of the dressing in a small jug. Add chicken to bowl; rub dressing all over chicken.

2 Rub extra oil all over corn; season. Cook corn on a heated oiled grill plate (or grill or barbecue), over medium-high heat, for 5 minutes or until charred. When cool enough to handle, cut kernels from cobs with a sharp knife.

3 Cook chicken, in batches, on heated oiled grill plate, over medium-high heat, for 4 minutes each side or until cooked through.

4 Place corn in a large bowl with orange, spinach and onion; toss gently to combine.

5 Serve chicken with corn salad, drizzled with the reserved dressing.

nutritional count per serving 27.9g total fat (6.1g saturated fat); 2215kJ (530 cal); 24.6g carbohydrate; 38.5g protein; 13.5g fibre

**PREP +
COOK TIME**
35 MINUTES
SERVES
4

PORK CUTLETS WITH SWEET & STICKY APPLE

We used red apples in this recipe, but green apples would also work well.

2 TABLESPOONS OLIVE OIL

4 X 235G (7½-OUNCE) PORK CUTLETS

4 MEDIUM RED APPLES (600G), UNPEELED

1 TABLESPOON SOY SAUCE

4CM (1½-INCH) PIECE FRESH GINGER (20G), GRATED FINELY

2 TABLESPOONS BROWN SUGAR

2 TEASPOONS FINELY GRATED ORANGE RIND

1 CUP (250ML) FRESHLY SQUEEZED ORANGE JUICE

1 MEDIUM RADICCHIO (200G), TRIMMED, LEAVES SEPARATED

1 Heat half the oil in a large frying pan over medium heat; cook pork for 5 minutes each side or until browned and cooked through. Remove from pan; cover to keep warm.

2 Cut apples in a variety of ways: sliced, halved, quartered and in wedges.

3 Heat remaining oil in same frying pan over high heat; cook apples, turning occasionally, until just tender and still hold their shape. Remove from pan.

4 Add sauce, ginger, sugar, rind and juice to same pan; bring to the boil. Reduce heat; simmer for 5 minutes or until sauce thickens. Return apples to pan; toss to coat in sauce.

5 Serve pork and radicchio with apple, drizzled with remaining sauce.

nutritional count per serving 11.5g total fat (2.2g saturated fat); 1454kJ (347 cal); 30.2g carbohydrate; 29.3g protein; 4.1g fibre

STIR-FRIED FISH WITH GAI LAN & CASHEWS

Gai lan, also known as gai lum or chinese broccoli, is available from Asian food stores as well as most supermarkets and greengrocers.

2 TABLESPOONS SESAME OIL

800G (1½ POUNDS) FIRM WHITE FISH FILLETS (SEE TIP)

500G (1 POUND) GAI LAN, CHOPPED COARSELY

4 GREEN ONIONS (SCALLIONS), SLICED THINLY LENGTHWAYS

⅓ CUP (80ML) KECAP MANIS

2 TEASPOONS SAMBAL OELEK

½ CUP (75G) RAW CASHEWS

2 LEBANESE CUCUMBERS (260G), CUT INTO LONG THIN MATCHSTICKS

1 Heat half the oil in a wok or large frying pan over medium-high heat; gently fry fish fillets, in batches, for 3 minutes or until browned lightly and cooked. Remove from wok.

2 Heat remaining oil in wok; stir-fry gai lan, onion, kecap manis, sambal oelek and cashews; stir-fry for 2 minutes or until gai lan is just wilted.

3 Remove wok from heat. Return fish to wok with cucumber; gently toss to combine, allowing the fish to naturally break into chunks.

nutritional count per serving 19.9g total fat (3.1g saturated fat); 1699kJ (406 cal); 6.4g carbohydrate; 47.5g protein; 4.9g fibre

tip Cooking the fish fillets whole in step 1 means that when you toss the fish through the mixture in step 3, it doesn't fall apart into tiny pieces, but naturally breaks into good sized chunks.

PREP +
COOK TIME
20 MINUTES

SERVES
4

**PREP +
COOK TIME**
45 MINUTES
SERVES
4

MUSHROOM, CAVOLO NERO & QUINOA RISOTTO

10G (½ OUNCE) DRIED PORCINI MUSHROOMS

½ CUP (125ML) BOILING WATER

2 TABLESPOONS OLIVE OIL

1 MEDIUM BROWN ONION (150G), CHOPPED FINELY

1 FLAT MUSHROOM (80G), CHOPPED COARSELY

200G (6 OUNCES) SWISS BROWN MUSHROOMS, SLICED THINLY

2 CLOVES GARLIC, CRUSHED

1 CUP QUINOA (200G), RINSED, DRAINED

1.25 LITRES (5 CUPS) SALT-REDUCED VEGETABLE STOCK

1 SPRIG FRESH THYME

100G (3 OUNCES) CAVOLO NERO (TUSCAN CABBAGE), SLICED THINLY

120G (4 OUNCES) GOAT'S CHEESE, CRUMBLED

⅓ CUP (25G) FINELY GRATED PARMESAN

4 EGGS

1 Place porcini mushrooms in a heatproof bowl with the boiling water. Stand for 5 minutes.

2 Meanwhile, heat oil in a medium frying pan over medium heat; cook onion, stirring, for 3 minutes or until soft. Add flat and swiss brown mushrooms; cook, stirring, for 3 minutes or until browned and tender. Add garlic; cook, stirring, for 1 minute or until fragrant.

3 Stir in quinoa, stock and thyme. Remove porcini mushrooms from water (reserve the soaking liquid); chop coarsely. Add porcini and soaking liquid to pan; bring to the boil. Simmer, uncovered, for 20 minutes until liquid is absorbed and quinoa is tender. Discard thyme. Add cavolo nero; stir until wilted. Remove pan from heat; stir in goat's cheese and half the parmesan.

4 Meanwhile, half-fill a large frying pan with water; bring to the boil. Break one egg into a cup, then slide into pan; repeat with remaining eggs. When all eggs are in pan, return water to the boil. Cover pan, turn off heat; stand for 4 minutes or until a light film of egg white sets over yolks. Remove eggs, one at a time, using a slotted spoon; place spoon on paper-towel-lined saucer to blot up any poaching liquid.

5 Serve risotto topped with eggs and remaining parmesan. Season with pepper.

nutritional count per serving 26.7g total fat (9.3g saturated fat); 2157kJ (516 cal); 38.6g carbohydrate; 27.7g protein; 6.3g fibre

SWEET & SPICY PORK SKEWERS

If you use bamboo skewers, soak them in water for at least 1 hour before use to prevent them splintering and scorching during cooking.

750G (1½ POUNDS) PORK FILLETS

6 CLOVES GARLIC, CRUSHED

1 TABLESPOON HONEY

2 TEASPOONS HOT PAPRIKA

¼ CUP FINELY CHOPPED FRESH FLAT-LEAF PARSLEY

1 CUP (250ML) OLIVE OIL

2 EGG YOLKS

1 CLOVE GARLIC, EXTRA, CRUSHED

1 TEASPOON FINELY GRATED LEMON RIND

2 TABLESPOONS LEMON JUICE

1 TEASPOON PREPARED HORSERADISH

500G (1 POUND) CELERIAC (CELERY ROOT), TRIMMED, PEELED

2 MEDIUM CARROTS (240G)

1 LARGE RED APPLE (200G)

¾ CUP (75G) WALNUTS, ROASTED, CHOPPED COARSELY

½ CUP FRESH FLAT-LEAF PARSLEY SPRIGS, EXTRA

1 Cut pork into 3cm (1¼-inch) pieces. Combine garlic, honey, paprika, chopped parsley and 1 tablespoon of the oil in a large bowl; add pork, toss to coat in mixture. Cover; refrigerate 3 hours or overnight.

2 Blend or process egg yolks, extra garlic, rind and juice until combined. With motor operating, add remaining oil in a thin, steady stream, until dressing thickens and is smooth. Stir in horseradish. Season to taste.

3 Using a mandoline or V-slicer, cut celeriac and carrots into matchsticks; cut apple into thin slices. Place celeriac and apple in a large bowl of water to prevent discolouration.

4 Thread pork onto skewers; discard marinade. Cook skewers, in batches, on a heated oiled grill plate (or grill or barbecue), turning, for 2 minutes each side, or until pork is browned and cooked through.

5 Drain celeriac and apple. Place in a large bowl with carrot, walnuts and parsley sprigs; toss to combine.

6 Serve pork skewers with salad, drizzled with dressing.

nutritional count per serving 77.67g total fat (12.5g saturated fat); 4164kJ (996 cal); 22.2g carbohydrate; 48.7g protein; 12.3g fibre

tip Prepared horseradish, preserved grated horseradish, is purchased in bottles from most supermarkets.

**PREP +
COOK TIME**
35 MINUTES
SERVES
6

CURRIED LENTIL & VEGETABLE SOUP

500G (1 POUND) BUTTERNUT PUMPKIN, PEELED, CHOPPED COARSELY

1 LITRE (4 CUPS) VEGETABLE STOCK

1 LITRE (4 CUPS) WATER

2 TEASPOONS OLIVE OIL

1 MEDIUM BROWN ONION (170G), CHOPPED FINELY

1 LARGE CLOVE GARLIC, CRUSHED

1 MEDIUM CARROT (120G), CHOPPED COARSELY

1 STALK CELERY (150G), TRIMMED, CHOPPED FINELY

1 FRESH BAY LEAF

3 TEASPOONS CURRY POWDER

1 CUP (120G) FROZEN PEAS

400G (12½ OUNCES) CANNED BROWN LENTILS, DRAINED, RINSED

¼ CUP (60ML) LEMON JUICE

¼ CUP FRESH CORIANDER (CILANTRO) LEAVES

1 Place pumpkin, stock and the water in a medium saucepan; cover, bring to the boil. Reduce heat; simmer, uncovered, for 5 minutes or until pumpkin is nearly tender.

2 Heat oil in a large saucepan over high heat; cook onion, garlic, carrot, celery and bay leaf, stirring, for 3 minutes or until softened. Add curry powder; stir until fragrant.

3 Add pumpkin mixture and peas to pan; simmer for 10 minutes or until vegetables are tender. Stir in lentils and juice. Remove and discard bay leaf.

4 Ladle soup into bowls; serve topped with coriander.

nutritional count per serving 2.9g total fat (0.5g saturated fat); 644kJ (154 cal); 19g carbohydrate; 9g protein; 8g fibre

PORK STIR-FRY WITH LIME & PEANUTS

800G (1½ POUNDS) PORK FILLETS, SLICED THINLY

¼ CUP (60ML) LIME JUICE

2 TEASPOONS GRATED FRESH GINGER

500G (1 POUND) CHOY SUM, CHOPPED COARSELY

2 TABLESPOONS WATER

2 MEDIUM CARROTS (240G), CUT INTO LONG THIN MATCHSTICKS

1 CUP FIRMLY PACKED FRESH CORIANDER (CILANTRO) LEAVES

4 GREEN ONIONS (SCALLIONS), SLICED THINLY

¼ CUP (35G) COARSELY CHOPPED ROASTED UNSALTED PEANUTS

¼ CUP FRESH VIETNAMESE MINT LEAVES

2 LIMES, CUT INTO CHEEKS

SWEET CHILLI DRESSING

1 TABLESPOON FISH SAUCE

1 TABLESPOON SWEET CHILLI SAUCE

2 TABLESPOONS LIME JUICE

1 FRESH SMALL RED CHILLI, CHOPPED FINELY

1 Place pork in a large bowl with juice and ginger; toss pork to coat in mixture. Cover; refrigerate 3 hours or overnight.

2 Make sweet chilli dressing.

3 Heat a lightly oiled wok or large frying pan; stir-fry pork, in batches, until cooked through. Remove from wok; cover to keep warm.

4 Stir-fry choy sum with the water in wok until just wilted.

5 Place pork and choy sum in a large bowl with carrot, herbs, green onion and dressing; toss gently to combine. Top with peanuts and mint. Serve with lime cheeks.

sweet chilli dressing Place ingredients in a screw-top jar; shake well.

nutritional count per serving 9.3g total fat (2.2g saturated fat); 1433kJ (342 cal); 8.8g carbohydrate; 51g protein; 7.5g fibre

tip Use a mandoline or V-slicer to cut carrot into thin matchsticks.

CHILLI CHICKEN
SAN CHOY BOW

1 TABLESPOON PEANUT OIL

2 CLOVES GARLIC, CRUSHED

10CM (4-INCH) PIECE FRESH GINGER (50G), GRATED FINELY

4 FRESH LONG RED CHILLIES, CHOPPED FINELY

1KG (2 POUNDS) MINCED (GROUND) CHICKEN

⅓ CUP (80ML) OYSTER SAUCE

230G (7 OUNCES) CANNED SLICED WATER CHESTNUTS, DRAINED, RINSED

2 CUPS (160G) BEAN SPROUTS

4 GREEN ONIONS (SCALLIONS), SLICED THINLY

12 ICEBERG LETTUCE LEAVES

⅓ CUP (50G) ROASTED UNSALTED CASHEWS

1 FRESH LONG RED CHILLI, EXTRA, SLICED THINLY ON THE DIAGONAL (OPTIONAL)

1 Heat oil in a wok or large frying pan; stir-fry garlic, ginger and chilli over high heat for 1 minute or until fragrant.

2 Add chicken to wok; stir-fry until browned all over. Add sauce, chestnuts, sprouts and green onion; stir-fry mixture until heated through.

3 Spoon chicken mixture into lettuce leaves; sprinkle with cashews and extra chilli.

nutritional count per serving 20.9g total fat (5.4g saturated fat); 1528kJ (365 cal); 7g carbohydrate; 35.4g protein; 3.4g fibre

PORK STEAKS WITH SAUTEED LENTILS

2 TABLESPOONS OLIVE OIL

1 MEDIUM RED ONION (170G), CHOPPED FINELY

2 CLOVES GARLIC, CRUSHED

6 SLICES PANCETTA (90G), CHOPPED FINELY

1 TABLESPOON FINELY CHOPPED
FRESH ROSEMARY

4 SPRIGS FRESH THYME

800G (1½ POUNDS) CANNED BROWN LENTILS,
DRAINED, RINSED

½ CUP (125ML) WATER

1 TABLESPOON LEMON JUICE

4 X 150G (4½-OUNCE) UNCRUMBED PORK
SCHNITZELS

1 MEDIUM LEMON (140G), HALVED CROSSWAYS

175G (5½ OUNCES) ASPARAGUS, TRIMMED,
SLICED THINLY LENGTHWAYS

1 Heat half the oil in a large frying pan over high heat; cook onion, garlic and pancetta, stirring, until onion softens. Add rosemary and 3 sprigs of the thyme; cook, stirring, for 1 minute or until fragrant. Add lentils and the water; reduce heat, simmer, uncovered, for 2 minutes or until water evaporates. Stir in juice.

2 Meanwhile, cut pork in half crossways. Heat remaining oil in a large frying pan over medium heat; cook pork, in batches, until browned both sides and cooked. Remove from pan; rest, covered, for 2 minutes.

3 Cook lemon halves, cut-side down, in pan for 3 minutes or until charred.

4 Boil, steam or microwave asparagus until just tender; drain. Season to taste.

5 Serve pork with lentils, asparagus and lemon, sprinkled with remaning thyme leaves. Season with pepper.

nutritional count per serving 15.8g total fat (3.8g saturated fat); 1987kJ (475 cal); 15g carbohydrate; 64g protein; 6.5g fibre

**PREP +
COOK TIME**
35 MINUTES
SERVES
4

FISH & ROASTED CORN WITH CAPSICUM SALSA

2 CORN COBS (500G), HUSKS INTACT

OLIVE OIL COOKING SPRAY

1 EGG YOLK

1 CLOVE GARLIC, CRUSHED

2 TABLESPOONS LIME JUICE

1 TEASPOON DIJON MUSTARD

²/₃ CUP (160ML) OLIVE OIL

½ TEASPOON SMOKED PAPRIKA

1 MEDIUM RED ONION (170G), CHOPPED FINELY

2 FRESH SMALL RED CHILLIES, CHOPPED FINELY

1 SMALL AVOCADO (200G), CHOPPED FINELY

1 SMALL GREEN CAPSICUM (BELL PEPPER) (150G), CHOPPED FINELY

1 SMALL YELLOW CAPSICUM (BELL PEPPER), CHOPPED FINELY

⅓ CUP COARSELY CHOPPED FRESH CORIANDER (CILANTRO)

4 X 200G (6½-OUNCE) FIRM WHITE FISH STEAKS

LIME CHEEKS, TO SERVE

1 Pull husks back away from the cobs and tie to secure. Remove and discard the silk from cobs. Spray corn and husks with oil. Cook corn on a heated oiled grill plate (or grill or barbecue) until browned lightly and just tender.

2 Blend or process egg yolk, garlic, juice and mustard until smooth. With motor operating, gradually add oil in a thin, steady stream; process until mayonnaise thickens slightly. Season. Stir in paprika.

3 Place onion, chilli, avocado, capsicums and coriander in a medium bowl; toss to combine. Season to taste.

4 Cook fish on heated oiled grill plate for 3 minutes each side or until browned and cooked.

5 Serve fish with salsa, corn, mayonnaise and lime.

nutritional count per serving 49.3g total fat (8.4g saturated fat); 2966kJ (710 cal); 15.7g carbohydrate; 46.6g protein; 9.3g fibre

tip Be careful when roasting the corn, especially if you use a barbecue with flames, as the husks may catch alight.

PORK WITH BEETROOT
MASH & SPROUT SALAD

500G (1 POUND) BABY BEETROOT (BEET), TRIMMED, CHOPPED COARSELY

1 SMALL KUMARA (ORANGE SWEET POTATO) (250G), CHOPPED COARSELY

1 TABLESPOON OLIVE OIL

4 PORK MID-LOIN CHOPS (1.2KG)

1 CUP (250ML) POURING CREAM

100G (3 OUNCES) GORGONZOLA CHEESE

300G (9½ OUNCES) BRUSSELS SPROUTS, TRIMMED, SHREDDED

50G (1½ OUNCES) SMALL RED-VEINED SORREL LEAVES

¼ CUP (35G) HAZELNUTS, ROASTED, CHOPPED COARSELY

MUSTARD DRESSING

1 TABLESPOONS WHOLEGRAIN MUSTARD

1 TABLESPOON EXTRA VIRGIN OLIVE OIL

2 TEASPOONS LEMON JUICE

1 Boil, steam or microwave beetroot and kumara, separately, until tender; drain. Place beetroot and kumara in a large bowl; mash to combine. Season to taste.

2 Meanwhile, heat oil in a large frying pan over high heat; cook pork for 5 minutes each side or until cooked through. Remove from pan; cover to keep warm.

3 Discard oil from frying pan, add cream and cheese; cook, stirring, over medium heat until smooth. Bring to the boil. Reduce heat; simmer for 2 minutes or until sauce thickens.

4 Meanwhile, make mustard dressing.

5 Place brussels sprouts, sorrel and hazelnuts in a medium bowl with dressing; toss gently to combine.

6 Serve pork with mash and salad, drizzled with sauce.

mustard dressing Whisk ingredients in a small bowl to combine; season to taste.

nutritional count per serving 47.2g total fat (21g saturated fat); 3271kJ (781 cal); 25.4g carbohydrate; 56.5g protein; 10.6g fibre

PREP +
COOK TIME

45 MINUTES

SERVES

4

HONEY SOY PORK WITH PINK GRAPEFRUIT & SNOW PEA SALAD

2 CLOVES GARLIC, CRUSHED

1 TABLESPOON OLIVE OIL

¼ CUP (90G) HONEY

1 TEASPOON FINELY GRATED FRESH GINGER

2 TABLESPOONS SOY SAUCE

2 TABLESPOONS LIME JUICE

800G (1½-POUND) TRIMMED PORK NECK

PINK GRAPEFRUIT & SNOW PEA SALAD

1 MEDIUM PINK GRAPEFRUIT (425G)

100G (3 OUNCES) SNOW PEAS, TRIMMED

⅓ CUP (80ML) EXTRA VIRGIN OLIVE OIL

1 TEASPOON FINELY GRATED LIME RIND

200G (6½ OUNCES) BABY SPINACH LEAVES

6 GREEN ONIONS (SCALLIONS), SLICED THINLY

⅓ CUP (40G) ROASTED UNSALTED CASHEWS

1 Combine garlic, oil, honey, ginger, soy sauce and juice in a large bowl; add pork, turn to coat in marinade. Cover; refrigerate 3 hours or overnight, turning pork occasionally in marinade.

2 Preheat oven to 180°C/350°F.

3 Remove pork from marinade; reserve marinade. Wrap pork in three layers of foil, securing ends tightly; place in a baking dish. Bake for 2 hours 20 minutes or until cooked. Stand for 10 minutes. Shred meat coarsely; cover to keep warm in cooking juices.

4 Make pink grapefruit and snow pea salad.

5 Serve salad topped with shredded pork.

pink grapefruit & snow pea salad Segment grapefruit, by cutting off the rind along with the white pith. Cut between membranes, over a small bowl to catch any juice, releasing segments; you need ¼ cup (60ml) juice, reserve. Boil, steam or microwave snow peas until tender; refresh in iced water. Drain. Place reserved juice, oil and rind in a screw-top jar; shake well. Season to taste. Place grapefruit segments and snow peas in a large bowl with spinach, green onion and cashews; drizzle with dressing.

nutritional count per serving 41.1g total fat (8.6g saturated fat); 2794kJ (668 cal); 26.5g carbohydrate; 47.5g protein; 3.2g fibre

SIDES

CREAMED SPINACH

prep + cook time 15 minutes **serves** 4

Melt 20g (¾oz) butter in a large frying pan; cook 600g (1¼lbs) trimmed spinach, stirring, until wilted. Add ½ cup pouring cream; bring to the boil. Reduce heat; simmer, uncovered, until liquid reduces by half.

nutritional count per serving 15.6g total fat (9.9g saturated fat); 710kJ (170 cal); 1.6g carbohydrate; 4.6g protein; 2.5g fibre

CAULIFLOWER GRATIN

prep + cook time 30 minutes **serves** 4

Preheat oven to 220°C/400°F. Boil, steam or microwave 750g (1½lbs) baby cauliflowers, cut into florets until tender; drain. Place in a shallow ovenproof dish. Melt 30g (1oz) butter in a saucepan, add 2 tablespoons plain (all-purpose) flour; cook, stirring, until mixture bubbles and thickens. Stir in 1¼ cups hot milk until smooth; cook, stirring, until mixture boils and thickens. Remove from heat; stir in ⅓ cup grated cheddar and 2 tablespoons finely grated parmesan. Pour over cauliflower; top with 2 teaspoons panko breadcrumbs. Bake 15 minutes or until browned.

nutritional count per serving 17.4g total fat (11.2g saturated fat); 1148kJ (274 cal); 13g carbohydrate; 14g protein; 5.2g fibre

MIXED BEAN SALAD WITH HAZELNUTS

prep + cook time 15 minutes **serves** 4

Boil, steam or microwave 250g (8oz) trimmed green beans and 250g (8oz) trimmed yellow beans until tender; drain. Combine warm beans with 60g (2oz) chopped butter, ⅓ cup finely chopped roasted hazelnuts, ½ cup torn fresh flat-leaf parsley leaves and 2 teaspoons finely grated lemon rind (or strips) in a medium bowl.

nutritional count per serving 18.4g total fat (8.1g saturated fat); 810kJ (194 cal); 2.2g carbohydrate; 3.3g protein; 3.7g fibre

ASIAN GREENS WITH CHAR SIU SAUCE

prep + cook time 25 minutes **serves** 4

Layer 350g (11oz) trimmed broccolini, 150g (5oz) snow peas, 2 halved baby buk choy and 1 thinly sliced fresh long red chilli in a large baking-paper-lined bamboo steamer. Steam, covered, over a large wok of simmering water for 5 minutes or until vegetables are just tender. Combine vegetables, 2 tablespoons char siu sauce and 2 teaspoons sesame oil in a large bowl. Heat 1 tablespoon peanut oil in a saucepan until hot; pour over vegetables, toss to combine. Top with 1 tablespoon toasted sesame seeds.

nutritional count per serving 8.8g total fat (1.3g saturated fat); 643kJ (153 cal); 8.6g carbohydrate; 6.8g protein; 5.8g fibre

**PREP +
COOK TIME**
1 HOUR
SERVES
4

VEGETABLE TAGINE

2 TEASPOONS OLIVE OIL

1 LARGE RED ONION (300G), CHOPPED COARSELY

2 CLOVES GARLIC, CRUSHED

4 BABY EGGPLANT (240G), HALVED LENGTHWAYS

500G (1 POUND) JAP PUMPKIN, CUT INTO THIN WEDGES

2 TEASPOONS GROUND CUMIN

2 TEASPOONS GROUND CORIANDER

2 TEASPOONS GROUND GINGER

½ TEASPOON GROUND CINNAMON

400G (12½ OUNCES) CANNED CRUSHED TOMATOES

2 CUPS (500ML) VEGETABLE STOCK

2 CUPS (500ML) WATER

300G (9½ OUNCES) OKRA, TRIMMED

1 TABLESPOON HARISSA

¾ CUP (200G) GREEK-STYLE YOGHURT

½ CUP FINELY CHOPPED FRESH FLAT-LEAF PARSLEY

½ CUP FINELY CHOPPED FRESH MINT

HARISSA CHICKPEAS

400G (12½ OUNCES) CANNED CHICKPEAS (GARBANZO BEANS), DRAINED, RINSED

1 TABLESPOON HARISSA

1 TABLESPOON OLIVE OIL

1 Make harissa chickpeas.

2 Heat oil in a large saucepan over medium heat; cook onion and garlic, stirring, for 5 minutes. Add eggplant and pumpkin; cook for 1 minute each side or until vegetables are lightly browned. Add spices; cook for 1 minute or until fragrant. Add tomatoes, stock and the water; bring to the boil. Reduce heat; simmer, covered for 15 minutes or until vegetables are just tender.

3 Meanwhile, boil, steam or microwave okra until tender; drain. Stir okra into tagine.

4 Fold harissa through yoghurt in a small bowl; season to taste.

5 Serve tagine topped with yoghurt mixture, harissa chickpeas and herbs. Season with pepper.

harissa chickpeas Preheat oven to 200°C/400°F. Oil a large oven tray; line with baking paper. Pat chickpeas dry with paper towel; place in a medium bowl. Add remaining ingredients to chickpeas; stir to combine. Season to taste. Spread chickpeas in a single layer on tray. Bake for 20 minutes, stirring three times during cooking, or until well browned and slightly crunchy.

nutritional count per serving 13g total fat (3.3g saturated fat); 1491kJ (356 cal); 39g carbohydrate; 13.7g protein; 15.2g fibre

tip Harissa is a paste made from dried red chillies, garlic, olive oil and caraway seeds. It can be used as a rub for meat, as an ingredient in sauces and dressings or eaten on its own, as a condiment. It is available ready-made from all Middle-Eastern food shops and some supermarkets.

SMOKY CHICKPEA STEW

1 SMALL RED CAPSICUM (BELL PEPPER) (150G), QUARTERED LENGTHWAYS

1 SMALL YELLOW CAPSICUM (BELL PEPPER) (150G), QUARTERED LENGTHWAYS

¼ CUP (60ML) EXTRA VIRGIN OLIVE OIL

1 MEDIUM RED ONION (170G), CHOPPED FINELY

2 CLOVES GARLIC, CHOPPED FINELY

3 TEASPOONS SMOKED PAPRIKA

PINCH SAFFRON THREADS

1 CINNAMON STICK

800G (1½ POUNDS) CANNED CHICKPEAS (GARBANZO BEANS), DRAINED, RINSED

400G (12½ OUNCES) CANNED DICED TOMATOES

2 CUPS (500ML) VEGETABLE STOCK

200G (6½ OUNCES) GREEN BEANS, HALVED LENGTHWAYS

100G (3 OUNCES) BABY ROCKET (ARUGULA)

1 Preheat oven to 220°C/425°F.

2 Place capsicum pieces on an oven tray; drizzle with 2 teaspoons of the oil. Roast 15 minutes or until tender.

3 Meanwhile, heat another 1 tablespoon of the oil in a deep, large frying pan over medium heat; cook onion and garlic, stirring, for 5 minutes or until soft. Add paprika, saffron and cinnamon; cook, stirring, 1 minute or until fragrant.

4 Add chickpeas, tomatoes and stock to pan; bring to the boil. Reduce heat; simmer, uncovered, over low heat for 12 minutes or until sauce thickens. Add beans; simmer, uncovered, for 2 minutes or until just tender. Season to taste.

5 Serve stew topped with capsicum and rocket, drizzled with remaining oil. Season with pepper.

nutritional count per serving 17.5g total fat (2.7g saturated fat); 1394kJ (333 cal); 26.7g carbohydrate; 12.7g protein; 11.2g fibre

serving suggestion Serve with grilled flatbread or couscous and greek-style yoghurt.

PREP + COOK TIME

40 MINUTES

SERVES

4

HOT & SOUR STEAMED FISH WITH THAI SALAD

4 X 200G (6½-OUNCE) FIRM WHITE FISH FILLETS

3 FRESH SMALL RED CHILLIES, SEEDED, CHOPPED FINELY

3 FRESH KAFFIR LIME LEAVES, SHREDDED FINELY

10CM (4-INCH) STICK FRESH LEMON GRASS (20G), CHOPPED FINELY

½ CUP LOOSELY PACKED FRESH CORIANDER (CILANTRO) LEAVES

½ CUP LOOSELY PACKED FRESH MINT LEAVES

150G (4½ OUNCES) SNOW PEAS, TRIMMED, SLICED LENGTHWAYS

2 FRESH LONG RED CHILLIES, SLICED THINLY ON THE DIAGONAL

2 GREEN ONIONS (SCALLIONS), SLICED THINLY

35G (1 OUNCE) SNOW PEA SPROUTS

1 LARGE FIRM MANGO (600G), CUT INTO LONG THIN MATCHSTICKS

½ MEDIUM PAPAYA (500G), HALVED, CUT INTO 2CM (¾-INCH) SLICES

LIME & SWEET CHILLI DRESSING

2 TEASPOONS SWEET CHILLI SAUCE

⅓ CUP (80ML) FISH SAUCE

⅓ CUP (80ML) LIME JUICE

2 TEASPOONS PEANUT OIL

1 CLOVE GARLIC, CRUSHED

½ FRESH LONG RED CHILLI, CHOPPED FINELY

½ TEASPOON GRATED FRESH GINGER

1 TEASPOON GRATED PALM SUGAR

1 Make lime and sweet chilli dressing.

2 Combine fish, small chilli, lime leaves and lemon grass in a large bowl with half the dressing. Cover; refrigerate for 30 minutes.

3 Place fish, in single layer, in a baking-paper-lined large bamboo steamer; steam, covered, over wok or large saucepan of simmering water for 10 minutes or until fish is cooked as desired.

4 Place herbs and snow peas in a large bowl with remaining ingredients and remaining dressing; toss gently to combine. Serve fish with salad.

lime & sweet chilli dressing Place ingredients in a screw-top jar; shake well.

nutritional count per serving 4.1g total fat (0.6g saturated fat); 1277kJ (305 cal); 18.8g carbohydrate; 44.3g protein; 5.3g fibre

tips We used blue eye trevally fillets in this recipe. Use a mandoline or V-slicer to cut the mango into thin, even-sized matchsticks.

PANEER, CHICKPEA & VEGETABLE CURRY

PEANUT OIL, FOR SHALLOW-FRYING

6 CURRY LEAF SPRIGS

2 TABLESPOONS PEANUT OIL, EXTRA

1 LARGE BROWN ONION (200G), SLICED THINLY

2 CLOVES GARLIC, SLICED THINLY

4CM (1½-INCH) PIECE FRESH GINGER (20G), GRATED

⅓ CUP (100G) BALTI CURRY PASTE

400G (12½ OUNCES) CANNED CHICKPEAS (GARBANZO BEANS), DRAINED, RINSED

400G (12½ OUNCES) CANNED DICED TOMATOES

½ CUP (125ML) WATER

400G (12½ OUNCES) PANEER CHEESE (SEE TIP)

150G (4½ OUNCES) GREEN BEANS, HALVED CROSSWAYS ON THE DIAGONAL

¼ CUP (60ML) POURING CREAM

1 Heat oil in a medium saucepan over high heat; shallow-fry 4 curry leaf sprigs for 10 seconds or until crisp. Drain on paper towel.

2 Heat half the extra oil in a large saucepan over high heat; cook onion, garlic and ginger, stirring, until onion softens. Add curry paste and remaining curry leaves; cook, stirring, for 1 minute or until fragrant.

3 Add chickpeas, tomatoes and the water; bring to the boil. Reduce heat; simmer, covered, for 5 minutes.

4 Meanwhile, cut paneer into 3cm (1¼-inch) pieces. Heat remaining oil in a large frying pan over medium heat; cook paneer, turning, until browned all over. Remove from pan; cool. Roughly crumble paneer.

5 Add beans and cream to curry; cook for 5 minutes or until beans are tender. Stir in paneer; cook until heated through. Serve topped with fried curry leaves.

nutritional count per serving 24g total fat (9.6g saturated fat); 2179kJ (521 cal); 19.5g carbohydrate; 23.7g protein; 7.1g fibre

tip Paneer is a fresh unripened cow's-milk cheese, originating in India, that is similar to pressed ricotta. It has no added salt and doesn't melt at normal cooking temperatures. Available in many major supermarkets (near the fetta and haloumi) and from Indian food stores. You can use fetta or haloumi instead, but the results won't be the same.

PREP +
COOK TIME
30 MINUTES
SERVES
4

**PREP +
COOK TIME**

1 HOUR
(+ REFRIGERATION)

SERVES
4

SPINACH & RICOTTA
FRIED GNOCCHI

If you have one, use a zester to create strips of lemon rind. If you don't have one, peel two long, wide strips of rind from the lemon, without the white pith, then cut them lengthways into thin strips.

450G (14½ OUNCES) SPINACH, TRIMMED

20G (¾ OUNCE) BUTTER

1 MEDIUM BROWN ONION (150G), CHOPPED FINELY

¾ CUP (180G) FRESH RICOTTA

½ CUP (75G) PLAIN (ALL-PURPOSE) FLOUR

2 EGG YOLKS

1¼ CUPS (100G) FINELY GRATED PARMESAN

PINCH GROUND NUTMEG

250G (8 OUNCES) TRUSS CHERRY TOMATOES

2 TABLESPOONS EXTRA VIRGIN OLIVE OIL

2 TABLESPOONS SHAVED PARMESAN

⅓ CUP (35G) WALNUTS, ROASTED, CHOPPED COARSELY

1 TABLESPOON FINELY GRATED LEMON RIND OR THIN STRIPS (SEE NOTE ABOVE)

1 Place spinach in a large saucepan of boiling water for 1 minute; drain. Rinse under cold water; drain well. Squeeze out excess liquid from spinach; chop coarsely.

2 Heat butter in a large frying pan over low heat; cook onion, stirring, for 8 minutes or until soft but not coloured. Stir in chopped spinach. Transfer mixture to a large bowl; stir in ricotta and flour, season. Stir in egg yolks, grated parmesan and nutmeg.

3 Using two teaspoons, shape ricotta mixture into 24 gnocchi-shaped ovals; place on a lightly floured tray. Cover; refrigerate 1 hour.

4 Preheat grill (broiler) to high. Place tomatoes on an oven tray; drizzle with half the oil. Season. Place under hot grill for 5 minutes or until lightly charred. Cover to keep warm.

5 Cook gnocchi in a large saucepan of boiling salted water, in batches, for 3 minutes or until they float to the surface. Remove from pan with a slotted spoon; drain on paper towel.

6 Heat remaining oil in a large frying pan over high heat; cook gnocchi, in two batches, sitrring occasionally, for 2 minutes or until browned lightly.

7 Serve gnocchi topped with tomatoes, walnuts, shaved parmesan and rind. Season with pepper.

nutritional count per serving 37g total fat (14.6g saturated fat); 2140kJ (511 cal); 18.3g carbohydrate; 24.5g protein; 4.8g fibre

SAUCES

CHIMICHURRI

prep time 10 minutes **serves** 4 (makes 1 cup)

In a small food processor, process 1 tablespoon red wine vinegar, ½ cup extra virgin olive oil, 2 halved cloves garlic, ½ teaspoon dried chilli flakes, 1 teaspoon sea salt flakes, 2 cups loosely packed fresh flat-leaf parsley leaves, 1 teaspoon dried oregano and 1 tablespoon lemon juice until finely chopped. Season. Transfer to a small bowl or jar; cover tightly. Refrigerate until ready to use.

nutritional count per serving 28.6g total fat (4.5g saturated fat); 1141kJ (273 cal); 0.7g carbohydrate; 1.6g protein; 4.2g fibre

goes with Barbecued or grilled beef, pork, chicken and fish.

ANCHOVY, GARLIC & LEMON BUTTER

prep time 10 minutes **serves** 8 (makes ⅔ cup)

Beat 125g (4oz) softened butter in a small bowl with an electric mixer until light and creamy. Beat in 2 crushed cloves garlic, 2 teaspoons finely grated lemon rind, 3 chopped anchovy fillets and 1 tablespoon finely chopped fresh flat-leaf parsley until combined. Season with freshly ground pepper.

nutritional count per serving 12.7g total fat (8.2g saturated fat); 488kJ (117 cal); 0.2g carbohydrate; 0.5g protein; 0.2g fibre

tip Freeze butter up to 3 months. Thaw in the fridge; stand 30 minutes at room temperature before use.

goes with Grilled steak, chicken or fish.

ROMESCO SWIRL

prep + cook time 20 minutes (+ cooling)

serves 6 (makes 1 cup)

Preheat oven to 180°C/350°F. Roast ⅓ cup blanched almonds on an oven tray 10 minutes or until lightly browned. Cool. Process nuts with 140g (4½oz) drained bottled fire roasted capsicum (bell peppers), 1 chopped clove garlic, 1 teaspoon smoked paprika, ½ teaspoon chilli flakes and 1 tablespoon sherry vinegar until smooth. With motor operating, gradually add ¼ cup extra virgin olive oil until combined. Transfer to a bowl; season. Swirl with 2 tablespoons sour cream.

nutritional count per serving 18.8g total fat (3.5g saturated fat); 801kJ (191 cal); 1.8g carbohydrate; 3.2g protein; 1.5g fibre

goes with Barbecued or grilled chicken or beef.

NAM JIM

prep time 10 minutes **serves** 6 (makes 1 cup)

In a small food processor (or with a mortar and pestle), process 2 halved cloves garlic, 3 large seeded and chopped fresh green chillies, 2 cleaned and trimmed coriander (cilantro) roots, 3 chopped shallots, 1½ tablespoons fish sauce, 1 tablespoon finely grated palm sugar and ¼ cup lime juice until combined.

nutritional count per serving 0.1g total fat (0g saturated fat); 100kJ (24 cal); 3.6g carbohydrate; 1g protein; 1.3g fibre

tip Even large chillies can be a little hot, so start with 1 or 2 chillies and add the last one to taste.

goes with Barbecued or grilled meat, chicken or fish.

QUINOA & CAULIFLOWER 'COUSCOUS'

¾ CUP (150G) RED QUINOA, RINSED WELL

1½ CUPS (375ML) WATER

1 MEDIUM CAULIFLOWER (1.25KG), TRIMMED

1 TABLESPOON EXTRA VIRGIN OLIVE OIL

1 LARGE BROWN ONION (200G), CHOPPED FINELY

2 TEASPOONS GROUND CUMIN

½ CUP (80G) COARSELY CHOPPED ROASTED PISTACHIOS

1 TABLESPOON DRIED CURRANTS

2 TEASPOONS FINELY CHOPPED PRESERVED LEMON RIND

¼ CUP (60ML) LEMON JUICE

¼ CUP (60ML) EXTRA VIRGIN OLIVE OIL, EXTRA

1 CUP COARSELY CHOPPED FRESH FLAT-LEAF PARSLEY

150G (4½ OUNCES) FETTA, CRUMBLED

1 SMALL POMEGRANATE (250G), SEEDS REMOVED (SEE TIP)

1 Place quinoa in a medium saucepan with the water; bring to the boil. Reduce heat to low; cook, covered, for 12 minutes or until the water is absorbed and quinoa is tender. Season to taste.

2 Meanwhile, cut cauliflower into florets; process, in batches, until very finely chopped.

3 Heat oil in a medium frying pan over high heat. Add onion, reduce heat to low; cook, stirring occasionally, for 10 minutes or until caramelised. Stir in cumin, then add cauliflower. Increase heat to medium; cook, stirring occasionally, for 6 minutes or until cauliflower is tender. Season to taste.

4 Add quinoa to pan with remaining ingredients; stir to combine. Season to taste.

nutritional count per serving 40.3g total fat (10g saturated fat); 2722kJ (651 cal); 39.5g carbohydrate; 23.9g protein; 16.4g fibre

tip To remove pomegranate seeds, cut a pomegranate in half crossways; hold it, cut-side down, in the palm of your hand over a bowl, then hit the outside firmly with a wooden spoon. The seeds should fall out easily; discard any white pith that falls out with them. Pomegranate seeds will keep in the fridge for up to a week. Fresh pomegranate seeds can sometimes be found in the fridge section of supermarkets and good greengrocers; you will need ½ cup (75g) for this recipe.

**PREP +
COOK TIME**

1¼ HOURS
(+ REFRIGERATION)

SERVES

6

SWEET CHILLI RIBS
WITH COLESLAW

1.5KG (3 POUNDS) PORK SPARERIBS

⅓ CUP (80ML) SWEET CHILLI SAUCE

1 TABLESPOON SOY SAUCE

¼ CUP (60ML) RICE WINE VINEGAR

2 CLOVES GARLIC, CRUSHED

1 TEASPOON GRATED FRESH GINGER

2 TABLESPOONS FINELY CHOPPED FRESH CORIANDER (CILANTRO)

½ MEDIUM SAVOY CABBAGE (850G), SHREDDED FINELY

6 GREEN ONIONS (SCALLIONS), CHOPPED FINELY

1 FRESH SMALL RED CHILLI, CHOPPED FINELY

½ CUP COARSELY CHOPPED FRESH MINT

½ CUP COARSELY CHOPPED FRESH FLAT-LEAF PARSLEY

¼ CUP COARSELY CHOPPED FRESH CORIANDER (CILANTRO), EXTRA

⅓ CUP (45G) ROASTED UNSALTED PEANUTS, CHOPPED COARSLEY

LIME DRESSING

2 TABLESPOONS LIME JUICE

2 TEASPOONS RICE WINE VINEGAR

⅓ CUP (80ML) PEANUT OIL

1 Place ribs in a large disposable baking dish. Combine sauces, rice wine vinegar, garlic, ginger and finely chopped coriander in a small bowl; pour all over ribs. Cover; refrigerate 3 hours or overnight.

2 Cook ribs in a covered barbecue, using indirect heat, following manufacturer's instructions, for 50 minutes or until browned all over and cooked.

3 Meanwhile, make lime dressing.

4 Place cabbage, green onion, chilli, herbs and peanuts in a large bowl with lime dressing; toss to combine.

5 Serve ribs with coleslaw.

lime dressing Place ingredients in a screw-top jar; shake well. Season to taste.

nutritional count per serving 25.8g total fat (6.4g saturated fat); 1717kJ (410 cal); 13g carbohydrate; 28.3g protein; 6.2g fibre

CHAR-GRILLED THAI SQUID SALAD

1.5KG (3 POUNDS) WHOLE BABY SQUID

2 CLOVES GARLIC, CRUSHED

1 TABLESPOON PEANUT OIL

170G (5½ OUNCES) ASPARAGUS, TRIMMED, SLICED VERY THINLY LENGTHWAYS

175G (5½ OUNCES) BROCCOLINI, TRIMMED

200G (6½ OUNCES) SUGAR SNAP PEAS, HALVED LENGTHWAYS

1 CUP LOOSELY PACKED FRESH MINT LEAVES

½ CUP LOOSELY PACKED FRESH CORIANDER (CILANTRO) LEAVES

2 LIMES, CUT INTO CHEEKS

CHILLI DRESSING

1 FRESH LONG RED CHILLI, CHOPPED FINELY

⅓ CUP (80ML) LIME JUICE

1 TABLESPOON PEANUT OIL

2 TEASPOONS FISH SAUCE

2 TEASPOONS BROWN SUGAR

1 Remove tentacles from squid hoods; cut tentacles in half. Cut squid in half lengthways. Using a sharp knife, score inside surface in a criss-cross pattern at 1cm (½-inch) intervals. Cut into thick strips. Combine squid, garlic and oil in a large bowl; season.

2 Cook squid on a heated oiled grill plate (or grill or barbecue), turning occasionally, until cooked through.

3 Meanwhile, make chilli dressing.

4 Boil, steam or microwave asparagus, broccolini and sugar snap peas, separately, until tender.

5 Place squid and vegetables in a large bowl with herbs and dressing; toss gently to combine. Serve salad with lime cheeks.

chilli dressing Place ingredients in a screw-top jar; shake well.

nutritional count per serving 11.6g total fat (2.3g saturated fat); 1119kJ (267 cal); 5.1g carbohydrate; 32g protein; 5.5g fibre

tip Use a mandoline or V-slicer to cut asparagus.

PREP + COOK TIME

40 MINUTES

SERVES

4

PREP + COOK TIME

1 ½ HOURS

SERVES

4

ROAST CHICKEN & PARSNIP MASH

1.8KG (3½-POUND) WHOLE FREE-RANGE CHICKEN

2 TEASPOONS OLIVE OIL

1 TEASPOON SEA SALT FLAKES

750G (1½ POUNDS) PARSNIPS, CHOPPED COARSELY

2 CLOVES GARLIC, CRUSHED

30G (1 OUNCE) BUTTER, CHOPPED

½ CUP (125ML) MILK

200G (6½ OUNCES) BROCCOLINI, TRIMMED

200G (6½ OUNCES) ASPARAGUS, TRIMMED

4 SMALL FRESH THYME SPRIGS

TOMATO CHUTNEY

1 TABLESPOON OLIVE OIL

1 SMALL RED ONION (100G), CHOPPED COARSELY

4 SMALL TOMATOES (520G), CHOPPED COARSELY

1 CLOVE GARLIC, CRUSHED

2 TABLESPOONS BROWN SUGAR

1 TABLESPOON BALSAMIC VINEGAR

1 Preheat oven to 220°C/425°F.

2 Wash chicken under cold water; pat dry with paper towel. Using kitchen scissors, cut along both sides of backbone of chicken; discard backbone. Place chicken, skin-side up, on chopping board; using the heel of your hand, press down on breastbone to flatten chicken.

3 Rub oil all over chicken, sprinkle with salt flakes; place chicken on an oiled wire rack over a baking dish. Roast, uncovered, for 20 minutes. Reduce oven to 180°C/350°F; roast, uncovered, 1 hour or until chicken is browned and cooked through. If chicken starts to overbrown, cover with foil halfway through cooking.

4 Meanwhile, make tomato chutney.

5 Boil, steam or microwave parsnip until tender; drain. Mash parsnip in a large bowl until smooth; stir in garlic, butter and milk. Push parsnip mash through fine sieve or food mill (mouli) back into same bowl. Season.

6 Boil, steam or microwave broccolini and asparagus until tender; season. Cover to keep warm.

7 Serve chicken on mash with broccolini and asparagus, topped with tomato chutney and thyme.

tomato chutney Stir ingredients in a large saucepan over medium heat until sugar dissolves; bring to the boil. Reduce heat; simmer, uncovered, for 1 hour, stirring occasionally, or until mixture thickens.

nutritional count per serving 39.7g total fat (13.4g saturated fat); 2990kJ (715 cal); 30.3g carbohydrate; 53.7g protein; 11.6g fibre

PRAWN & SQUID
KELP NOODLE SALAD

900G (1¾ POUNDS) KELP NOODLES (SEE TIP)

500G (1 POUND) SQUID HOODS

500G (1 POUND) UNCOOKED MEDIUM PRAWNS (SHRIMP), PEELED, DEVEINED, TAILS INTACT

2 TABLESPOONS PEANUT OIL

2 LIMES, CUT INTO CHEEKS

¼ CUP (60ML) PEANUT OIL, EXTRA

¼ CUP (60ML) RICE WINE VINEGAR

1 TABLESPOON SAMBAL OELEK

1 TABLESPOON FISH SAUCE

2 TABLESPOONS GRATED PALM SUGAR

½ MEDIUM GREEN PAPAYA (500G), CUT INTO LONG THIN MATCHSTICKS

1 MEDIUM RED ONION (170G), SLICED THINLY

1 CUP MICRO SHISO (BABY PERILLA LEAVES)

1 FRESH PURPLE CHILLI, SLICED THINLY

1 Cook noodles in a large saucepan of boiling water for 10 minutes; drain.

2 Meanwhile, cut squid hoods in half lengthways. Using a sharp knife, score inside surface in a crisscross pattern at 1cm (½-inch) intervals. Halve squid, then cut each strip diagonally into thirds.

3 Combine squid, prawns and oil in a large bowl; season.

4 Cook squid and prawns on a heated oiled grill plate (or grill or barbecue) over high heat, squid for 2 minutes and prawns for 3 minutes or until just cooked.

5 Place lime cheeks, cut-side down, on heated grill plate for 2 minutes or until charred.

6 Whisk extra oil, rice wine vinegar, sambal oelek, fish sauce and palm sugar in a small jug.

7 Place noodles and seafood in a large bowl with papaya, onion and dressing; toss to gently combine.

8 Serve salad topped with herbs, chilli and charred lime.

nutritional count per serving 24.9g total fat (4.7g saturated fat); 1931kJ (461 cal); 20g carbohydrate; 35.9g protein; 6.5g fibre

tip Kelp noodles do not go tender like regular noodles, they still retain their crunch.

**PREP +
COOK TIME**

45 MINUTES

SERVES

4

PORK & MANGO CURRY

1 TABLESPOON PEANUT OIL

2 TABLESPOONS YELLOW CURRY PASTE

400ML (12½ OUNCES) CANNED COCONUT CREAM

500G (1 POUND) PORK FILLET, CUT INTO 1CM (½-INCH) THICK STRIPS

100G (3 OUNCES) SUGAR SNAP PEAS

1 LARGE MANGO (600G), PEELED, SLICED THINLY

1 LARGE ZUCCHINI (150G), HALVED LENGTHWAYS, SLICED THINLY

1 FRESH LONG RED CHILLI, SLICED THINLY

1 TABLESPOON FRESH VIETNAMESE MINT LEAVES

½ CUP FRESH CORIANDER (CILANTRO) LEAVES

1 CUP (80G) BEAN SPROUTS

1 MEDIUM LIME, CUT INTO WEDGES

1 Heat oil in a medium saucepan over medium-high heat. Add paste; cook, stirring for 1 minute or until fragrant. Stir in coconut cream; bring to the boil.

2 Add pork to sauce; simmer, uncovered, for 4 minutes or until pork is just cooked. Add peas, mango, zucchini and half the chilli; cook, stirring, until heated through.

3 Sprinkle with mint, coriander and remaining chilli. Serve with bean sprouts and lime wedges.

nutritional count per serving 29.3g total fat (20g saturated fat); 1978kJ (472 cal); 18.6g carbohydrate; 31.8g protein; 5.3g fibre

serving suggestion Serve with roti, or any flatbread you prefer, and mango pickles.

DESSERTS

ROASTED PEAR WITH COCONUT YOGHURT

prep + cook time 20 minutes **serves** 4

Preheat oven to 200°C/400°F. Cut 2 medium pears in half lengthways. Heat 20g (¾oz) butter in an ovenproof frying pan over medium-high heat until lightly browned. Add pear, cut-side down; cook for 4 minutes or until browned. Turn pear over. Transfer pan to oven; roast for 15 minutes or until pears are just tender. Serve pears topped with 170g (5½oz) coconut yoghurt, 2 tablespoons toasted shredded coconut, 2 tablespoons toasted flaked almonds and a pinch of ground cinnamon.

nutritional count per serving 17.3g total fat (11.2g saturated fat); 922kJ (220 cal); 13.9g carbohydrate; 2.2g protein; 2g fibre

tips Cooking time may vary depending on the ripeness of the pears. For even lower carbs use plain yoghurt instead of coconut yoghurt.

SOFT-SET YOGHURT PANNA COTTA

prep + cook time 20 minutes (+ cooling & refrigeration)

serves 4

Combine 300ml pouring cream, ¼ cup pure maple syrup and 2 teaspoons vanilla extract in a medium saucepan over low heat. Sprinkle 1 teaspoon powdered gelatine over cream mixture; stir until mixture is hot and gelatine has dissolved. Do not boil. Pour cream mixture into a medium heatproof bowl; cool to room temperature. Whisk in 1 cup plain yoghurt. Pour into four ¾ cup serving glasses; refrigerate for 4 hours or overnight. Serve with 200g (5½oz) sliced strawberries.

nutritional count per serving 31.1g total fat (20g saturated fat); 1700kJ (406 cal); 24.7g carbohydrate; 6.8g protein; 0.7g fibre

Savoury bites

AVOCADO
CHERRY TOMATOES
BOILED EGG
CELERY/CUCUMBER STICKS
SNOW PEAS
CANNED TUNA
OLIVES

Delicious dips

GUACAMOLE
HUMMUS
TZATZIKI
EGGPLANT DIP

Dose of dairy

CHEESES
NATURAL YOGHURT
SMOOTHIES

Make & take

BLISS BALLS
SWEET POTATO CHIPS
CHEESY CAJUN POPCORN
PEANUT BUTTER COOKIES
CHEESE BISCOTTI

Fruit treats

STRAWBERRIES
FRESH FIGS
RASPBERRIES
APRICOTS
WATERMELON
PASSIONFRUIT

Nuts

PISTACHIOS
ALMONDS
HAZELNUTS
UNSALTED PEANUTS
BRAZIL NUTS
PECANS
WALNUTS

Low CARB SNACKS

In between meals, it's all too easy to reach for a high-carb junk food fix to satisfy that craving. While chips and chocolate bars fill the gap, they don't do your body any favours. Re-think the way you snack by making some of these nutritious treats.

PREP + COOK TIME

30 MINUTES

MAKES

24

SEEDED PARMESAN CRISPS

These crisps would also work well crumbled over salads instead of croutons.

2 CUPS (160G) FINELY GRATED PARMESAN

1 TABLESPOON WHITE CHIA SEEDS

1 TABLESPOON FLAXSEEDS (LINSEEDS)

1 TABLESPOON WHITE SESAME SEEDS

1 Preheat oven to 180°C/350°F. Line two large oven trays with baking paper.

2 Place level tablespoons of parmesan in mounds on trays. Flatten mounds to about 7.5cm (3 inches) across, leaving 2.5cm (1 inch) between rounds. Combine seeds in a small bowl; sprinkle ½ teaspoon of seed mixture on each round. Season lightly with freshly ground black pepper.

3 Bake crsips for 12 minutes or until melted and lightly golden. Cool on trays. Transfer to airtight container.

nutritional count per crisp 2.8g total fat (1.4g saturated fat); 157kJ (37 cal); 0.1g carbohydrate; 2.8g protein; 0.2g fibre

tip Store crisps in an airtight container for up to 1 week.

CRUSTLESS BACON & TOMATO QUICHES

Quiches can be kept refrigerated for up to 3 days or transfer to an airtight container and freeze for up to 1 month.

250G (8 OUNCES) BACON SLICES, TRIMMED, CHOPPED COARSELY

6 GREEN ONIONS (SCALLIONS), CHOPPED

100G (3 OUNCES) FETTA, CRUMBLED COARSELY

12 SMALL WHOLE FRESH BASIL LEAVES

100G (3 OUNCES) HEIRLOOM CHERRY TOMATOES, HALVED LENGTHWAYS

6 EGGS

½ CUP (125ML) POURING CREAM

1 Preheat oven to 180°C/350°F. Grease a 12-hole (⅓ cup/80ml) muffin pan; line bases with baking paper.

2 Cook bacon in a medium frying pan over medium heat, stirring, for 5 minutes or until crisp. Add green onion; cook, stirring, for 2 minutes or until onion is soft. Drain on paper towel.

3 Divide bacon mixture, fetta, basil and tomatoes, cut-side up, between holes. Beat eggs and cream in a medium jug; season. Pour mixture into holes.

4 Bake quiches for 18 minutes or until a thin-bladed knife inserted into the centre comes out clean. Cool in pan for 5 minutes before turning out on a wire rack. Serve warm or cooled.

nutritional count per quiche 10.8g total fat (5.5g saturated fat); 572kJ (137 cal); 0.8g carbohydrate; 9.2g protein; 0.2g fibre

SWEET POTATO CHIPS

Sweet potato and kumara chips will stay fresh in an airtight container for up to 2 days.

2 SMALL PURPLE-SKINNED WHITE SWEET POTATO (320G)

2 SMALL KUMARA (ORANGE SWEET POTATO) (500G)

VEGETABLE OIL, FOR DEEP-FRYING

1 Scrub vegetables lightly and wash well; pat dry. Trim ends of vegetables. Using a mandoline or V-slicer, slice vegetables lengthways into 1mm slices.

2 Preheat the oil in a large saucepan to 150°C/300°F. Deep-fry white sweet potato, in batches, until beginning to brown around the edges. Remove from oil with a slotted spoon; drain well on paper towel. When cooled, if any chips are not completely crisp, deep-fry again for 30 seconds; drain on paper towels. Repeat with kumara.

3 Sprinkle chips lightly with salt before serving.

nutritional count per serving 5.8g total fat (0.8g saturated fat); 611kJ (146 cal); 19.8g carbohydrate; 2.7g protein; 2.5g fibre

NORI SESAME CHIPS

The nori sheet edges will have a rippled effect when cooking. Keep nori chips in an airtight container for up to 2 weeks.

10 YAKI NORI SHEETS (25G)

1½ TABLESPOONS SALT-REDUCED SOY SAUCE

2½ TEASPOONS SESAME OIL

1½ TABLESPOONS WHITE SESAME SEEDS

1 Preheat oven to 150°C/300°F. Line three large oven trays with baking paper.

2 Place two sheets of nori, shiny-side up, on each tray. (If two sheets don't fit on one tray, cook one at a time.)

3 Combine soy sauce and sesame oil in a small bowl. Brush half the soy mixture on nori sheets on trays; sprinkle with half the sesame seeds.

4 Bake nori for 8 minutes or until crisp. Transfer to wire racks to cool.

5 Repeat with remaining nori sheets, soy mixture and sesame seeds, re-using trays and baking paper.

6 Cut each sheet into six pieces before serving.

nutritional count per piece 0.3g total fat (0.05g saturated fat); 21kJ (5 cal); 0.1g carbohydrate; 0.2g protein; 0.02g fibre

PREP +
COOK TIME

20 MINUTES

MAKES

60 PIECES

PREP +
COOK TIME

1 HOUR
(+ COOLING)

MAKES

2¼ CUPS

PREP TIME

15 MINUTES

MAKES

1⅓ CUPS

ROASTED CARROT HUMMUS

Serve this dip with seeded parmesan crisps on page 183.

4 MEDIUM CARROTS (480G), QUARTERED LENGTHWAYS

4 CLOVES GARLIC, UNPEELED

1 TABLESPOON EXTRA VIRGIN OLIVE OIL

⅓ CUP (80ML) EXTRA VIRGIN OLIVE OIL, EXTRA

400G (12½ OUNCES) CANNED CHICKPEAS (GARBANZO BEANS), DRAINED, RINSED

2 TABLESPOONS HULLED TAHINI PASTE

2 TABLESPOONS LEMON JUICE

2 TABLESPOONS WATER

1 TEASPOON SEA SALT FLAKES

1 Preheat oven to 200°C/400°F.

2 Combine carrots, garlic and oil in an ovenproof dish. Bake for 40 minutes or until tender; cool slightly. Reserve pan juices. Squeeze garlic from skins; discard skins.

3 Blend or process carrot, garlic and reserved pan juices with remaining ingredients until smooth.

nutritional count per 2 tablespoons 8.4g total fat (1.3g saturated fat); 440kJ (105 cal); 4.7g carbohydrate; 1.9g protein; 2.5g fibre

tip This dip will keep, covered, in the fridge for up to 4 days.

SPICY GUACAMOLE

Serve this dip with seeded parmesan crisps on page 183.

1 LARGE RIPE AVOCADO (320G), HALVED

½ SMALL RED ONION (50G), CHOPPED FINELY

1 LARGE ROMA (EGG) TOMATO (90G), CHOPPED FINELY

2 TABLESPOONS FINELY CHOPPED FRESH CORIANDER (CILANTRO)

1 TABLESPOON LIME JUICE

¼ TEASPOON TABASCO OR HOT CHILLI SAUCE, OPTIONAL

1 Scoop avocado into a medium bowl; mash coarsely with a fork.

2 Add remaining ingredients; stir to combine. Season to taste with salt.

nutritional count per 2 tablespoons 6g total fat (1.3g saturated fat); 261kJ (62 cal); 0.7g carbohydrate; 0.8g protein; 1.1g fibre

tip This dip is best made close to serving.

SPICED YOGHURT, CUCUMBER & HERB DIP

1 LEBANESE CUCUMBER (130G), UNPEELED

1 TEASPOON SEA SALT FLAKES

½ CUP LOOSELY PACKED FRESH CORIANDER (CILANTRO) LEAVES

1 CUP LOOSELY PACKED FRESH MINT LEAVES

2 CLOVES GARLIC, CRUSHED

1 FRESH LONG GREEN CHILLI, SEEDED, CHOPPED COARSELY

½ TEASPOON GROUND CUMIN

1 CUP (280G) GREEK-STYLE NATURAL YOGHURT

500G (1 POUND) RED RADISHES, TRIMMED, LARGE ONES HALVED AND QUARTERED

1 Halve cucumber lengthways; remove seeds. Coarsely grate cucumber. Toss cucumber and salt together in a medium bowl. Place in a sieve; stand for 5 minutes. Squeeze cucumber with your hands to remove excess liquid. Transfer to a medium bowl.

2 Meanwhile, blend or process herbs, garlic, chilli, cumin and 1 tablespoon of the yoghurt until smooth.

3 Add herb mixture to cucumber in bowl with remaining yoghurt; stir until well combined.

4 Serve dip with radishes.

nutritional count per 2 tablespoons 2.1g total fat (1.2g saturated fat); 229kJ (55 cal); 5.8g carbohydrate; 2.3g protein; 1.3g fibre

tip Dip is best made on day of serving, but can be kept refrigerated for up to 3 days.

PREP TIME

15 MINUTES

MAKES

1½ CUPS

**PREP +
COOK TIME**
40 MINUTES
MAKES
24

LITTLE BANANA COCONUT CAKES

You will need 1 large overripe banana for this recipe.

4 EGG WHITES

60G (2 OUNCES) BUTTER, MELTED

⅓ CUP (50G) COCONUT SUGAR

⅔ CUP (80G) GROUND ALMONDS

⅓ CUP (50G) WHOLEMEAL SELF-RAISING FLOUR

⅓ CUP (100G) MASHED OVERRIPE BANANA (SEE NOTE ABOVE)

½ CUP (25G) FLAKED COCONUT

½ TEASPOON GROUND CINNAMON

1 Preheat oven to 180°C/350°F. Grease two 12-hole (1-tablespoon/20ml) mini muffin pans.

2 Using a fork, lightly whisk egg whites in a medium bowl until combined. Add butter, coconut sugar, ground almonds and flour; stir until combined. Stir in banana.

3 Spoon mixture into holes; top with flaked coconut.

4 Bake cakes for 15-20 minutes or until browned and cooked. Turn cakes top-side up onto wire rack to cool. Serve sprinkled with cinnamon.

nutritional count per cake 4.5g total fat (2g saturated fat); 278kJ (66 cal); 4.6g carbohydrate; 1.6g protein; 0.4g fibre

tip These can be kept in an airtight container for up to 2 days or frozen for up to 3 months.

SEED & NUT BARS

On cooling, the peanut butter mixture becomes firm and starts to set. You may need to use your hands when incorporating into the other ingredients. When adding chocolate in the choc-chip variation ensure peanut butter mixture is cool otherwise the chocolate will melt.

½ CUP (80G) ALMONDS KERNELS (NATURAL ALMONDS), CHOPPED COARSELY

½ CUP (50G) WALNUTS, QUARTERED

¼ CUP (40G) WHITE SESAME SEEDS

¼ CUP (50G) PEPITAS (PUMPKIN SEED KERNELS)

¼ CUP (35G) SUNFLOWER SEEDS

¾ CUP (210G) CRUNCHY PEANUT BUTTER (SEE TIPS)

⅔ CUP (160ML) RICE MALT SYRUP

2 CUPS (40G) PUFFED MILLET

2 TABLESPOONS WHITE CHIA SEEDS

2 TABLESPOONS FLAXSEEDS (LINSEEDS)

1 Preheat oven to 180°C/350°F. Grease a 20cm x 30cm (8-inch x 12-inch) slice pan. Line base and two opposite sides with baking paper, extending the paper 5cm (2 inches) over sides.
2 Place almonds, walnuts, sesame seeds, pepitas and sunflower seeds on a large oven tray in a single layer. Bake 10 minutes or until browned lightly and fragrant. Transfer to a large heatproof bowl.

3 Meanwhile, stir peanut butter and rice malt syrup in a small saucepan over low heat until combined.
4 Add syrup mixture to nut mixture with puffed millet, chia seeds and flaxseeds; stir until well combined. Press mixture firmly into pan. Refrigerate for 4 hours or overnight.
5 Remove slice from pan; cut into 24 bars.

nutritional count per bar 11.2g total fat (1.5g saturated fat); 653kJ (156 cal); 8.2g carbohydrate; 4.8g protein; 1g fibre

tips You can use any type of nut butter or sunflower butter instead of peanut butter. For a crisper bar, bake at 180°C/350°F for 10 minutes or until lightly browned. Cool in pan.

FLAVOUR VARIATIONS

CHOC-CHIP Stir 50g (1½oz) chopped sugar-free dark chocolate into mixture before pressing into pan. Drizzle top with 50g (1½oz) melted sugar-free dark chocolate.

nutritional count per bar 13g total fat (2.6g saturated fat); 735kJ (176 cal); 8.4g carbohydrate; 5.1g protein; 1g fibre

COCONUT Omit the pepitas and sunflower seeds and add ¾ cup (60g) shredded unsweetened coconut. Sprinkle the top with ¼ cup (20g) toasted shredded unsweetened coconut.

nutritional count per bar 12.4g total fat (3.2g saturated fat); 704kJ (168 cal); 8.6g carbohydrate; 4.5g protein; 1g fibre

PREP + COOK TIME

45 MINUTES
(+ REFRIGERATION)

MAKES

24 BARS

PREP +
COOK TIME

35 MINUTES
(+ COOLING)

MAKES

4 CUPS

TRAIL MIX

1 CUP (140G) ROASTED SALTED PEANUTS

1 CUP (160G) ALMOND KERNELS
(NATURAL ALMONDS)

½ CUP (70G) WHOLE SKINLESS HAZELNUTS

½ CUP (100G) PEPITAS (PUMPKIN SEEDS)

1 CUP (50G) FLAKED COCONUT

2 EGG WHITES, BEATEN LIGHTLY

45G (1½-OUNCE) PACKET LEMON AND
HERB DUKKAH

½ TEASPOON TABLE SALT

¼ CUP (40G) DRIED CURRANTS

1 Preheat oven to 180°C/350°F. Line two oven trays with baking paper.

2 Combine nuts, pepitas and coconut in a large bowl.

3 Combine egg white, dukkah and salt in a small bowl; add to nut mixture. Stir until well combined. Divide mixture between trays in a single layer.

4 Bake for 10 minutes. Sprinkle each with currants; bake a further 8-10 minutes or until browned lightly and fragrant. Cool on trays.

5 Separate trail mix into small clusters. Store in an airtight container.

nutritional count per ¼ cup 18.6g total fat (3.4g saturated fat); 925kJ (221 cal); 4.9g carbohydrate; 7.6g protein; 2.4g fibre

tip Trail mix can be kept in an airtight container at room temperature for up to 2 weeks.

CAULIFLOWER, QUINOA & ASPARAGUS BITES

These bites will keep in an airtight container in the fridge for up to 3 days.

2 TABLESPOONS WHITE QUINOA

350G (11 OUNCES) CAULIFLOWER, CHOPPED

300G (9½ OUNCES) ASPARAGUS, TRIMMED, CHOPPED COARSELY

3 EGGS, BEATEN LIGHTLY

¼ TEASPOON GROUND NUTMEG

½ CUP (50G) GRATED MOZZARELLA

⅓ CUP (50G) FINELY GRATED PARMESAN

1 GREEN ONION (SCALLIONS), SLICED THINLY

1 Preheat oven to 180°C/350°F. Grease a 12-hole (⅓ cup/80ml) muffin pan. Cut out twelve 12cm (4¾-inch) squares from baking paper; line holes with squares.

2 Rinse quinoa in cold water; drain. Soak quinoa in ¼ cup (60ml) water in small saucepan for 15 minutes. Place over heat; bring to the boil. Reduce heat; simmer, covered, for 5-8 minutes or until water is absorbed. Remove from heat; stand 10 minutes. Fluff with fork. Cool.

3 Meanwhile, boil, steam or microwave cauliflower and asparagus, separately, until tender; drain. Refresh asparagus in cold water; cool. Reserve asparagus tips.

4 Combine, egg, nutmeg, mozzarella, parmesan and green onion in a large bowl. Season. Add cauliflower, asparagus and quinoa; mix well. Spoon mixture evenly into holes. Top with reserved asparagus tips.

5 Bake for 20 minutes or until golden brown. Leave in pan for 5 minutes; transfer to a wire rack to cool.

nutritional count per bite 3.6g total fat (1.8g saturated fat); 290kJ (69 cal); 2.4g carbohydrate; 5.8g protein; 1.3g fibre

PREP +
COOK TIME

50 MINUTES
(+ SOAKING &
COOLING)

MAKES 12

ROASTED SESAME
EDAMAME BEANS

500G (1 POUND) EDAMAME (SOY BEANS), SHELLED (SEE TIP)

2 TEASPOONS OLIVE OIL

2 TEASPOONS BLACK SESAME SEEDS

2 TEASPOONS WHITE SESAME SEEDS

½ TEASPOON SESAME OIL

½ TEASPOON SALT FLAKES

1 Preheat oven to 220°C/425°F. Line an oven tray with baking paper.

2 Place ingredients in a medium bowl; stir to combine. Spread mixture onto tray.

3 Bake for 15 minutes or until golden.

nutritional count per serving 7.5g total fat (0.6g saturated fat); 476kJ (114 cal); 6.6g carbohydrate; 6.1g protein; 0.2g fibre

tip You can use fresh or frozen (thawed) edamame; available from Asian food stores and some supermarkets. To quickly thaw the beans, place in a heatproof bowl, top with hot water; stand for 1 minute. Drain, then shell.

CHEESY CAJUN POPCORN

Cooled popcorn will keep in an airtight container for up to 3 days.

1 TABLESPOON OLIVE OIL

25G (¾ OUNCE) BUTTER

¼ CUP (60G) POPPING CORN

2 TEASPOONS CAJUN SEASONING MIX

2 TEASPOONS SALT FLAKES

½ CUP (40G) FINELY GRATED PARMESAN

1 Heat oil and butter in a medium saucepan over medium-high heat until starting to bubble.

2 Add popping corn, seasoning mix and salt; cover pan with a tight fitting lid. Cook, shaking pan occasionally, for 3-5 minutes or until popping has stopped.

3 Remove pan from heat. Add parmesan to popcorn; stir until well coated.

nutritional count per ½ cup 9.1g total fat (3.3g saturated fat); 516kJ (123 cal); 6.7g carbohydrate; 3.5g protein; 1.1g fibre

PREP +
COOK TIME
10 MINUTES
MAKES
3 CUPS

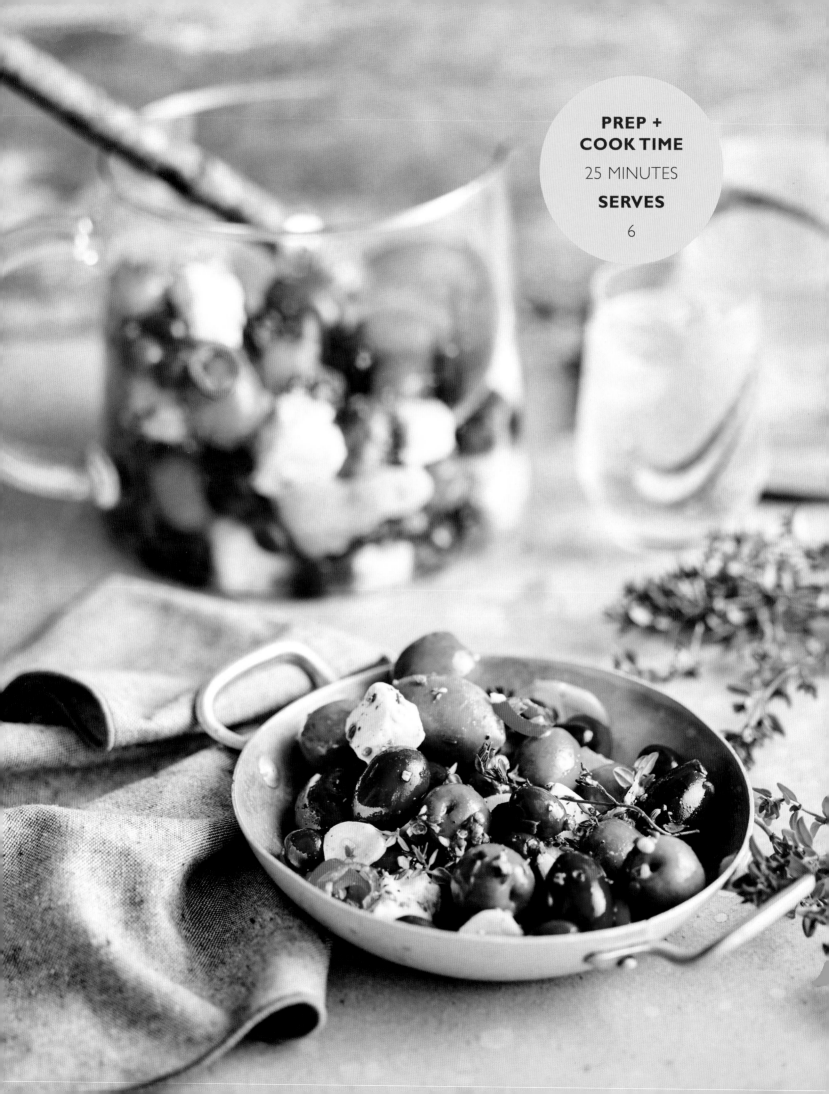

**PREP +
COOK TIME**
25 MINUTES
SERVES
6

ROASTED MIXED OLIVES & FETTA

Use pitted olives, if you prefer.

1 TEASPOON FENNEL SEEDS

1 TEASPOON CUMIN SEEDS

1 TEASPOON CORIANDER SEEDS

1 MEDIUM LEMON (140G)

300G (9½ OUNCES) MIXED OLIVES

1 TEASPOON FRESHLY GROUND BLACK PEPPER

¼ CUP (60ML) OLIVE OIL

2 TABLESPOONS SHERRY VINEGAR

2 CLOVES GARLIC, SLICED THINLY

1 FRESH LONG RED CHILLI, SLICED THINLY

200G (6½ OUNCES) FIRM FETTA, CUT INTO CUBES

3 FRESH THYME SPRIGS

1 Preheat oven to 180°C/350°F. Line an oven tray with baking paper.

2 Lightly crush the seeds in a mortar and pestle. Dry-fry crushed seeds in a small frying pan over medium heat, shaking pan frequently, for 1 minute or until fragrant.

3 Using a vegetable peeler, peel rind from lemon, avoiding any white pith. Cut rind into long thin strips.

4 Combine olives, rind, pepper, oil, vinegar, garlic, chilli, fetta, thyme and toasted crushed seeds in a medium bowl. Arrange olive mixture on tray.

5 Bake for 8 minutes or until hot. Serve warm.

nutritional count per serving 27.3g total fat (7.8g saturated fat); 1208kJ (289 cal); 2.1g carbohydrate; 7.3g protein; 2.3g fibre

PEA, CHICKPEA & HAZELNUT FALAFEL

½ CUP (60G) FROZEN PEAS, THAWED

125G (4 OUNCES) CANNED CHICKPEAS
(GARBANZO BEANS), DRAINED, RINSED

50G (1½ OUNCES) FETTA, CRUMBLED

2 TABLESPOONS COARSELY CHOPPED MINT

1 FRESH LONG GREEN CHILLI, SEEDED,
CHOPPED FINELY

1 EGG

¼ CUP (25G) HAZELNUT MEAL

1 TABLESPOON WHITE SESAME SEEDS

¼ CUP (30G) FINELY CHOPPED HAZELNUTS

VEGETABLE OIL, FOR SHALLOW-FRYING

1 MEDIUM LEMON (140G), CUT INTO WEDGES

MINT YOGHURT

½ CUP (140G) GREEK-STYLE YOGHURT

1 TABLESPOON LEMON JUICE

1 TABLESPOON FINELY CHOPPED FRESH MINT

1 Place peas, chickpeas, fetta, mint, chilli, egg and hazelnut meal in a food processor; pulse until coarsely chopped and combined. Season. Shape tablespoons of mixture into balls; flatten slightly. Toss falafel in combined sesame seeds and chopped hazelnuts. Place falafel on an baking-paper-lined oven tray. Refrigerate for 30 minutes.

2 Meanwhile, make mint yoghurt.

3 Heat oil in a medium frying pan over medium-high heat; shallow-fry falafel, in batches, for 5 minutes or until golden brown. Drain on paper towel.

4 Serve falafel with mint yoghurt and lemon wedges.

mint yoghurt Combine ingredients in small bowl.

nutritional count per serving 16.6g total fat (4.3g saturated fat); 990kJ (236 cal); 9.5g carbohydrate; 10.5g protein; 4.1g fibre

PREP + COOK TIME

30 MINUTES
(+ REFRIGERATION)

SERVES 4
(MAKES 12)

**PREP +
COOK TIME**
30 MINUTES
(+ FREEZING &
REFRIGERATION)
MAKES 16

SUGAR-FREE COCONUT CHOCOLATE BARS

We used 99.8% sugar-free chocolate, available from health food stores and pharmacies. These bars can be stored in an airtight container in the refrigerator for up to 1 week.

2½ CUPS (190G) SHREDDED COCONUT

2 TEASPOONS STEVIA

⅔ CUP (160ML) COCONUT CREAM

2 TEASPOONS VANILLA EXTRACT

300G (6 OUNCES) SUGAR-FREE DARK CHOCOLATE, CHOPPED FINELY

50G (1½ OUNCES) BUTTER

1 Combine coconut, stevia, coconut cream and half the extract in a medium bowl. Divide mixture into 16 portions; shape each portion into a 6cm (2½-inch) log. Place logs on a baking-paper-lined oven tray. Freeze for 1 hour or until firm.

2 Place chocolate and butter in a small microwave-safe bowl. Microwave on HIGH (100%) in 30-second bursts, stirring, until melted and smooth. Add remaining extract; stir until smooth. Cool to room temperature.

3 Dip bars, one at a time, into chocolate mixture to evenly coat; allow excess to drain, then return to tray. Refrigerate for 30 minutes or until firm.

nutritional count per bar 20.8g total fat (14.9g saturated fat); 897kJ (214 cal); 2.7g carbohydrate; 2.3g protein; 0.1g fibre

tip Stevia comes from the leaf of a plant, so is promoted as a natural sweetener. It is processed into a white powder that can be used in a similar way to sugar. It has a minimal effect on blood glucose levels and has no kilojoules, so it can be a useful way to reduce your sugar intake.

SUGAR-FREE
APPLE & ALMOND FRIANDS

These friands can be made a day ahead. Store in an airtight container.

2 CUPS (240G) GROUND ALMONDS

¼ CUP (35G) SELF-RAISING FLOUR

1 TEASPOON BAKING POWDER

1 TABLESPOON STEVIA

1 TEASPOON GROUND CINNAMON

4 EGG WHITES, BEATEN LIGHTLY

120G (4 OUNCES) BUTTER, MELTED

1 MEDIUM RED APPLE (150G), GRATED COARSELY

¼ CUP (20G) FLAKED ALMONDS

1 Preheat oven to 200°C/400°F. Grease a 9-hole oval (⅓ cup/80ml) friand pan.

2 Combine ground almonds, flour, baking powder, stevia and cinnamon in a large bowl. Add egg white, butter and apple; stir to combine. Spoon mixture evenly into holes. Top with flaked almonds.

3 Bake friands for 18-20 minutes or until a skewer inserted in centre comes out clean. Leave friands in pan for 5 minutes before turning, top-side up, on a wire rack to cool.

nutritional count per friand 27g total fat (5.6g saturated fat); 1268kJ (303 cal); 6.5g carbohydrate; 8g protein; 2.9g fibre

tip Stevia comes from the leaf of a plant, so is promoted as a natural sweetener. It is processed into a white powder that can be used in a similar way to sugar. It has a minimal effect on blood glucose levels and has no kilojoules, so it can be a useful way to reduce your sugar intake.

**PREP +
COOK TIME**

20 MINUTES
(+ REFRIGERATION)

SERVES

4

ORANGE & MINT RICOTTA WITH RASPBERRIES

You can use either fresh or packaged ricotta in this recipe.

1 MEDIUM ORANGE (240G)

1 CUP (240G) RICOTTA

½ CUP (140G) GREEK-STYLE YOGHURT

1 TABLESPOON FINELY CHOPPED FRESH MINT

250G (8 OUNCES) FRESH RASPBERRIES

2 TABLESPOONS SHELLED PISTACHIOS, CHOPPED COARSELY

½ CUP FRESH MICRO MINT OR BABY MINT LEAVES

1 TABLESPOON HONEY

1 Using a vegetable peeler, peel rind from half the orange, avoiding any white pith. Cut rind into long thin strips; reserve. Finely grate remaining rind.

2 Press ricotta through a fine sieve into a medium bowl. Add yoghurt, grated rind and chopped mint; mix well. Refrigerate for 30 minutes.

3 Place reserved rind strips in a small heatproof bowl. Cover with boiling water; stand for 1 minute or until softened. Drain well.

4 Divide three quarters of the raspberries among four 1-cup (250ml) serving glasses; spoon ricotta mixture on berries. Top with pistachios, remaining raspberries, rind strips and baby mint leaves; drizzle with honey.

nutritional count per serving 9.7g total fat (4.7g saturated fat); 872kJ (208 cal); 18.4g carbohydrate; 8.9g protein; 5.1g fibre

BLISS BALLS

PISTACHIO & CRANBERRY

prep time 20 minutes (+ refrigeration) **makes** 35
Process 1 cup shelled pistachios until finely chopped; reserve. Process another 1 cup shelled pistachios until finely chopped. Add 200g (6½oz) chopped medjool dates and ½ cup dried unsweetened cranberries; process until well combined. Add about 2 teaspoons hot water; process until mixture comes together. With damp hands, roll 2 level teaspoons of mixture into balls. Roll balls in reserved nuts to coat; place on a baking-paper-lined oven tray. Refrigerate for 1 hour.

nutritional count per ball 1.8g total fat (0.2g saturated fat); 187kJ (45 cal); 6.4g carbohydrate; 0.8g protein; 0.4g fibre

CACAO & HAZELNUT

prep time 20 minutes (+ refrigeration) **makes** 30
Process 1 cup roasted skinless hazelnuts until finely chopped; reserve. Process another 1 cup roasted skinless hazelnuts until finely chopped. Add 200g (6½oz) chopped medjool dates, 2 tablespoons cacao powder and ½ teaspoon ground nutmeg; process until well combined. Add about 2 teaspoons hot water; process until mixture comes together. With damp hands, roll 2 level teaspoons of mixture into balls. Roll balls in reserved nuts to coat; place on a baking-paper-lined oven tray. Refrigerate for 1 hour.

nutritional count per ball 5.8g total fat (0.2g saturated fat); 342kJ (81 cal); 5.7g carbohydrate; 1.6g protein; 0.9g fibre

Bliss balls will keep in an airtight container in the fridge for up to 2 weeks.

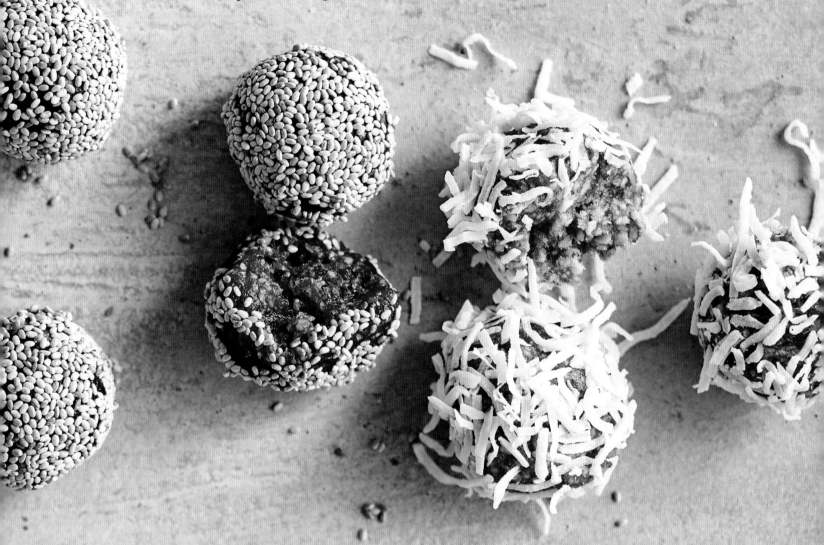

MACADAMIA & FIG

prep time 20 minutes (+ refrigeration) **makes** 30
Process 1 cup macadamias until finely chopped. Add 200g (6½oz) chopped medjool dates, 75g (2½oz) soft and juicy dried figs, 2 tablespoons white chia seeds and ½ teaspoon ground cinnamon; process until well combined. Add about 2 teaspoons hot water; process until mixture comes together. With damp hands, roll 2 level teaspoons of mixture into balls. Roll balls in 1 cup white chia seeds to coat; place on a baking-paper-lined oven tray. Refrigerate for 1 hour.
nutritional count per ball 6.5g total fat (0.7g saturated fat); 403kJ (96 cal); 6.9g carbohydrate; 1.8g protein; 2.5g fibre

APPLE & PEPITA

prep time 20 minutes (+ refrigeration) **makes** 35
Process 1 cup natural sliced almonds until finely chopped. Add 200g (6½oz) chopped medjool dates, 50g (1½oz) coarsely chopped dried apple, ¼ cup shredded coconut and ½ cup pepitas (pumpkin seeds); process until well combined. Add about 2 teaspoons hot water; process until mixture comes together. With damp hands, roll 2 level teaspoons of mixture into balls. Rolls balls in 1 cup shredded coconut to coat; place on a baking-paper-lined oven tray. Refrigerate for 1 hour.
nutritional count per ball 6g total fat (3.3g saturated fat); 359kJ (86 cal); 6.1g carbohydrate; 1.5g protein; 0.5g fibre

PEANUT BUTTER
COOKIES

These cookies will keep in an airtight container for up to 1 week.

1 CUP (280G) NO ADDED SUGAR CRUNCHY PEANUT BUTTER

¼ CUP (90G) HONEY

1 TEASPOON BICARBONATE OF SODA (BAKING SODA)

1 EGG, BEATEN LIGHTLY

1 Preheat oven to 180°C/350°F. Line two oven trays with baking paper.

2 Combine peanut butter, honey, bicarbonate of soda and egg in a medium bowl. Drop 1 tablespoon of the mixture onto trays, about 4cm (1½ inches) apart.

3 Bake cookies for 10 minutes or until lightly browned. Cool on trays; cookies will firm on cooling.

nutritional count per cookie 8.5g total fat (1g saturated fat); 511kJ (122 cal); 6.3g carbohydrate; 5g protein; 0g fibre

**PREP +
COOK TIME**
30 MINUTES
(+ COOLING)
MAKES
17

**PREP +
COOK TIME**
30 MINUTES
(+ REFRIGERATION)

MAKES
20 BALLS

SUGAR-FREE
CHOC ALMOND BALLS

We used 99.8% sugar-free chocolate, available from health food stores and pharmacies. These balls will keep in an airtight container in the refrigerator for up to 2 weeks.

100G (3 OUNCES) SUGAR-FREE DARK CHOCOLATE, CHOPPED FINELY

½ CUP (140G) 100% ALMOND SPREAD (NO ADDED SUGAR)

100G (3 OUNCES) SUGAR-FREE DARK CHOCOLATE, CHOPPED FINELY, EXTRA

1 TABLESPOON FLAKED ALMONDS, CHOPPED, TOASTED

1 Place chocolate into a medium heatproof bowl over a medium saucepan of simmering water (don't let water touch base of bowl); stir until melted and smooth. Remove bowl from heat.

2 Stir almond spread into melted chocolate until smooth and well combined. Spread mixture onto a baking-paper-lined oven tray. Refrigerate for 15 minutes or until firm.

3 Spoon teaspoons of mixture onto another baking-paper-lined oven tray. Refrigerate 10 minutes. Roll into balls; refrigerate for a further 20 minutes or until firm.

4 Melt extra chocolate until smooth. Dip balls, one at a time, into melted chocolate; allow excess chocolate to drain, then return to tray. Sprinkle with flaked almonds. Refrigerate for 30 minutes or until firm.

nutritional count per ball 8.6g total fat (3g saturated fat); 392kJ (93 cal); 0.8g carbohydrate; 2.2g protein; 1g fibre

tip You can also melt the chocolate in the microwave. Place in a microwave-safe dish, then microwave on HIGH (100%) in 30-second bursts, stirring until melted and smooth.

SUGAR-FREE CRANBERRY CHOCOLATE SNACK BARS

We used 99.8% sugar-free chocolate, available from health food stores and pharmacies. When measuring honey, lightly spray the measuring cup with oil first and the honey will slide out more easily.

2½ CUPS (50G) PUFFED RICE

½ CUP (60G) PECAN NUTS, CHOPPED

⅓ CUP (65G) PEPITAS (PUMPKIN SEEDS)

¼ CUP (35G) DRIED UNSWEETENED CRANBERRIES, CHOPPED COARSELY

2 TABLESPOONS LSA (SEE TIP)

1 TABLESPOON WHITE SESAME SEEDS

½ CUP (180G) HONEY

1 TEASPOON VANILLA EXTRACT

½ TEASPOON SALT FLAKES

45G (1½ OUNCES) SUGAR-FREE DARK CHOCOLATE, CHOPPED COARSELY

1 Preheat oven to 150°C/300°F. Grease a 20cm (8-inch) square cake pan; line base and two opposite sides with baking paper, extending the paper 5cm (2 inches) over the sides.

2 Combine puffed rice, nuts, pepitas, cranberries, LSA and sesame seeds in a large bowl.

3 Place honey, extract and salt in a small saucepan over medium heat; cook, stirring, for 2 minutes or until mixture just comes to a simmer. Pour honey mixture over dry ingredients; stir through until evenly coated. Cool for 5 minutes. Add chocolate; stir until combined. Transfer mixture to pan; pressing down firmly with the back of a spoon.

4 Bake for 30 minutes or until golden brown. Cool in pan. Cut into 16 bars.

nutritional count per bar 6.9g total fat (1.3g saturated fat); 548kJ (131 cal); 14.6g carbohydrate; 2.2g protein; 0.7g fibre

tip LSA is a ground mixture of linseeds, sunflower seeds and almonds. It is available from supermarkets and health food stores.

**PREP +
COOK TIME**
50 MINUTES
(+ COOLING)

MAKES
16 BARS

**PREP +
COOK TIME**
35 MINUTES
(+ COOLING)
MAKES
30

APRICOT MUESLI COOKIES

When measuring honey, lightly spray the measuring cup with oil first and the honey will slide out more easily. These cookies will keep in an airtight container for up to 1 week.

2 CUPS (240G) RAW NO-ADDED-FRUIT MUESLI WITH SEEDS AND NUTS

1 CUP (160G) WHOLEMEAL SELF-RAISING FLOUR

½ CUP (80G) FINELY CHOPPED DRIED APRICOTS

80G (2½ OUNCES) BUTTER, MELTED

⅓ CUP (120G) HONEY

1 EGG, BEATEN LIGHTLY

1 EGG WHITE, BEATEN LIGHTLY

1 Preheat oven to 180°C/350°F. Line two large oven trays with baking paper.

2 Combine muesli, flour and apricots in a medium bowl. Make a well at the centre. Add combined butter, honey, egg and egg white; stir until well combined.

3 Using damp hands, roll level tablespoons of dough into balls. Place balls on trays, about 4cm (1½ inches) apart. Flatten with a fork.

4 Bake cookies for 12 minutes or until lightly browned. Cool on trays; cookies will firm on cooling.

nutritional count per cookie 3.7g total fat (1.8g saturated fat); 405kJ (97 cal); 13.2g carbohydrate; 1.9g protein; 1.6g fibre

CHEESE BISCOTTI

These biscotti will keep in an airtight container for up to 1 week. If they soften, return to oven to re-crisp. For a gluten-free option, use gluten-free self-raising flour instead.

1 CUP (120G) GROUND ALMONDS

½ CUP (80G) WHOLEMEAL SELF-RAISING FLOUR

2 TEASPOONS DRIED OREGANO LEAVES

½ TEASPOON BAKING POWDER

¼ TEASPOON CAYENNE PEPPER

½ CUP (40G) FINELY GRATED PARMESAN

1 CUP (120G) COARSELY GRATED CHEDDAR

2 EGGS

¼ CUP (60ML) OLIVE OIL

1 Preheat oven to 180°C/350°F. Line an oven tray with baking paper.

2 Combine ground almonds, flour, oregano, baking powder and cayenne pepper in a medium bowl. Add parmesan and cheddar; mix well.

3 Whisk eggs and oil in a small jug. Add egg mixture to cheese mixture. Using your hands, bring the mixture together. Turn dough out onto lightly floured surface. Shape, then roll mixture into a 25cm (10-inch) log. Place log on tray; flatten slightly.

4 Bake for 35 minutes or until lightly browned. Leave on tray for 15 minutes.

5 Reduce oven to 160°C/325°F.

6 Using a large serrated knife, cut log, diagonally into 1cm (½-inch) slices. Place slices, in a single layer, on an oven tray. Bake for 15 minutes. Turn biscotti over. Bake for a further 10-15 minutes or until lightly browned. Cool on wire racks.

nutritional count per piece 9.3g total fat (2.6g saturated fat); 480kJ (115 cal); 2.7g carbohydrate; 4.7g protein; 1g fibre

**PREP +
COOK TIME**
1 HOUR 20 MINUTES
(+ COOLING)

MAKES
20 PIECES

PREP TIME
20 MINUTES
(+ REFRIGERATION)

MAKES
12 BALLS

CHEESE & HERB BALLS

125G (4 OUNCES) CREAM CHEESE, AT ROOM TEMPERATURE

75G (2½ OUNCES) FRESH GOAT'S CHEESE, AT ROOM TEMPERATURE

⅓ CUP FINELY CHOPPED FRESH FLAT-LEAF PARSLEY

1 TABLESPOON FINELY CHOPPED FRESH CHIVES

1 Combine cheeses in a medium bowl.

2 Roll 2 level teaspoons of mixture into balls. Roll balls in combined herbs. Place balls on a baking-paper-lined oven tray. Refrigerate for 1 hour.

nutritional count per ball 4.6g total fat (3g saturated fat); 216kJ (51 cal); 0.3g carbohydrate; 2g protein; 0.2g fibre

tip These cheese balls can be stored in an airtight container in the refrigerator for up to 1 week.

GREEN SUPER JUICE

prep time 5 minutes **serves** 3

Blend 1 chopped lebanese cucumber, 2 trimmed celery sticks, 2 large trimmed kale leaves, 50g (1½oz) spinach leaves, 1 medium cored green apple, ½ peeled lemon, 1 sprig fresh mint, 1 cup coconut water and 1 cup ice cubes on high speed for 1 minute or until smooth. If required, stop the blender and push the ingredients down before blending again.

nutritional count per serving 0.3g total fat (0.1g saturated fat); 289kJ (69 cal); 12.8g carbohydrate; 1.9g protein; 3.3g fibre

ALMOND & AVOCADO PROTEIN SMOOTHIE

prep time 5 minutes **serves** 2

Blend 1 cup unsweetened almond milk, 1 tablespoon vanilla-flavoured protein powder, 2 tablespoons almond butter, ½ medium ripe avocado, 1 tablespoon honey, ½ medium banana and 1 cup ice cubes on high speed for 1 minute or until smooth.

nutritional count per serving 34.9g total fat (4.6g saturated fat); 1889kJ (451 cal); 24g carbohydrate; 9.7g protein; 4g fibre

DRINKS

CREAMY RASPBERRY SMOOTHIE

prep time 5 minutes (+ standing) **serves** 2

Place ⅔ cup raw cashews in a medium bowl; cover with cold water. Stand at room temperature for 3 hours. Drain; rinse well. Blend drained cashews with 1 cup coconut water, 1 cup frozen raspberries, 1 tablespoon maple syrup, ½ peeled lime and 1 cup ice cubes for 1 minute or until smooth.

nutritional count per serving 23.1g total fat (4.1g saturated fat); 1564kJ (374 cal); 28.1g carbohydrate; 9.5g protein; 8g fibre

SUMMER SUNRISE

prep time 10 minutes **serves** 2

In this order, place ½ cup coconut water and the juice of 1 medium orange, then 1 medium cored apple, ½ small peeled and cored ripe pineapple and 1cm (½-in) piece sliced fresh ginger in a blender. Add 1 cup ice cubes; blend on high speed for 1 minute or until smooth.

nutritional count per serving 0.4g total fat (0.2g saturated fat); 517kJ (124 cal); 25.8g carbohydrate; 1.5g protein; 4.2g fibre

KALE CHIPS

These kale chips will keep in an airtight container for up to 2 weeks.

450G (14½ OUNCES) KALE

1 TABLESPOON EXTRA VIRGIN OLIVE OIL

½ TEASPOON CRUSHED SEA SALT FLAKES

1 Preheat oven to 190°C/375°F; place three large oven trays in the oven while preheating.

2 Remove and discard kale stems from leaves. Wash leaves well; pat dry with paper towel or in a salad spinner. Tear kale leaves into 5cm (2-inch) pieces; place in a large bowl, then drizzle with oil and sprinkle with salt. Using your hands, rub oil and salt through the kale. Spread kale, in a single layer, on trays.

3 Bake kale for 10 minutes. Remove any pieces of kale that are already crisp. Return remaining kale to the oven for a further 2 minutes; remove any pieces that are crisp. Repeat until all the kale is crisp. Cool.

nutritional count per serving 2.3g total fat (0.3g saturated fat); 135kJ (32 cal); 1.2g carbohydrate; 0.9g protein; 1.2g fibre

GLOSSARY

ALLSPICE also known as pimento or jamaican pepper; so-named because it tastes like a combination of nutmeg, cumin, clove and cinnamon. Available whole or ground.

ALMONDS

blanched brown skins removed from the kernel.

flaked paper-thin slices.

ground also called almond meal; almonds are powdered to a coarse flour-like texture.

slivered small pieces cut lengthways.

BAKING PAPER also called parchment or baking parchment; a silicone-coated paper that is primarily used for lining baking pans and oven trays so cooked food doesn't stick, making removal easy.

BEANS

borlotti also called roman beans or pink beans, can be eaten fresh or dried. Interchangeable with pinto beans due to their similarity in appearance – pale pink or beige with dark red streaks.

broad (fava) available dried, fresh, canned and frozen. Fresh should be peeled twice (discarding the outer long green pod and the beige-green tough inner shell); frozen beans have had their pods removed but the beige shell still needs removal.

butter cans labelled butter beans are, in fact, cannellini beans. Confusingly butter is also another name for lima beans (dried and canned); a large beige bean having a mealy texture and mild taste.

cannellini a small white bean similar in appearance and flavour to other white beans (great northern, navy or haricot), all of which can be substituted for the other. Available dried or canned.

kidney medium-sized red bean, slightly floury in texture, yet sweet in flavour.

snake long (about 40cm/16 inches), thin, round, fresh green bean; Asian in origin with a taste similar to green beans. Are also known as yard-long beans because of their (pre-metric) length.

white a generic term we use for canned cannellini, haricot, navy or great northern beans belonging to the same family; all can be used.

BEETROOT (BEETS) firm, round root vegetable.

BICARBONATE OF SODA (BAKING SODA) a raising agent.

BREADCRUMBS, PANKO (JAPANESE) are available in two varieties: larger pieces and fine crumbs. Both have a lighter texture than Western-style breadcrumbs. They are available from Asian grocery stores and most supermarkets.

BROCCOLINI a cross between broccoli and chinese kale; it has long asparagus-like stems with a long loose floret, both are edible. Resembles broccoli but is milder and sweeter in taste.

BURGHUL also called bulgar wheat; hulled steamed wheat kernels that, once dried, are crushed into various sized grains. Used in Middle Eastern dishes such as felafel, kibbeh and tabbouleh. Is not the same as cracked wheat.

BUTTER use salted or unsalted (sweet) butter; 125g (4 ounces) is equal to one stick of butter.

CAPERS grey-green buds of a warm climate shrub (usually Mediterranean); sold dried and salted or pickled in a vinegar brine. Rinse before using.

CAPSICUM (BELL PEPPER) also called pepper. Comes in many colours: red, green, yellow, orange and purplish-black. Be sure to discard seeds and membranes before use.

CARDAMOM a spice native to India and used extensively in its cuisine; can be purchased in pod, seed or ground form. Has a distinctive aromatic, sweetly rich flavour.

CELERIAC (CELERY ROOT) tuberous root with knobbly brown skin, white flesh and a celery-like flavour. Keep peeled celeriac in acidulated water to stop it discolouring. It can be grated and eaten raw in salads; used in stews; mashed like potatoes; or sliced and deep-fried as chips.

CHAR SIU SAUCE a Chinese barbecue sauce made from sugar, water, salt, fermented soya bean paste, honey, soy sauce, malt syrup and spices. It can be found at most supermarkets.

CHEESE

fetta Greek in origin; a crumbly textured goat- or sheep-milk cheese having a sharp, salty taste. Ripened and stored in salted whey.

fetta, persian a soft, creamy fetta marinated in a blend of olive oil, garlic, herbs and spices; available from most major supermarkets.

goat's made from goat's milk, has an earthy, strong taste; available in both soft and firm textures, in various shapes and sizes, and sometimes rolled in ash or herbs.

haloumi a firm, cream-coloured sheep-milk cheese matured in brine; haloumi can be grilled or fried, briefly, without breaking down. Should be eaten while still warm as it becomes tough and rubbery on cooling.

mozzarella soft, spun-curd cheese; originating in southern Italy where it was traditionally made from water-buffalo milk. Now generally made from cow's milk, it is the most popular pizza cheese because of its low melting point and elasticity when heated.

parmesan also called parmigiano; is a hard, grainy cow-milk cheese originating in Italy. Reggiano is the best variety.

pecorino the Italian generic name for cheeses made from sheep milk; hard, white to pale-yellow in colour. If you can't find it, use parmesan instead.

ricotta a soft, sweet, moist, white cow-milk cheese with a low fat content and a slightly grainy texture. The name roughly translates as 'cooked again' and refers to ricotta's manufacture from a whey that is itself a by-product of other cheese making.

CHICKPEAS (GARBANZO BEANS) an irregularly round, sandy-coloured legume. Has a firm texture even after cooking, a floury mouth-feel and robust nutty flavour; available canned or dried (soak for several hours in cold water before use).

CHILLI generally, the smaller the chilli, the hotter it is. Use rubber gloves when seeding and chopping fresh chillies as they can burn your skin. Removing seeds and membranes lessens the heat level.

CHOY SUM a member of the buk choy family; easy to identify with its long stems, light green leaves and yellow flowers. Stems and leaves are both edible, steamed or stir-fried.

CINNAMON available in pieces (called sticks or quills) and ground into powder; one of the world's most common spices.

COCONUT

cream obtained commercially from the first pressing of the coconut flesh alone, without the addition of water; the second pressing (less rich) is sold as coconut milk. Available in cans and cartons at most supermarkets.

flaked dried flaked coconut flesh.

milk not the liquid inside the fruit (coconut water), but the diluted liquid from the second pressing of the white flesh of a mature coconut. Available in cans and cartons at most supermarkets.

shredded thin strips of dried coconut.

sugar is not made from coconuts, but the sap of the blossoms of the coconut palm tree. The refined sap looks a little like raw or light brown sugar, and has a similar caramel flavour. It also has the same amount of kilojoules as regular white (granulated) sugar.

CORIANDER (CILANTRO) also known as pak chee or chinese parsley; a bright-green leafy herb with a pungent flavour. Both stems and roots of coriander are also used in cooking; wash well before using. Also available ground or as seeds; these should not be substituted for fresh as the tastes are completely different.

CORNFLOUR (CORNSTARCH) available made from corn or wheat (wheaten cornflour, gluten-free, gives a lighter texture in cakes); used as a thickening agent in cooking.

CREAM

pouring also called pure or fresh cream. It has no additives and contains a minimum fat content of 35%.

thickened (heavy) a whipping cream that contains a thickener. It has a minimum fat content of 35%.

CUMIN also known as zeera or comino; has a spicy, nutty flavour.

CURRY PASTES some recipes in this book call for commercially prepared pastes of varying strengths and flavours. Use whichever one you feel best suits your spice-level tolerance.

massaman rich, spicy flavour reminiscent of Middle Eastern cooking; favoured by southern Thai cooks for use in hot and sour stew-like curries and satay sauces.

tikka in Indian cooking, the word "masala" loosely translates as paste and the word "tikka" means a bite-sized piece of meat, poultry or fish. Tikka paste is any maker's choice of spices and oils, mixed into a mild paste, frequently coloured red. Used for marinating or for brushing over meat, seafood or poultry, before or during cooking instead of as an ingredient.

DAIKON also called white radish; this long, white horseradish has a wonderful, sweet flavour. After peeling, eat it raw in salads or shredded as a garnish; also great when sliced or cubed and cooked in stir-fries and casseroles. The flesh is white but the skin can be either white or black; buy those that are firm and unwrinkled from Asian food shops.

DUKKAH an Egyptian specialty spice mixture made up of roasted nuts, seeds and an array of aromatic spices.

EDAMAME (SHELLED SOY BEANS) available frozen from Asian food stores and some supermarkets.

FENNEL a white to very pale green-white, firm, crisp, roundish vegetable about 8-12cm (3¼-4¾ inches) in diameter. The bulb has a slightly sweet, anise flavour but the leaves have a much stronger taste. Also the name of dried seeds having a licorice flavour.

FISH FILLETS, FIRM WHITE blue eye, bream, flathead, snapper, ling, swordfish, whiting, jewfish or sea perch are all good choices. Check for small pieces of bone and use tweezers to remove them.

FISH SAUCE called nam pla (Thai) or nuoc nam (Vietnamese); made from pulverised salted fermented fish, most often anchovies. Has a pungent smell and strong taste, so use sparingly.

FLOUR

plain (all-purpose) a general all-purpose wheat flour.

self-raising plain flour sifted with baking powder in the proportion of 1 cup flour to 2 teaspoons baking powder.

GAI LAN also known as chinese broccoli, gai larn, kanah, gai lum and chinese kale; used more for its stems than its coarse leaves.

GINGER, FRESH pink or red in colour, paper-thin shavings of ginger pickled in a mixture of vinegar, sugar and natural colouring. Available from Asian food shops.

HARISSA a Moroccan paste made from dried chillies, cumin, garlic, oil and caraway seeds. Available from Middle Eastern food shops and supermarkets.

HOISIN SAUCE a thick, sweet and spicy Chinese paste made from salted fermented soya beans, onions and garlic.

KAFFIR LIME LEAVES also known as bai magrood. Aromatic leaves of a citrus tree; two glossy dark green leaves joined end to end, forming a rounded hourglass shape. A strip of fresh lime peel may be substituted for each kaffir lime leaf.

KECAP MANIS a thick soy sauce with added sugar and spices. The sweetness comes from the addition of molasses or palm sugar.

KUMARA (ORANGE SWEET POTATO) the Polynesian name of an orange-fleshed sweet potato often confused with yam.

LEMON GRASS a tall, clumping, lemon-smelling and -tasting, sharp-edged grass; the white part of the stem is used, finely chopped, in cooking.

LSA A ground mixture of linseeds (L), sunflower seeds (S) and almonds (A); available from supermarkets and health food stores.

MAPLE SYRUP, PURE distilled from the sap of sugar maple trees found only in Canada and the USA. Maple-flavoured syrup or pancake syrup is not an adequate substitute for the real thing.

MIZUNA a mustard green from Japan where it is traditionally used in soups and other cooked main dishes. It's often found in mesclun, but its mild, aromatic jagged green leaves can also stand alone. Refrigerate in a plastic bag, unwashed, for up to 5 days.

MUSHROOMS

flat large, flat mushrooms with a rich earthy flavour. They are sometimes misnamed field mushrooms, which are wild mushrooms.

porcini also known as cèpes; the richest-flavoured mushrooms. Expensive, but because they're so strongly flavoured, only a small amount is required.

shiitake, fresh also known as chinese black, forest or golden oak mushrooms; although cultivated, they are large and meaty and have the earthiness and taste of wild mushrooms.

swiss brown also known as cremini or roman mushrooms; are light brown mushrooms with a full-bodied flavour.

NUTMEG a strong and pungent spice ground from the dried nut of an evergreen tree native to Indonesia. Usually found ground but the flavour is more intense from a whole nut, available from spice shops, so it's best to grate your own.

OIL

cooking spray we use a cooking spray made from canola oil.

olive made from ripened olives. Extra virgin and virgin are the first and second press, respectively, of the olives; "light" refers to taste not fat levels.

peanut pressed from ground peanuts; most commonly used oil in Asian cooking because of its high smoke point (capacity to handle high heat without burning).

sesame used as a flavouring rather than a cooking medium.

OKRA also known as bamia or lady fingers. A green, ridged, oblong pod with a furry skin. Native to Africa, this vegetable is used in Indian, Middle Eastern and South American cooking. Can be eaten on its own; as part of a casserole, curry or gumbo; used to thicken stews or gravies.

ONIONS, GREEN (SCALLIONS) also called, incorrectly, shallot; an immature onion picked before the bulb has formed. Has a long, bright-green edible stalk.

PINE NUTS not a nut but a small, cream-coloured kernel from pine cones. Toast before use to bring out their flavour.

POLENTA also known as cornmeal; a flour-like cereal made of ground corn (maize). Also the name of the dish made from it.

POMEGRANATE dark-red, leathery-skinned fruit about the size of an orange filled with hundreds of seeds, each wrapped in an edible lucent-crimson pulp with a unique tangy sweet-sour flavour.

PRESERVED LEMON RIND a North African specialty; lemons are quartered and preserved in salt and lemon juice or water. To use, remove and discard pulp, squeeze juice from rind, rinse rind well; slice thinly. Once opened, store under refrigeration.

QUINOA pronounced keen-wa; is a gluten-free grain. It has a delicate, slightly nutty taste and chewy texture.

RADICCHIO a red-leafed Italian chicory with a refreshing bitter taste that's eaten raw and grilled. Comes in varieties named after their places of origin, such as round-headed Verona or long-headed Treviso.

ROASTING/TOASTING desiccated coconut, pine nuts and sesame seeds roast more evenly if stirred over low heat in a heavy-based frying pan; their natural oils will help turn them golden brown. Remove from pan immediately. Nuts and dried coconut can be roasted in the oven to release their aromatic essential oils. Spread them evenly onto an oven tray then roast at 180°C/350°F for about 5 minutes.

SAFFRON available ground or in strands; imparts a yellow-orange colour to food once infused. The quality can vary greatly; the best is the most expensive spice in the world.

SAMBAL OELEK also ulek or olek; an Indonesian salty paste made from ground chillies and vinegar.

SILVER BEET also called swiss chard; mistakenly called spinach.

SOY SAUCE made from fermented soya beans. Several variations are available in most supermarkets and Asian food stores. We use japanese soy sauce unless stated otherwise.

SPINACH also known as english spinach and, incorrectly, silver beet.

SUGAR

brown very soft, finely granulated sugar retaining molasses for its characteristic colour and flavour.

caster (superfine) finely granulated table sugar.

coconut see Coconut

white (granulated) coarse, granulated table sugar, also called crystal sugar.

SUMAC a purple-red, astringent spice ground from berries growing on shrubs flourishing wild around the Mediterranean; adds a tart, lemony flavour to food. Available from major supermarkets.

TOFU also called bean curd; an off-white, custard-like product made from the "milk" of crushed soybeans. Comes fresh as soft or firm, and processed as fried or pressed dried sheets. Fresh tofu can be refrigerated in water (changed daily) for up to 4 days.

WATERCRESS one of the cress family, a large group of peppery greens. Highly perishable, so must be used as soon as possible after purchase. It has an exceptionally high vitamin K content, which is great for eye health, and is an excellent source of calcium.

YOGHURT we use plain full-cream yoghurt in our recipes.

greek-style plain yoghurt strained in a cloth (muslin) to remove the whey and to give it a creamy consistency.

ZA'ATAR a Middle Eastern herb and spice mixture which varies but always includes thyme, with ground sumac and, usually, toasted sesame seeds.

ZUCCHINI also called courgette; small, pale- or dark-green or yellow vegetable of the squash family. Harvested when young, its edible flowers can be stuffed and deep-fried.

CONVERSION CHART

MEASURES

One Australian metric measuring cup holds approximately 250ml; one Australian metric tablespoon holds 20ml; one Australian metric teaspoon holds 5ml.

The difference between one country's measuring cups and another's is within a two- or three-teaspoon variance, and will not affect your cooking results. North America, New Zealand and the United Kingdom use a 15ml tablespoon.

All cup and spoon measurements are level. The most accurate way of measuring dry ingredients is to weigh them. When measuring liquids, use a clear glass or plastic jug with the metric markings.

The imperial measurements used in these recipes are approximate only. Measurements for cake pans are approximate only. Using same-shaped cake pans of a similar size should not affect the outcome of your baking. We measure the inside top of the cake pan to determine sizes.

We use large eggs with an average weight of 60g.

DRY MEASURES

METRIC	IMPERIAL
15G	½OZ
30G	1OZ
60G	2OZ
90G	3OZ
125G	4OZ (¼LB)
155G	5OZ
185G	6OZ
220G	7OZ
250G	8OZ (½LB)
280G	9OZ
315G	10OZ
345G	11OZ
375G	12OZ (¾LB)
410G	13OZ
440G	14OZ
470G	15OZ
500G	16OZ (1LB)
750G	24OZ (1½LB)
1KG	32OZ (2LB)

LIQUID MEASURES

METRIC	IMPERIAL
30ML	1 FLUID OZ
60ML	2 FLUID OZ
100ML	3 FLUID OZ
125ML	4 FLUID OZ
150ML	5 FLUID OZ
190ML	6 FLUID OZ
250ML	8 FLUID OZ
300ML	10 FLUID OZ
500ML	16 FLUID OZ
600ML	20 FLUID OZ
1000ML (1 LITRE)	1¾ PINTS

LENGTH MEASURES

METRIC	IMPERIAL
3MM	⅛IN
6MM	¼IN
1CM	½IN
2CM	¾IN
2.5CM	1IN
5CM	2IN
6CM	2½IN
8CM	3IN
10CM	4IN
13CM	5IN
15CM	6IN
18CM	7IN
20CM	8IN
22CM	9IN
25CM	10IN
28CM	11IN
30CM	12IN (1FT)

OVEN TEMPERATURES

The oven temperatures in this book are for conventional ovens; if you have a fan-forced oven, decrease the temperature by 10-20 degrees.

	°C (CELSIUS)	°F (FAHRENHEIT)
VERY SLOW	120	250
SLOW	150	300
MODERATELY SLOW	160	325
MODERATE	180	350
MODERATELY HOT	200	400
HOT	220	425
VERY HOT	240	475

INDEX

STREET ART OF THE REVOLUTION

STREET ART

OF THE REVOLUTION
Festivals and Celebrations in Russia 1918-33

Edited by VLADIMIR TOLSTOY, IRINA BIBIKOVA, CATHERINE COOKE

with 220 illustrations, 85 in colour, and 4 maps

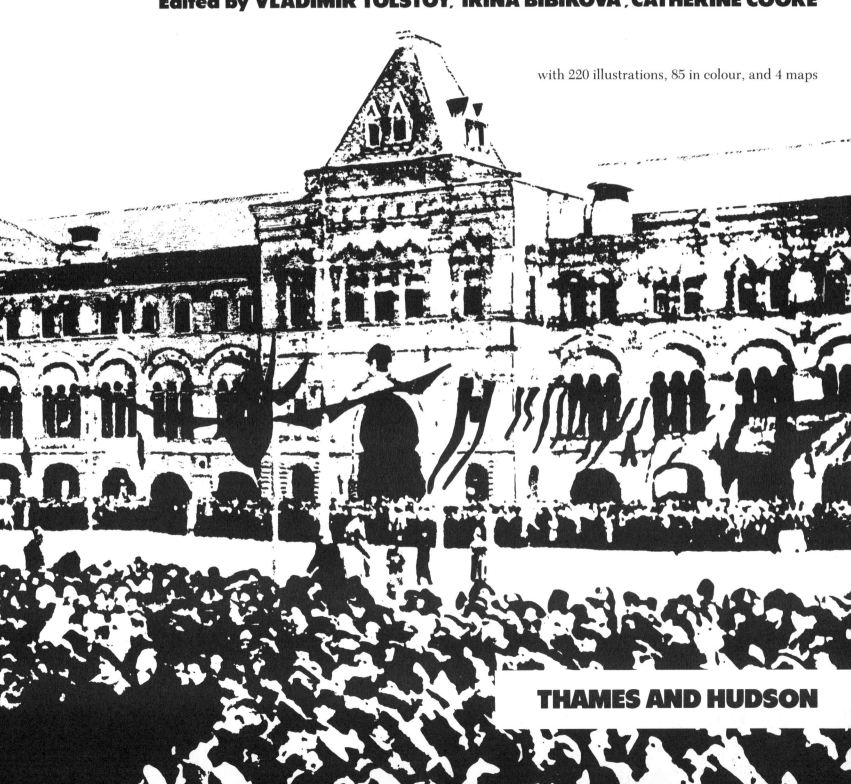

THAMES AND HUDSON

Contents

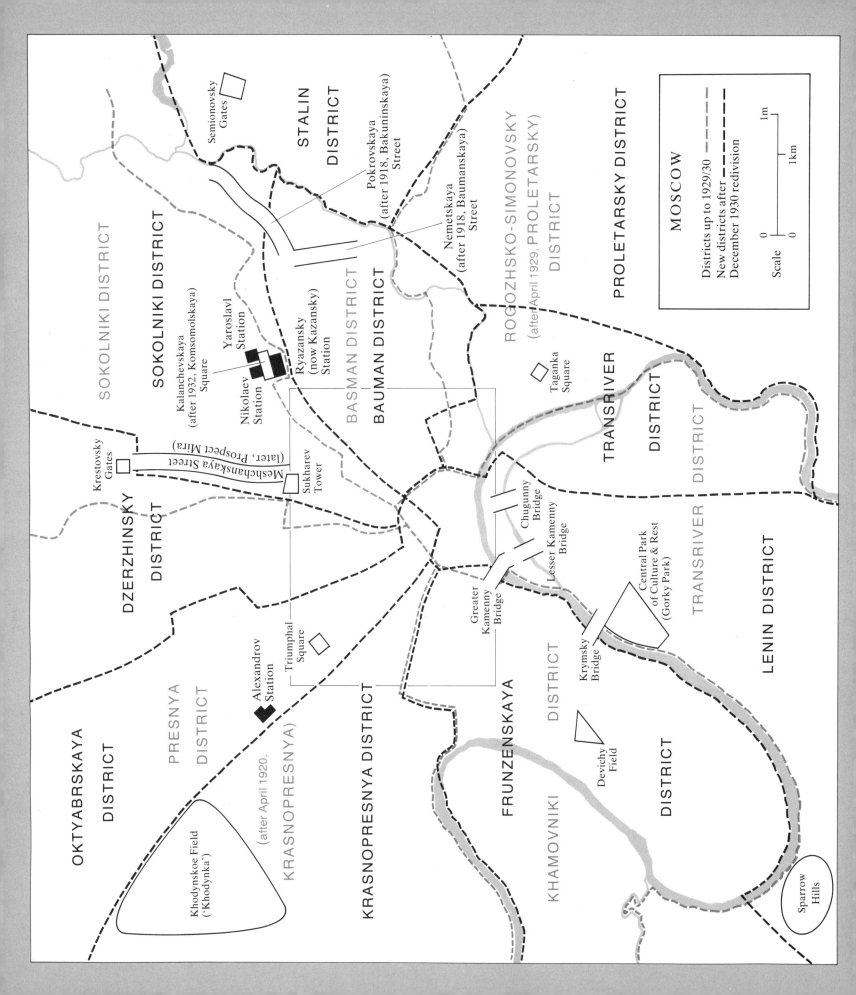

MOSCOW

Districts up to 1929/30 — — —
New districts after — —
December 1930 redivision

Scale

1m

1km

STALIN DISTRICT

Semionovsky Gates

Pokrovskaya (after 1918, Bakuninskaya) Street

Nemetskaya (after 1918, Baumanskaya) Street

SOKOLNIKI DISTRICT

ROGOZHSKO-SIMONOVSKY (after April 1929, PROLETARSKY) DISTRICT

PROLETARSKY DISTRICT

Kalanchevskaya (after 1932, Komsomolskaya) Square

Yaroslavl Station

Nikolaev Station

Ryazansky (now Kazansky) Station

BASMAN DISTRICT

BAUMAN DISTRICT

Taganka Square

TRANSRIVER DISTRICT

Krestovsky Gates

Meshchanskaya Street (later, Prospect Mira)

Sukharev Tower

TRANSRIVER DISTRICT

DZERZHINSKY DISTRICT

Chugunny Bridge

Lesser Kamenny Bridge

Central Park of Culture & Rest (Gorky Park)

LENIN DISTRICT

Greater Kamenny Bridge

Krymsky Bridge

Triumphal Square

Alexandrov Station

FRUNZENSKAYA DISTRICT

Devichy Field

OKTYABRSKAYA DISTRICT

PRESNYA DISTRICT

(after April 1920, KRASNOPRESNYA)

KRASNOPRESNYA DISTRICT

KHAMOVNIKI DISTRICT

DISTRICT

Khodynskoe Field ('Khodynka')

Sparrow Hills

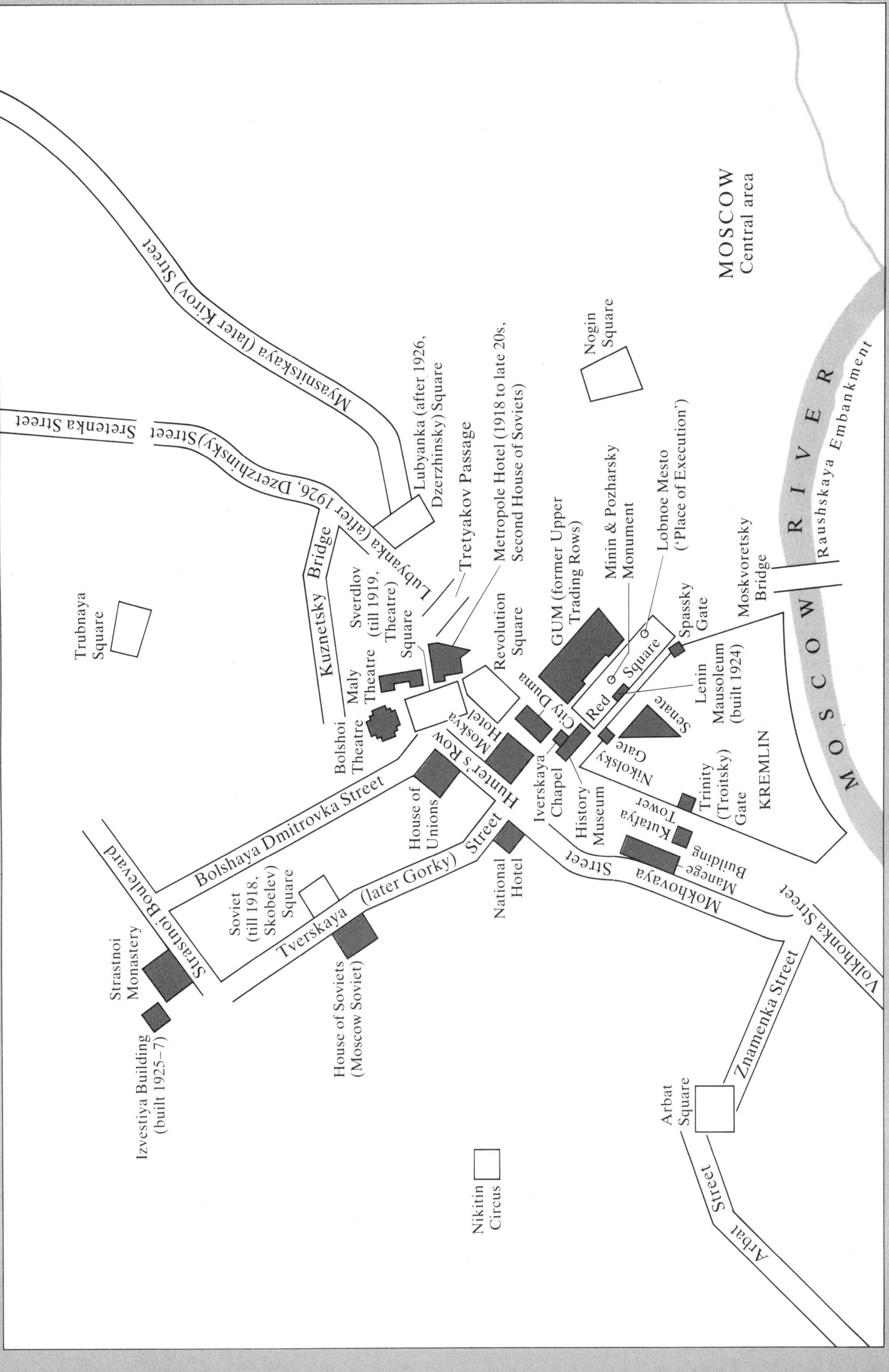

MOSCOW
Central area
Myasnitskaya (later Kirov) Street
Sretenka Street
Lubyanka (after 1926, Dzerzhinsky) Street
Lubyanka (after 1926, Dzerzhinsky) Square
Tretyakov Passage
Metropole Hotel (1918 to late 20s, Second House of Soviets)
Kuznetsky Bridge
Trubnaya Square
Nogin Square
Sverdlov (till 1919, Theatre) Square
Maly Theatre
Bolshoi Theatre
Revolution Square
GUM (former Upper Trading Rows)
Minin & Pozharsky Monument
Lobnoe Mesto ('Place of Execution')
Spassky Gate
Moskvoretsky Bridge
MOSCOW RIVER
Raushskaya Embankment
Red Square
City Duma
Moskva Hotel
Senate
Lenin Mausoleum (built 1924)
Nikolsky Gate
Iverskaya Chapel
History Museum
Trinity (Troitsky) Gate
KREMLIN
Kutafya Tower
Manege Building
Hunter's Row
House of Unions
Bolshaya Dmitrovka Street
Strastnoi Boulevard
Soviet (till 1918, Skobelev) Square
Tverskaya (later Gorky) Street
National Hotel
Mokhovaya Street
Volkhonka Street
Znamenka Street
Strastnoi Monastery
House of Soviets (Moscow Soviet)
Izvestiya Building (built 1925–7)
Arbat Square
Arbat Street
Nikitin Circus

Editor's Note:
In numerous cases the authors of documents have continued to use old names – either pre-Revolutionary ones or other officially superseded versions – simply out of habit and familiarity. Where a street, building, etc., appears in the documents under two different names, both are given here and, where possible, the official date of change, but this may not be accurately reflected in their usage.

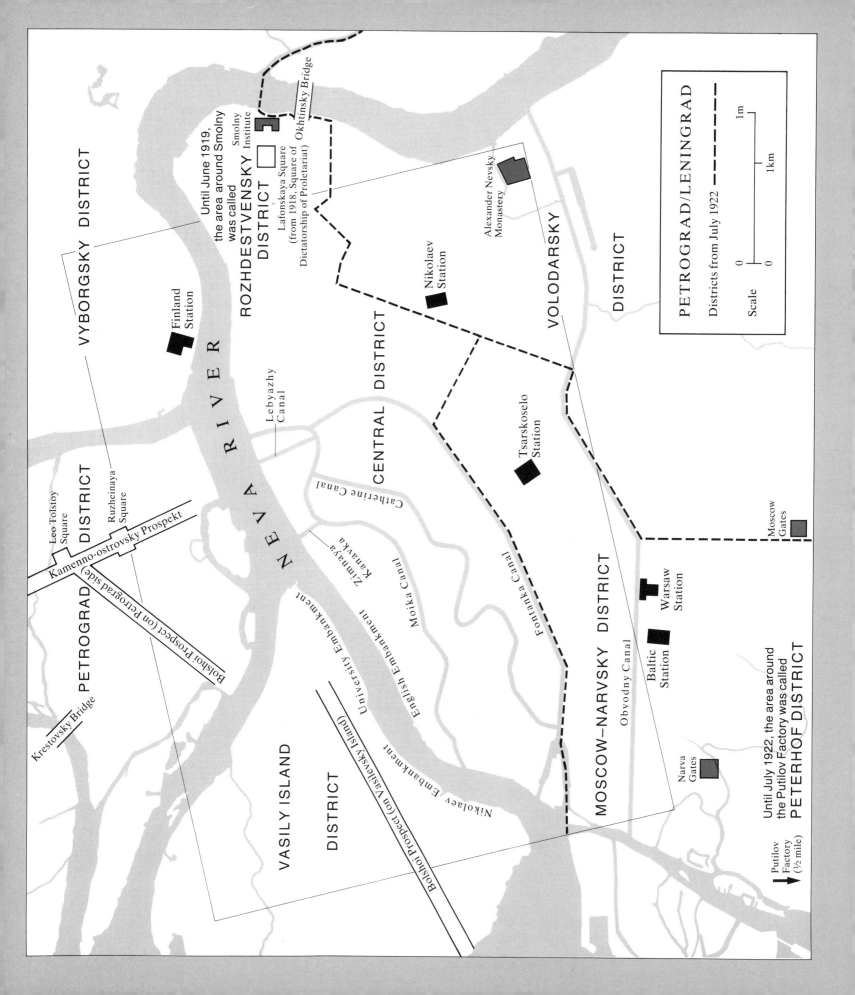

PETROGRAD/LENINGRAD

Scale

Districts from July 1922 - - - -

0   1m

0   1km

VYBORGSKY DISTRICT

PETROGRAD DISTRICT

Krestovsky Bridge

Kamenno-ostrovsky Prospekt

Leo Tolstoy Square

Ruzheinaya Square

Bolshoi Prospect (on Petrograd side)

Finland Station

NEVA RIVER

Lebyazhy Canal

ROZHDESTVENSKY DISTRICT

Smolny Institute

Until June 1919, the area around Smolny was called Lafonskaya Square (from 1918, Square of Dictatorship of Proletariat)

Okhtinsky Bridge

Alexander Nevsky Monastery

VOLODARSKY DISTRICT

Nikolaev Station

CENTRAL DISTRICT

Tsarskoselo Station

VASILY ISLAND DISTRICT

Bolshoi Prospect (on Vasilyevsky Island)

Nikolaev Embankment

University Embankment

English Embankment

Zimnaya Kanavka

Moika Canal

Catherine Canal

Fontanka Canal

Obvodny Canal

MOSCOW–NARVSKY DISTRICT

Warsaw Station

Baltic Station

Moscow Gates

Narva Gates

Putilov Factory (½ mile)

Until July 1922, the area around the Putilov Factory was called PETERHOF DISTRICT

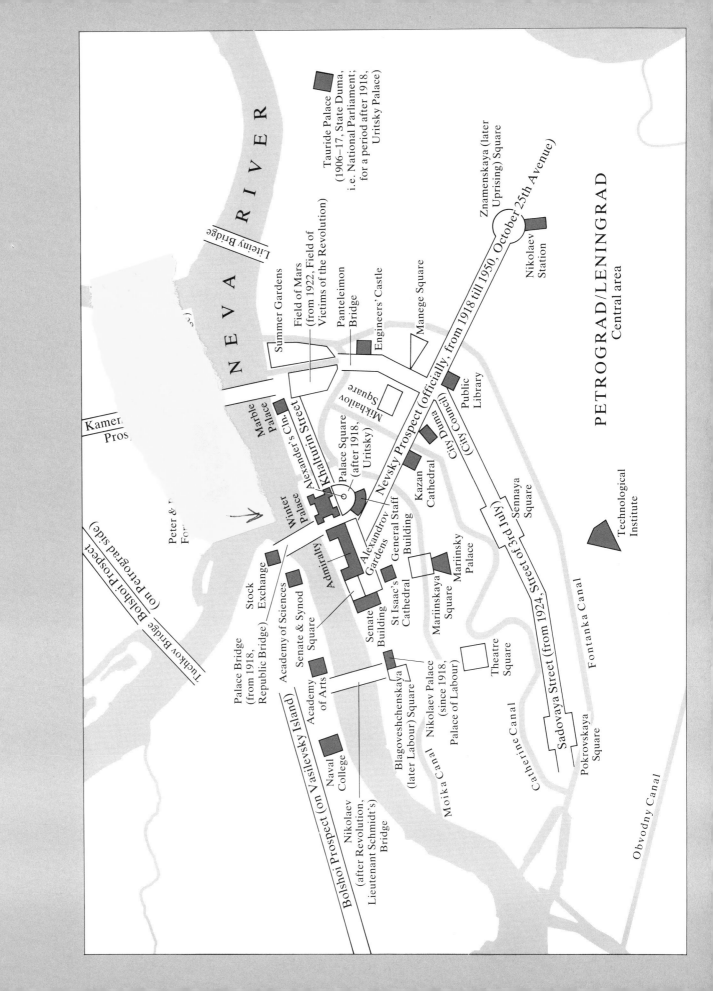

N E V A   R I V E R

Liteiny Bridge

Kamer...
Pros...

Peter & ...
For...

Tuchkov Bridge (on Petrograd side)
Bolshoi Prospect (on Petrograd side)

Bolshoi Prospect (on Vasilevsky Island)
Nikolaev (after Revolution, Lieutenant Schmidt's) Bridge

Naval College

Palace Bridge (from 1918, Republic Bridge)

Academy of Sciences

Stock Exchange

Academy of Arts

Senate & Synod Square

Senate Building

Blagoveshchenskaya (later Labour) Square

Nikolaev Palace (since 1918, Palace of Labour)

Moika Canal

Catherine Canal

Sadovaya Street (from 1924, Street of 3rd July)

Pokrovskaya Square

Obvodny Canal

Fontanka Canal

Technological Institute

PETROGRAD/LENINGRAD
Central area

Znamenskaya (later Uprising) Square

Nevsky Prospect (officially, from 1918 till 1950, October 25th Avenue)

Nikolaev Station

Sennaya Square

Public Library

City Duma (City Council)

Kazan Cathedral

Manege Square

Engineers' Castle

Panteleimon Bridge

Field of Mars (from 1922, Field of Victims of the Revolution)

Summer Gardens

Marble Palace

Alexander's Cln.

Khalturin Street

Palace Square (after 1918, Uritsky)

Mikhailov Square

Winter Palace

Admiralty

Alexandrov Gardens

General Staff Building

St Isaac's Cathedral

Mariinskaya Square

Mariinsky Palace

Theatre Square

Tauride Palace (1906–17, State Duma, i.e. National Parliament; for a period after 1918, Uritsky Palace)

Art born of the October Revolution

Introduction by VLADIMIR TOLSTOY

THE OCTOBER REVOLUTION which took place in Russia in 1917 transformed the face of the contemporary world. Nationally and internationally, it also had a decisive influence on the fate of art.

Within Russia itself, the Revolution changed the ideas and content of art, its forms and methods, and above all changed the audience to which it was addressed. From that time onwards, Soviet art became actively involved in the struggle for national transformation. After the 1917 Revolution, the prophetic words uttered by Lenin at the time of the first Russian revolution in 1905 began to come true. Under socialism, Lenin had insisted, art would no longer serve the elite of society, that 'upper ten thousand suffering from boredom and obesity; it will rather serve the millions and tens of millions of labouring people, the flower of the country, its strength and its future.'[1]

In some respects, there was a complete break with what avant-gardists of those days called 'the old art'. In other respects, however, the active participants in the Revolutionary epoch manifested a very strong feeling for their links with the progressive democratic strivings of Russian social thought in the nineteenth century, as well as a strong conviction that the October Revolution finally inaugurated the period when humanity's highest aspirations could be realized. As if anticipating revolution, Russian artistic culture at the turn of the century had been overflowing with an animation and potency whose destiny was yet to be revealed. The new Soviet regime gave an opportunity for these trends to find fulfilment.

In the years following the Revolution, the main focus was on various forms of mass agitational art. There was a flowering of innovation in such genres as the political poster, newspaper and magazine graphics, oratorical poetry and heroic theatre, mass dramatizations and popular street processions, murals for agitational trains and decorations for the streets in celebration of Revolutionary anniversaries. In these often new forms of mass agitational

1. V. I. Lenin, *Polnoe sobranie sochinenii* (*Complete Collected Works*), vol. 12, p. 104.

art, there was always a live and direct echo of the events of the Revolution itself. In this, as the new Soviet government's famous Commissar of Public Education A. V. Lunacharsky put it, 'there was undoubtedly a happy confluence of the strivings of the youthful branches of art, and the aspirations of the crowd.'[2]

The real architectural arenas for these great Revolutionary events and their later commemoration and celebration were of no small importance in themselves. Of course the people who were creating history did not particularly select special 'architectural backcloths' for their real-life dramas. But the great beauty of many of the sites of Revolutionary events – the Winter Palace, the Smolny Institute, the Field of Mars, the Tauride Palace in Petrograd, or Red Square and the Kremlin in Moscow – will always remain in the popular memory as being a symbolically significant and artistically expressive dimension of the events themselves. Suffice it to look at episodes from the *Storming of the Winter Palace* or from Eisenstein's film *October* to see how the significance of events is emphasized by their magnificent environments. The temporary decorations erected for the celebration of Revolutionary anniversaries in Moscow and Petrograd/Leningrad, as depicted in this book, give us invaluable documentary evidence of that environment itself, while also conveying the historic meaning of the events being celebrated.

The fundamental initiative which set this train of state festivals in motion was taken by Lenin himself in April 1918. The very young Soviet republic was enjoying a brief breathing space from the troubles and difficulties which arose after the signing of the Brest-Litovsk Peace treaty in February that year, and as socialist Russia entered its first spring of freedom there was a period for enjoying the practical realization of the dream of many revolutionary generations before them.

Lenin was working on a plan for technical and scientific work in the new Russia. He was worrying about the best way to develop radio and cinema. With leading architects he was discussing plans for reconstructing Moscow as the new capital of the new republic. He was concerned with policies for artistic education and for preserving the country's heritage of cultural monuments from any threats of vandalism. In the midst of this he launched his 'Plan of Monumental Propaganda'.

Presenting the plan to Lunacharsky, Lenin reminded him of the treatise entitled *Civitas Solis* by Tommaso Campanella, one of the first utopian socialists from the Renaissance. Campanella had described an ideal town whose walls would all be decorated with frescoes, to provide young people with a visual education in natural science and history and to arouse civic

---

2. A. V. Lunacharsky, 'Pervoe Maya 1918g (The First of May 1919) in *Vospominaniya i vpechatleniya* (*Reminiscences and Impressions*), Moscow 1968, p. 209.

feelings. 'It seems to me', said Lenin, 'that this is far from naive, and that with certain changes, we could take his idea on board and put it into practice now. I would call what I have in mind "monumental propaganda".' The essence of his idea consisted in the fact that 'short but expressive inscriptions should be placed in various significant places, on suitable walls or on special constructions. These inscriptions should contain the most basic Marxist principles and slogans as well as, perhaps, tightly worked out formulations evaluating one or another great historical event . . . Even more important than these slogans are in my opinion statues – be they busts or bas-reliefs of figures and groups.' They would not be 'of marble, granite and gold incised lettering' but 'modest, and let everything be temporary'.[3]

The link between Lenin's monumental propaganda plan and the general enthusiasm of the Revolutionary period for festivals is very significant. It is also important that the roots of Lenin's ideas date back to the humanistic traditions of the Renaissance and the experience of previous revolutions, in particular to the Paris Commune and the French Revolution. The idea coincides with that of Robespierre, delivered to the Convention on 7 May 1794, when he said that the motherland ought to educate its citizens and use popular festivals as an important means of performing such civic education. 'Man is nature's greatest phenomenon', declared Robespierre, 'and the most magnificent of all spectacles is that of a large popular festival.'[4]

However, such historical continuities in no way belittle the novelty and originality of Lenin's proposals. In the entirely new phrase 'monumental propaganda' we can see a reflection of the conception of the artist's social role which was inaugurated with the socialist revolution. We see the aspiration to link fine arts with other forms of mass agitational and propaganda work in the name of larger tasks of ideological education.

On 12 April 1918 the Soviet of People's Commissars passed the decree 'On the Monuments of the Republic' which was published two days later. This historic decree established quite specific tasks for monumental propaganda and revolutionary celebrations. By its nature the plan had a double social function: it was both educational and propagandist. Both these functions were now aspects of art's main task in society, which was to be a participator in the all-embracing business of 'building socialism'. In a conversation with Clara Zetkin Lenin said 'our workers . . . have earned the right to a truly great art'.[5] Lenin shared Tolstoy's view that art must 'have a theme which is significant and important for the working mass and not just for an idle

3.   A. V. Lunacharsky, 'Lenin o monumentalnoi propagande' (Lenin on Monumental Propaganda), in the book *Lenin i izobrazitelnoe iskusstvo* (*Lenin and Fine Art*), Moscow 1977, pp. 318–20.
4.   Quoted in: Zh. Terso, *Pesni i prazdnestva Franstuskoi revoliutsii* (*Songs and Festivals of the French Revolution*) Moscow 1933, pp. 139–40.
5.   K. Tsetkin (C. Zetkin), 'Vospominaniya o Lenine' (Memories of Lenin', in the book *Vospominaniya o Vladimire Iliche Lenine* (*Reminiscences of Vladimir Ilich Lenin*), vol. 5, Moscow 1969, p. 17.

minority'.[6] In relation to all forms of popular education Lenin emphasized that 'it would be the greatest and most terrible mistake which a Marxist could make to think that the millions of craftsmen and peasants could emerge from the darkness along the straight line of pure Marxist education'. These simple people, he said, 'must be approached in such a way that their interest is awakened – they must be roused from all directions and by all manner of means.'[7]

Reminiscences of the architect N. D. Vinogradov, who was charged with realizing the plan of monumental propaganda in Moscow, indicate Lenin's clear understanding of how such re-education could be served by such actions. Vinogradov met Lenin for the first time several days after the suppression of the Socialist Revolutionary rebellion and asked him whether this decree 'On the Monuments of the Republic' really deserved the over-riding importance which Lenin was according it. He replied: 'This decree is extremely important. After all you cannot liquidate illiteracy immediately. Just imagine: a statue to a revolutionary has been put up. There is a solemn ceremony . . . An imaginative speech is made . . . and imperceptibly we are achieving our first goal: we have touched the soul of an illiterate person.'[8] The extraordinary way in which a truly mass culture of festivals took off after the Revolution was a testimony to the effectiveness of their appeal to the illiterate Russian population.

The majority of artists at that time had only the most hazy understanding of Marxist theories, and it is natural that they expressed their revolutionary mood in ways that were spontaneous, and in rebellious gestures against established canons. We see such tendencies very clearly in the poetry and theatre of those post-Revolutionary years just as we do in the ideas about architecture and the posters, panels and decorations for the mass festivals. Revolutionary romanticism, a tense expressiveness, the language of academic allegory and stylization, everyday realism, Cézannist Post-Impressionism, folk prints and many other things, all went into the melting pot of revolutionary creativity to produce often unexpected results. The arts of this period tried, consciously or unconsciously, to lay the foundations for a unity of what had previously been different and separate branches of the arts, and in many of these festive celebrations we see this exemplified by the attempts to weld all available media into a great synthetic event.

The intention was fundamentally to convey something of the historic purpose of the social changes through which they were living to those very people who had in fact created that history: the working masses. As

6.   V. D. Bonch-Bruevich, *Lenin v Petrograde i Moskve 1917–20* (*Lenin in Petrograd and Moscow 1917–20*), Moscow 1966, p. 35.
7.   V. I. Lenin, *Polnoe sobranie sochinenii*, vol. 45, p. 26.
8.   Quoted in: A. Yusin, 'Nachalos v 1905–m' (It Began in 1905), *Pravda*, 16 December 1975.

Lunacharsky put it to his audience at the opening of the Free Art Educational Studios in Petrograd in October 1918, 'The need has arisen to change the external appearance of our towns as rapidly as possible, in order to express our new experiences in an artistic form as well as to get rid of all that is offensive to the feelings of the people.'[9] The task was all-embracing: the environment had to be brought to the point where it corresponded to the great social changes whose scale was not yet generally grasped. Each of the city-wide revolutionary celebrations recorded here generated works which aimed at linking architecture and urban space. They were monumental in scale, in their content, in the epic nature of their language, and in the extent to which they actively invaded the lives of individuals in the city.

The fact that all this was achieved with temporary structures of ephemeral materials makes the surviving documentary evidence even more valuable. The photographs which are published here, in many cases for the first time, show us what these syntheses of the Revolutionary towns and the first Soviet art actually looked like. We see clearly how the mass became the real hero of events, and how its belief in the future was directly expressed in its re-enactments.

Fifteen years is a short time in history, but our country travelled a long way in the fifteen years after 1917. Soviet power had first to conquer the country, and despite the foreign intervention, to win a Civil War which ended only in 1921–22 with the final victories of the Bolsheviks over the counter-revolutionaries. The economy had to be rebuilt out of ruin created by war and famine. Economic strength revived through Lenin's initiatives in the New Economic Policy of the early twenties, before it gave way to the major drive for industrialization and the first Five Year Plan of 1928–32.

The material assembled here covers the whole of this period, from 1918 to 1933, through every form of documentary record: photographs, press reports, official documents and reminiscences of participants. It is no use approaching this material with abstract aesthetic standards. Mass agitational art has to be judged in the light of the social struggle from which it emerges, and the aspirations of the people themselves in that period. With those criteria we can evaluate the creative effort on its own terms, and in relation to its work. Very relevant here is the judgment of the Italian Communist and philosopher Antonio Gramschi: 'The first stones of the new world, however coarse and unpolished they may be, are more beautiful than the sunset of a world in agony, and its swan songs.'[10]

9.   A. V. Lunacharsky, *Rech proiznesennaya na otkrytii Petrogradskikh GSKhUM* (*Speech delivered at the opening of the Petrograd State Free Art-study Studios*), 10 October 1918, Petrograd, 1918, p. 27.
10.   Antonio Gramschi, 'Iz tiuremnykh tetradei' (From Prison Notebooks), *Izbrannye proizvedeniya* (*Selected Works*), vol. 3, Moscow 1959, p. 34.

The Design of Revolutionary Celebrations

Introduction by IRINA BIBIKOVA

FROM THE VERY FIRST YEAR after the October Revolution public festivals began to play an important role in the political and artistic life of Russia. They were not only one of the most powerful means of agitation on behalf of Soviet power, but they also embodied in bright, exciting forms that everyone could understand, the people's dreams and hopes for a glorious future. The artists and craftsmen who designed and created these public events were faced with complex tasks and they discovered opportunities for bold, creative experiments and pursuits. The very scale of the work was unusual, as whole towns were decorated and there were thousands in the crowds of participants. The artists' creations were not displayed in enclosed museum galleries or exhibition halls but on the open spaces of squares and streets where they were seen not by individuals or small groups but by the broad masses.

In that synthesis of the arts which dealt with artistic aspects of the revolutionary festivals, painters, sculptors, architects, producers, musicians and scenery designers each tried to find their own solution to the tasks which led to an unusually diverse range of experiments and explorations. For those fifteen years which form the chronological frame of this book, the designs for festive celebrations followed a more complicated path of development than, probably, any other form of art in Russia. It is hard to find a single great name among the artists and cultural activists of that period which was not associated in one way or another with works for these festivals. It was a time of vigorous amateur art among the masses, when art clubs existed in almost every factory. Such activity found its most spirited embodiment in arrangements for revolutionary festivals. The festivals became an intergral part of life in our country and designs for them, with their sharp political aim and topical character, became a kind of illustrative chronicle reflecting the basic stages in the history of the Soviet state.

Despite the significance of this major social and artistic phenomenon, it has remained little studied to this day and the literature does not illuminate

it in all its complexity. It is true, however, that even at the end of the
twenties and the beginning of the thirties, apart from articles in the
periodical press (some of which are published in this collection), there were
a number of general publications on this theme. One of the very first was the
overview of recent experience assembled by the Committee for Sociological
Study of the Arts in Leningrad, published in 1927 as *Mass Festivals*, from
which discussions are published here as Documents 59, 60, 63 and 64.
E. Ryumin's book of the same title followed in the next year, with O. V.
Tsekhnovitser's from Moscow entitled *Demonstrations and Carnivals. For
the Tenth Anniversary of the October Revolution*. The early thirties saw a
considerable literature developing. A. S. Gushchin in Moscow published
three studies in as many years: *Fine Art in Mass Festivals and
Demonstrations*, in 1930; *The Experience of Organizing Mass Festivals* in
1931, and the photographic collection *Design of Mass Festivals during
Fifteen Years of the Dictatorship of the Proletariat* in 1932. Another from
Tsekhnovitser, *Festivals of the Revolution*, appeared in Leningrad in 1931.
A. S. Magidson, whose early work in 1927 and 1931 is described in her own
words here (Documents 78 and 87), was co-author of two studies which
appeared in 1932. With Yu. P. Shchukin she published *The Design of Mass
Festivals and Demonstrations*, and these two authors were joined by A. D.
Kuznetsova for *Designing the City for the Days of Revolutionary Festivals*.
Analyses and descriptions in these books, many of whose authors were
participants in the work, have great value as the evidence of eye-witnesses,
and in 1933 some documents in this field were among those assembled by I.
Matsa in his *Soviet Art over 15 Years: Materials and Documentation*.

The forties and fifties saw relatively little published on this topic, though
in 1949 the first academic dissertation in the field was presented by B. Stifel
as *Festival Decorations of the Russian City*. General books like L. I.
Lebedev's *Soviet Art of the Period of the Foreign Intervention and Civil
War* (1949) contained some information on these events, and my
collaborator here, V. P. Tolstoy, published more in his article 'Materials on
the History of Agitational Art during the Civil War Period' in 1953, and in
his book *Soviet Monumental Painting* (1958). Both these publications
illustrated designs for the streets of Moscow and Leningrad during the early
post-Revolutionary festivals, many of them published there for the first time.

Alongside works on the history of revolutionary festivals, there also
appeared a number of studies which attempted to provide a theoretical
discussion of festivity as a specific phenomenon of social and cultural life. V.
I. Chicherov's *The Winter Period in the Russian Farming Calendar* (1957)
can be pointed to as one of the early works of this sort.

In the sixties and more especially the seventies, popular festivals attracted
more and more attention from researchers who considered them as some of
the most important elements in the history of culture. The press carried on a

broad discussion of the idea of reviving traditional customs and creating new ones – revolutionary, everyday, professional, artistic and sporting. They also published many reminiscences of artists who had participated in their design and there were also a number of publications giving new information on the theme.

Two retrospective exhibitions in 1962 and 1967 showed works of Soviet mass agitational and decorative art and gave a deeper understanding of the problem. Many previously unseen designs, sketches and photographs of decorated towns and columns of demonstrators were exhibited for the first time since they had been created. The second exhibition, in the State Tretyakov Gallery, was particularly important in making this widely known. The exhibits were fully illustrated in the catalogue and *Mass Agitational Art in the First Years after October* (1971). The authors of the latter collection gathered and published many previously unpublished documents on the design and organization of festivals in 1918. In 1973 the publishing house 'Artist of the RSFSR' issued a small paperback book by O. V. Nemiro called *A Festival has Come to Town*.

It cannot be said, therefore, that this subject has no literature, but the material hitherto available has certain important limitations. In particular, the majority of these studies has been devoted exclusively to the work of well known artists, and they have limited themselves to the few years immediately following the 1917 Revolution. Very little attention was paid to the amateur art of the mass of the population, though this in fact played an enormous part in all the festive rituals. There were numerous workers' clubs which over a series of years organized most of the agitational processions, political carnivals, dramatizations and other forms of what we generally refer to as 'demonstrations'. This non-professional activity remains to be seriously researched even now, but is accorded its proper place here through balanced quotation.

An attempt to analyse the broader social and philosophical aspects of these events was made in 1978 by A. I. Mazaev in his book *The Festival as a Socio-cultural Phenomenon*. This was an important contribution to our understanding of these events, but it had two major shortcomings. Firstly it relied solely on secondary sources for its material; and secondly it contained no illustrations.

The selection of documents assembled here represents an attempt to portray the revolutionary festivals of the years 1918 to 1933 in a more balanced but authentic way, through press and official documents of the time and through reminiscences of the artists themselves. The result, we hope, is a far richer presentation of the reality of this important phenomenon of early Soviet history.

Thus this material explains the organizational structure of these festivals. It portrays the conflicts between the various artistic trends for which these festivals were an important field. It indicates the diversity of views to be found in the press of the time, as to the success or otherwise of the various aesthetic approaches, and of the attitudes of the masses themselves to what the artists, professional and amateur, offered them. Through this material something is communicated of the importance which the initiative of the masses themselves had in the organization of these festive events. At the same time the reminiscences of the artists reveal the atmosphere of general enthusiasm in which they worked and the extraordinary nature of the tasks with which they were faced.

Many of the photographs and design sketches reproduced here are being published for the first time, in particular those of the later twenties and early thirties. In combination with the verbal documents they provide a vivid picture of the various types and methods of festival design that succeeded each other as the twenties developed into the thirties, and in unprecedented detail they indicate the imaginative diversity of the work achieved.

It was less than six months after the Revolution, on 12 April 1918, that the Soviet of People's Deputies of the new regime issued the Decree which set this whole process in motion. This fundamental document appears here as Document 1. Despite the extremely critical situation that had developed within the young Soviet nation as a result of the Civil War and foreign intervention, it was decided that the workers' festival of 1 May, and the Revolutionary anniversary of 7 November, should be celebrated throughout the country. (Thanks to a discrepancy between the European and Old Russian calendars, the 'October' Revolution occurred on 7 November Western style). Festival commissions were set up for both occasions which worked in close contact with such bodies as the Fine Arts Department of the RSFSR Commissariat for Education, the Executive Committees of the Moscow and Petrograd Soviets of Workers' and Soldiers' Deputies, the Proletkult (Proletarian Culture) organization and the trade unions. Festival commissions were also set up under the executive committees of district Soviets and at certain major enterprises. Thus, a centralized system of organization took shape during preparations for the first revolutionary festivals, a system which existed with little alteration for several years.

The tremendous enthusiasm caused by the victory of the October Revolution gave a special and unique flavour to the first festival celebrations. Triumphal arches and tribunes were erected on the squares, avenues and streets of Moscow, Petrograd and other cities, individual buildings and entire architectural ensembles and bridges were decorated and adorned. In the years immediately following the Revolution, Soviet emblems began to emerge such as the hammer and sickle, the five-pointed star and the monogram of the RSFSR. The characteristic attributes of classical art, such as chariots, laurel wreaths and sacrificial altars, were also widely used. The theme of revolution was revealed through symbolic and allegorical images taken from ancient art and the celebrations of the French Revolution, or through heroic images of the new owners of the land, the workers and peasants, in styles ranging from the realistic through the generalized to the stylized.

Revolutionary festivals were a major phenomenon in the political and artistic life of the country and were given extensive coverage in the contemporary press. Newspaper and journal articles described and commented on the festival designs, expressing differing and often diametrically opposed views. Thus Lunacharsky, for instance, giving his impressions of the festive decoration of Petrograd for May Day 1918, wrote approvingly of the post-Cubist and Futurist decoration. Comparing his account in Document 6 with that of Dobuzhinsky, in Document 8, we find two totally different appraisals of the same festival. Dobuzhinsky offers many criticisms, fundamentally questioning the right of festival designers to 'explode' the historically formed architectural image of the city by covering the walls of its monumental buildings with 'new art' works. Indeed most commentators expressed a negative view of the decoration of Petrograd during these May Day celebrations of 1918, which had been done mainly by the artists of the so-called Leftist, or abstractionist, trend in Russian art.

Sadly, very few sketches and photographs of the designs for the 1918 May Day celebrations in Petrograd have survived, which makes it difficult to judge the accuracy of the various contemporary views. Moscow was much luckier in this respect. Archives of the avant-garde artist and architect brothers, the Vesnins (now part of the Shchusev Museum of Architecture) contain twenty sketches by them for the decoration of Red Square and three sketches for Skobelev Square. They were faced with a particularly difficult task for Red Square: the decoration of one of the most original national monuments of old Russian architecture which combines the beautiful spires of the Kremlin towers and the intricate, multi-coloured domes and side-chapel of St Basil's Cathedral – all the wealth of eighteenth-century colourful decoration – with the austere smoothness of the fortress walls, to form a unique architectural ensemble. The Vesnin brothers produced a series of different picturesque and whimsical compositions out of standards, banners, flags and draped material. Their rhythmic repetitions and overall colour range, based on combinations of various reds, ensured a unified spatial treatment of the square, emphasizing its elegance and magnificence. They did not attempt to set their design in contrast with the existing architectural ensemble, but tried merely to make the square look more festive.

A much larger contingent of creative workers of widely differing artistic trends, from masters of the academic school to representatives of the Left Front of Art, the Constructivist group LEF, took part in the decoration of

Moscow and Petrograd for the first anniversary of the October Revolution. Many interesting and unique compositions were created, consisting chiefly of huge decorative paintings intended to bear the main artistic message. In effect, this was the first time that contemporary art, so fully and diversely represented, had been put on display for the popular masses to judge, a point stressed in all the articles written at the time.

Pumpyansky's analysis of the Leningrad decorations for the 1918 celebrations gave three basic ways of dealing with the relationship between the festive decor and the architectural forms of the decorated buildings, an issue particularly significant for Petrograd where many people, like Dobuzhinsky, considered it blasphemy to destroy the 'severe and elegant' appearance of its ensembles with bright and loud panels. For artists from the pre-Revolutionary group of aesthetes called 'The World of Art', and for almost all architects, the answer was to be particularly careful with the appearance of the town and to use, in the main, decorative elements which would give the buildings a still more festive and elegant appearance. Examples of such an approach can be seen in Pumpyansky's own design for the Admiralty or in V. A. Shchuko's design for the decorations for the Tauride Palace. The second approach can be seen in the work of painters of a 'left' tendency. Their designs Pumpyansky considered 'audacious and contemporary', and he cited Natan Altman's decorations for Uritsky (or Palace) Square as being one of the most successful pieces of work of this type.

In Moscow with its picturesque variety of buildings, where each period has added its own particular stamp, the question of how festive decorations should relate to the existing architecture did not seem so important. Here there were broader opportunities for the artist's creative initiative, and diversity increased continuously as several designers worked on almost every subject and often one designer had a very different style from the other. As an example of one large, unified subject, Hunter's Row was decorated according to the designs of the young artists I. V. and O. V. Alekseev and, as Documents 14 and 15 show, it was very positively received by many contemporaries. Another example is Soviet Square where, with some variations, the Vesnins' design for the May Day celebrations was repeated. As far as other squares and constructions were concerned, V. Kerzhentsev was somewhat typical in considering that their decorations often showed a 'complete lack of co-ordination' (Document 15).

Criticism of the Moscow decorations reflected this somewhat fragmented character and was usually concerned with description and analysis of individual works. However, while approving or disapproving of individual pieces, most writers pointed to the need for a different approach to the decorations in the city – one based on entire ensembles. Thus Kerzhentsev urged that 'When organizing future celebrations . . . the decoration of each square should be assigned to one artist or to a well-established group', specifically in order to 'avoid a repeat of such blatant disharmony' (Document 15).

Underlying such details of the approach, however, the cardinal question which would define the future development of mass festivals remained that of whether artists could meet the expectations of the popular masses and could make their work accessible to them. From the overwhelming majority of contemporary authors, regardless of their own sympathies and aesthetic criteria, the answer was in the negative. Both the critics Pumpyansky and Kerzhentsev, for example, thought that the artists were still too 'individualistic' and had failed to understand what was the mass's level of experience. Other critics noted how 'alienated and puzzled' the crowds had seemed to be by Lebedev and Altman's decorations for that first Revolutionary anniversary in Petrograd. Lunacharsky, on the other hand, as the Commissar responsible, described the city of Petrograd as looking 'unforgettably beautiful' and raved about the enthusiasm with which the artists had participated (Document 6). The more typical critics, however, had to confess that neither the symbolic images nor the allegorical ones, and still less the formalist ventures of the 'leftists', gave a convincing visual expression of these themes, which had such importance for the workers' own lives and understanding of the Revolution's aspirations.

From early 1919 onwards, agitational propaganda at revolutionary festivals steadily shifted its focus onto more topical themes and a more comprehensible and realistic interpretation of its chosen subject-matter. Increasing importance was accorded to the workers' own active participation in generating the visual material of the festivities. Thus on 24 March 1919 a resolution of the Moscow Soviet's Presidium was passed which declared: 'All Moscow's artistic affairs should be carried out in close association with and under the strict control of the Moscow proletariat . . . the artistic sub-committee is guided by neutrality in relation to different artistic tendencies, placing the aesthetic needs of the proletariat higher than the pretensions of individual artistic groups.'[1] An analogous resolution was published on 10 April 1919 by the Executive Committee of the Petrograd Soviet: 'Under no circumstances may the arrangements for the May Day festivities be given into the hands of the Futurists from the "Fine Arts" department. A special commission has been entrusted with the job of attracting trade unions and other workers' organizations to the task.'[2]

After 1918 the decoration of the cities with enormous painted panels was

1. Statement of the presidium of Moscow City Soviet on the decorations for Moscow, published in the newspaper *Vechernaya Izvestiya Mossoveta* (*Evening Bulletin of Moscow Soviet*), 24 March 1919.
2. Statement of the Executive Committee of the Petrograd City Soviet on the creation of a committee for dealing with the celebrations on 1 May 1919, published in *Izvestiya Petrogradskogo Soveta* (*Bulletin of the Petrograd Soviet*), 10 April 1919.

not repeated on such a scale but this first 1918 attempt to create monumental works had a lasting influence on the course of subsequent Soviet art.

Later celebrations took on a different character. Theatrical productions began to occupy a special place and the leading role passed from artists to producers. Theatre activists approached the organization of celebrations differently from painters. They did not try to make the working masses immediately familiar with all the range of artistic tendencies abounding in those years: they turned, on the contrary, to the traditional forms familiar to the popular masses – raree-shows, carousels, Punch and Judy shows, booths with jesters, street criers, circus turns – and they added a revolutionary content. Similarly, the artists preparing the famous 'windows' of the Russian Telegraph Agency, ROSTA, when seeking a more accessible form of decorative art, turned to the model of the traditional peasant print, or *lubok*, to which the working masses could relate directly.

Many well known stage workers and theatre artists worked on the scenarios and staging of little scenes to be played on a quickly erected dais or on a stage on a tram or bus. They designed the scenery for such dramatizations and accompanied the performances round the town. Thus, for example, on May Day 1919 in Moscow, Piotrovsky remained on the platform all the time, 'giving guidance and instructions to the lively group of circus performers'. On May Day 1920 in Petrograd other famous producers and theatre workers including S. E. Radlov travelled with their performances on tram platforms. It was typical that most of the performers in these dramatizations put on in the years immediately after the Revolution were professional like the producers.

The reflection on stage of the first years after October 1917, with their revolutionary romanticism and their elevated spiritual zeal, was not and could not be limited merely to satirical-grotesque performances, sketches, recitations, circus numbers and so on, even though these certainly played an agitational role. The heroic struggle demanded other, more monumental forms. 'There is probably no such "super-practical" people in the world that would not experience the over-powering need to reflect the greatest moments of their life and their history by creating monuments. This feeling of magnificence, of the monumental nature of what is happening or has been monumentous in the past is given concrete, tangible shape by the power of art. . . . Essentially it is all the same if it is made out of bronze or plaster, whether it is to last for a millennium or for one day. . . . Such performance-monuments, splendid one-day events, were four times created in Petersburg in the short period from May to November 1920', wrote Radlov, one of the best-known organizers, scenario-writers and producers of such dramatizations.[3] The extent to which these monumental theatrical

3.   S. E. Radlov, *10 let v teatre* (*Ten Years in the Theatre*), Leningrad 1929, pp. 238–44.

spectacles corresponded to the feelings of the masses is shown by the fact that such performances, with thousands of participants, took place in towns all over the country and always, at the most emotional moments, the spectators themselves took an active part in the performance.

One of the first such participatory events was the performance of Sophocles's *King Oedipus* that took place in Tretyakov Passage, which runs between Nikolsky and Lubyanka Squares in Moscow, on May Day 1920 (Document 39). It was the first performance in the open air with a huge number of participants who included both amateur actors from the Red Army and professional actresses in the female roles.

The most famous such performances were the mass dramatizations in Petrograd. The organizers of these also looked to tradition, and to the antique rather than to Russian traditions. The primary hero of these performances was the people, the part they played being akin to that of the chorus in the original Greek tragedies, but the whole was given a completely original treatment which made these Petrograd dramatizations into a wholly new artistic phenomenon.

Thus the great musical performance of *The Anthem of Liberated Labour* was played out on the steps of the Petrograd Stock Exchange portico. Here both Red Army divisions and professional actors took part, making a total of two thousand people. The spectators, of whom there were about thirty-five thousand, were on the square in front of the Stock Exchange building, on the Neva Embankment or on the adjacent streets. The same Stock Exchange building formed the backdrop and stage for another magnificent dramatization entitled *Towards a World Commune*, performed on 19 July 1920 during the Second Congress of the Third International (Document 41). On this occasion there were already twice as many participants as before. Now four thousand people took part in the performance: members of workers clubs, students from theatre schools, Young Communists, Red Army soldiers and sailors. An interesting sketch for the production has been preserved, done by Altman, which shows a similarity to his decorations for Uritsky Square on the first anniversary of the Revolution in October 1918. The sketch shows the juxtaposition of contrasting compositions on surfaces brightly decorated with geometrical shapes, using the architectural forms of the Stock Exchange and the softness of its colours. This design was not chosen, however, and the performance took place using rather trite backcloths of draped materials.

For this event too we have interesting examples both of the analytical processes that were beginning to happen in response to early experiments, and equally of differences of opinion, some positive, some negative. Thus the article by P. Kudelli discussing this performance presents it in quite a negative light (Document 41). Kudelli seems to be evaluating the performance by the same criteria as for an ordinary theatrical performance aimed at an ordinary theatre audience. He was probably unaware of the complex problems faced by the producers of those spectacles. For their stages they had enormous areas of water and land, they were dealing with casts of thousands and their audiences consisted of tens of thousands of people. Another commentator, Piotrovsky, not represented here, pointed out the innovatory nature of these two dramatizations, however. He drew attention to the varied and witty use which had been made of the architectural character of the Stock Exchange itself, so that parallel and contrapuntal actions took place at the portico, on the steps and on the ramps. He pointed to the way in which the stage was surrounded by the real world and the way in which the Stock Exchange itself was a definite symbol. A third innovation, in Piotrovsky's opinion, was the use of real things in the action as well as theatrical, illusory effects. Real cars and cannon were introduced into the performance. The troops in a ceremonial marchpast retained their own real movements. Even in the representational procession of world nationalities, there were some delegates of real trade unions, and genuine shop-floor emblems alternated with symbols that were manifestly props.

Most spectacular of all these Petrograd dramatizations, of course, in both scale and conception, was *Storming the Winter Palace*, staged in Uritsky Square for the October celebrations of 1920 (Documents 43 and 44). Here the scale of operation was so large that the main producer, Yevreinov, was assisted by ten others, for a performance whose action took place on two specially constructed stages joined by a bridge, and inside the Winter Palace itself.

The result, as Yevreinov described it, was to make 'three stages . . . appear simultaneously. Two conventional stages and one real, historical stage', on each of which a different acting style and set of conventions was applied (Document 43). The Winter Palace itself participated through light effects as a gigantic actor in the drama. Here the total number of participants was ten thousand, including actors from professional troupes and amateur clubs, soldiers and sailors.

Such performances as these, wholly new in synthesizing the different arts, required strict discipline, tight organization and the subordination of all participants to the will of the producer, if the overall message and story of the perfomance was to be clearly preserved and communicated.

The agitational effect of these dramatizations and their artistic role were very significant. They contained a monumental reflection of the heroism of the struggle and victory in the Civil War, and they reflected it on a corresponding scale, presented in a highly emotional but concise form accessible to everyone. The participation of thousands was the most important factor in these performances. The masses, like the chorus in ancient Greek theatre, embodied the main ideas of the dramas and magnified their emotional content and tension. This arose naturally through mass 'infection' among such a large number of participants and was conveyed to the spectators. The definition of popular festivities given by Lunacharsky applies particularly to these mass dramas: in an article in *Vestnik teatra* (Theatre Courier) in 1929 he wrote that the organization of celebrations must be in such a way that 'a natural upsurge of the masses on the one hand and the enthusiastic and utterly sincere intention of the leaders on the other blend together'.[4]

After 1920 these mass dramatizations with thousands of participants were not repeated. The theme of enthusiasm for the struggle with the old and for victory over it, always at the heart of these dramas, fully accorded with the mood of the masses during the stormy epoch of the Civil War. However, it did not relate so closely to the tasks of production propaganda in the reconstruction period when the basic themes of agitation became the building of the economy and an increase in labour productivity.

With the change in theme came a change in character. This was revealed most fully in the decorations of the cities, which were very modest, using mainly flags, paint, material and garlands of greenery.

Workers' amateur activity, despite the fact that it had essentially no traditions, blossomed in the mid-twenties. In its pre-revolutionary past, the proletariat had only the experience of meetings, demonstrations and May Day gatherings where creativity showed itself through ardent political speeches. After the Revolution, 'for several months every crossroads in Petrograd and other Russian towns was a public platform. Heated arguments and meetings arose on trains, in trams, everywhere. . . . Everyone had the complete right to express his feelings and thoughts whatever they might be.' Thus wrote John Reed in *Ten Days that Shook the World*. There was an unrestrainable desire to show oneself actively, to say one's own word, one's own truth. This was a unique kind of political activity, for workers did not yet know any form of artistic self-expression.

The practice of the twenties went even further than the theory. Workers wanted not only to get to know professional art but also to perform themselves. Almost every factory and enterprise had its own art clubs; indeed there were so many that, as Viktor Shklovsky wrote in 1921, 'No one knew what to do with the clubs. They multiply like protozoa and neither the absence of heating, nor the shortage of food nor the Entente can restrain their development.'[5]

For all members of clubs and circles, participation in the festivals was a creative opportunity. Texts, illustrations and photographs have been preserved from which we can judge the extent of the work and the

4. A. V. Lunacharsky, 'Teatr i revolyutsiya' (Theatre and Revolution), *Vestnik teatra* (*Theatre Courier*), 1929, no. 65, pp. 1–2.
5. V. Shklovsky, in *Zhizn iskusstva* (*Life of Art*), 1921, March, p. 1.

enthusiasm and zeal with which it was carried out. The twenties were the years when the amateur art of the workers determined the general character of the celebrations. Their contributions included banners with slogans and diagrams, industrial and agricultural machinery (sometimes in action), displays and hand-outs of products or colossal substitutes for them floating above the crowds, lorries carried complicated models of entire factories or trains or residential buildings, there were huge masks and grotesque figures in political caricatures.

The theme of industrial production was also presented in the musical arrangements for the festivals, such as the symphony of sirens which was organized by Proletkult and the Conservatoire for the sixth anniversary of the Revolution in Moscow.

The amateur art of the workers remained dominant in the festivals throughout the twenties. Towards the end of the decade, professionals from the different arts began to play a more important role. Thus several major architects worked on decorations for the tenth anniversary of the Revolution. However, the festivals had a completely different character from those of the early years after the Revolution. In the May and October celebrations of 1918, every artist and architect working on city decorations could decide themselves how to decorate their allotted place, be it one separate panel as often in Moscow, or a whole architectural ensemble as in Petrograd. From 1927, however, special attention was paid to the artistic unity of the entire decoration of the town. The Academy of Arts organized a special artistic and decorations subcommission which checked the numerous designs for the decoration of architectural monuments and also looked at sketches of different types of festival products and organized an exhibition of these.

For theatrical performances also the tenth anniversary glanced back to the art of the years immediately after the Revolution. Thus in Leningrad there were once again grandiose dramatizations in the open air, the most spectacular of which was played on the Neva between Republic and Equality Bridges, the Peter and Paul Fortress and Ninth January Embankment. The same people were involved as in 1920 (Petrov, Radlov, the musical arranger Wehrlich) and they re-used many of the creative devices of that year but on a more magnificent scale, including huge expanses of water and dry land. If, as Radlov wrote, in the performances of 1920 'a mass of people was the main material from which our spectacle was moulded', then in 1927 'we must include among the performers mine-carriers, cutters, factory chimneys, tugs, rowing boats, emblems in lights, letters in fire, people of the six-metre size desired by the producer and in modest numbers people of the normal and unsatisfactory six-foot size.'[6]

6. S. E. Radlov, *10 let v teatre.*

Introduction

The decorations of the cities for the May and October celebrations in the period of the first Five Year Plan (1928–32) moved in a different direction. Here the enormous tasks of the industrialization of the country, the reconstruction of agriculture and the installation of gigantic new construction sites became the themes of all decorative work.

If the dream of a bright, free life had been illustrated by symbols and allegories at the celebrations in the first years after the Revolution, in the thirties the enormous, life-important task of creating a powerful industrial state was reflected in the gigantic three-dimensional constructions made as models of machines and of new construction sites. They were an artistic image of a generalized machine born of the artist's creative imagination. Music, radio, cinema, movement and various pyrotechnical effects, all these were also used to amplify the theatrical spectacle. Amateur art continued to develop but was oriented not towards mass celebrations as in the twenties but towards the numerous productions in individual workers' clubs.

What these documents and photographs show is effectively a sequence of stage sets created from the streets of Moscow and Petrograd/Leningrad over a period of fifteen years, with varying themes, techniques and intentions.

In the first year after the Revolution, the approach was a relatively conventional one: the first anniversary was celebrated by hanging the streets and squares with vast panels and decorative features created by the leading young talents in Russian painting, sculpture and architecture. Through the next two years, 1919–1920, the celebrations of May and October featured grandiose historical dramatizations with thousands of participants. In the twenties these gave way to colourful processions of industrial or political floats, in great carnivals of enormous grotesque figures. By the end of the decade, through the years 1928–1933, the imagery and message shifted again, to colossal models of machines and new construction sites, and dynamic, 'working' structures were accompanied by light music and loudspeaker commentaries. The cumulative result was not only a set of images and techniques which added much to the development of visual propaganda and agitational work, but which represented some of the most interesting aspects of early Soviet art.

My principal collaborator in the assembly of this material has been Nadezhda Levchenko of the Central State Archive of the Economy of the USSR, and I am also much indebted to my colleagues at the Research Institute of the Academy of Arts of the USSR. Further thanks are also due to V. P. Yaroshevskaya from the Leningrad Archive of Literature and Art, and to N. M. Khvostenkova and S. R. Levin of the Central State Archive of the Economy of the USSR, for extensive help in the completion of the project.

PART 1
1918-19

The Artists are Mobilized

THE PERIOD AFTER the October 1917 Revolution saw the Soviet Union emerge as an industrial state, out of the chaos and economic ruination produced by the 1917 Revolution and the four years of Civil War which followed. At the outbreak of the First World War in 1914 Russia had been expanding economically, even booming, but after the Bolshevik victory it would spend the rest of the twenties trying to get back to those pre-War levels of industrial output and growth.

Even such urbanization and industrialization as had been achieved before the War was slight in a country whose population was still essentially composed of peasants. Europe and America had a century of the industrial revolution behind them but it was only fifty years before the War, in 1861, that the bulk of the Russian population acquired the legal right to obtain their personal freedom from serfdom. There were already significant numbers of 'free' peasants, many of whom were engaged in trade and industry. But the legal act of Emancipation in 1861 changed attitudes – some rooted in religion and some merely habitual – that had been intensely inimical to modernization. The energies released were vast, and on the eve of the War, Russia was the fasted growing economy in the world.

While the incompetent leadership and disastrous handling of the War by Russia's stagnant establishment were the final provocations for the Revolution, many of the predisposing tensions derived precisely from this burgeoning of industrial and urban life within a society too rigid to absorb its thrust. There was enough of an urban industrial workforce to constitute a working class which Lenin's revolutionaries could lead, if not properly to constitute the true proletariat of European political theorists like Marx. At the top of the social hierarchy, however, was a tiny ossified class of aristocrats and officials who enforced Russia's rigid pyramid of social ranks. Along with international leaders who propped them up in power, these figures appear here vigorously caricatured in both the documents and the photographs of the post-Revolutionary festivals. Their government had been unable to handle either the problems of the War front itself, or wartime tensions at home. Still less was it able to handle the pressures of profound social change required by the rapid technical modernization.

As Soviet attempts at modernization again reminded us in the 1980s, Russia never took part in that long evolutionary process which created a bourgeoisie in Europe. The country was equally untouched by the movements of Renaissance and Enlightenment which brought Europe its philosophically sophisticated legal and moral systems and a concomitant political maturity. Behind the closed intellectual boundaries carefully preserved by the Orthodox church, with only a small elite ever exposed to Western culture, the whole social structure was fatally vulnerable to disintegration once the First World War brought the economy to its knees. The ebullience we see in the festivals of the first post-Revolutionary years partly reflects the energy of a population genuinely overjoyed at having rid themselves of that prodigal, intellectually moribund White autocracy whose demise they re-enacted so festively. The more orderly celebrations of the late twenties and early thirties, on the other hand, represented demonstrations to the Soviet population itself of how its efforts at industrial and social reconstruction were progressing, and injunctions to work even harder.

Between these two periods lay another, the middle twenties, of extraordinary social transformation. Extreme austerity and worsening housing conditions were the background to a complete social re-structuring that produced new classes of cultural and industrial leaders. For these organizers and designers of a new social order the brief was to mould a more collectively oriented mentality out of traditional individualism; to foster a capability for industrial work and an adaptation to urban life amongst a still-peasant population; to build a literate and therefore educable population from an almost entirely illiterate one; to assert relative rationality over fatalist and mystical habits of thought.

Underpinning these ambitious social programmes ran a series of steps in economic policy which themselves gave rise to cultural phenomena – as well as to subjects for lampoon or celebration. Thus the rationing and austerity resulting from the emergency economic policy of War Communism gave way at the end of the Civil War in 1921 to a partial re-institution of the free enterprise economy and market. This was Lenin's New Economic Policy, or NEP, and like Gorbachev's somewhat parallel policy of the 1980s, it was conceived as a pragmatic way of breathing life back into the moribund corpse of the economy.

As ever, such a situation allowed some to profiteer, and as the country regained its feet enough to assert political principles over sheer survival, this new bourgeoisie of so-called NEP-men were also increasingly the object of political lampoon in the festivals, as in broader media. In 1923/4, the economy had started, in the common phrase of the time, 'to wake up from its ten-year sleep'; over the next three years or so it was to be gradually brought under tighter management until it was possible, albeit crudely, to set production targets and to measure their degree of fulfilment – even in some cases to actually achieve them.

Soviet economic reconstruction in the twenties was a trial and error process of learning, of trying to build a socialist, centrally planned economy on the ground at the same time as the underlying theory and practical techniques were being formulated for its operation. In 1926/7 it was possible to discuss 'long-term', and eventually 'five year' plans as meaningful statements of intent, if not as definitely realizable intentions, and the years 1928–32 officially saw the Soviet Union's 'First Five Year Plan' come and go as the modern world's first experiment in operating such an economic approach.

These broad stages of initial reconstruction which created the Soviet Union determined much else in Soviet life, and they are reflected in the public festivals described here with a natural and even automatic directness. They were essentially a combination of celebration, exhortation, catharsis and passage rites on a national scale. The three-part division of the material here is based on these periods. Thus Part 1 embraces the first celebrations of the event of Revolution, in 1918–19, which were achieved despite the exigencies of War Communism and nationwide Civil War. Part 2, 1920–26, traces the development of the two new national festivals, of May Day and the Revolutionary anniversary, through the inauguration of the NEP, the revival of the economy and the major re-structurings of community and public life around socialist principles. Even by this time the festivals have become established elements of Soviet life which vigorously reflect changing national concerns and changing views of their own proper function and character. Part 3, 1927–33, depicts a country which already sees itself – at least in the government centres of Moscow and Leningrad pictured here – operating concertedly as a national unit. It is on course to its first Five Year Plan for economic and social development, and is battling to fulfill it not in five years, but in only four.

This material offers a fascinating and direct window into the great process of reconstruction and the stages – even particular campaigns – through which it went. As such, it richly complements more conventional histories of the period and deserves to be read alongside them. It also shows the development of a genre of public event that was part visual art, part educational theatre, and part consciousness-raising, participatory 'happening'. We see the parameters of the genre themselves evolving through active discussion and criticism of each event. There are changing views on the extent to which such events should be celebratory or educational; should be a participatory or a spectator activity; should follow an officially prescribed plan or be aggregated from a series of spontaneous events conceived by popular contributors. There are arguments about appropriate visual languages and the different visual techniques for conveying specific themes in relation to the population's level of understanding.

From the encyclopaedic two-volume Soviet edition of this book I have selected here documents which bring out these two stories: of changing social purpose and changing social event. As Irina Bibikova has said of her original larger collection, the focus is not upon the big-name artists who normally (and properly) dominate in histories of Soviet art in this period. On the contrary, the intention has been to present a balanced picture of how these festivals developed in the Soviet Union's two main cities, Moscow and Petrograd/Leningrad, and most of it shows a movement of genuinely popular self-expression in which the 'art', if the word is appropriate at all, is highly naive. When the great names appear it is as working members of a larger community team. The early festivals were something of a battlegound between avant-garde styles – all then popularly known as 'futurist' – and more traditional realism. Even the art students of the famous VKhUTEMAS school in Moscow, whose role was at times considerable, contributed more as skilled caricaturists than as abstractionists. Then, also in Moscow, we see such pioneer avant-gardists as the Stenberg brothers working as professionals in this field right through to 1933 and beyond, managing designs for the Red Square area in all festivals. But the main contributors to this effort were the anonymous amateur artists and handymen of innumerable factories and local soviets. Where there is artistic innovation, therefore, it is usually the result of a direct and unselfconscious attempt to find forceful means of communicating certain inherently original or unprecedented messages. The working models of industrial processes, the live graphs and charts of the later years, are a rich example of pragmatic innovation in this way. Artistic innovation in the sense of an application of avant-garde artistic languages tended to be unsuccessful precisely because, by all accounts, these languages were generally unintelligible to the masses. Contemporaneous discussions of this problem appear in the documents here, and are important first-hand evidence of the reasons for what is traditionally presented by art history as the 'tragic demise' of the avant-garde.

At this level of style and story-line, the relationship between new and old, between innovation and established traditions of these festivals is relatively easy to understand from the documents themselves. What is less apparent for a Western reader is the extent to which the whole phenomenon of such street processions and public festive events was itself deeply traditional in Russia, preserved in urban life long after they had disappeared elsewhere precisely because of Russia's slow development compared to that of Western Europe.

Vladimir Tolstoy writes in his introduction here of how the Revolution 'changed the ideas and content of art [in Russia], its forms and methods, and . . . the audience to which it was addressed.' In some fields that is certainly powerfully the case, but in these festivals perhaps less so than in any other. The prototypes of 'monumental art' to which he refers in Campanella's *Civitas Solis*, for example, are precedents more for the static side of Lenin's 'monumental propaganda' programme, for the new monuments and the slogans blazed across public buildings, than for the dynamic participatory events in the streets themselves. References to the precedent for a 'large popular festival' in the Paris Commune and Robespierre come closer to the early Soviet festivals. But the population of Soviet cities did not participate en masse in these events because they were sanctioned by the French as proper expressions of a revolutionary situation. They participated because such events were traditional, even habitual, in the everyday life of a Russian. The content changed with the Revolution. The targets of the lampoons changed. The story-line of the comic playlets in the street booths ' changed, and increasingly the playlets were carried around the streets on lorries, but the great street festival on this model was an extremely ancient Russian phenomenon still current right up to the Revolution.

Like much else in Russia, its strongest roots were in religious practice. Thus from the late fifteenth century dramatized Bible stories were acted out in Russian Orthodox churches. A better-known phenomenon of the Orthodox ritual were the processions in which icons were carried across the village or through the town as part of religious festivals. These *krestnye khody* – literally 'walkings of the cross' – are familar from numerous paintings of the nineteenth-century realist schools, who were the first to make such events of ordinary life acceptable as subjects for 'art'. Before the Revolution, as well as afterwards, the street processions of trade-union or workers-movement banners represented a direct extension of this habitual form of community ritual.

While Bible stories were enacted in church, it was the church's stiff opposition to any form of secular acting which delayed for several centuries the development of any tradition of theatre in special buildings, as a secular art form like that inherent in European culture. Thus theatrical activity, for entertainment and as an expression of cultural concerns, established itself first in Russia as an outdoor event where a group of strolling players, probably with performing animals, used whatever background they might find as they toured from village to village across Russia. By the eighteenth century, when major regional and national fairs became regular events of the trading and social calendar, temporary booths called *balagans*, which could be reassembled, were erected on fairgrounds to stage little productions for the simple townsfolk and peasants. It was standard practice that such major state events as the signing of peace treaties or the coronation of a Tsar were likewise celebrated by street processions and public fairs, and the same open spaces were naturally used for the festivals of the Soviet period.

One of the first such festivals that is well documented visually was the extensive celebration under Peter the Great for Russia's signature of the Treaty of Nystad with Sweden. One public festival took place in St Petersburg in September 1721, followed by a five-day long masquerade in Moscow that started on 31 January 1722. Fifty years later the peace concluded with Turkey in 1775 was celebrated with vast quasi-theatrical performances on the Khodynskoe Field in Moscow, and elaborate fireworks were a regular feature. Every year the Shrovetide festival of *Maslenitsa* took a similar form, with every type of procession, fairground entertainment and the traditional *balagans* providing miniature theatrical sideshows in the main squares of the towns. The Field of Mars, St Isaac's Square and Admiralty Square, were all traditional sites for these great public carnivals in St Petersburg.

Even after Peter moved the capital north to his new city, old Moscow remained the sacred site for coronations of the Tsar and hence for the elaborate public festivals traditional on these occasions. Thus the last pre-Revolutionary coronation, of Nicholas II in May 1896, was celebrated not only by a public festival on the Khodynskoe Field but by street processions and extensive decorations. The increasingly affluent new bourgeois of Moscow were mostly still peasants at heart and loved to besport themselves in the streets and parks on any pretext. At the turn of the century the Moscow entertainments magnate M. V. Lentovsky was running a lucrative business of regularly satisfying their fancies. Just as architects like Rastrelli contributed to designs for triumphal arches and firework displays in the eighteenth century, or as the future Constructivist architects such as the Vesnin brothers would do after the Revolution, so the coronation of Nicholas gave the young Fedor Shekhtel, later Moscow's greatest architect of the Art Nouveau, the opportunity to demonstrate the skills learnt in work for Lentovsky on a state occasion and across the whole city.

All this was part of the traditional fabric of Russian life. References to the French Revolution legitimated its continuation as a 'socialist' event, but certainly should not be taken to suggest that such events were only inaugurated in Russia under socialism. What was new was a more sharply political edge to the lampoons, and the scale on which public participation was orchestrated into single theatrical events in the immediately post-Revolutionary years. Later, as subsequent documents show, the events reverted in some respects to the more traditional, less participatory form, where specific organizations laid on processions and other entertainments for the population at large as spectators.

For all the early sanctifying of such events by socialist precedent, the continuing use of traditional popular forms was itself a conscious act of Leninist cultural policy. In the theoretical debates on this topic that preceded and followed the Revolution itself, two broad views of the proper sources of socialist culture were in contention: that which broadly held that socialist culture was something to be created ex nihilo by the proletariat itself in the Revolutionary situation (generally associated with the Proletkult organization), and that to which Lenin himself adhered, which built upon the still-valid elements of previous culture. The latter prevailed, and was the basis of what emerged later under the name of Socialist Realism. One of the key texts here came from Lenin's famous speech 'On the task of the youth leagues' in 1920, where he said: 'Only with some real understanding and precise knowledge of the culture created by the whole development of mankind, only through a reworking of that, can we build a proletarian culture. The latter is not clutched out of the air; it is not an invention of those who call themselves "experts in proletarian culture". Such things are nonsense. Proletarian culture must be the natural and logical development of those reserves of knowledge and experience which humanity has built up under the yoke of capitalist society.'

It is not until the early thirties, when the process of re-establishing this orthodoxy was in train on most cultural fronts to quell the pluralism of the twenties, that we find this principle and the reference back to Russian traditions taking priority over references to utopian and French socialist precedents in the literature on these festivals. Precisely this quotation from Lenin forms the epigram, for example, to the officially published handbook of 1932 by Kuznetsova, Magidson and Shchukin to which Bibikova has already referred, *Designing the City for Days of Revolutionary Festivals*. The book places the events of the early Soviet years in the context of popular traditions in cultures as far flung as Japan, New Guinea and eighteenth-century England, as well Revolutionary France and pre-Revolutionary Russia. To the Russian workers of the twenties, however, whom we see enjoying themselves in the photographs here, most of that was theory. They were out on the streets because it was a traditional thing to do in Russia. The content might be new but the activity was entirely familiar to them.

The documents of Part 1, numbers 1–36, cover the two years 1918 and 1919. The first document is the Decree of April 1918 which launched the whole programme of such festivals in the Soviet era, and is signed by Lenin as Chairman of the Council of People's Commissars (Sovnarkom); by Stalin as one of the Council and by Lunacharsky, as Commissar for Public Education. Documents 2–5 describe the planning and realization of the first great Soviet May Day a month later. In Moscow such famous avant-garde artists as Vladimir Tatlin, Alexander Rodchenko and Nadezhda Udaltsova already appear working alongside well established architects like Victor Vesnin, Alexei Shchusev and Nikolai Vinogradov, and producing a combination of sequinned banners and portraits of Marx that exactly reflected the synthesis of old and new, popular and political, which these events represented. The same flavour prevailed in Petrograd – still then the capital – where Lunacharksy noted in his diary for that day that in the combination of youthful artists with popular enthusiasm 'not everything has been a success, but already something great and delightful is being set in motion.'

Documents 8 and 9 show how the questioning about what it all meant was already under way. In the critiques of celebrations for the first anniversary of the Revolution itself, more specific discussions of the relative merits of avant-gardism and traditional realist painting prefigure the direction that later designs for these events would take. As the birthplace of the Revolution, Petrograd was decorated at every significant public point by a team of artists and architects as eclectic as that in Moscow, and here too general issues of policy were already emerging. Should there be an overall plan, or should 'individual initiative and personal enthusiasm' be given its head locally throughout the city? Was 'modern art . . . or futurism . . . equal to the demands of the great historical moment', and capable of expressing 'the rhythm, experiences and feelings of the revolutionary popular masses?' Indeed, were the professional artists really interested in engagement with 'the proletariat and its daily life' at all?

By May Day 1919, the local soviets had taken a hand in the planning of content as well as form, so that a more didactic, less purely celebratory event resulted. By that autumn, the effects of War Communism and the Civil War were beginning to constrain the budgets and enforce 'the strictest possible economy in coloured fabric' and electric lights. However the documents of these first two years show these biannual festivals of May Day and the Revolutionary anniversary firmly inscribed into the Soviet calendar as the great ritual festivals of the new atheist, Marxist-Leninist state, and the unique range of drawings preserved from these two years manifest to the role still being played by professional artists in their planning.

1 *Setting up the process*

Decree of the Soviet of People's Commissars, 'On Monuments of the Republic'

12 April 1918

To mark the great revolution that has transformed Russia, the Soviet of People's Commissars decrees:

1   Monuments erected in honour of the tsars and their servants and of no historical or artistic interest, should be removed from the streets and squares, some stored away and others put to some utilitarian use.

2   In accordance with an agreement with the Arts Boards of Moscow and Petrograd, a special commission of People's Commissars for Education and the Property of the Republic and the head of the Fine Arts Department of the Commissariat for Education are entrusted with the task of determining which monuments to remove.

3   The same commission is to mobilize artists and organize a broad competition for the design of monuments to celebrate the great days of the Russian Socialist Revolution.

4   The Soviet of People's Commissars expresses the wish that by 1 May some of the more monstrous statues will have already been removed and the first models of new monuments set out for the masses to see.

5   The same commission is also urgently required to organize the city's decoration for 1 May and to replace inscriptions, emblems, street names, coats of arms etc., with new ones reflecting the ideas and mood of revolutionary working Russia.

6   Regional and Provincial Soviets of Workers', Peasants' and Soldiers' Deputies should also begin this work only in accordance with the instructions of the above-mentioned commission.

7   The necessary resources will be allocated on presentation of estimates and explanations of those estimates.

Chairman of the Soviet of People's Commissars:
V. Ulyanov [Lenin]
People's Commissars: A. Lunacharsky, Stalin
Secretary of the Soviet: Gorbunov

Dekrety sovetskoi vlasti (Decrees of Soviet Power), Vol. 2, pp. 95–6.

May Day Celebrations 1918

MOSCOW

2 *The Planning Stage*

From the minutes of a meeting of the Arts Board of the Moscow Soviet of Workers' and Soldiers' Deputies, on the Organization of the 1918 May Day Celebrations in Moscow

14 April 1918

Those present: V. A. Vesnin, V. A. Vatagin, S. I. Dymshits-Tolstaya, A. I. Ivanov, A. V. Kuprin, P. V. Kuznetsov, P. P. Malinovsky, A. A. Morgunov, S. V. Noakovsky, V. Y. Tatlin, N. A. Udaltsova, A. V. Shchusev.

Topic discussed: the organization of the May Day celebrations.

Opening the discussion, the Chairman pointed to the two tasks facing those delegated by the board to participate on the Moscow Soviet's Commission for Festival Preparations.

1   The organization of an orderly and beautiful mass parade.

2   The decoration of the graves of fallen comrades on Red Square, the starting point of proletarian festivals.

After a stormy exchange of opinions it was decided:

1   to elect a board of three persons. V. A. Vesnin, Y. Korotkov and A. Rodchenko.[1] General instructions were adopted after discussions;

2   that the task of the Arts Board is to draw up a general plan for the festival organization, giving details of the creative initiative to be taken by the workers' districts and indicating the relevant professional artistic organizations in such cases when the districts request help. Special attention should be paid to the adornment of the graves of fallen comrades at the foot of the Kremlin walls and to the decoration of Red Square. Members of the Board are requested to provide draft designs for the adornment of the graves and the square. The adornment of the graves is

1
3–5

entrusted to the same board of three persons with the involvement of the trade unions of sculptors, painters and architects.

Chairman: P. P. Malinovsky
Secretary: Oranovsky

TsGAORSS of the City of Moscow, f.528, op.5, d.115, l.38–39.

1. Documents show that A. M. Rodchenko did not take part in the arrangement of the 1918 May Day celebrations and was replaced by the artist F. F. Fyodorovsky on the board with V. A. Vesnin and Y. Korotkov (see: GAMO, f.66, op.1, d.76, l.162).

3   *The Design Stage*

Recollections of the artist N. M. Chernyshev of his work in the team designing decorations for Moscow's Transriver district for May Day 1918

At the end of April, the Transriver District Soviet suggested to a group of young artists, S. Gerasimov, M. A. Dobrov, A. G. Yakimchenko . . . and myself, that we assist in the festival arrangement, to which we willingly agreed.

The notes in my thin diary for 22 April 1918 read: 'Oleinik from the People's Festival Section telephoned to ask whether I would like to decorate Moscow.'

As I recall, S. Gerasimov undertook the design of Transriver District Soviet and the workers' parade, while I was given the task of decorating the four bridges: Lesser Kamenny, Greater Kamenny, Chugunny and Moskvoretsky.

It was a responsible task. The columns of workers were to cross these bridges on their way to Red Square. But how was I to go about it? The country was in economic ruin and people were hungry. All I had was a limited amount of red calico and even fewer green conifer branches. I could make no structures. I had to fasten the garlands and banners directly onto the street lamps which were rather well placed for this purpose along the bridge, and also on the telegraph poles. And, it goes without saying, that we had very little time in which to accomplish it all.

However, my rough sketches were approved without a hint of bureaucracy. The estimates were precise and we economized on each inch in order to make as many flags as possible.

I recall once I was on the bridge, still in my soldier's greatcoat, showing two workers what length to make the flags. When they began to tear up the piece of calico, there were several angry remarks from passers-by: 'You could make shirts out of that, instead of wasting it on flags!' snarled the discontented onlookers. Nevertheless, when finished, the bridges looked splendid. We kept to my original sketches. Indeed they are also the final sketches: done in pencil on grey paper, but carefully maintaining diversity for each of the four bridges, both at the entrance to the bridge and along the profile of the bridge itself. These same sketches, cut into strips, were also used as working drawings.

Personal archives of N. M. Chernyshev

MAY DAY, 1918

May Day, 1918, Moscow, the Kremlin and Red Square

1 (*previous page*) Sketch for the decoration of Trinity and Kutafya Towers of the Kremlin by the Vesnin brothers, Alexander and Victor.

2 Photograph showing an informal popular parade or 'demonstration' passing through Red Square beneath the Bolshevik Party leaders, assembled on the rostrum by the Kremlin walls.

3 The Vesnins' designs for the decoration of Red Square and the Kremlin, perspective sketch showing the whole design for Red Square.

4 Their sketch for treatment of the rostrum and fraternal graves along the Kremlin wall of Red Square.

5 Their preliminary sketch for decoration of the saluting base in Red Square.

May Day, 1918, Moscow, the Kremlin and Red Square

6 (*right*) The Vesnins' sketch for decorating the Armoury Tower of the Kremlin and, 7 (*below*), for the Tainitskaya Tower.

May Day, 1918, Moscow, Skobelev (from later in 1918, Soviet) Square

8 Decorations on the Moscow City Soviet building on Tverskaya Street (later Gorky Street), which forms the west side of Skobelev Square. The initials M.S.R.D. stand for Moscow Soviet of Workers' Deputies, and the slogans read 'Long live the Federation of Soviet Socialist Republics!' and 'Proletariat of all countries, unite!'

9 Preliminary sketch for decorating the building by the Vesnins.

May Day, 1918, Moscow, Skobelev (from later in 1918, Soviet) Square

10   The District Fire Station, which faces the City Soviet building from the east, with a speaker's tribune and rostrum erected on the site of the Skobelev monument in the centre of the square, bearing the slogan 'Long live the Third International!' (In 1925 this Fire Station was demolished and replaced by the new Institute of V. I. Lenin.)

11   (*below right*) Part of the popular parade walks up Tverskaya Street towards Skobelev Square, with its banners from various local district soviets and factories proclaiming 'Long live the Russian Socialist Federated Soviet Republic!' and 'Proletariat of all countries unite!'

12   (*below*) A motor car decorated with a globe and a portrait of Marx, in honour of 'the 100th Jubilee of his birth', forming the Union of Metal Workers' float in a Moscow street parade.

13   (*right*) The former Mariinsky Palace, where the main painted panel proclaims 'Build the Red Army!'

14   A general view of Palace Square, with a large painted panel by V. I. Kozlinsky on the facade of the Winter Palace, left, and screens around the Alexander Column, right.

15   (*next page*) Part of one of the numerous popular parades which flowed from Petrograd all day towards the focal point of events in Palace Square. This banner calls for an uprising of 'the whole world of hungry slaves which is branded by a curse'.

4   *Preparation on the eve of May Day*

5   *Events of the Day*

From a report on the preparations for the 1918 May Day celebrations in Moscow, in the newspaper *Izvestiya*

1 May 1918

The Kremlin has been a hive of activity since early in the morning of 30 April. . . .The entrances are being decorated with greenery and plants. Buildings which suffered during the October Revolution are being carefully draped in order to hide the damaged parts. . . . Artists, architects and sculptors organizing the decoration of the Kremlin and the city have been coming and going all day long. The chief artists are Fyodorovsky, Bogatov, Yasinsky and Meshkov, the chief architects, Vesnin, Polyakov and Vinogradov, and the sculptors, Vatagin and others.

The main entrance to the Kremlin has been decorated particularly well. The rounded Kutafya Tower is draped all round in red material and hung with posters reading 'Long live the World Republic!' and so on. Two banners with artistic depictions hang on each side of the tower. Further up, on the bridge, are two rows of flags. The decoration of Trinity Tower is especially magnificent: a large decorative sheet bearing a slogan hangs from each of the four sides. In the middle is a large painting of a red angel, its wings radiant in the distance, and the emblem of socialism depicted against a blue background.

A banner with slogans also flaps outside the building of the Soviet of People's Commissars.

Opposite the entrance to the Kremlin, in the middle of the square rises a huge banner seven to eight arshins [approximately 5 to 6 metres] long, edged with gold trimming and tassels. The drawings on the banner are the work of the finest artists. . . .

The building of the Central Executive Committee (Senate House) has been artistically decorated and seems ablaze amid a fire of red material. The red flags have been removed from the walls of the Kremlin buildings and the round shields have been painted by students from the Stroganov College. The state coats of arms and the tsarist emblems have been covered with red material on which the emblems of the new Russia have been painted.

Izvestiya VTsIK, no. 87, 1 May 1918

From a report on the 1918 May Day celebrations on the streets of Moscow, in the newspaper *Izvestiya*

3 May 1918

The streets

Lubyanka Square was swamped in red. The countless silk, velvet and other banners, embroidered with sequins and glass beads were quite dazzling to the eye. One focus of attention was the metal workers' vehicle, draped in red material and bearing a huge globe with a portrait of Marx on it.

The vehicles of the workers' collective were also striking. On one a band played, while the other was covered in greenery and flowers arranged in the shape of an arch.

Another wonderful spectacle was the Sokolniki District lorry, decked out from top to bottom in flowers. Invalids walked on crutches behind the maimed soldiers' lorry.

Next came the machine-gunners, on foot with their guns loaded onto horses. They were followed by the Alexandrovsky College Training School. A detachment of sailors, smartly dressed in black, marched past, followed by firemen and then a float displaying emblems of agricultural work. Children paraded past all holding little red flags. . . . Detachment after detachment of the army of labour, the army of the Revolution. . . .

Speeches were given and a series of meetings held on Skobelev Square in front of the Moscow Soviet. [This square, with the former Dresden Hotel, was decorated by a group of artists under A. I. Ivanov.] The column of the stage workers' trade union was particularly interesting; on the front lorry, beneath a poster reading 'Free Worker', representatives of the most important kinds of labour stood at their machines; on the second lorry was a band, and behind it an allegorical group depicting Russia heralding peace to all peoples.

There were performers in the costumes of all nationalities, a peasant woman with a sheaf of rye in her arms, boys holding rakes and sickles, and nearby the courageous figures of soldiers holding red banners. And above them all stood Russia with a palm sprig in her hands.

In front of the Moscow Soviet, the participants in these

1, 3

12

10, 11

pictures sang the 'Internationale', the 'Marseillaise' and other revolutionary songs to the accompaniment of the band.

Red Square

The Kremlin wall was hung with flags from Nikolsky Gate to Spassky Gate. An obelisk, draped in red and black canvases, towered above the communal grave of victims of the October Revolution.

A rostrum was erected nearer Spassky Gate, on which stood the members of the Central Executive Committee and representatives of the Moscow Soviet. The Place of Execution (*Lobnoye Mesto*) was covered in black canvas and an enormous crimson flag fluttered on top.

The columns of people streamed endlessly along the wall, past the communal grave and the rostrum, the bands and banners at the head of each column. As they passed the grave, they lowered their banners and the bands played solemnly. . . .

Other districts

In the Presnya District, which is mainly inhabited by workers, the people generally responded very enthusiastically to this proletarian festival, and the small houses were painted red and covered with workers' slogans, summoning people to fight for the happiness of all. . . .

All the railway stations were beautifully decorated: Alexandrov Station looked grand, Ryazansky Station, still under construction, was colourful, and Nikolaev Station was rigidly austere in accordance with its style.

The decoration of the Yaroslavl Station was particularly splendid with the words 'Peace and the brotherhood of peoples!' printed in large white letters on a red background right above the entrance. A long red banner with the inscription: 'Long live the Third International!' hung on the pediment. A vast red sheet with the inscription: 'Long live the Soviet Federative Republic!' was wrapped round the station's tower.

The festivities continued on the streets and in the theatres of Moscow until late in the evening. . . .

The lights on the House of Soviets and the House of Unions shone bright against the darkness.

The fountain on Theatre Square looked most effective, bedecked with garlands of electric lights.

Izvestiya VTsIK, no. 88, 3 May 1918

PETROGRAD

 The atmosphere and events

Extract from A. V. Lunacharsky's diary for 1 May 1918, describing the May Day festivities in Petrograd

. . . Many of the city's streets and squares have been decorated, in some places with great taste, to the honour of the artist organizers.

The posters

Of course, I am absolutely certain that the posters will be criticized. After all, it is so easy to criticize the Futurists. In essence, all that remains of Cubism and Futurism is the precision and force of the general form and the brightness of colour so essential for painting intended for the open air and for a giant audience with hundreds of thousands of heads.

And how enthusiastically the young artists devoted themselves to their task! Many of them worked for 14–15 hours at a stretch on huge canvases. And having painted a giant peasant and a giant worker, they then drew in bold letters: 'We will not surrender Red Petrograd' or 'All Power to the Soviets'. Without doubt we witnessed the searching of the young merge with the searching of the crowd.

Not everything has been a success, but already something great and delightful is being set in motion. . . .

I went to the Neva and was met by a truly magical fairytale! . . .

During the day, the fleet, bedecked with thousands of flags, made the splendid Neva river so beautiful that my heart, though full of troubles, leaped with delight. I think that all those who saw this sight, and half of Petrograd saw it, would agree that it was unforgettably beautiful and tremendously exciting.

In the evening an amazing battle between light and darkness began. Dozens of searchlights cast shafts of light that flashed like white swords through the air. Their bright beams rested on the palaces, fortresses, ships and bridges and snatched from the night first one, then another beauty of our enchanting Rome of the North.

Up shot rockets and down fell many-coloured stars.

In the strange, pale motion of the searchlight beams, the fountains and clouds of smoke created an epic poem, a symphony of fire and darkness in all the variations of light and shade and created an impression of awe-inspiring splendour. Salutes were sounded from the Peter and Paul Fortress.

Yes, the celebration of May Day has truly been made official. It has been celebrated by the state. The might of the state was evident in many ways. But is it not intoxicating to think that the state, until recently our worst enemy, now belongs to us and has celebrated 1 May as its greatest festival?

And yet, take my word, if this festival had only been official, it would have produced nothing but coldness and emptiness.

But no, the popular masses, the navy, the Red Army – all true working people put their efforts towards it. And we can therefore say that this festival of labour has never been so beautiful.

A. V. Lunacharsky, *Vospominaniya i vpechatleniya* (Reminiscences and Impressions), Moscow, 1968, pp. 208–9, 211–12.

7   *The city decorated*

From a report on the 1918 May Day celebrations in Petrograd, in the newspaper *Izvestiya*

Yesterday, Petrograd ceremonially celebrated 1 May.
15   Early in the morning, long processions began moving from all over the city towards the Field of Mars – the central point of the May Day parade.

The city was magnificently decorated. Garlands of red flags stretched all the way along Nevsky Prospekt and across all the bridges over the Neva. Buildings were colourfully adorned with red banners and May Day posters.

The buildings of the City Duma, the Public Library, and
3, 14   the Mariinsky, Winter and Marble Palaces were decorated with huge paintings. Statues of the former tsars were covered with strips of red material.

Izvestiya VTsIK, no. 88, 3 May 1918. The report must have been written on 2 May but not published until 3 May.

8   *What did it all mean?*

M. V. Dobuzhinsky, 'A bomb or a firecracker: a conversation between two artists', from the newspaper *New Life*

4 May 1918

ARTIST A   Well, you must admit we have witnessed the birth of a new era in art: on 1 May we, artists, finally took our revolutionary banners out onto the streets and just look how delightfully the creations of new art adorned the city. At last, we have declared war on the despotism of architectural lines which have imprisoned the artist's free eye for long enough! Don't you see how creative artists have finally moved off in step with the progressive proletariat, and how, much in the way bourgeois structures in the state are being swept away, there is now a rebellion in art too, against the hypnotic idea of 'austere harmony' that has been so adored and extolled by poets and artists before us? Well, enough is enough! We have dropped a bomb.

ARTIST B   I do not know how, but I shall have to put a damper on your enthusiasm. First of all, I did not find at all delightful the new 'beauty' which you pasted up all over the city and which you so welcome. You can surround Michelangelo's David with the finest Raphaels and Rembrandts but you will not produce a new artistic delight. I can see that you have indeed declared war on, or rather your contempt for, architecture. But then why do you not strike out more courageously, destroy whatever fails to meet your notions of beauty, cover things completely, disguise, transform. But I hardly think that by randomly sticking up patches and plasters, albeit in the form of the most brilliant paintings and posters, on buildings which you have declared 'outlawed', you can triumph over the latter. Alas, they continue to stand as unshakeable and magnificent as before, while your posters perish in the unequal fight and hang torn by the counter-revolutionary wind. Just take a look at Alexander's Column: how pathetically those feeble matchstick-like poles, with one bold poster attached to the side, huddle round the base. What a futile assault, like a frog attacking an ox!

ARTIST A   All the same, the fact is what matters: the banner of rebellion has been raised and even if it has been frayed in the fight, the shreds are triumphant shreds. Just allow us to summon up our strength again and if you think this first battle was our Narva, then give us at least until 5 May and you'll have a Poltava to glorify Karl Marx. [The Battle of Narva in 1700 was a serious defeat for Petrograd's founder, Peter the Great, whereas the Battle of Poltava in 1709 was one of his greatest victories. *Ed.*]

ARTIST B   I do not believe in a Poltava, either in May or later, because, like Peter the Great, you don't want to learn from your enemy. You don't want to learn architecture, the elements which comprise its eternal strength and soul – stability and harmony – for it is precisely these things that you find deeply alien and unacceptable. And I do not believe you will ever create new decorative thought on a broad scale. In the grip of your megalomania, you have wasted an enormous quantity of canvas (those in need would be green with envy if they knew how much), and if, instead, it could have been used for flags, banners, garlands, ribbons or I don't know what else – what expanse for the artist's invention! – a far more 'festive occasion' and a far more joyful spectacle would have been created. But then, in your heart of hearts, you may not be rejoicing (perhaps this is understandable). You simply had to demonstrate your ability to paint a brush-stroke twenty metres long or an enormous talented blot. But just remember how beautiful the sun-pierced clouds of multi-coloured flags were on the masts of our unfortunate ships – just like a Japanese print by Hiroshige, but then you had nothing to do with that. . . .

ARTIST A   Evidently you are quite incapable of ridding yourself of all these hackneyed and obsolete flags and garlands. Try to understand: we want new forms, bold, perhaps even coarse, but massive forms, and we are breaking away from rotten traditions.

ARTIST B   Do you really think that just any coloured thing slapped on a building represents a symbol of new beauty? Or that the paper streamers wrapped like macaroni round the hoofs of Klodt's Horses are a triumph? By the way, talking of statues. You are so particular about ugliness in sculpture, your eye is sickened by the little statuette in front of the Admiralty (it is indeed rather skinny), but what about the two great boors as high as the facade, stretched out beneath the pediment of the palace, do they seem beautiful and relevant next to Rastrelli's rococo? There is something here that I don't quite understand. After all, is this not disrespect for one's own *oeuvre*? Hardly a suitable frame! Of course, you will say that I am becoming retrospective again, but let me remind you that even under Peter the Great huge pictures and banners were erected on festive occasions, but then whole architectural cartouches, triumphal arches and special 'iconostases' were built for them on the streets and squares, and they made an imposing and theatrically magnificent sight.

ARTIST A   Let me repeat that all this is archaeological rubbish. A new art is now emerging that has no time for reactionary forms of court magnificence and theatricality. We are pioneers of new aesthetic joys and the people will follow us.

ARTIST B   I saw the people on 1 May, and I saw their 'joy', or rather laughter. But there are various kinds of laughter and I fear it may have been more scoffing, alas directed at you. It is bad when even your own do not recognize you. . . . To put it bluntly, my poor man, you've defeated yourselves. However, it's a very good thing that this festival was such an excellent test; now, I think that for many (though probably not for you, who are so truly narcissistic) it is clear that a slap in the face given undeservedly (and your 'bold art' is precisely a slap in the face of Petrograd), punishes only the one who gives it. I think the best thing you could do is not to triumph but humbly to repent.

Forgive my harsh judgment but it is such a shame that the marvellous opportunities you were given to create a simple, harmonious and splendid decorative whole were used merely to make a chaotic, motley mess. There is only one thing that can perhaps excuse you and that is this 'festival', so inopportunely arranged, which could not inspire anyone or evoke that mood of 'fun' and joy without which there is no art, however new it might want to seem, and without this soul in creative work, boldness is merely impertinence, naïveté is stupidity and talent merely creates a nonsense! And your 'bomb' is nothing but a fire-cracker!

Novaya zhizn (New Life), no. 83, 4 May 1918

The negative view expressed by Dobuzhinsky and a number of other authors on the artistic decoration of Petrograd for the 1918 May Day celebrations was provoked not only by the general style of the decorative designs, chiefly done by artists of the Left Front of Art, but also by a lack of experience in this kind of monumental art that was to be perceived within the spatial and architectural environment of the city. As far as one can judge from the few surviving photographs and also from the comments of contemporaries, the painted canvases that decorated the city in May 1918 were neither related to the architectural forms of the buildings which they adorned, nor did they form a unified artistic whole. Such disparate and in many ways random works naturally could not be set in contrast to the magnificent monuments of architecture, something Artist A tries to do in the dialogue above. However, the issue of such contrasts came up again during the celebration of the first anniversary of the October Revolution, when artists tried to solve it on a more professional level by producing designs encompassing entire architectural ensembles.

That lack of experience in this kind of work also affected the designs of the 1918 May Day demonstration, which was still very modest and inexpressive, a point noted by contemporaries. For instance, Alexander Blok wrote in his diary, 1 May 1918: 'This morning, soldiers and sailors with neat little red posters have been marching to military music in exemplary Nicholas II formation.' [*Zapisniye knizhki 1901–1920* (Notebooks), Moscow, 1965, p. 404.]

In the period between the two festivals, of 1 May and 6 November 1918, the issue of the nature of festival design in the city was discussed in the press on several occasions. Widely varying opinions and suggestions were voiced, many of which were subsequently reflected in practice. The following article by P. M. Kerzhentsev is an example.

9 Art on the streets

Extract from the article 'Art on the streets' by P. M. Kerzhentsev, in the journal *Creative Work*

July 1918

The world shift towards socialism that we are now witnessing is pushing artists towards a new path. The building of theatres, halls, clubs, circuses, monumental arcades and galleries is drawing the attention of architects. The decorative adornment of building, mural painting and the effects of the grouping of buildings will begin to provide an outlet for the creativity of artists. More than this, art is breaking out of walls onto the streets. Just as it is used to strive for the confined space of private homes where it was met by select connoisseurs, now it will burst out in search of freedom onto the streets and squares, where it will be admired by the masses as a whole.

What a great deal has to be done! If you take a walk round the city today with this thought of beauty and this dream of art triumphant on the streets, you will see the total chaos of facades, the discordance of buildings bordering squares, the garish combination of colours, the dull tones of clothing. And you will be struck by the absence of sound and singing, the drabness of the crowds, the empty bandstands along the boulevards, the disordered triteness of the shop signs.

Now we have the chance to concern ourselves with the city's artistic integrity; we can create a harmony of the parts and districts of the city; we can work to ensure restraint in the style of individual corners and squares; we can think about the visual effect of house colour, place artistic controls on new buildings and reconstruction work, and concern ourselves with achieving an integral overall impression of the city. Some things will have to be destroyed, others skilfully disguised, and others highlighted. A broad field of activity is opening up for architects and artists.

But, while concerning ourselves with the architectural lines of the city and the colour effect of facades, we must also search for new ways to introduce the street to beauty. Recently, a certain Futurist hung a picture on the corner of Kuznetsky Bridge. [This is the name of a central Moscow street, which formerly spanned a small river that was diverted underground in the nineteenth century. *Ed.*] The newspapers commented ironically, but in reality, the idea underlying the act was good. Why should the walls of houses and special shop windows not be turned into permanent exhibitions? Why should people go into a building or inside the walls of a gallery, why not let pictures and sculptures come out instead to meet people? Maybe soon, there will be special pavilions and shop windows displaying works of art rather than the tempting hams and neckties of today.

Why do artists expend their efforts and talent on painting murals that only a few dozen people will see, and on décor that grows shabby within a couple of years, instead of thinking, if not about murals, about the new and original colouring of houses? What unexplored expanses await the decorator who decides through a combination of two or three tones, to turn a drab, uni-colour house facade into a bright and colourful carpet, transforming the monotonous, factory-like building with its rows of windows into an asymmetrical patch of true painting!

How much room for expression there is in the skilful use of tree planting, the arrangement of flowerbeds and the planting of creepers which adorn walls now with greens, now with reds and yellows!

Youth theatre groups are organizing wandering troupes of five to ten persons, with light screens for scenery and a kind of medieval moving stage (on a cart or lorry), and with an especially simplified repertoire, no doubt somewhat exaggerated (predominantly biting satire, farces and pantomimes).

Itinerant theatre should create its own new repertoire and different stage methods that suit the special conditions of performing on city squares for passing crowds. Any true actor will be happy to perform on this mobile stage, willingly acting, reciting or improvising on it.

These performances by wandering troupes should become a part of everyday life, just like children's 36 Petrushka [Punch and Judy] shows, wandering puppets, 37 *skomorokhs* [wandering minstrels-cum-clowns] and reciters, etc.

Less frequently, there will be processions along the city streets and celebrations on city squares. Apart from May Day and 25 October, other days, even those bearing no relation to political events, will be celebrated with festivals and street processions. Why should there not be a spring festival, a day of renewal and good cheer that not only celebrates the birth of new life in nature, but also the beginning of a new free age of socialist development? We could choose a day to celebrate the harvest and autumn fruit-picking season and turn it into a peasant festival at a symbolic moment marking the fraternal unity of town and country, worker and peasant.

So, there is a fascinating world of completely new creative achievement ahead for anyone who wants to work towards introducing art to the democratic streets.

Art itself, by breaking out of enclosing walls on to the city squares, will be transformed under the influence of those masses whom it is now to serve.

Tvorchestvo (Creative Work), no. 3, July 1918, pp. 12–13.

First Anniversary of the October Revolution

MOSCOW

10 *Planning: new ideas*

From a report on the organization of celebrations for the first anniversary of the October Revolution in the newspaper *Izvestiya*

25 September 1918

The last meeting of the Council of the Moscow Soviet's Popular Education Department Board discussed the organization of celebrations for the anniversary of the October Revolution.

During open discussions on this matter the view was expressed that the anniversary should be a repetition of the experiences of the October Revolution and for this reason it was decided that Comrade Lunacharsky's proposal should form the basis of plans for the festival's arrangement.

The meeting elected a special commission to work out the details of the festival. This commission concluded that the festivities by no means have to be of an official kind like the May Day celebrations, but should have a profound inner meaning with the masses reliving the upsurge of the revolution. The festivities will last for three days. They should begin with public lectures in the city's districts to explain the meaning and significance of the Revolution to the masses and to review preceding historical epochs. Obelisks should be unveiled the same day. On the second day, poetry and prose readings should be given and relevant works of drama staged in the evening. The third day will be devoted to parades and national festivities. . . .

Izvestiya VTsIK, no. 208, 25 September 1918

11 *The programme*

Resolution of the Moscow Soviet of Workers' and Soldiers' Deputies on the celebration of the First Anniversary of the October Revolution

28 September 1918

1 To organize the celebration of the October Revolution over the course of one and a half days.
2 The first evening should be devoted to military revolutionary agitation in the form of lectures, reports, meetings, pageants and music.
3 The second day will be devoted to a public parade from the districts to the centre and to the unveiling of a number of statues, memorial plaques, etc.

In the evening, cafés, theatres, cinemas and other entertainments should be open and free of charge. . . .

GAMO, f.66, op.3, d.819, l.55.

12 *The themes*

From a report by the Information Bureau of the Festival Committee on the organization of the First Anniversary of the October Revolution in Moscow

Not later than *30 October 1918*

No parades are planned for the evening of 6 November, the first day of the celebrations, and only meetings, lectures, concerts and plays will be organized. However, the proceedings of this first evening are to be rounded off with gatherings on the main squares of each district, the purpose of which is to be the symbolic destruction of the old world and the birth of the new system of the Third International.

For these purposes, each district is required to choose a central rallying point on one of its main squares and publicly to announce . . . that on this square, at 9 p.m. on 6 November, the old imperialist world will be burnt and the new world born.

A special commission should be set up immediately to organize this event, and should be given the following instructions: a figure representing the old imperialist regime, which must personify the latter in all aspects, should be made out of lightweight material by either local or central artists and decorators. All the foundations of the old regime should be used, such as capitalists, priests, policemen, cannons, shells, guns, etc.

The figure representing the modern-day pillar of international imperialism should occupy the main position amidst the emblems of the old world. It should be set up in a safe place on the square, after everything needed to burn it has been prepared, and at 9 p.m., after the relevant speeches, it will be set alight. Then, the emblem of the new, socialist system should be raised above the ashes of the old regime, in the form of a banner bearing an

33 inscription such as The Third International, though the choice of inscription should depend on the inventiveness of each district's organizers.

Before being burned, the figure of the old regime should be clothed in old tsarist flags, which should be collected in abundant quantities from local inhabitants or from the archives of official institutions, etc.

The city district should organize a burning of the old regime on the Place of Execution on Red Square.

GAMO, f.66, op.3, d.814, l.43.

13   *Events in the city's main squares*

Extracts from a report in *Pravda* on the festive decorations of Moscow streets for the First Anniversary of the October Revolution

9 November 1918

The city has never looked so splendid. . . . On Znamenka Street the attention is drawn to the painted red columns of the former Alexandrov Military School, adorned with the eloquent inscription: 'Peace to the Hovels, War to the Palaces!' . . .

As one looks at what the genius of the proletariat has

16 created in Soviet Square, as one looks at its splendid

17 artistic decoration, one truly senses that the old system has gone forever and will never again rise from the dead. The

18 building of the Moscow Soviet is bedecked with greenery, red stars bearing depictions of the RSFSR coat of arms, and red posters with inscriptions. Above the Soviet itself hangs a huge poster which reads: 'The proletariat has nothing to lose but its chains, and it will gain the whole world'. . . . Huge red posters hang at the entrance to, and all around,

23 the square. . . . Theatre Square is a colourful mass of flags,

24 garlands and large painted posters. . . . Special platforms intended for bands and speakers have been erected, and adorned with different brightly coloured fabrics . . .

Revolution Square
At the entrance to the square, busts of Karl Marx and Friedrich Engels, the two founders of Communism, stand on a red and white base. On one side of the monument is the inscription 'The revolutionary whirlwind thrusts back all that resist it' and on the other 'The liberation of workers is the task of workers themselves'.

Beside the monument to our great teachers stands a

21 white block (representing the White Guards) pierced and

22 cracked by a red wedge (representing the great Red Army). [This was by N. Ya. Kolli. *Ed.*] Splendid paintings surround the historic square.

The red building of the History Museum is decorated with shields of different colours bearing the names of world revolutionary leaders such as Lenin, Liebknecht.

Pravda, no. 242, 9 November 1918

FIRST ANNIVERSARY, 1918

First Anniversary of the Revolution, 1918, Moscow, the former City Duma building

16   Sketch of a panel intended for this building by S. V. Gerasimov, entitled 'Master of the earth'.

17   The building decorated with much red drapery over the entrance, left, the slogan 'Communism is our victory torch', centre, and N. M. Chernyshev's painted panel 'Science and Art bring their gifts to Labour', right.

First Anniversary of the Revolution, 1918, Moscow, Soviet Square (former Skobelev Square)

18 (*left*) The Moscow City Soviet building, with banners proclaiming 'The proletariat has nothing to lose but its chains', and with the initials of the Russian republic, the RSFSR.

19 The view looking north up Tverskaya Street past the facade of the Moscow City Soviet building, left. A banner hanging across the street bears the new name of the square which opens off to the left, 'Soviet Square'.

20 (*inset*) Looking towards the Fire Station, which has already lost its tower, past the new obelisk erected to designs by D. P. Osipov in place of the Skobelev monument.

First Anniversary of the Revolution, 1918, Moscow, Revolution Square

21 (*right*) Nikolai Kolli's sketch for his building-sized structure depicting 'the Red Wedge cleaving the White bloc'.

22 Kolli's 'Red Wedge' structure erected on Revolution Square, with the ancient Kitai-Gorod walls, now demolished, visible beyond it. Whereas the sketch shows it bearing the slogan 'Bands of Reds', this view bears the slogan 'Bands of White Guardists'.

First Anniversary of the Revolution, 1918, Moscow, Theatre Square

23   (*right*) The Maly Theatre, with a central painted panel depicting the exploits of Stepan Razin (see p. 73) by Pavel Kusnetsov.

24   Alexander Kuprin's sketch for his panel on the theme of 'Art' for the Nezlobin Theatre.

First Anniversary of the Revolution, 1918, Moscow, Theatre Square

25, 26 (*facing page*) Details of Alexander Osmerkin's panels for the building of Zimin's theatre: (*far left*) over the left side of the theatre entrance, 'A House Painter' and (*near left*) over the right side, 'A Carpenter'.

Red Square

27, 28 (*this page*) Popular parades moving southwards through Red Square with the History Museum behind them. 28 (*below*) includes the shopping complex of GUM (former Upper Trading Rows), right, and the banner in the foreground reads 'Let us direct our path towards the shining life'.

29 (*next page*) I. V. Alekseev's design sketches for the decoration of Hunter's Row, where abstractly decorated wooden kiosks stood in front of the rows of small shops advertising their meat, fish, fruit, vegetables and eggs.

14 *Streets, lights and Lenin*

Report in *Izvestiya* on the festive decoration of Moscow for the First Anniversary of the October Revolution

9 November 1918

The decoration of the Moscow Streets
. . . . A crowd has gathered on Trubnaya Square beside what looks like a scaffold. But no, the people are not preparing a place of execution, nor a bloody spectacle in honour of their festival. They are placing on its pedestal the massive creation 'Human Thought', by artist Merkurov, with the help of ropes and pulleys.

Tverskaya Street, all the way from Strastnoi Monastery to Hunter's Row, is decorated with red material, greenery and banners with slogans, stretched from one side of the street to the other: 'The October Revolution has given power to the people!', 'Long Live Soviet power!', etc.

An exhibition entitled 'One year of the dictatorship of the proletariat' is on display in what used to be Filippov's Bakery. On a red poster are the words: 'The bright new world of labour has come to replace the old world'. . . .

29   Hunter's Row with its unprepossessing, fish-smelling stalls is beyond all recognition. Painted, toy-like houses with little front gardens and naive yellow sunflowers have been arranged in two rows.

The public garden in front of the Bolshoi Theatre has been magically transformed into the Chernomor garden. The trees have been wrapped in mauve muslin and the painted paths appear flooded with moonlight. Several rows of red trimming have been stretched right round the square and flap in the wind.

The illuminations
Dusk quickly falls and the lights of the illuminations go on all over the city.

What an unforgettable, fairytale night! . . . The streets are lit as if it were peacetime. The buildings shine with multi-coloured lights, and the sky, lit up by searchlights and full of pink, fluffy clouds, seems strangely mysterious and beautiful.

The House of Unions and Lubyanka Square resemble a radiant fiery castle floating in the air . . .

The mysterious dark silhouettes of the Kremlin walls and towers stand out against a sky lit by searchlights and the glow from the illuminations, and from time to time rockets rise and fall in cascades of stars, frightening flocks of birds to the delight of the crowd.

The Kremlin chimes play the 'Internationale' and strike nine. The crowd moves towards the Place of Execution. It is time for the village *kulak* to be burned. [A *kulak* was an embourgeoisé peasant. *Ed.*]

A stuffed figure bobs up and down over the heads of the crowd, and one of the members of the Poor Committee, standing on top of the former Place of Execution, puts a blazing torch to it.

The flames instantly engulf the effigy of the kulak and the wind disperses the burning shreds, forcing the crowd to move back suddenly, grumbling as it does so. . . .

An armoured car drives up and down Tverskaya Street letting off loud firecrackers, which make the crowd run screaming in different directions. Lorries carrying bands

34
35   and mobile stages with costumed performers drive around the streets giving concerts.

The illuminations and noisy street celebrations continue late into the night both in the centre and in the outlying districts.

The unveiling of memorial plaques
The procession approaches the plaque. The band plays the funeral march and all banners are lowered. This is a solemn moment.

'A year ago,' says Comrade Smidovich, 'the people decided to transfer power to the Soviets. It is the desire of the Soviet, elected by the people, that we now unveil this memorial plaque to our comrades who fell in the fight for liberation. The Soviet requests you, Vladimir Ilyich Lenin, to unveil this plaque.'

Comrade Lenin goes up the steps to the plaque and unveils it. We see the figure of a woman, representing freedom, holding a palm branch. Above her is the inscription 'The October Revolution' and below 'To those who fell in the struggle for peace and brotherhood'. The plaque is the work of Konenkov, done in the style of Vrubel. . . .

As the funeral march ends, Lenin ascends the rostrum: 'Comrades! We are unveiling a monument to the advance fighters of the October Revolution of 1917. The finest members of the working mass gave their lives, having started the uprising for the liberation of all peoples from imperialism, for the cessation of wars between nations, for the overthrow of the reign of capital, for socialism . . .'

The entire square responds to its leader with lengthy cheering and clapping.

Comrade Lenin descends from the rostrum and joins Comrades Steklov, Smidovich, and others. He looks healthy and in good spirits, and chats and jokes with those around.

The parades

27   The columns of marchers are beginning to file past the plaque. The square looks splendid with the sun shining
28   brightly in the rippling sea of purple banners.

The original artistic posters of the trade unions stand out amidst the ordinary banners, and above the marchers' heads sail painted cut-out depictions of chemists in white coats, dockers bent double beneath their loads, print-workers at their machines, etc.

What a furore the food industry workers' union causes with its depiction of a shop-keeper, a bull's head and, most important of all, golden brown loaves of bread.

The procession of Futurist posters makes a strange and beautiful sight, dazzling the eye with its diversity of colour and design.

Next come the Poor Committee, representatives of Orlov, Tambov and Tula Provinces dressed in coarse cloth, public organizations, the People's Court, Proletkult, students from various academic institutions, and workers from all the city's districts.

The huge Presnya district causes general delight with its allegorical procession: people on carts dressed up as peasant women and soldiers in the chains of serfdom, followed by Freedom standing with her chains broken.

32   The float of the International Union of Circus Artists with its huge globe appears on the square and stops opposite the memorial plaque. . . .

The parade unveils statues on its return to the districts.

The illuminations and noisy celebrations on the streets of Moscow continue late into the night, much helped by the circus artists who perform on specially built stages on Trubnaya Square, in Hunter's Row and in the Nikitin Circus, and elsewhere. . . .

Izvestiya VTsIK, no. 244, 9 November 1918

15   *Harmonies and disharmonies*

From the article 'After the festivities' by V. Kerzhentsev, published in the magazine *Art*

November 1918

. . . Only one square in Moscow created an impression of wholeness as a result of its overall decorative unity, and that was Soviet Square. There was a kind of magnificent and austere solemnity, and I would even say a pleasant feeling of massiveness in the long red banners hung thickly
19   round the obelisk, in the posters stretched across
20   Tverskaya Street, and in the garlands of greenery. The dark red tone of most of the banners went well with this massiveness. I do not much care for the obelisk itself, but adorned in green and purple, even it blended well with the general appearance of the square and with the House of Soviets.

Despite all the energy spent by artists, none of the other squares in Moscow left such an impression of unity of design, and often there was a surprising lack of correspondence in the decoration of even one and the same building. . . .

When organizing future celebrations, special care should be taken to avoid a repeat of such blatant disharmony. The decoration of each square should be assigned to one artist or to a well-established group.

As for specific details, one should mention two exceptionally successful decorations, namely the stalls on
29   Hunter's Row and the fence on Tverskaya Street not far from the National Hotel. The artist who painted the dull wooden stalls on Hunter's Row managed to find gay colours exceptionally evocative of all Russian festivals, of the colourful patchwork of Russian bazaars and the brightly painted designs on little old Moscow houses. The bouquets, flowers and patterns were so simply and clearly drawn that one could not help smiling at them in delight. I still cannot pass these stalls without turning round to admire once more the harmony of fantastical colours and carefree, vivid designs. There are no slogans or symbols on these stalls, nor is there any clever idea behind them, but they have succeeded in evoking a festive mood and infecting the onlooker with a sense of inexplicable delight, which is the main requirement of any decoration. . . .

The painting of the awful fence on Tverskaya Street, which has been an eyesore for passers-by for more than a year now, is almost as fine, though totally different. This painting cannot be seen at one glance, and the artist evidently took this into account, because he has split his painting into several individual episodes which are revealed to the onlooker as he passes by. The group of men with raised arms, and its central piece, evidently depicting the birth of a new world out of chaos, is particularly fine. It is so pleasant to know that the two finest decorations are painted directly onto buildings and therefore cannot be removed to the stores and sheds of the October committee.

Iskusstvo (Art), no. 6, November 1918, p. 3.

16 *Changing demands on art*

From the article 'The first national exhibition' by N. G. Mashkovtsev, published in the journal *Working World*

24 November 1918

The first celebration of the October Revolution will be recorded in the chronicles of Russian art as a major event. The Revolution has summoned art onto the streets. It has forced painters to decorate the facades of buildings and sculptors to turn to monumental sculpture. . . .

The October Revolution celebrations of 1918 represent the beginning of the development of art under new conditions.

So many artistic groups participated in the celebrations and the decorations which transformed the streets of Moscow during the festivities were so magnificent that one can justly call this festival the First National Art Exhibition. Here lies the festival's value and significance for art. Of course, one cannot speak of the unified decorative style. Of course, one could have wished for greater co-ordination, and yet surely one cannot ask this of

artists who, for the first time, have placed their creations in the merciless environment of open air and sunlight. However, there was great resourcefulness and ingenuity in the decorations of certain buildings. . . .

The huge paintings on the Second Building of the Moscow Soviet were well done. The gloomy building of the History Museum was quite transformed by decorative shields in strong shades of red. The decorations on the Food Committee building were less successful, resembling the small pictures from *Jugend*, the journal of young German artists, enlarged into decorations. The large painting of Stenka Razin (by the artist P. Kuznetsov), hanging on the Maly Theatre, seemed rather colourless and faded. The artist obviously had not taken into consideration the strength of light outside. No doubt the painting would have created a quite different impression inside an exhibition hall. . . .

There were certain cases of decorative insensitivity. For example, the painted bushes in the public garden on Theatre Square provoke downright indignation. Beauty achieved by such methods is as unreal as the beauty of trees in French parks, trimmed into the shape of cubes, cones, fences, etc. This is yet another of those decadent Futurist ideas, and it has no place in a proletarian festival. . . .

This is a brief account of the designs for the October Revolution celebrations. Art desperately needs the crossfire of opinions, criticism and arguments. And now we must create the conditions for nation-wide discussion of art, just as we created the conditions for its exhibition.

Rabochii mir (Working World), no. 18, 24 November 1918, pp. 34–5.

17 *Realism and avant-garde*

Extracts from the article 'Two years of Russian art and artistic activity' by A. A. Sidorov, published in *Creative Work* in 1919

The October Revolution celebrations of 1918 were a real triumph of colour. Straightaway one can say that the paintings coped with their task more successfully than the sculptures. Many huge 'posters', as one is forced to call them, were truly superb and even though some clashed with one another or with the general 'style' of the building or square, these shortcomings are simple to eliminate.

However, I would like, at least briefly, to touch on an issue which has already excited the artistic world of Moscow, namely the apparently preferential 'patronage' given by Soviet power to left-wing artistic trends.

Of course, much is the result of misunderstandings, but I will not go into them now. The leaders of Soviet policy in the arts have declared on many occasions that they are happy to support any lively, creative trend in art. But there seemed some connection, essentially between 'left-wing' art and the revolutionary construction of life, in the fact that Futurists, Suprematists (there are now so many of them) have made it their sacred goal to 'revolutionize' people's sight, just as any revolution does to the consciousness. But again, let us not stop at this issue, which keeps coming back to concepts of art, democratic or proletarian, intended for the people. I would merely like to point out that the attempt at monumental decoration of the city exclusively by 'left art' (Red Army Day) was not a success. I would, however, like to recall a few of the pictorial decorations for the October Revolution celebrations of 1918 which will, I believe, go down in the history of Russian art. First and foremost, these were the paintings on the building of the former Painting School on Myasnitskaya Street. This was the first time they had been put on display. They were done by the studio of I. Mashkov, one of the few first-rate modern painters. Of course, the colours are incomparably better in reality than in photographs. But the figures of the worker and sailor in delightful garlands of fruit, figures powerfully and cheerfully drawn, were truly worthy of the language which the art of a proletarian country must speak. The monumental portrait of Lunacharsky, the People's

Commissar for Education, was less successful, as were all the portraits done for this festival. There seems a certain deliberate haste about it, but then one would like to remember it as an artistic reflection of the face of a man who has determined Soviet policy in art for the last two years.

One other aspect of the Soviet government's activity in decorating the city worthy of attention is the commemorative bas-relief plaques which have already been set into the walls of many buildings, thus leaving, in contrast to the paintings and posters, a permanent recollection of the union of art and life. Some of these plaques are excellent; others, on the contrary, are definitely unsuccessful. But it was in precisely this genre that Konenkov created the large plaque on Red Square, a work that reflects, perhaps best of all, the revolutionary ideal of our day. Few could rise to the task of setting a work of modern sculpture into the Kremlin wall, above the communal graves. Konenkov passed the test with flying colours. . . . This is something so new in design, so creatively unexpected, that the appearance of this relief alone is sufficient to refute the pessimistic fears of those who believed that art would die during the socialist revolution.

On the whole, a great deal has been done. Art has moved closer to life than ever before. But of course much still remains to be done. We are on the right path, and that, perhaps, is sufficient for the moment.

Tvorchestvo (Creative Work), no. 10–11, 1919, p. 43.

PETROGRAD

18 *Allocating the tasks*

List of places to be decorated in Petrograd, compiled by
the Festival Committee for the First Anniversary of the
October Revolution of the Petrograd Soviet of Workers'
and Soldiers' Deputies, published in the newspaper
Northern Commune

23 October 1918

	Name of place	*Artist allocated to design decorations*
57	Ruzheinaya Square	B. M. Kustodiev
	Lafonskaya Square	I. G. Langbard
	Blagoveshchenskaya Square	A group of artists under G. M. Bobrovsky
	Nikolaev Bridge	V. I. Shukhayev
101	Alexander Nevsky Monastery	S. V. Chekhonin
54–56	Admiralty building	M. V. Dobuzhinsky
38–41	The Field of Mars	L. V. Rudnev
	Peter and Paul Fortress, the Square by the Exchange, Palace Bridge and the road leading to Liteiny Bridge	D. M. Iofan
84, 85	City Duma building	S. P. Ivanov
67, 68	Police Bridge	V. V. Lebedev
87	Trinity Square	V. N. Meshkov
62, 63	Theatre Square	K. S. Petrov-Vodkin
46–53	Palace Square[1]	N. I. Altman
44, 45	Znamenskaya Square	V. D. Baranov-Rossine
	Vasilyevsky Island District Soviet	S. L. Abugov
	Bolshoi Prospekt & corner of Kamenno-ostrovsky Prospekt	I. I. Brodsky
	Sadovaya St., corner of Nevsky Prospekt	A. Y. Karyev
64	Okhtinsky Bridge	I. A. Puni
70, 71	Zimnaya Kanavka	D. P. Shterenberg
88, 89	Trinity Bridge	E. Y. Shtalberg
72	Senate and Synod Square	S. S. Serafimov
	Ligovka St., corner of Obvodny Canal	A. Y. Belogrud
65, 66	Liteiny Bridge	Society of Artists and Architects, OAKh, (S. Grower)
	Mariinskaya Square	P. S. Naumov
	Kazan Square	Y. V. Guretsky
	Institute of Technology and Square	K. A. Veshchilov and group
	Tsarskoselo Station Square	F. F. Kovarsky

	Name of place	*Artist allocated to design decorations*
	Warsaw Station Square	A. P. Udalenkov
	Finland Station Square	I. V. Simakov
	Baltic Station Square	A. S. Schwarz
90	Anichkov Bridge	S. O. Ovsyannikov
	Mikhailov Square	A. B. Regelson
	Novoderevenskaya Square and District Soviet	A. A. Yefimov
	Bolshaya Zelenina St. and Krestovsky Bridge	G. P. Lyubarsky
	Tuchkov Bridge	S. F. Simkhovich, R. A. Gabrikov
	Petrograd Soviet	S. M. Dudin
	Moscow Gate	Y. M. Cheptsov
	Kirochnaya St., Liteiny Prospekt	V. I. Kozlinsky
	Panteleimon St. and the Neva embankment in the area of Okhta	A. B. Lakhovsky
	Simeonov St., Liteiny Pr., Sennaya Square	S. V. Spirin
	Nevsky Prospekt, corner of Liteiny Pr.	N. A. Tyrsa
	Admiralty District Soviet	V. S. Shcherbakov
	1st Line of Vasilyevsky Island, corner of Bolshoi Prospekt	G. K. Savitsky
78	University Square	V. L. Simonov
	Chernyshev Bridge and Square	D. K. Stepanov
	Izmailov Prospekt	K. I. Gorbatov
	Square of the Five Corners	P. A. Pillanovsky
91	Panteleimon Bridge linked to Summer Gardens	K. K. Bikshe
73	Uritsky Palace (or Tauride Palace)	V. A. Shchuko
	Villieue Clinic Square	Kuindzhi Society (S.M. Zeidenberg)
	Okhtinsky District	Group of artists (M. A. Kerzin)
	Arcade	N. I. Kravchenko
	English Embankment near to the marine pier	Boris Grigoriev
	Pokrovskaya Square	M. M. Adamovich
	Peterhof District Soviet	V. S. Shcherbakov
	Narva Square	Society of Independent Artists
80	Rozhdestvensky District and General Headquarters building	M. A. Kerzin and group
81, 82	Zamoskovsky District and the District Soviet	S. N. Makletsov
	Narva District and District Soviet	Society of Independent Artists
77	Vasilyevsky Island Harbour	V. V. Mazurovsky (Petrograd Society of Artists)
	Vladimir Square	Y. K. Rudnitszky
	Zabalkanskaya Square and Bridge	K. V. Dydyshko
	Bridge of Nikolaev Square	L. A. Leifert

Name of place	Artist allocated to design decorations
94, 95 Sampsonievsky Bridge	A. R. Diderichs and V. A. Alvang
Michael the Archangel Square	I. F. Porfirov (Society of Assistance to Russian Artists)
Stock Exchange Bridge	V. A. Voloshinov
Pushkin Public Garden	V. P. Belkin
Corner of Vvedenskaya St. and Bolshoi Prospekt	S. V. Priselkov
79 Nikolaev Embankment from the Bridge to Naval College	P. I. Smukrovich
Lesnoi (graves of victims of October Revolution)	D. P. Buryshkin
Manege Square	Proletkult
79 Naval College	V. V. Emme

Severnaya kommuna (Northern Commune), no. 137, 23 October 1918

Additional allocations of artists are quoted from archival sources in *Agitatsionno-massovoye iskusstvo pervykh let Oktyabrya* (Mass Agitational Art of the First Years after the Revolution), Moscow, 1971, pp. 53–5, as follows:

Name of place	Artist allocated to design decorations
Embankment of Catherine Canal (near Nikolsky Market)	I. Murzich, M. Rundaltsev
60, 61 Smolny Institute	Y. M. Guminer, under the guidance of A. A. Andreyev (Proletkult)
75, 76 Labour Square and Palace of Labour	I. G. Langbard
74 Engineer's Castle	A. A. Plitman
Military Commissariat (on Admiralty Prospekt)	S. Rositsky
Izmailov Square	N. F. Lapshin
86 The arches 'Rest' and 'The Triumph of Labour' on Liteiny Prospekt	A. B. Lakhovsky and Y. Z. Buvshtein
Putilov Factory	F. Tikhonov, V. Chernov
Bolshoi Prospekt on Vasilyevsky Island	F. F. Buchgolts
Baltic Shipbuilding Factory	A. M. Arnshtam
Blagoveshchenskaya Square	N. F. Lapshin, T. P. Chernyshev and V. V. Volkov

1 Palace Square: a short while after the assassination of Petrograd Cheka (secret police) chief M. S. Uritsky in the General Staff Headquarters building on this square in August 1918, it was renamed Uritsky Square, and appears under that name in subsequent documents.

19 *Artists recollect: Petrov-Vodkin*

The artist Kuzma Petrov-Vodkin recalls his work on decorations for the First Anniversary of the Revolution

62
63 For the first anniversary of the Revolution I painted *Stenka Razin and Vasilisa the Wise*. This was a huge painting, 7 *sazhens* by 4 [approximately 15 by 8.5 m], which hung in Theatre Square. It was an important and interesting work which, according to a resolution of the Art Workers' Trade Union, was to have been preserved, but it somehow found its way into the backyard of some local Soviet and was later used for foot-bindings, because the canvas was relatively good. I did it with a group of thirteen of my students, and we worked on it day and night, as they say. You must remember that at this time nothing was available and we had to resort to such measures as highjacking horses and cabs and driving round the city confiscating whatever we could.

I remember when I had completed the rough sketches, I went to Maxim Gorky and showed him what I wanted to do. 'Folktales are fine', he replied, 'but I'm not so sure about this one of *Ivan the Fool*? Now we aren't fools, are we? I don't think this would work very well.' *Ivan the Fool* was the third painting I did. Ivan scratching his head, then bathing in bourgeois milk and finally becoming a tsarevich. These paintings did have some success but we did not even keep a record of them.

I recall that when I saw the parades passing in front of *Stenka Razin*, I felt for the first time that I was in my place, that my work was where it should be.

Excerpt from a stenographic record of an evening given in Petrov-Vodkin's honour on 9 December 1936, preserved in NBA AKh SSSR, f.7, op.42, 1936, d.46, l.15.

20 *Artists recollect: Altman*

The artist Natan Altman recalls his work on decorating Palace Square for the First Anniversary of the Revolution

I set myself the task of changing the historical image of the square, and transforming it into a place where a revolutionary people would come to celebrate its victory.

I decided not to decorate the square. The creations of Rastrelli and Rossi required no decoration. I wished instead to contrast the new beauty of a victorious people with the beauty of imperial Russia. I did not seek harmony with the old but contrast with it. I placed my constructions not on the buildings but between them, where the streets opened the square (at the corner of the Winter Palace and the road leading to the bridge, at the entrance to Khalturin Street, between the Guards' Headquarters and General Staff building, where there was a wide passage to the chapel, above the arch of Herzen Street at the corner of the General Staff building and Nevsky Prospekt). Only three vast paintings, almost the height of the buildings, were placed in front of the facades. One hung above the gates of the Winter Palace depicting a worker diagonally unfolding a banner which read 'He who was nothing will be everything', and two posters on the semi-circles on the facade of the General Staff building: on one side a peasant holding a banner printed with the words 'Land to the Working People', and the other on the opposite semi-circle a worker with a banner bearing the slogan: 'Factories to the Working People'.

Palace Square is enclosed by buildings, except for the Nevsky Prospekt side, where there are none. There used to be a tree-lined avenue there, and being late autumn, all the leaves had fallen and only the bare branches remained. I erected constructions round the branches and covered them with green material. Once again the trees turned green.

In the centre of the square, a rostrum was built round the base of the column in the space between it and the four lamp posts. It was a high dais with steps on all four sides. The four lamps at the corners were enclosed in huge red cubes positioned on stands and at night they glowed. A construction was erected around the column itself. On top of the platform were tongues of fire leaping upwards. This construction stood at the very base of the column and enclosed it. It was put together out of planes of different shape and size, painted yellow, orange and red.

I had to put up quite a fight to be allowed to break the monopoly of the colour red for festival design, and use all the colours of the spectrum in creating a festive street design.

N. Altman, *Vospominaniya* (Reminiscences), in the Manuscript Department of the Saltykov-Shchedrin Public Library, Leningrad, f.1126.

21 *Events of the day*

Report in *Izvestiya* on the festive decorations of Petrograd for the First Anniversary of the October Revolution

9 November 1918

The celebration of the anniversary of the Great October Revolution began at 12 o'clock at night when the population of the city was informed of the start of the great day by twenty-five bursts of cannon fire from the battlements of the Peter and Paul Fortress.

Despite the relatively unpropitious weather, St Petersburg looked festive.[1] The decoration of the squares and buildings was finished in good time and by morning the city was a picture of unprecedented beauty. Enormous banners stretched right across the streets and the flags, etc., added to the general impression. As early as 8 o'clock in the morning, long lines of people coming from all over the city, stretched along the streets, empty of all traffic, towards the place where the celebrations were to take place. The celebrations were opened first at the Smolny Institute. Here, wrapped in red material, stood a monument to the great leader Karl Marx.

At 10 o'clock, delegations from the Red Army, the Navy and the city's districts began arriving at the Smolny Institute with banners and standards. Sometime after 11 o'clock the Second City District arrived. A band played the 'Internationale' and Comrade Lunacharsky appeared on the rostrum and addressed everyone with a few brief words of welcome. . . .

To the sounds of the 'Internationale', Comrade Punin, Commissar for the Fine Arts, pulled the cover from the statue. There were shouts of 'Hurrah!' and 'Long live the world social revolution!' Then, on behalf of the Fine Arts Section, Comrade Punin presented Lunacharsky with a china statue of Karl Marx, made at the State China Factory. . . .

On the Neva
In accordance with a planned programme, the sailors of the Red Navy arranged the ships in specific positions along the Neva. Aviators also took part in the celebrations. The Neva looked magnificent in the evening. Garlands were hung from one ship to the next and all the vessels were lit

by electric effects. Rockets were fired from the ships and exploded loudly in the air. The celebrations continued until midnight.

On the streets of Petrograd

58–61 The Smolny Institute was one of today's main focal points. In the morning the square was extremely busy with the final preparations being made for the celebrations. The railings were artistically decorated, and banners with

73 slogans were on display. . . . The Uritsky Palace was decorated in an austere and constrained style: the railings were draped with red material and garlands and a huge red sheet hung down from the roof. . . . Znamenskaya Square, near Nikolaev Palace, and the Znamenskaya Hotel were very effectively decorated with many posters and banners with revolutionary calls. The Admiralty district was one of the most beautifully decorated districts in the city.

Several streets have been renamed in honour of the anniversary of the revolution.

Izvestiya VTsIK, no. 244, 9 November 1918

1. Although the city had been renamed Petrograd back in 1914, habit died hard, and the report does indeed refer to 'St Petersburg' here.

22 *Lessons learned*

From the report on the decoration of Petrograd for the First Anniversary of the Revolution published in the newspaper *Life of Art*

9 November 1918

There were two ways of decorating the stony face of Petrograd for the planned mass celebrations. The first was the path of a single will, encompassing all the details of a general plan. But this would have prevented individual initiative and the personal enthusiasm of individual masters of eloquent and symbolic form.

The second way was to leave decisions up to the artists and organizations themselves, in each specific case. Here

there would have been no limit to decorative imagination. But there would also have been the danger of an anarchic and random approach. The festival's overall arrangement would have been split into thousands of unforeseen and unrelated parts. In fact, a middle way was chosen. Whole architectural ensembles were put at the disposal of individual artists, so that whatever could be seen at one glance, would be merged into a single impression. What was the result? Despite the haste of the preparations and the fact that parts of the planned decorations could not be carried out, in many cases, these impressions were both harmonious and impressive. What an improvement from 1 May when the very mood of the city proletariat's austere and cultural festival was compromised by amateurish Futurist work, with the walls of splendid buildings being draped in paintings in the style of enlarged *lubki* [popular prints]. This time, it was not the character of the grotesque, of gigantic caricatures that prevailed, but a higher pitch of festive enthusiasm. In some cases, it was the form rather than the subject of the decorative constructions that was the source of the impression

46–53 (Uritsky Square, Police Bridge), and the form, colouring and positioning of the cloth boards, the wooden towers, the obelisks and the arches were all striking in their self-sufficient expressiveness. . . .

Meanwhile, the street festival only reached its peak with the appearance of another element – light. The illuminations, the immense glow which hung above Petrograd for two nights, was also not organized according to a general plan. On Nevsky Prospekt, where one recalls

42 the huge triangle of lights with the tower of Nikolaev

84 Station as its peak, Lassalle's House [the former City

85 Duma building] clothed in light, the glow inside the colonnade of Kazan Cathedral as well as certain monograms and banners, whole other sections and groups of buildings were plunged in darkness. The most magnificent festival of light was played out on the Neva where the Navy's fleet and the shore were illuminated and the chains of electric lights were pierced by soaring firework rockets. Many recall this spectacle of fire on the Neva as the visual culmination of the festival celebrations.

Zhizn iskusstva (Life of Art), no. 9, 9 November 1918

First Anniversary of the Revolution, 1918, Moscow, painted panels

30 (*right*) Detail of a sketch by G. V. Fedorov for a panel showing 'Stepan Razin issuing his call to the poor'. Stepan (or Stenka) Razin was a Cossack who in 1670 led oppressed Cossack peasants on a military campaign along the Volga River and then threatened the Tsar's defences of Moscow. Eventually he was executed near the Lobnoe Mesto in Red Square in June 1671 (where a statue to him was erected on May Day 1919 – see Document 27). He became a popular hero and was taken up by the revolutionary movement in Russia, hence his frequent use as a subject of Revolutionary mythology in these festivals.

31 Detail of a sketch by M. V. Eberman for a panel on the theme of 'Labour'.

1918-19

First Anniversary of the Revolution, 1918, Moscow, Red Square

32 (*left*) Members of the Moscow Union of Circus Artistes (MSATs).

33 (*above right*) Crowds at the north-east entrance to Red Square. The banner proclaims 'Long live the Third International' on behalf of 'The Workers of Moscow Soviet'.

On the streets

34, 35 (*right*) Tableau showing 'The funeral of autocracy'; and (*below right*) Strastnaya Square: A tram with Labour slogans from VSNKh, the Supreme Economic Soviet.

First Anniversary of the Revolution, Moscow, 1918, on the streets

36, 37   Costume designs by I. I. Zakharov and N. N. Agapeva for street traders dressed as Punch (*right*) and to carry a placard (*below*).

First Anniversary of the Revolution, 1918, Petrograd, the Field of Mars

38 (*above right*) K. I. Gorbatov, sketch for banners and an archway onto the Field of Mars.

39 (*below right*) Lev Rudnev, proposals for the evening illuminations on the Field of Mars.

40 (*below*) Rudnev's squared-up drawing for the banner to fly from the obelisk on the Field of Mars, depicting the flying figure of Glory.

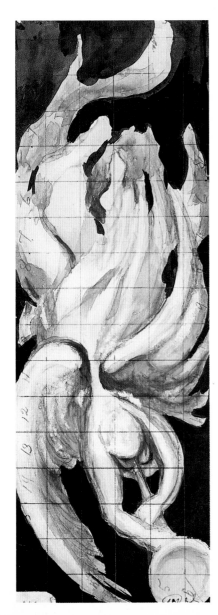

*First Anniversary of the Revolution, Petrograd,
the Field of Mars*

41 Rudnev's design for the obelisk, arch and
decorative panels in place. The overall theme
was 'To the memory of the victims of the
Revolution', and the text over the archway
reads 'To the host of the great ones who have
departed this life, the sons of Petrograd join
with them in the name of the flowering of life.'

First Annniversary of the Revolution, 1918, Petrograd, Uprising Square

42 (*right*) In the centre of the square, typographic panels covering Paolo Trubetskoy's statue of Alexander III carry slogans on the role of art: the upper one, for example, reads 'Art is one of the means of unifying the people'.

43 (*below*) Looking towards the central tower of the Nikolaev (now Moscow) Station.

First Anniversary of the Revolution, 1918, Petrograd, Uprising Square

44 (*right*) V. D. Baranov-Rossiné's squared-up sketch for a panel inscribed 'There is no higher calling than that of soldier of the socialist revolution', to be part of the decoration of Uprising Square.

45 (*below*) His squared-up sketch for a panel inscribed 'The 365 revolutionary days'.

23 *Successes and shortcomings*

From the article 'The October Revolution celebrations and the artists of Petrograd' by Lev Pumpyansky, published in the journal *The Flame*

5 January 1919

As I review the artistic decoration of Petrograd for the anniversary of the October Revolution, I am forced to begin by repeating my earlier assertions that contemporary art, on the whole, has not been equal to the demands made of it by the great historical moment. Artists were ill-prepared to carry out the tasks put before them both for external reasons, in the sense that they lacked organizational and technical experience, and, what is much more important, for inner reasons.

In the first respect, artists can be cleared of much of the blame. The decoration work was begun late and artists had less than a week to prepare sketches (and for such an occasion!). Materials (canvas, paints, boards, etc.) were received late and with great difficulty, and in some places either materials or manpower were in short supply. This left five days to a week for the completion of the actual designs, often of immense size and complexity. Owing to these circumstances, barely a fifth of what had been planned was completed by the day of the celebrations, and one can only judge the remainder from the sketches exhibited in the Palace of Labour.

If one adds to this the bad weather, the wind and rain which on the very first day, tore and drenched many of the works displayed, one can only be surprised at the extraordinary, festive and rich impression which Petrograd none the less created during the celebrations.

Also evident was a lack of technical experience of this type of decorative work, and indeed, where could Russian artists possibly have acquired such experience? Yet this is merely the external aspect, which can easily be rectified with practice in future. Far more important were the shortcomings that resulted from a disparity between the spiritual make-up and rhythm of modern art and the rhythm, experiences and feelings of the revolutionary popular masses. The blunders caused by these shortcomings are not so simple to correct because they are deeply connected with the painful crisis in modern art during recent decades, known as individualism, i.e., the isolation and alienation of the artist's personality from the surrounding environment, on the whole, the greatest fault of bourgeois culture.

Never has there been such a diversity of trends in art, nor has the rivalry between individual artistic groups been so intense, and never has the abyss of mutual incomprehension dividing artist and public been so deep as today. It would be a wise idea to give this some thought.

. . . The October Revolution celebrations which were, in accordance with the generous idea of its organizers, like a huge street exhibition of contemporary art (owing to the involvement of artists of all trends), provided us with a marvellous opportunity to become acquainted with its main groups.

The designs fall into three categories roughly corresponding to the right-wing, centre and left-wing of contemporary art. Those artists whom we may call the centre generally based their concepts on the outstandingly beautiful and harmonious overall architectural ensembles of classical Petrograd. The distinctive feature of this group was its caring attitude to the existing, fully-formed artistic 'face' of Petrograd, which it was neither possible nor necessary to change in a few days. Consequently, it was necessary only to supplement and enhance the given basis with a few architectural and pictorial details to make the whole ensemble look festive while not destroying its overall style and spirit. Such was the centre group, which included almost all the authors of architectural designs and painters from the 'World of Art' circle, until recently the most significant and progressive trend in Russian art, which played a prominent role in interpreting and providing a proper evaluation of ancient art. Among the works which one can assign to this central group are the decorations of the Tauride Palace (the architect Shchuko), Lafonskaya Square (the architect Langbard), Kazan Cathedral (the artist Guretsky), Anichkov and Panteleimon Bridges, and the Admiralty (Dobuzhinsky). . . .

In contrast with the experts on style and the enthusiastic connoisseurs of the beauty of the past stands the left wing, a group of bold, young trail-blazers who disclaim the past: 'Futurists' as they are publicly known, incorrectly in the sense of the precise meaning of the term but instinctively correct as a general description of this group's striving towards the future.

73

90

54–56

What is it that the 'Futurists' are endeavouring to do? They are drawn to the previous group, from which they historically originate, by the fact that they also take the demands of style as their point of departure, i.e., certain abstract, formal correlations of lines, colour, material, etc. But the profound distinction between the two trends is that the Futurists do not feel obliged in the expression of their artistic ideas to fit in with the 'alien' work of the great classic architects who created the old Petersburg. Instead, they express their own view, youthful, bold and modern, if a little 'tactless' with respect to their elders. In certain cases the result was an irritating dissonance; for instance, many will no doubt recall the obvious failure of the 'Left' group during the May Day celebrations, when even the boldest paintings hung pathetically against the magnificent facades of our palaces, making the latter ugly and failing miserably to rival them. But evidently, the lesson of the May celebrations did not fall on deaf ears. This time, the more earnest artists of the left trend in art operated not by the laws of harmony, but by the laws of opposition and contrast. An almost exemplary solution to this task was provided for Palace Square in the design by the artist Altman, which unfortunately, was only approximately carried out by the architect. The artist did not vie with the old masters but ingeniously placed next to them something totally new and contrasting. The square in front of the Winter Palace is strictly architectural. Altman supplemented it with purely pictorial impressions: the former strives for symmetry and completeness, the latter for sharpness, suddenness and whim, the former is uniform in colour, the latter is brightly coloured, the first splendid, rounded and three-dimensional, the latter flat, angular and disturbing; the two support one another magnificently.

46–53

In spite of certain weak points, especially the rather sickly combination of orange, crimson and watery-green tones, this undoubtedly represents a correct new principle capable of broad application in the future.

The third trend, encompassing the conservative right wing of contemporary Russian art, stands quite apart. It consists of naturalists of all possible shades who derive material for their work directly from life, and recreate this life 'as it is', without purifying it in the crucible of a specific artistic view of the world, and without transforming it into the motionless, enclosed forms of style. Such is the distinction between the naturalists and not only the left

wing, who either make no use of real forms (e.g. Lebedev's decoration of Police Bridge), or break them down in their work until they are unrecognizable (Altman's 'peasant' on the arch of the General Staff building, Shterenberg's 'blacksmith's striker' on the embankment side of the Winter Palace), but also the artists of the centre and the subjective realists such as Boris Grigoriev (the English Embankment) or Professor K. S. Petrov-Vodkin (the decorations on Theatre Square). All these contain a clear narrative idea and bear the vivid mark of the author's own original personality. For example, Boris Grigoriev did a delightfully refreshing sketch for a portrait of Walt Whitman and had the original idea of decorating the bridge with cube-shaped lanterns, fabric covered and hand painted with quotations from the great author of 'Blades of Grass', which seemed to 'whisper' Whitman's thoughts to the chance passer-by, 'whoever you are'. It is very rare for today's representatives of extreme naturalism to possess this spiritual freedom with respect to the real world. Usually, they subordinate themselves to reality rather than subordinating it. I will not however embark on a criticism of individual works of this third group, which were very poor both artistically and technically.

62
63

Plamya (The Flame), no. 35, 1919, pp. 11–14.

24 *Are the artists with us?*

From an unpublished article by V. Kerzhentsev entitled 'My reproach to artists'

10 February 1919

Since the Revolution, many Russian artists, especially young ones, have begun to work with Soviet power. They deserve both honour and fame for this.

Today, many hundreds of artists, sculptors and art teachers work in the various institutions of the People's Commissariat for Education with the aim of popularizing art. During the Revolution celebrations last year, artists made a tremendous effort to establish a new beauty in popular festivals.

This is all very well, but there is still one big 'but', which begins a string of reproaches directed at even the most active figures in the arts in Soviet Russia.

I claim that our artists have still not fully understood the tasks of the moment and still shut themselves up in their studies, continuing their former individualist existence, divorced from life and the interests of the working masses.

No doubt people will object that it was artists who decorated the city for the October Revolution celebrations, that it is artists who are erecting statues in the city's squares and public gardens, and that it is artists who are conducting 'monumental propaganda' by setting bas-reliefs and inscriptions in the walls of buildings.

But these tasks were imposed from above. In this case, artists did not show their own initiative. They had no such plan of their own. In other words, they had not yet personally sensed the beating of the collective pulse and the desire of the collective will. . . . Why have these energetic, talented and inquiring artists turned in on themselves and become so divorced from the spiritual needs of the working class, and why do they so scornfully ignore our daily life?

Yes, Soviet Russia has every right to direct these reproaches at her artists. The proletariat has good reason to ask artists why they disregard its daily life and do not attempt to transform its humdrum, everyday existence into a beautiful and delightful festival?

A typed manuscript dated 10 February 1919 preserved in TsGAORSS, Moscow, f.967, op.1, d.109, l.2.

May Day Celebrations 1919

25 *Instructions to the local Soviets*

From a resolution of the Presidium of the All-Russia Central Executive Committee on the 1919 May Day Celebrations, published in *Pravda*

25 April 1919

1   The organization of the proletarian May Day festival is the responsibility of the local Soviets.
2   All institutions and enterprises serving transport (loading, unloading, etc.), all public canteens, hospitals, sanitary facilities, and all light, sewerage and water works, etc., should continue functioning as normal or set up a duty rota.
3   According to instructions, strict economical use is to be made of coloured materials and fabrics for all kinds of decoration, and also of electrical illumination. . . .
   Chairman of the VTsIK: M. Kalinin.
   Secretary of the VTsIK: L. Serebryakov

Pravda, no. 87, 25 April 1919

MOSCOW

26 *Themes and approaches*

From the plan of the Theatrical Department of Narkompros on the organization of Moscow decorations for May Day 1919, published in the journal *Theatre Courier*

29 April–2 May 1919

In proposing the plan below for the arrangement of the May Day festivities, the Theatrical Department of

Narkompros believes it necessary to point out that this plan provides only a general outline and thus gives broad opportunities for those organizations and persons responsible to show initiative. The outlines proposed by the Theatrical Department are based on the following fundamental idea: 1 May is the day on which the international solidarity of the proletariat is celebrated, a festival of spring labour. The whole festival should therefore be given a vivid spring flavour . . . the celebrations should take us out of buildings into the open air, onto the noisy streets, wide squares, public gardens and lawns.

The themes of these decorations should be the following: an arch of factory labour, an obelisk of agricultural labour, arches and obelisks of trade unions, science, art and literature, and arches dedicated to revolutionary figures. In order to impart a distinctive flavour to the whole festival, banners and emblems should be designed for each professional organization participating in the festivities. It would also not be out of place to create drawings not only of posters, banners and badges, but also of costumes that allegorically represent the meaning and significance of the proletarian festival.

No matter how brightly decorated the festival's exterior, it loses its entire inner meaning without the direct participation of the broad popular masses as a lively crowd.

On this day, theatres should stage their plays exclusively in the open air. Stages are being erected on the city's squares, crossroads and park areas. Mobile scenery is being transported on baggage waggons and lorries can already serve as stages for troupes of actors. Of course, the programmes of these spectacles should use a cheerful and vivid repertoire with a clearly expressed revolutionary idea.

Vestnik teatra (Theatre Courier), no. 22, 29 April–2 May 1919, p. 3.

27 *Political clowns*

From a report on the 1919 May Day celebrations in Moscow, published in *Pravda*

3 May 1919

. . . There is a strange procession along Strastnoi Boulevard: Durov the Clown is travelling down the street with his animals on several leads.

The procession is surrounded by large crowds. The carts are entwined with flags with slogans. On the first cart is a shield, on the second a small locomotive puffs and whistles, wrapped in a sash with the inscription: 'Revolution is the Locomotive of History'.

On the following cart is a 'carrion-crow' creature, dressed in a Prussian uniform and reminiscent of either Wilhelm or Herr Noske. . . .

Next comes a hyena in a cage. The cage is decorated with the coat of arms of the Romanov family and the inscription 'Capitalism'.

The procession comes to a halt and Durov, surrounded by little children, begins a performance with a dog. Durov plays a commanding officer of the tsarist army and the dog plays the lowest rank. The ingenious Durov portrays a picture of previous mockery of soldiers. Both adults and children are amused.

Then a tramcar with circus performers stops on Lubyanka Square. The jokes of the clown are drowned by bursts of laughter, a balalaika is strummed and a performer in the costume of a boyarina dances in the Russian style. The spectators can barely keep from joining in the dance. . . .

Throughout the city the squares are crowded and the theatres full. Proletkult is depicting the 'Entente': the Krylov Quartet has found the best approach to the 'peace' conference in Paris. The audience immediately grasps the sense of the fable. Children's theatres are filled with uncontrollable laughter. . . .

The first rays of the spring sun which peeped out on May Day after a series of grey days lit up Moscow in its festive attire. Naturally, not one building was without at least a few red flags, but certain streets and buildings in the centre were literally swamped in greenery and red material, on which glittered the golden words of slogans.

What is more, there was a pleasant absence in the decorations of last year's enormous posters and paintings of the latest 'futurist' forms of art. Here and there among the greenery one could see a portrait of Marx, Lenin or some other revolutionary leader and this time, the participation of 'painting' was successfully limited to this alone. The overall impression of the embellished streets and squares was one of simplicity and modesty, and simple harmonies without mannerisms do not draw the inquisitive eye to trivialities and the unnecessary. . . .

109
110
111

Some of the processions were led by allegorical groups, depicting labour, the alliance between the proletarians and the countryside etc. A tram went past with children wearing red caps and shirts and a French tank, a trophy from Odessa, rolled heavily towards the assembly point. Then a vehicle decorated with a horn of plenty rushed past scattering newspapers and brochures. Up in the blue sky soared aeroplanes, occasionally letting go of newspapers and leaflets, like flocks of white birds. . . .

106
107

By midday, the broad expanse of Red Square was barely able to accommodate the arriving masses. Symbolically dominating the square was a colossal star with the emblem of the RSFSR. Posters with slogans on the unity of proletarians throughout the world had been hung on both sides of the memorial plaque in the Kremlin wall. The monument to Stepan Razin awaited its forthcoming unveiling ceremony on the former place of execution. Comrade Sverdlov's grave was covered in flowers and greenery. Medallions of Marx and Lenin stood out vividly on the Kremlin wall.

Pravda, no. 93, 3 May 1919

28 *Problems of re-use*

In reminiscences in his personal papers, the artist N. Chernyshev recalled that on the facade of the State Department Store GUM (the old Upper Trading Rows, along Red Square), hung his painting 'Science and Art bring their gifts to Labour', and S. V. Gerasimov's 'The

Owner of the Land'. Both paintings had originally been done to decorate the building of the former City Duma, just round the corner, for the first anniversary of the October Revolution.

. . . Our paintings were hung in the middle of the facade, opposite the main saluting rostrum. I recall that as I passed by them on the pavement, I noticed on the ground below a lot of dry paint which had cracked and fallen off as a result of rolling and unrolling the canvas with a glue-based painting.

PETROGRAD

29 *Discussing approaches*

Report on the discussion of a May Day decoration plan for the streets and squares of Petrograd, published in the newspaper *Art of the Commune*

16 March 1919

A committee under the chairmanship of N. I. Altman has been set up at the Arts Section of the Department of Fine Arts [IZO], to plan the decoration of the streets and squares for 1 May.

The first meeting of the committee, held on 7 March, was attended by members of the Board of Arts and Crafts, Comrades Baranov-Rossiné, Karev, Matveyev, Rudnev and Shkolnik.

The meeting was opened with a speech by Altman. All discussions should bear in mind, he said, that May Day is a celebration both of the unity of working people all over the world and of the rebirth of humanity. The decorations should be based on a unified artistic plan. The lack of a co-ordinated system of designs, such as was seen last November during the celebrations of the Revolution, cannot be allowed. Individual points along the parade route should be decorated, as well as places where large numbers of people will gather.

Comrade Rudnev regards it as essential that the street decorations be done properly, above all technically. They should be more or less sturdy. It is not enough to decorate the streets merely with flags and emblems.

Decorations on the city's squares should correspond closely to the architectural ensembles.

Comrade Karev believes that the basis of decorating a square should be either to destroy the idea of the old architecture, or to introduce an element of entertainment and festivity, which is what 1 May is, from the international point of view.

Comrade Shkolnik thinks it unwise to decorate the streets with different depictions. He believes that a uniform type of poster should be produced and hung all over the city.

Comrade Rudnev suggests that the decorations be monumental.

At the end of the meeting, the committee began to draw up a detailed plan for the decoration of the capital city which is to be implemented through the announcement of several competitions.

Iskusstvo kommuny (Art of the Commune), no. 9, 16 March 1919

Soviet on the appointed squares and streets half an hour before the parade starts out along its route.

Each column is to be headed by a standard bearer from the Executive Committee, followed by a band and choir, and then by the local committee of the Petrograd Committee of the Russian Communist Party (Bolshevik), members of the district executive committee, the plenum

114 of the district Soviet, the Red Army and Navy carrying guns decorated with greenery and ribbons. Then will come the Communist Youth League (Komsomol) followed by children over twelve, trade unions, factory organizations, commissariats, co-operatives as well as cultural, educational and other organizations.

Each column should be ten to twelve people wide. Children under twelve, in the charge of teachers, will form two rows along the route set for each district's parade and the marchers will pass between them.

While the marchers are forming, women workers will go round the columns with shields decorated with badges offering the latter for sale. The Red Army and Navy will receive badges free of charge through their units.

Krasnaya gazeta (The Red Newspaper), no. 94, 30 April 1919

30 *Composition of the processions*

From the report on the procedure for the 1919 May Day parade in Petrograd, published in the *The Red Newspaper*

30 April 1919

At 8 o'clock in the morning of 1 May there will be a salute of seven shots to mark the start of the parade, and decorated vehicles with leaflets, posters and badges will depart to all districts from the Palace of Labour. Each vehicle will carry a trumpeter heralding the start of the parade. All participants should gather at their district

31 *Themes*

From a report by the Petrograd Soviet on the plan for a float procession during the 1919 May Day festivities, published in the newspaper *Petrograd Pravda*

25 April 1919

The columns of marchers are to be organized according to district, and will proceed along the streets of Petrograd according to a set plan, past the communal graves on the Field of Mars, taking up specially allocated positions

113 where rostrums will be erected for speeches. Then there will be a magnificent procession of floats, constructed by the Arts Committee of the Commissariat for Education.

These floats will represent 'the old and the new world'. In front will be four floats depicting life under the old system. This will be a dragon intended to personify the capitalist system, a two-headed eagle, and a float

112 portraying the classes, nobility and all the paraphernalia of the old regime. A border post will separate these from the floats of 'the new world', a labour float and floats presenting a general picture.

A striking evening spectacle is also to be organized on the Neva river.

Petrogradskaya Pravda (Petrograd Pravda), no. 75, 25 April 1919

32 *Flags and greenery*

An account of the festivities from *The Red Newspaper*

3 May 1919

. . . There were almost no painted panels to be seen on the streets. The organizers had to limit themselves to red flags, but this in no way diminished the general ceremony and splendour of the occasion. . . .

There were several particularly original floats in the ceremonial procession. For example, the Baltic Factory had placed a huge globe on a lorry, with a dark blue ribbon with the inscription 'Internationale' in place of the equator.

There were beautiful floats: vehicles in the form of tents

115 made out of fir branches and decorated with flags. Red-painted aeroplanes circled the sky from early in the morning.

Krasnaya gazeta (The Red Newspaper), no. 96, 3 May 1919

Second Anniversary of the October Revolution

33 *Central planning*

From the decree of the Party Central Executive Committee, VTsIK, 'On the Celebrations to mark the Second Anniversary of the October Revolution'

6 October 1919

1.   In view of the difficult situation, instruct the commission to distribute the 50,000,000 roubles allocated by the Council of People's Commissars for the October Revolution anniversary celebrations in the following manner: 40,000,000 should be given as allowances to the families of Red Army soldiers and 10,000,000 should be used to reinforce written and oral propaganda on that day. . . .
4.   The orders are for the strictest possible economy of coloured material and other fabrics for all types of decorations, and also of electrical illuminations.

SU, no. 49, 1919, p. 478.

PETROGRAD

34 *Modest scale*

From an editorial in the newspaper *Life of Art*

20–21 September 1919

. . . The celebrations of the second anniversary of the October Revolution will be of a more modest nature. In all probability the festival [in Petrograd] will be limited to one day.

Nevertheless the broad popular masses will participate in the festivities. The festival will be organized with the help of artists and performers of all classes. All kinds of theatre will have a special part to play in the celebrations.

Zhizn iskusstva (Life of Art), no. 247–8, 20–21 September 1919

35 *Competitions*

Report on the design competition for festive decoration of Petrograd, from the newspaper *Life of Art*

5 June 1919

Rules have been worked out for the competition announced by the archaeological department of the Commissariat for Education for the festival decorative design of Uritsky Square, Alexandrov Gardens from the Admiralty to the Senate building, the Palace Bridge and the squares in front of the Exchange.

The best designs will be awarded prizes of 30,000, 25,000, 20,000, 15,000 and 10,000 roubles.

The jury will be composed of representatives of various government institutions, social and artistic organizations. In total the jury will be comprised of forty people. All those taking part in the competition will receive 1,500 roubles to cover the cost of purchasing materials.

Zhizn iskusstva (Life of Art), no. 155, 5 June 1919

Further competitions were later announced by the Trade Union of Art Workers for other areas, for posters, banners, emblems, a medal, floats and a special journal cover, giving work 'for forty-three artists' in total.

Zhizn iskusstva (Life of Art), no. 268, 15 October 1919

36 *Singing crowds*

From a report on the Petrograd celebrations for the Second Anniversary of the Revolution, in the newspaper *Petrograd Pravda*

9 November 1919

There was an extraordinary throng of people on the Field of Mars and from 12 o'clock until 2 o'clock workers and soldiers marched endlessly past with banners, which they reverentially lowered over the unforgettable graves. This marchpast was accompanied by the funeral march and a salute from the Peter and Paul Fortress. . . .

There was a constant stream of men and women workers, soldiers and sailors with banners, posters, bands and revolutionary songs stretching from the Field of Mars to the Smolny Institute along October 25th Avenue and Soviet Avenue. Then the demonstration returned to the various districts after the unveiling of the monument to the victims of the revolution. The entire proletariat of St Petersburg [*sic*] took part in this splendid demonstration.

Petrogradskaya Pravda (Petrograd Pravda), no. 256, 9 November 1919

116
117
118

First Anniversary of the Revolution, 1918, Petrograd, Natan Altman's designs for Uritsky (former Palace) Square

46　(*right*) West side view of the Alexander Column.

47　(*far right*) Altman's drawing for the north (Winter Palace) side of the rostrum around the Alexander Column (facing left in 46).

48　(*below*) Altman's design drawing for the whole square: showing the Winter Palace on the left, the Alexander Column, centre, and Central Staff building, right.

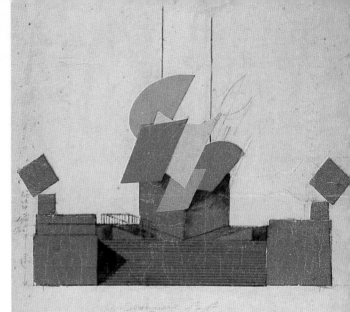

ПРОЛЕТАРИИ ВСЕХ СТРАН СОЕДИНЯЙТЕСЬ

First Anniversary of the Revolution, 1918, Petrograd, Altman's designs for Uritsky Square

49, 50 (*facing page*) Reproductions by Altman himself, in 1969, of panels he did for decorating the General Staff building in 1918; 49 (*far left*) has the theme 'Land to the Working People'; 50 (*left*) has the theme 'Factories to the Working People'.

51 (*below left*) Altman's original sketch for the whole General Staff complex, with these panels to left and right of the main arch. In memoirs, Altman recalled that the final colours were exactly as projected in his designs. He also commented that he had tried to juxtapose a 'new beauty' to the classical architecture, not to compete with it.

52 (*right*) Another 1969 reproduction by Altman, for the panel 'He who was nothing will be everything', placed in the centre of the Winter Palace facade.

53 (*below*) Central detail from an earlier re-painting by Altman, showing the whole Winter Palace facade. Left and right of this central portion were horizontal banners reading 'Art to the workers'.

1918-19

First Anniversary of the Revolution, 1918, Petrograd, Mstislav Dobuzhinsky's designs for the Admiralty complex

54　(*right*) Squared-up sketch for the decorative elements of ship and flags to be erected over the pediment of the Admiralty's side elevation in Dobuzhinsky's scheme.

55　(*below*) His sketch for the Admiralty's side elevation.

56　(*bottom*) His sketch for decorating the whole river frontage of the Admiralty.

Ruzheinaya Square

57　(*facing page*) Boris Kustodiev's sketch for his panel on the theme of 'The Reaper'.

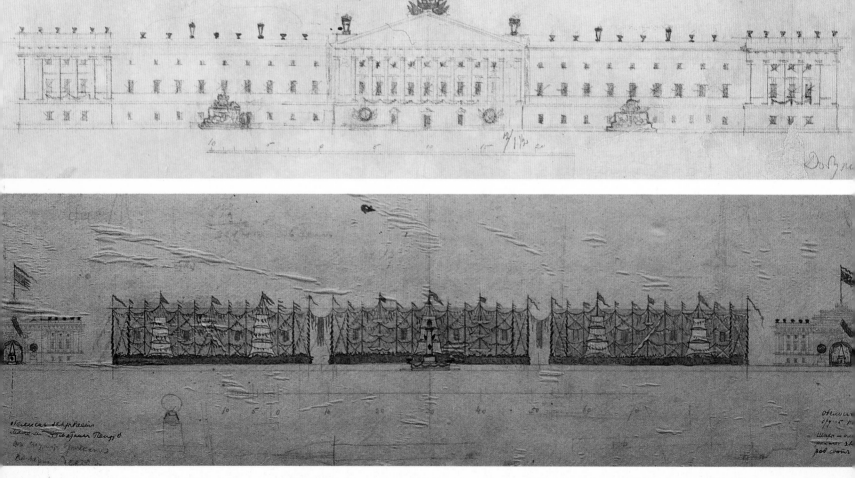

First Anniversary of the Revolution, 1918, Petrograd, the Smolny Institute

58 (*above*) The archway created at the main entrance to the Smolny Institute to designs of I. G. Langbard. The slogan 'Proletariat of all countries unite' was picked out in lights and the main arch, banners, etc., were in bright red.

59, 60 Ya. M. Guminer, two sketches for panels to decorate the interior of the Smolny building. 59 (*right*) has the theme 'Glory to the heroes who by their lives have given birth to the world revolution', and 60 (*below*) reads: 'Proletkult: the creativity of the proletariat is the guarantee of the world commune'.

61 (*below right*) Design by an anonymous team of artists for decorating the Smolny Institute's main facade.

First Anniversary of the Revolution, 1918, Petrograd, decoration of Theatre Square by Kuzma Petrov-Vodkin

62   Petrov-Vodkin's sketch for the overall treatment of Theatre Square.

63   His sketch for a panel about the exploits of Stepan Razin.

First Anniversary of the Revolution, 1918, Petrograd, Liteiny Bridge and the Okhta district

64 (*left*) Ivan Puni, squared-up sketch for a panel on the theme 'Armed workers in a motorcar'.

65 (*right*) Vladimir Kozlinsky, squared-up sketch for his panel honouring the 'RSFSR'.

66 Kozlinsky's squared-up sketch for a panel bearing the slogan 'Long live the Red Navy'.

First Anniversary of the Revolution, 1918, Petrograd, Vladimir Lebedev's scheme for Narodny (People's, former Police) Bridge

67, 68   Lebedev's squared-up sketches for two panels. 67 (*right*) has the theme 'Long live the Red Army'; 68 (*below*) 'Long live the International'.

1918-19

First Anniversary of the Revolution, 1918, Petrograd

69 (*right*) Nikolai Tyrsa, sketch for decorating a Petrograd street.

Palace Embankment and Zimnaya Kanavka

70, 71 David Shterenberg's squared-up drawings for decorative panels. 70 (*below right*) depicts 'The sun of freedom'; 71 (*below left*) a worker with a rifle.

First Anniversary of the Revolution, 1918, Petrograd

72 (*above*) A. I. Klein, sketch for a panel for the former Synod building on the theme 'The old world has collapsed, a new world is imminent'.

73 (*right*) Vladimir Shchuko, sketch for the decoration of the Tauride Palace.

74 (*below*) A. A. Plitman, design for decorating the external elevation of the Engineer's Castle.

First Anniversary of the Revolution, 1918, Petrograd, Labour (former Blagoveshchenskaya) Square

75 (*right*) I. G. Langbard's designs for decorating a tram stop.

76 (*far right*) His design for a decorative arch.

Harbour area

77 (*below*) F. F. Bukhgolts and V. V. Mazurovsky, sketch design for decorative arches in the harbour area of Vasilyevsky Island.

First Anniversary of the Revolution, 1918, Petrograd

78, 79 (*facing page*) G. K. Savitsky, V. N. Kuchumov and V. L. Simonov, sketch for decorating the Academy of Sciences (*above*); P. I. Smukrovich and V. V. Emme, decorations for the Neva embankment in front of the Naval College (*below*).

80 (*above*) The local Soviet in Rozhdestvensky District: panels by K. F. Lekht and B. N. Gererdov. The poster on the front railings advertises a free concert.

81, 82 Two sketches by S. N. Makletsov. 81 (*right*) is for the facade of a local building, and 82 (*far right*) is his squared-up drawing for its central panel. A worker with Red Banner reading 'Oct(ober) Rev'(olution) spears a crowned snake representing the old regime.

83 (*below*) Street banners. Left: 'Workers will come to the village in order to rouse the whole multi-million body of the poor peasantry to fight for socialism'. Right: 'The Red Army is rescueing the workers' and peasants' revolution. Before spring we must have an army of three million'. Oddities of alphabet and spelling may indicate a semi-illiterate artist.

First Anniversary of the Revolution, 1918, Petrograd, S. O. Ivanov's design for the City Duma

84 Ivanov's sketch for the decoration of the former City Duma or City Hall (known as Lassalle's House) on Nevsky Prospect.

85 Photograph of the former City Duma building showing Ivanov's decorative scheme executed in most of its details.

First Anniversary of the Revolution, 1918, Petrograd

86 (*right*) A. B. Lakhovsky and Ya. Z. Buvshtein, sketch, for a triumphal arch on the theme of 'The Triumph of labour', for erection on Liteiny Prospect opposite Simeonov Street.

87 (*below*) V. N. Meshkov, sketch for decoration of Trinity Square.

First Anniversary of the Revolution, 1918, Petrograd, bridges

88, 89 (*right and below*) E. Ya. Shtalberg and P. I. Sokolov, sketch and photograph of Equality Bridge.

90 (*facing page, above*) S. O. Ovsyannikov, decorations for Anichkov Bridge, which carries Nevsky Prospect over the Fontanka Canal: banners at the southern end of the bridge.

91 (*right*) K. K. Bishke, decorations on Pestel Bridge.

92 (*below*) Nikolai Tyrsa, decoration of a bridge.

First Anniversary of the Revolution, 1918, Petrograd, bridges

93 (*above*) D. K. Stepanov, sketch for decorating Lomonosov Square and Chernyshev Bridge.

94, 95 (*right and below*) A. R. Diderikhs and V. A. Alvang, sketches for the decoration of Stepan (Stenka) Razin Bridge: sections across the bridge showing side views of the ships to be created around its abuttments, and plan of the whole bridge and its long elevation, showing the eight ships and their sails.

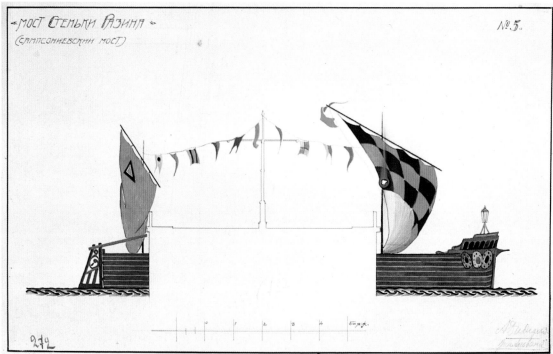

First Anniversary of the Revolution, 1918, Petrograd

96   (*right*) A. R. Eberling, sketch for a panel entitled 'From ruination to creation'.

97, 98   (*below left and right*) Squared-up sketches by an unknown artist for two panels depicting 'Glory'.

99   (*bottom*) M. I. Agulyansky, sketch for a panel entitled 'The furnace of a metallurgical plant'.

First Anniversary of the Revolution, 1918, Petrograd

100   A parade of workers from the city tramways. Slogans on the front banner read: 'Proletariat of all countries unite! All power to the labouring masses! Workers of the Electric Tramway Station'.

101   Sergei Chekhonin, sketch for a panel entitled 'Death to the oppressors' for decorations around the Alexander Nevsky Monastery.

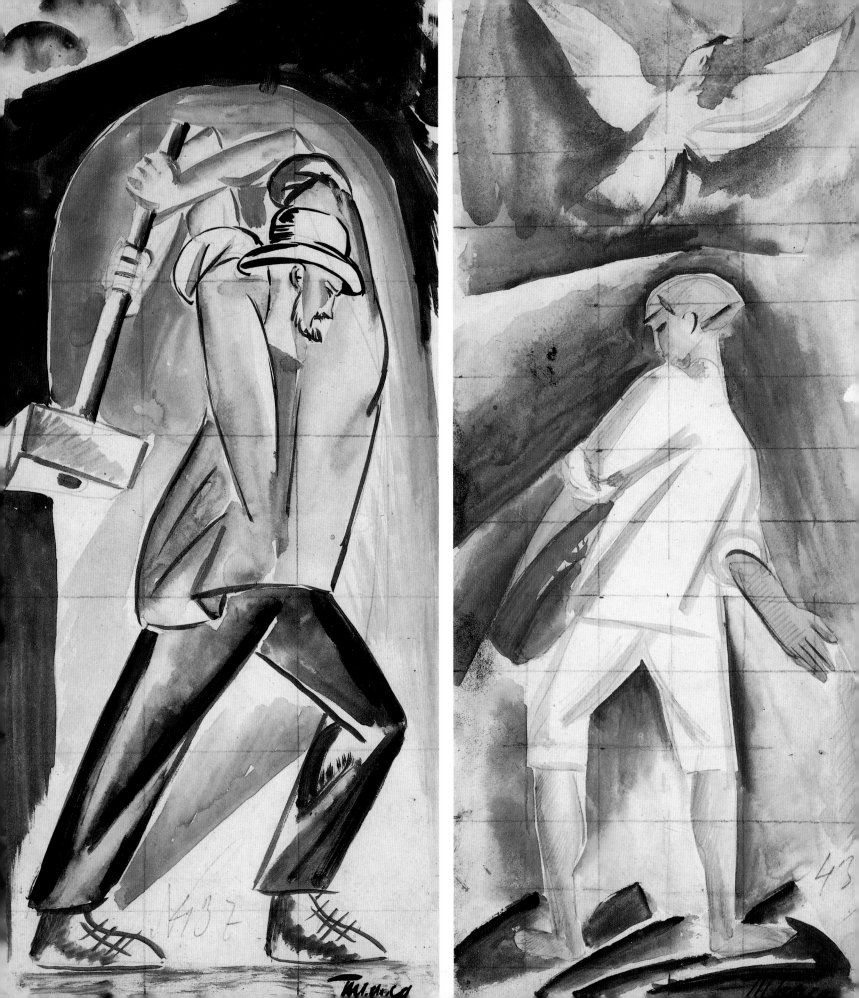

First Anniversary of the Revolution, 1918, Petrograd

102, 103 (*facing page*) Squared-up sketches by Nikolai Tyrsa for a panel showing 'A worker with a hammer' (*far left*), to decorate the corner of Liteiny and Nevsky Prospects; (*left*) for a panel showing 'Young man sowing seed'.

104 (*right*) V. S. Savrog, a banner reading 'Everyone to the defence of the revolution!'

105 (*below*) T. P. Chernyshev, squared-up sketch for a panel entitled 'The call', to decorate the Metalworking Plant near the Okhta River in eastern Petrograd.

MAY DAY, 1919

May Day, 1919, Moscow

106 (*right*) A lorry bearing the message 'Long live socialism' enters Red Square at the north end past the History Museum.

107 (*below*) A horse-drawn wagon passes through Red Square bearing the slogan 'Proletariat of the world unite!' In the background is the GUM building, and a banner for the Russian Communist Party, the RKP.

108 (*far right*) A unique picture in the collection: the only photograph, from Irina Bibikova's own collection, showing the artists who created the festival decorations at work: the painters Ilya Mashkov, Andrei Goncharov and G. I. Lazarev, sitting in front of their completed festival panel on the theme *Vsevobuch* (meaning obscure), Moscow 1919.

May Day, 1919, Moscow

109, 110   Two sketches by A. A. Lebedev-
Shuisky. 109 (*right*) a squared-up sketch for a
panel entitled 'Encounter of the military
visitors'; 110 (*below*) sketch for a panel
entitled 'The Red Army soldiers attack'.

111   (*far right*) Sketch by Alexander Kuprin
for a panel bearing the slogan 'Away with
idleness! Glory to labour!'

May Day, 1919, Petrograd

112   (*right*) A lorry moving through the streets bearing a symbolic cage of pre-Revolutionary and White 'types' entitled 'Before they did the biting, now they are frightened'.

113   (*below*) A rostrum in Uprising Square inscribed 'Greetings to the true leaders of the socialist revolution', masking the Trubetskoy statue of Alexander III.

114, 115   (*facing page*) Show floats from the street processions. In 114 (*above*) sailors with a naval band process through Petrograd streets on a lorry decorated as a warship. In 115 (*below*) a motorcar draped in branches from fir trees carries paintings of 'White' and 'Red' figures towards the Trinity Bridge.

SECOND ANNIVERSARY, 1919

Second Anniversary of the Revolution, 1919, Petrograd

116   (*right*) The archway erected at the entrance to the Smolny Institute.

117   (*below left*) A procession with banners bearing Arabic inscriptions and Islamic symbols, apparently representing Red conquests of southern and central Asian republics, combined with the name of 'The Political Section' and slogans welcoming 'The Third Communist International'.

118   (*below right*) Uprising Square, where a circular fortress has symbolically imprisoned the statue of Alexander III.

PART 2
1920-26

Mass Performances and Spectacles

THE THIRD YEAR of these revolutionary festivals, 1920, was conspicuous for the boldness of the concepts both proposed and realized. Two years of practice had given the various organizers confidence in achieving practical and popular success, but content, scale and overall concepts were still open to bold experimentation. Thus after a clear reassertion by Lunacharsky in Document 37 that only 'organization' would produce something 'of a higher order' than mere 'lively noise of festively dressed people', the documents on 1920 show us five entirely distinct conceptions of the form such a festival could or should take.

The events actually staged in Petrograd in May and in Moscow in November 1920 were of a traditionally Russian festive kind, and combined the two components distinguished by Lunacharsky in his article. The 'mass' component was represented by converging 'movements of the mass public' that culminated in some 'action or elevated, symbolic ceremony' at a focal point in the city. The 'intimate' component was the direct descendant of the *balagans*, sideshows and clowns of traditional fairs. They had become 'revolutionary cabarets' comprising 'fiery speeches, recital of satirical verse, clowns caricaturing enemy forces, or topical dramatic sketches', performed 'on trams, lorries or simply on tables or barrels'.

As documents from later years show, some variant on that combination would become the norm. But the wider circumstances of 1920 contained little that was normal. Dreadful austerity was compounded by continuing uncertainty as to the ultimate fate of the new regime, and coincided with – perhaps helped to fire – an extraordinary burgeoning of avant-garde artistic activity. The possibility of harnessing vast manpower and energy to new purposes was still fresh, and no small sense of liberation derived from the ending of the Western powers' post-war blockade of Russia in January 1920. Thus Document 38, from the following month, records one of the most daring conceptions of the decade. It came from Alexei Gan, an artist in the Theatrical Section of Lunacharsky's cultural commissariat (Narkompros), who eighteen months later emerged as the principle theorist of a new relationship between artistic and political activity under the name of Constructivism. Gan's proposal for May Day preceded by a mere six weeks the founding in Narkompros's Art Section of the famous research forum INKhUK (the Institute of Artistic Culture). From here in 1922 Gan's manifesto *Constructivism* would 'declare uncompromising war on art' as the 'illustration of sacred history', and replace it by 'Constructivism, as a phenomenon of our age, which arose in 1920 amidst the "mass action" leftist painters and ideologists'. His May Day proposal to make the entire population enact 'the Communist city of the future' already proffered the same radical redefinition of 'artistic activity'.

Gan's project was not accepted, and the actual events of that May Day in Moscow represented a different concept of the public festival, the *subbotnik*, first launched a year previously and soon to become another characteristic phenomenon of Soviet public life. The very opposite of a holiday, except in spirit, this was (and still is) a Saturday when the populace gives a free day's work for the public good, in a relaxed and cheerful communal spirit. On the May Day *subbotnik* of 1920, the only entertainment was a late-night performance of Sophocles in Tretyakov Passage – which, as Bibikova has noted, was the first such open-air production on a mass scale.

The fourth type was demonstrated by the Petrograd celebrations for the Second Congress of the Third International in July 1920, and was one development of this Moscow innovation. As a story of revolutionary events since the founding of the First Socialist International (the Paris 1871 Commune), it shared some of the same subject-matter of Gan's proposal. Conceptually however, it was only traditional theatre writ large, and served to demonstrate the inappropriateness of 'tedious slowness' and 'dull prose' to a mass spectacle.

The November celebrations in Petrograd that year offered yet a fifth model – one whose drama (as well as the avant-garde artists' participation) has made it so famous as to appear a type, but which took place only once. This was the great mass 're-enactment' *Storming the Winter Palace*. With ten thousand people and rich theatrical effects, this on-site replay of how the Tsar's palace had been 'stormed' by Revolutionaries in 1917 was far more dramatic (and more damaging to the building) than the original event. Documents 43 and 44 are the director's own account and a journalist's commentary.

Lenin's New Economic Policy (NEP), was adopted by the Russian Communist Party's Tenth Congress in March 1921. The Moscow May Day celebrations that year, like most festivals thereafter, were dominated by economic and industrial themes and sharply topical political propaganda.

From this period onwards, descriptions of the events themselves are self-explanatory. It is the commentators' asides which illuminate the changing larger context. Thus in Document 46 the inward-looking 'family atmosphere' of a somewhat 'frowning' Moscow in November 1921 reflects the famine of that winter, while the exchanges of 'business reports' reflect the new expansion of private trading under NEP. Reference in the same document to 'the new beginnings of everyday life' is at one level a statement of relief that 'peacefully . . . reconstructing our real surroundings' is possible again after the upheavals of the Civil War. At another, it refers to the great campaign for a 'reconstruction of everyday life', the *perestroika byta*, which launched the cultural and social-psychological dimension of the Revolution programme. A year later, the *Izvestiya* report in Document 48 reminds us poignantly that 'this is the first October festival without the thunder of weapons at the front and without the bony spectre of a hungry death'.

If civil war, foreign intervention and famine were now past, so too were the headier days of avant-garde experimentation in the visual language of these festivals. 'This time, in contrast with previous years when futurism [ie, avant-gardism] dominated', wrote *Izvestiya*, everything was kept 'realistic' and hence 'more accessible to the untutored observer.' So it continued to be. The battles were now largely economic, and nicely symbolized in Document 49 with a float where 'Soviet co-operation' beats the life out of an over-rich private merchant called 'NEP-mug . . . with a huge model hammer'.

Late December 1922 saw the creation of the USSR as a single state, and in Document 50 the Communist Party recognizes it could now relax that 'rigid centralization of festivities' which was 'only necessary before to demonstrate the strength and power of the Soviet Republic to the West.' The 'foreign diplomatic presence in Moscow this year' was another reflection of the new world standing. As ever more innovative than Petrograd, largely under the influence of Proletkult, Moscow enjoyed a 'Symphony in A' on steam heating-pipes and factory sirens for the Revolutionary festival of 1923.

On 21 January 1924 Lenin died. Ten days later, the Second Congress of Soviets approved the new Constitution, and renamed Petrograd in his memory. Through February and March the new nation started establishing diplomatic relations successively with Britain, Italy, Austria, Norway and Sweden. It had much to celebrate, but as Document 55 records, this 'first May Day since Lenin's death' was 'funereal'. For all the treaties, the external political threat remained, and vast caricatures of capitalist politicians were increasingly used to ensure that the populace did not forget it. But the most interesting phenomenon then, at mid-decade, was the development of self-conscious analysis of the genre itself and the emerging typologies of festival production.

At the start of the decade there was still debate about whether ancient Greek myth could be appropriate subject-matter for allegorical presentation in Soviet festivals. By mid-decade that illusion of the intelligentsia that the workers were like them had gone. The subject-matter of allegory now was 'the triumph of socialism', 'the independence of the USSR' or the old Marxist theme of 'linking the town and the countryside'. Also gone was the illusion that the workers shared the intelligentsia's enthusiasm for abstraction in art.

May Day Celebrations 1920

37 *More than entertainment*

From an article by People's Commissar for Education
A. V. Lunacharsky 'On popular festivals', published in the
journal *Theatre Courier*

27 April–2 May 1920

. . . In general, any genuine democracy strives naturally
towards popular festivals. Democracy presupposes the free
life of the masses.

In order for the masses to make themselves felt, they
must outwardly manifest themselves, and this is possible
only when, to use Robespierre's phrase, they are their own
spectacle.

If organized masses march to music, sing in unison or
perform some extensive gymnastic manoeuvres or dances,
in other words, organize a kind of parade, then those
other, unorganized masses clustering round on all sides of
the streets and squares where the festival takes place, will
merge with the organized masses, and thus, one can say:
the whole people manifests its soul to itself. . . .

We must, however be on our guard against
entertainment alone. Some people believe that collective
creativity means a spontaneous, independent
manifestation of the will of the masses. But until social life
teaches the masses some kind of instinctive compliance
with a higher order and rhythm, one cannot expect the
throng to be able by itself to create anything but a lively
noise and the colourful coming and going of festively
dressed people.

This celebration should be organized just as anything
else in the world that has a tendency to produce a
profound aesthetic impression.

I think that this year's May Day festival will be a major
step forward in this sense.

Popular festivals should without fail be divided into two
quite different acts. Into a mass demonstration, in the
proper sense of the word, which presupposes the
movement of the masses from the outskirts to one centre,

121
122

or, if there are too many people, to 2–3 centres, where
some central action, such as an elevated symbolic
ceremony, takes place. This could be a performance, vast,
decorative, a firework display, it could be satirical or
ceremonial, or it could be the burning of enemy emblems,
etc., accompanied by loud choral singing, by harmonious
and many-voiced music, bearing the nature of celebration
in the proper sense of the word.

The second act would be celebrations of a more intimate
kind either indoors, where all premises are turned into a
kind of revolutionary cabaret, or out of doors: on trams,
moving lorries, or simply on tables, barrels, etc. Here all
kinds of activity are possible such as fiery revolutionary
speeches, the recital of satirical verse, performances by
clowns with some kind of caricature of enemy forces, or
topical dramatic sketches, and much much more. But, it is
essential that any dramatized variety show of this kind is
tendentious. It would be good if it is imbued with
uncontrollable, uninhibited laughter, etc.

Vestnik teatra (Theatre Courier), no. 62, 27 April–2 May 1920, p. 13.

MOSCOW

38 *A constructive approach*

A proposal for the organization of the May Day festivities
on the streets of Moscow, drawn up by the Section of Mass
Performances and Spectacles of the Theatrical
Department of the Commissariat for Education,
Narkompros, published in the journal *Theatre Courier*

5–8 February 1920

The task facing the Section of Mass Performances and
Spectacles from the first moment of its activity has been to
work out the first scenario of mass action, and to work out
a magnificent drama in which the whole city would be the
stage and the entire proletarian masses of Moscow the
performers. What is more, the Section has chosen the

correct path. The scenario should be written by the masses themselves in the process of collective work and collective discussion.

The Section is working out only the general principles, a plan for the festivities, which will then be sent for discussion by various proletarian groups: clubs, studios, committees, etc. The detailed work of these groups will serve as material for the final scenario.

Initially, the Section proposed the idea of using an ancient myth as the theme of the festivities, interpreted symbolically in the sense of the struggle of the proletariat against capitalism. The myth of Prometheus was suggested, a myth both rich in content and extensively developed in world literature.

But then the section came to the conclusion that it would be wrong to restore Greek myths during the celebration of 1 May. They are alien to the proletarian masses and in no way reflect the latter's own ideology or feelings.

The first proletarian festival should protect the purity of its idea from any deposits of alien cults, from Biblical myths or Christian rites, even from the civic festivities of the French Revolution.

The Section acknowledged May Day to be an integral festival of proletarian culture and adopted A. M. Gan's suggestion of basing it on the idea of the International, from which the international festival historically emerges as the first act of mass creativity on a world scale.

The content of the festivities is to be the history of the three Internationals. The proletariat, having travelled in the course of history the path to socialism via three internationals, must travel this path during the May Day celebrations in theatrical forms, giving a vivid portrayal of the great achievements of the October Revolution, the Soviet system and of the transition to forms of socialist life. A. M. Gan has elaborated in detail the decorative side of the festivities, the lay-out of the 'stage' on which the festivities are to develop, and which will ultimately expand to envelop not only the entire city of Moscow, but even its outskirts.

The overall task of this decorative plan is to imagine the Communist city of the future. All the squares on which the action is to take place will be named after sciences and arts. For example, Geography Square – with a huge globe on which the continents are painted in the red shades of a flaming world revolution – Astronomy Square, Political Economy Square, and so on.

The streets will be decorated with red flags and shop windows with satirical depictions on themes of a topical nature. Somewhere out of town (possibly at Khodynka) a field of the International will be set up with a wireless station and an aerodrome. The main action of the festivities will be played out on this field.

The part of the festival scenario elaborated in most detail by the Section is the prologue, which is outlined in the following form: early in the morning a loud siren will sound from Sparrow [now Lenin. *Ed.*] Hills, which will be answered by the horns of all the city's factories.

At this signal, cavalry patrols, motor-cycles and vehicles will leave the seventeen outposts of Moscow for the district squares, summoning citizens onto the streets. On the district squares they will be awaited by agitation collectives who will draw the people into active participation in the festival. Here the act of the First International will be performed.

On its completion, the masses will start moving towards the centre, passing along the streets and squares of the sciences and the arts. In the centre the celebration of the Second International will be held.

Finally, the crowds of citizens will move towards the field of the International where the collapse of the Second International will be played out, followed by the emergence of the Third and the transition to a socialist system. Along the way, intervals for rest and food will be organized, which will also take the form of theatre.

This is the basic outline of the plan for the May Day festivities. The Section is aware of the immense difficulties involved in putting this plan into practice. Its vast scope requires the use of totally new methods, and new creative devices.

Rehearsals with performers will have to take the form of manoeuvres with whole groups of people. The vast number of performers will mean that gestures and voices will have to be forgotten. Instead sound and movement will have to be regarded as elements from which to mould the theatrical part of the festivities.

The Section also has to devise methods to involve the masses in the festival action. In this area, V. S. Smyshlyaev has suggested a series of measures that would involuntarily force the masses to move away from passive contemplation to active participation, and would turn them from spectators into performers. The methods include: a series of easily surmountable obstacles along the route of the procession, the arrangement of the crowd into columns which would move in a previously determined direction under the guidance of organized groups, the ascent of steps and slopes, etc.

A number of ideas were also put forward at that first debate on 'mass participation' organized by the section in the Moscow Proletkult.

Mass pantomimes, the dramatization of all aspects of the procession, of rest and food intervals, the use of historical places connected with memories of revolutionary events, should all form part of the festival programme.

It must, however, be acknowledged that the very nucleus of the festivities has not yet been found; there is still only a vague outline of how the movement of individual collectives will be transformed into a harmonious, general 'participation' that is both theatrically fine and fascinating for the performers.

The newness of work in this field, with forms that are so majestic and so vast, fully explains the difficulty of every step. But the collective genius of the proletariat must overcome these difficulties and ultimately create a scenario that corresponds fully to the immensity of the tasks facing it.

Vestnik teatra (Theatre Courier), no. 51, 5–8 February 1920

When this same set of proposals was published in shortened form in the journal *Artistic Life* it was accompanied by the comment that:

The experience of such festivities, even if they are not completely successful, will nevertheless not be lost: it will accustom the masses to the concept of 'collective action' and mass theatre.

Khudozhestvennaya zhizn (Artistic Life), no. 2, 1920, pp. 25–6.

39 *A working subbotnik*

From a report on the organization of the 1920 May Day celebrations in Moscow, published in the journal *Theatre Courier*

27 April–2 May 1920

A May Day Committee, headed by O. D. Kameneva and organized by the Artistic Sub-section, has outlined the plan for the celebrations. The main principle of the decorative side is that there will be no new large painted posters on the streets of Moscow. Old posters, used in past popular festivals will be put on display again. On this occasion, coloured material, coloured paper and above all greenery will form the decorative materials used. . . . In amongst the greenery and patches of colour will be slogans such as 'May Day is a festival of labour, long live glorious labour'. . . . 'Down with parasites, landowners and the bourgeoisie!', 'Everything for the first great May Day *Subbotnik*' [day of voluntary labour. *Ed.*], 'Our May Day *Subbotnik* is a hundred times more frightening for the world bourgeoisie than all previous May Day demonstrations', . . . 'Down with laziness, glory to labour!', and many others. Red, Soviet and Triumphal Squares will be decorated by a collective from a camouflage school. Round the city thirty-five canteens will be decorated, two for adults and two for children for each district. All clubs and factories will also be adorned. Work on this day should be joyful and festive. . . .

At about 11 o'clock in the evening, a spectacle will take place on Tretyakov Passage. A troupe of the Third Battalion of a Guards Regiment . . . will perform Sophocles' tragedy *King Oedipus*. In the words of those staging the play, it is only a rough sketch, in view of the brevity of its preparation. Red Army men with a love of acting and professional actors at present doing national service will participate, and the women's roles will be played by actresses who permanently work with the troupe. The performance will be illuminated by search lights.

Vestnik teatra (Theatre Courier), no. 62, 27 April–2 May 1920, p. 13.

PETROGRAD

40 *Entertainments*

From the programme of the May Day Committee of the Petrograd Soviet of Workers' and Soldiers' Deputies, on mass entertainments during the 1920 May Day celebrations, published in the newspaper *Life of Art*

1–3 May 1920

These entertainments, which will begin at 7 o'clock in the evening at the sound of a signal from the Peter and Paul Fortress, are divided up according to the institutions organizing them and their venue:

A   Entertainments in the city centre

B   Entertainments organized in the city's districts.

Entertainments are being organized by the following establishments:

1   The Petrograd Theatrical Department.

2   State Academy Theatres.

3   The Musical Department.

4   The Narkompros Club Section.

5   The political departments of the Military Commissariat and the Baltic Fleet.

. . . .The Narkompros Club Section is organizing a pantomime-type dramatization in all districts on the theme of 'slave labour, transforming into joyous construction'. The dramatization will be staged on mobile tramcars at the following places:

a   Trinity Bridge.

b   The square in front of St Isaac's Cathedral.

c   Uprising Square (*Ploshchad Vosstaniya*).

d   At the Moscow Gates (in the morning before the procession).

In the afternoon stages on trams and lorries will run round the city, from which the following productions will be given:

1   Radlov (2 stages) – *The Monkey Informer* and *The Intrigues of Capitalism and the Magic Concertina.*

2   Solovyov – *The Happiness of King Mahomet's Planet* and *The Love of Petrushka, who loves pears.*

3   Rappoport – *The Wooing* and *Mandragora*. . . .

Entertainments in the city centre, in turn, are distributed thus:

Near the Summer Gardens gondolas with singers, mandolin players and guitarists will glide along the Neva, the Fontanka, the Moika and the Lebyazhy Canals. The Military Commissariat will set up a group of fanfare trumpeters on the upper terrace of the Engineer's Castle facing the Summer Gardens, and the Commissariat's political department (under the direction of N. N. Arbatov) will stage the tragedy *Hippolytus* on the steps beneath this terrace.

The former Archangel Choir will perform several songs on a raft on the pond in the Summer Gardens; one of the troupes which travelled round the town will give a performance from its repertoire near the avenue along the side of Revolution Victims' Square, while on the square around the 'sleeping Psyche', a troupe from the Academic Opera and Ballet Theatre will perform Glück's opera *The May Queen*, illuminated by a searchlight erected on the Peter and Paul Fortress. . . .

The Petrograd Theatrical Department will organize an improvised show and a balalaika group on a platform in front of the pavilion on the Fontanka side of the gardens while a troupe of the Military Commissariat's Political Department will stage *Petrushka* on the central stage beside the small pavilion. . . .

A photograph and cinema committee has taken measures to record all the May Day pageants. Films with May Day slogans will be shown on some streets, chiefly in working-class workers' districts.

Zhizn iskusstva (Life of Art), no. 439–41, 1–3 May 1930

Second Congress of the Third International

PETROGRAD

41 *A mass dramatization*

From P. Kudelli's article 'A new pageant at the portal of the Stock Exchange', published in *Petrograd Pravda*

21 July 1920

The portal of the Stock Exchange, to which in times gone by only the trotters of stockbrokers and those in search of easy profit used to drive, has once again been disturbed by an unusual spectacle. On May Day we saw *The Overthrow of the Autocracy* here, and on 19 July, a splendid new mass dramatization entitled *Towards a World Commune* took place in honour of the Second Congress of the Third International.[1]

What can we say about it? I would so much like just to praise it, just to find expression in eulogies, because undoubtedly the future will perceive such pageants as a vital part of every public festival, and that is why every attempt in this area is so dear to us, but unfortunately we cannot give a totally favourable reaction.

Towards a World Commune encompasses far too complicated events from the First International down to our day, including both the February and October of the great Russian Revolution. Not everyone could compile an artistic fictional scenario round all these historical events. Indeed this is something only a major artist could do after a more or less detailed study of the revolutionary movement in the principal European countries over more than half a century of the life of mankind. The haste with which the scenario was written could be felt in everything, in the scenario itself and in its performance.

The scenario did not give a clear picture of the epoch. We saw nothing but a dramatization of dull prose, written with the aim of giving a historical study from the First to the Third International.

This dullness led to tedious slowness and utterly inartistic prose.

Petrogradskaya Pravda (Petrograd Pravda), no. 159, 21 July 1920

1 Kudelli made a mistake here, since the dramatization in front of the Stock Exchange on May Day 1920 was *The Anthem of Liberated Labour*, not *The Overthrow of the Autocracy*, though such a mistake is surprising as more than 30,000 inhabitants of Petrograd saw the dramatization performed.

MAY DAY, 1920

May Day, 1920, Petrograd, designs by the Lebedevs for a tram carrying a mobile theatre group

119   Sarra Lebedeva, two sketches for satirical posters to decorate the mobile tramway theatre, caricaturing the White Russian General Denikin (left) and 'Ruination' (right).

120   (*below*) Vladimir Lebedev, sketch for a poster panel on a mobile theatre platform to be carried round Petrograd on a tram. The slogan between the flail and chains says of the imperial figure above 'This is a museum-piece citizen!!! Gather round and have a good stare!!!'

May Day, 1920, Petrograd

121 A motorcar decorated with hammer, flags, greenery and a model globe, in the streets.

122 A tramcar moves through crowds in the Field of Mars area, bearing the slogans 'Long live the First of May' and 'Long live Communists of the whole world!' The banner in the right foreground, apparently borne by 'The 35th Soviet School', declares that 'The path to the new way of life lies through the school'.

SECOND COMINTERN CONGRESS, 1920

Second Congress of the Third International, July 1920, Petrograd, mass performance on the Stock Exchange steps

123   Scene from the mass enactment of *Towards a World Commune* on the Stock Exchange steps, described by Khudelli in Document 41 as attempting to portray a 'far too complicated' sequence of historical events, and clearly using a trivial and traditional form of decoration far removed from Altman's bold conception (see next page).

124   The popular participants on the side colonnades. The banners above them wish long life to the Third International and urge 'the proletariat of the world to unite' in various languages. The performers' banners read 'Land to the people', 'Factories to the workers', 'Power to the soviets' and 'The blood of Hungarian workers calls us to vengeance'.

Second Congress of the Third International, July 1920, Petrograd, mass performance on the Stock Exchange steps

125, 126 (*above and right*) Natan Altman, two variants of a proposal for decorating the Stock Exchange building as a stage set for the mass dramatization of *Towards a World Commune.* Both variants involve visually splitting the colonnade into two parts by wrapping only the outer three columns in red cloth; then building a garden of green triangles and prisms in the centre and raising a vast golden sphere over the colonnade to create a coloured abstraction of the play itself. In one variant the slogan on the pediment is 'Proletariat of all countries unite!'; in the other it is 'The Sun of the October Revolution has risen'.

127 (*below*) Boris Kustodiev, a painting of 1921 recording celebrations on Uritsky Square to honour the Second Congress of the Third International. The Winter Palace forms the background, and the base of the Alexander Column stands on the right.

THIRD ANNIVERSARY, *1920*

*Third Anniversary of the Revolution, 1920,
Petrograd, mass theatrical re-enactment,
'Storming the Winter Palace'*

128   The moment of attack from Red side to
White across the connecting bridge.

129   Yuri Annenkov's design sketch for the re-
enactment, showing the General Staff building
divided into the Red side, with factories, and
the White, with Tsarist throne room, and
connecting bridge (see Document 44).

Third Anniversary of the Revolution, 1920, Petrograd, mass theatrical re-enactment, 'Storming the Winter Palace'

130 (*above left*) Around the Throne Room on the White side, where the banner, left, advertises 'The Freedom Loan'.

131 (*below left*) Amidst the factories of the Red side.

132 (*above right*) Workers who in early scenes were 'disorganized' became co-ordinated and turned into Red Guards. They threaten the bourgeois.

133 (*below right*) Close-up of the bourgeoisie around their money-bags contemplating 'The Freedom Loan', with Kerensky presiding.

MAY DAY AND THIRD CONGRESS, 1921

May Day, 1921, Moscow, Sverdlov Square

134   (*below*) Decorative installation diagrams and statistics about the national importance of oil 'for a better life and a shorter route to a great future'.

Third Congress of the Third International, May 1921, Petrograd

135   (*right*) Liubov Popova and Alexander Vesnin, design for a theatricalized parade of the troops, showing the old city on the left and the new mechanized city on the right.

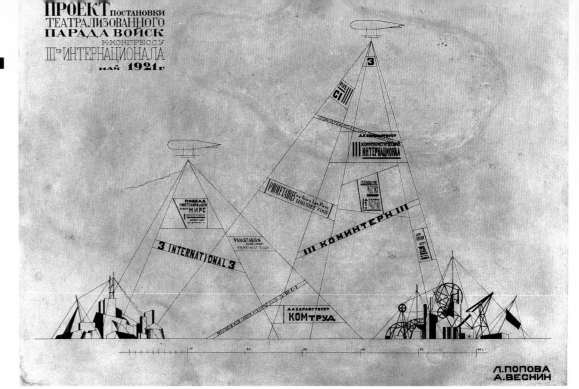

Third Anniversary of the October Revolution

MOSCOW

42 *Conventional celebrations*

From a report on the plan for celebrating the Third Anniversary of the Revolution in Moscow, published in the journal *Theatre Courier*

9–17 October 1920

The arts section of MONO (the Moscow Department of Education) has drawn up a plan for the artistic sphere of the October Revolution festivities, approved at the present time by the Celebration Commission. This plan envisages four parts: decorations, theatres and concerts, cinematography and children's entertainments.

All canteens and clubs in Moscow will be decorated for the festivities – some with monumental decorative frescoes, paintings and sculptures on educative and propaganda themes, others with temporary decorations.

A special competition for architects, artists and sculptors has been organized for the purpose of the strictly artistic decoration of the central squares. The problem of decorating squares should not be solved through paintings alone. At the same time a contest will be held for models reproducing the three central squares in Moscow: Soviet Square, Red Square and Sverdlov Square. The streets and buildings will be decorated with slogans, and it has been decided not to undertake large decorative works in view of the altogether limited quantity of materials, especially paint. . . .

It has been decided to send Moscow workers' theatre groups with revolutionary and classical repertoires and Proletkult workshops, and studios and schools of the Theatrical Department [of MONO] to villages outside Moscow.

In the sphere of cinema special pictures on the October Revolution and revolutionary slogans will be issued for the celebrations.

Cinemas will work longer hours and special film screens will be erected on the streets.

Vestnik teatra (Theatre Courier), no. 70, 9–17 October 1920, p. 14.

PETROGRAD

43 *To storm the Winter Palace*

From an interview with N. N. Yevreinov, Director of the mass dramatization of *Storming the Winter Palace*, to be enacted on Uritsky Square on 6 November 1920, published in the newspaper *Life of Art*

30–31 [sic] September 1920

N. N. YEVREINOV   The collective of authors comprised ten of Petrograd's best directors and this team worked enthusiastically and extremely smoothly. All the same, an immense project was handed to the director, namely myself, and as a theatrical historian and theoretician I can assure you that the production is of unprecedented complexity. Three stages are to appear simultaneously: two conventional theatrical stages and one real, historical stage. On the first stage, events will be portrayed in the style of comedy; on the second, in the style of a heroic drama, and on the third, in the style of a battle. The director will have to find a common denominator, some purely theatrical style, to unify all three.

. . . Our method of work will be artistic simplification. But it is not enough to co-ordinate the three styles, we also have to co-ordinate mass action on these three platforms, or stages. This co-ordination, incidentally, is ingeniously achieved by plunging each platform by turns into darkness and brightly illuminating the area of the theatrical arena to which the spectator's attention should be drawn.

The action will take place not only on the stages, but also on a bridge between them and on the ground, across which the Provisional Government will run attempting to escape from the pursuing proletariat, and in the air where aeroplanes will soar and bells and factory sirens will sound.

Apart from ten thousand performers – actors and persons mobilized from the drama groups of the Red Army and Navy units – inanimate characters will also take part in the production. Even the Winter Palace itself will be involved as a gigantic actor, as a vast character in the play which will manifest its own mimicry and inner emotions. The director must make the stones speak, so that the spectator feels what is going on inside, behind those cold red walls. We have found an original solution to this problem, using a cinematographic technique: each one of the fifty windows of the first floor will in turn show a moment of the development of the battle inside.

In the form of silhouetted groups, pieces of the immense action will light up and vanish in the darkness until everything ends with the finale of shots, hooters and sirens, and lighting effects: fireworks and flags.

Zhizn iskusstva (Life of Art), no. 596–97, 30–31 September 1920

44 *Action*

From the article by N. Shubsky, 'On Uritsky Square', describing the mass dramatization of *Storming the Winter Palace*, published in the journal *Theatre Courier*

30 November 1920

. . . Towards evening the rain died down and the inhabitants of St Petersburg arrived, perhaps not in the number that had been expected, but none the less, at an approximate estimate, at least thirty thousand. And this whole mass of people, who had streamed in from all sides of the city, stood with its back to the Winter Palace, facing the arch of the General Headquarters, where a huge stage had been constructed, consisting of two platforms – a white and a red – connected by a bridge and filled with structures and scenery . . . representing factories and enterprises on the red platform and a 'throne room' on the white platform.

At 10 o'clock a gun boomed and the commander's platform attached to Alexander's Column gave the signal to start. The arched bridge flashed and eight trumpeters gave an introductory fanfare. Then they vanished again into the darkness. In the silence Litolf's 'Robespierre', performed by the symphony orchestra of the Political Administration of the Petrograd Military District, sounded splendid. And the show began.

It proceeded alternately on the white platform, the red or on the bridge between them.

The characters on the white platform were Kerensky, the Provisional Government, dignitaries and grandees of the old regime, the women's batallion, the *junkers*, bankers and merchants, front-line soldiers, cripples and invalids, enthusiastic ladies and gentlemen of a conciliatory type.

The red platform was more 'impersonal'. There it was the mass that reigned, first drab, foolish and unorganized, but then increasingly active, orderly and powerful. Roused by 'militias', it turned into the Red Guard, made fast with crimson banners.

The action was built on the struggle between the two platforms. It began with the Bolshevik June uprising and ended with the square on which the fate of the powerless ministers was decided.

The bridge between the two worlds was the arena of their clashes. This is where people fought and killed, here people triumphed and from here they retreated.

The first light that illuminated the whites showed their triumph in caricatured form. To the strains of the 'Marseillaise', arranged as a Polonaise, Kerensky appeared before the expectant ladies and gentlemen. The actor who played Kerensky, dressed in the characteristic khaki, captured the premier's gestures very well and provoked particular attention among the crowd. . . .

But meanwhile the revolution continued. . . . The red platform became more organized after suffering losses; troops went over to the side of the 'Leninists'. And the ministers sitting at a table peacefully in their top hats, rocked amusingly in their seats, like little Chinese idols.

Then came the moment of escape and vehicles started rumbling near the steps leading down from the white platform to the wooden pavement.

There they rushed, caught by the beam of a searchlight, and artillery roared. The air resounded with the volleys fired from the *Aurora*, anchored on the Neva, the rattle of rifles and machine guns.

Then the action transferred to the Winter Palace. Light would flash on in the windows of the sleeping giant and the figures of people fighting would be visible. The attack ended. The Palace was captured. The banner of the victors appeared deep purple out of the darkness above the palace. Five red stars lit up on the pediment. Then rockets went up and diamond-like stars lit up the sky, and waterfalls of fireworks gushed down in a rain of sparks.

The 'Internationale' sounded and the parade of the victors began, illuminated by the searchlights and fireworks. . . .

This is a general outline of what the spectators gathered on Uritsky Square witnessed in the course of an hour and a quarter.

Vestnik teatra (Theatre Courier), no. 75, 30 November 1920, pp. 4–5.

May Day Celebrations 1921

MOSCOW

45 *New emphasis*

From a report on the May Day celebrations in Moscow published in the newspaper *Izvestiya*

4 May 1921

On the eve of the holiday Moscow was beautifully tidied and decorated. The city was unrecognizable. Nature herself came to the aid of the artists and decorators. A light shower bathed the streets and trees, giving them a fresh spring appearance. . . .

The streets were already full of life at ten o'clock in the morning. Everyone was making his or her way to Theatre Square, Strastnaya Square and Red Square.

The entire avenue leading to the Bolshoi Theatre was covered and hung with artistic posters depicting the various branches of industry in the Republic. There were also explanatory diagrams and figures. There was a 'living' diagram showing coal output in a very beautiful and original way using especially constructed red columns. This original exhibition attracted the attention of workers who immediately started discussions about the fuel, timber and so on illustrated in the diagram. The entrance to the Bolshoi Theatre was barricaded by a stage constructed for Proletkult's presentation.

During the day in different areas of Moscow – and late at night on Strastnaya Square – there were readings of the ROSTA Living Newspaper [ROSTA was the Russian Telegraph Agency. *Ed.*]. The readings were accompanied by misty news pictures projected on large screens. These 'living newspapers' were enormously successful with the public.

Izvestiya VTsIK, no. 94, 4 May 1921

134

Fourth Anniversary of the October Revolution

MOSCOW

46 *For the children*

Extract from a report on the celebration of the Fourth Anniversary of the October Revolution in various districts of Moscow, published in *Pravda*

9 November 1921

The streets are quiet just as they were yesterday. There are no hurriedly constructed platforms decorated with red panels; nor are there any new futurist posters proclaiming our victories. Everything looks just as it does every day. There is not even one crowd of demonstrators gathering early to mark the coming fourth anniversary of proletarian rule in Moscow; there is not even one extra shout to be heard in this populous city. Outwardly the city is frowning and concentrated. It is as if Moscow had shut itself up in its own shell. Life seems to have gone inwards and to have ensconced itself inside the factories, clubs and professional organizations.

People are going to meetings but there is somehow a family atmosphere. Business reports take their turn with reminiscences about the days of the revolution. Then there are concerts and plays are performed. The new beginnings of everyday life are put into the framework of our transition towards the peaceful construction of our real surroundings. Here there is a factory building crowded with workers. There are men and women. A sea of heads. It sways and swells with a gentle buzz. The weak attempts at decoration are hardly noticeable; there is a narrow thread of pine twigs and something resembling little flags over the cornice. However, the very iron girders stretching from wall to wall and the exposed emptiness above them give the evening a feeling of solemnity. The stage, brightening up one corner of the hall, is colourful with revolutionary slogans on red panels.

In the districts:

On 6 and 7 November proletarian Moscow joyfully celebrated the great days when workers gained their emancipation. The celebrations were modest in character. During the day on 6 November children's festivals were organized in all areas; these attracted tens of thousands of workers' children to theatres, clubs and children's establishments. At night, evenings of reminiscences took place in meeting halls, at theatres and in workplaces with hundreds of thousands of proletarians taking part.

Pravda, no. 256, 9 November 1921

PETROGRAD

Press reports on the Fourth Anniversary celebrations in Petrograd indicate their restraint.

There were only modest decorations in the streets with just a few decorated points in the city and some illuminations in the evenings to remind us of the important day of the October Revolution anniversary.

Krasnaya gazeta (The Red Newspaper), no. 231, 9 November 1921

May Day Celebrations 1922

MOSCOW AND PETROGRAD

47 *Modest and quiet*

Press reports on the May Day celebrations of 1922 in both Moscow and Petrograd indicate that like those of Petrograd for the previous October anniversary, they were modest and restrained.

Izvestiya VTsIK, no. 96, 3 May 1922
Krasnaya gazeta (The Red Newspaper), no. 94, 3 May 1922

Fifth Anniversary of the October Revolution

MOSCOW

48 *After Civil War*

Extract from an article by Z. Richter, 'The decorative attire of Moscow on the eve of the fifth anniversary of the Great October Revolution', published in *Izvestiya*

5 November 1922

We are on the eve of the greatest proletarian festival, the Red equivalent of Christmas. Moscow in the evening sparkles with lights and is herself like a Christmas tree decorated with flags. . . . It is early winter, more like spring. There are sledges and the horns and sirens of lorries laden with greenery and new cars merrily decked with red flags, there is the hustle and bustle of pre-holiday crowds . . . and the man in the street is hung about with packets and purchases. It is the first October festival without the thunder of weapons at the front and without the bony spectre of a hungry death. Moscow is hurriedly decorating herself with greenery and flags. Red Square – the place of the parade – can be seen framed by the ancient arches of the Iverskaya Chapel. A red stone platform in the style of the Kremlin walls has been erected and towering above it is a gigantic monument of a worker greeting the people – this monument is formless at the moment under its sacking cover [the sculptor was F. K. Lekht; see next document. *Ed.*]. Craftsmen and sculptors are busy beside the monument; they look like magicians or wizards as they finish off its installation by the light of a bonfire. On the wall, surrounded by garlands of greenery, is already blazing the slogan 'Glory to the fallen, fight to the end for the living'. On the empty square, army divisions are rehearsing for the parade like extras in an unlit, empty theatre. They are dressed in brand new regimental uniforms with stripes of various colours which, moving around, resemble a gaily coloured kaleidoscope. On Theatre Square, by the Soviet building on Tverskaya

Street, there are mountains of greenery and hammers clang as artists and decorators climb up firemen's ladders to decorate the buildings. This time, in contrast with previous years when futurism dominated all, the decorations and posters keep to a simple, realistic style, more accessible to the untutored observer.

Izvestiya VTsIK, no. 251, 5 November 1922

49 *Industry and the Forces*

Extract from a report about the celebration of the Fifth Anniversary of the Revolution in Moscow, from *Pravda*

9 November 1922

On the streets of Moscow

In the Rogozhsko-Simonovsky district:
The district came to life very early in the morning. Groups of workers came from all directions to gather at the meeting points. Taganka Square was decorated with flags. In the middle of the square there was a decorative tableau showing workers, peasants and Red Army soldiers in the sunrise glow of the Revolution. At the entrance to the square there were ornamental gates with slogans. . . .

In the Khamovnichesky district:
The meeting point of this district – the Soviet Building – was decorated with portraits of Marx and Lenin, with greenery and posters. Men and women workers gathered for eleven o'clock in the morning. Workers from the Goznak factory came with their band. Workers from the Kauchuk (Rubber) factory came with a model of an airship emblazoned with the slogan 'Red rubber for the red air force'. The strains of revolutionary songs could be heard from all directions.

In the Bauman district:
. . . A procession stretched for about a mile and a half from

the Soviet Building. There was an endless line of demonstrators along Nemetskaya Street. Workers from the Fourth State Mill erected a mill with turning sails on a lorry. A full-size portrait of Comrade Lenin was artistically painted on the wall of the Spartacus Club Building. . . .

In the Krasnopresnya district:
Separate workers' divisions gathered from early morning on Georgievskaya Square heading for the Krasnopresnya District Committee Building. The crowd grew larger every minute. At the head of the procession a memorial plaque was carried with the words 'To the eternal memory of those who fought for the October Revolution'. This was followed by the banners of the regional committee and the Young Communist League and by innumerable posters with slogans.

The procession heading for Red Square began to the sounds of an orchestra. There was a long chain of workers from the Trekhgornaya Factory, the Miussky Tram Park, the Alexandrov Railway, the Dukat Factory and others. On one float a large model steam engine – the railway workers' emblem – emerged from behind red banners. On the corner of Strastnaya Square there were two decorated steamers on wheels with the slogan 'Three cheers for the skipper of the ship of the universal revolution, Comrade Lenin'. . . .

Tverskaya Square in its entirety was turned into a workers' camp and was drowning in red paint and in the greenery decorating the buildings. There was an unremitting buzz of voices and music. People's faces were happy and festive. In the air could be seen a line of aeroplanes. 'Three cheers for the Red Air Force' sounded the loud collective greeting. . . .

In the Transriver district:
The District Soviet and the District Committee headed the procession. They were followed by a group of seamen with a large model of a dreadnought of the 'Marat' class called Comintern. Behind the dreadnought there was a mine-carrier of the 'Novik' class. Behind these vessels there was a large procession of 'Knights' bearing caricatures of Poincaré, Lloyd George and others.

Workers from the former Mikhelson Factory (now called Vladimir Ilyich) came to the demonstration with a large peat machine; the factory has produced forty such machines now at work in Kashirka and other places. Every

137

136

single factory and enterprise of the Transriver district came to the demonstration with an original emblem of its products. . . .

On Red Square:
Strings of red flags were attractively hung out on Red Square, along the Kremlin wall, in front of the communal graves and on both sides of the rostrums. Near to the platforms erected for the guests of the Comintern hung a white monolith, about four and a half metres in height, depicting a worker holding a hammer and an anvil in one hand and, in the other, a hat with which he greets the approaching demonstration. This is the work of the sculptor Lekht and was brilliantly produced under exceptionally unfavourable conditions. There was such a frost that, in order to be able to make the statue, it was necessary to work under a tarpaulin to warm up the surrounding atmosphere and to heat the freezing water on a fire. Behind the rostrum there was a row of specially painted revolutionary pictures, in enormous frames, along the whole length of the square by the communal graves.

A Day of Symbols:
These festivities marking the October Revolution are a total and splendid examination of what the revolution has achieved. And every moment of the celebrations, every part of each event becomes automatically a symbol in the consciousness of the masses, of all who take part and of all who watch. It is only necessary to listen to the conversations and to the orators' speeches. . . .

Nevertheless, the sense of order and balance in the mass movements is remarkable. The astonishment and joy of those who watch from the Comintern rostrum is noticeable: it is all in such contrast to the Asiatic chaos, lack of discipline and contagious disorder which the entire bourgeois ideological world is always sounding off about. . . .

A new stone rostrum having the architectural form of the Kremlin walls and towers has been erected on the square itself and seems to be a symbol of our new strength. It is now no longer the same quickly knocked up dais from which the speeches of our revolutionary leaders have rung for the last four years. Now, this year, it is from one of the strongholds of the Kremlin that the calls for freedom sound, tolling the knell for all the old world.

The white and very artistic figure of the worker greeting the demonstrators is a new symbol of enormous enthusiasm.

Opposite there is another symbol. There is a colourful panel, on the pedestal of the monument to Minin and Pozharsky, and it shows a worker, surrounded by a glittering rainbow of fire, and hammering red-hot iron with such powerful strokes that sparks like lightning penetrate throughout the universe.

Above the rostrum, like a shining scarlet cobweb, flutters the fine silk banner of the RSFSR, raised by a pulley. . . .

In the sea of banners there were extraordinarily many unexpected symbolically commanding ideas. In the procession there were battleships, carriages, printing machines, mills and steam engines. Workers from the Alexandrov Factory even had smoke coming from the chimney of their varnished locomotive. With a huge model hammer, workers from the 'Soviet Co-operative' were beating a bearded private merchant called Nep-mug. [NEP-men were those who took advantage of private enterprise incentives under Lenin's New Economic Policy, or NEP, to make money for themselves ruthlessly. *Ed.*] Surrounded by howls of laughter a huge worm crawled along with a smoking capitalist astride it. The conviction could be felt that from here, from this demonstration, the political satire and propaganda would fly out and would hasten round the whole world to become popular with workers all over the globe.

Products of our factories were hoisted on poles and carried ceremoniously on high. Hovering above the crowds were colossal cigarettes, boots and pencils which were well-sharpened and the size of tree trunks.

'It's hard to write but to fight is easy' joked the Red Army soldiers. And the columns of demonstrators floated past with their thousands of banners and symbols. Symbols, symbols, everywhere there were shining, splendid, bright symbols of bright hopes.

Pravda, no. 253, 9 November 1922

May Day Celebrations 1923

MOSCOW

50 *A truly festive occasion*

Extract from the minutes of a meeting of the Regional May Day Commission of the Moscow Committee of the Russian Communist Party about the celebrations for 1 May 1923 in Moscow

20 April 1923

1   We listened to a debate: about the principles of the celebrations:

a   After a short informative address by Comrade Mikhailov [Secretary of the Moscow Committee] on the forthcoming celebrations of 1 May, opinions were given about the principles which should determine the entire character and direction of the celebrations this year. Opinions divided in the following way: Comrades Zheltov [Moscow Soviet], Okulova [Political Education Department], Alexandrov [Moscow Committee of the Young Communist League] and Yakovlev [Commandant of the City], held that we should finally move away from the compulsory and warlike atmosphere which has characterized previous May day celebrations. Strict demonstrations and parades only exhaust the workers and even evoke some discontent. This week the participation of some million demonstrators is expected and it would take until late in the evening for them all to cross Red Square so that all the festive part of the celebrations would come to nothing. The First of May should be a truly festive occasion allowing workers, enterprises and districts a true freedom of action as well as independence and initiative. All the festivities should be concentrated in local areas and should be characterized by walks in the countryside, dances, carnival processions, singing, street theatre, etc.

We should reject the rigid centralization of the festivities which was only necessary before to demonstrate the strength and power of the Soviet Republic to the West.

Comrades Mikhailov, Breslav [Political Administrator of the Moscow Military District], Goncharova [Propaganda Section] and Antonov [Moscow Trade Union Organization] disagreed with the opinions of Comrades Zheltov *et al*. They held that a demonstration of the power of the Soviet Republic and of the trust which the working masses have in it is politically essential this year because of the foreign diplomatic presence in Moscow and the members of the Communist International gathering for the May Day celebrations. Transferring festivities to local areas would disperse the celebrations and would make it impossible to calculate the results of the day. If the demonstration and the parades give the day too military a flavour, then measures must be taken to blend an artistic and carnival element into the general demonstration and it would be possible to do this. The Moscow-wide scope of the demonstration also has an educational significance for the worker, evoking in him a feeling of collective consciousness.

b   About the parade.

c   About the slogans which should accompany the celebrations.

When a vote took place as to whether there should be a rigidly centralized all-Moscow demonstration or to reject this in favour of local festivities, the commission was equally divided. There were four votes for the demonstration (Mikhailov, Breslav, Goncharova and Antonov) and four votes against the demonstration (Zheltov, Okulova, Alexandrov and Yakovlev); there were four votes for the organization of the parade (Mikhailov, Breslav, Yakovlev and Antonov) and four against (Goncharova, Okulova, Zheltov and Alexandrov). . . .

d   The following slogans were chosen:

i   The struggle with the international bourgeoisie

ii   The culture front

iii   The rebirth of the economy

2   We heard a report on the creation of a sub-committee: It was decided to establish the following sub-committees: Artistic (Okulova, Sukhanov, Alexandrov, Dashkova and Pletnev); Route (Yakovlev and one representative from each of the districts); Literature and Publishing (Stukov, Vasilchenko and Ginzburg); Economic and Budget (Samsonov); Children's (Krupenina). . . .

For the Chairperson Goncharova
Secretary Kovalenko

GAMO, f.66, op.12, d.1244, l.191.

138
139

51 *Fun in the streets*

Extract from a report on the May Day festivities in the districts of Moscow, published in the newspaper *Workers' Moscow*

3 May 1923

The Bauman district:
At the head there was a tank and an armoured car – these headed the Cherkizov column. They were a gift from the Red Army armoured tank factory on the occasion of 1 May and they set off first. Behind them came the radio factory. They had set up a field radio-station on a lorry. The other Cherkizov enterprises followed one by one.

From Blagushi by the Semyonovsky Gates the colour of it stretched, with workers from the Icarus, Mastyazhart, Semyonov, Rais and other factories.

The Icarus plant displayed one of its products – a real aeroplane with its internal workings open.

Komsomol members with their carnival chariots were spread out along Pokrovskaya Street. Everyone was on the receiving end, especially priests. There was a real bell-tower and a weeping priest – everything was done in an inimitable way. Every factory wanted to better all the others with its inventiveness. And each of them did something original.

The Rogozhsko-Simonov (Taganka) district:
There are decorated trams. People in disguise. The carnival is coming. On the rostrum are Comrades A. V. Lunacharsky, V. V. Kuibyshev and others.

The Sokolniki district:
In Sokolniki columns of demonstrators marched for five hours without ceasing. They passed along the decorated streets in a majestic way, calmly, with music and songs. To meet the columns went a long line of decorated trams and cars filled to bursting-point with gaily dressed children. . . .

The three stations and the customs halls on Kalanchevskaya Square were drowning in greenery and red calico. The brightly painted Sukharev area was unrecognizable and bands thundered out into the quiet residential Meshchanskaya Street and beyond the Krestovskaya Gate. . . .

At the head of the columns of demonstrators were groups of people who were brightly dressed in costumes of many different nationalities; amusing little scenes of street theatre took place there and then on the march. These gave rise to lots of laughter. With a group of steam-engine workers from the Oktyabrsky Railway you could see a distorted Mussolini; apparently Poincaré could not take such a picture of tightly knit workers, he stood fidgeting with his hands and eyeing the crowd with a glassy stare.

The former Blandov Factory staged a sketch about capitalism. Comrade G. V. Chicherin walked at the head of the Red Sokolniki bakers and drew after him a long pack of foreign leaders. Leather-workers carried an immense banner of red leather – strong for future battles and useful for the boots of Red Army men.

Sewing-workers had a banner showing a seamstress at a machine. Mill-workers chose for their slogan 'A sack of rye flour weighing four poods'. [A pood was a traditional Russian measure equivalent to 16.5 kg. *Ed.*]

There were processions in neat rows of chemists, pastry-cooks, transport workers, builders with a model of a six-storey building, workers from Rusanov Park in their canvas work-clothes and a colourful group from the Sokolniki carriage-repair works.

A car called 'Red Knight' drove right up to the rostrum. On the car in a huge galosh were Poincaré, Vanderveld and other 'nobility' with a priest at their head. They were holding two-foot long baby's dummies in their hands and were sucking them. . . . Aeroplanes, like cranes, were hovering over Sokolniki and the Babaevky Factory had a model aeroplane fluttering over the street shaking out little boxes of delicious chocolates.

Heavy garlands hung from the observation tower of the Sokolniki fire brigade, a fountain of water leapt higher than the tower and fireman desperately slid one after the other down ropes to the ground. Speeches thundered from the rostrums and there was street theatre and displays of art from workers' clubs.

In the evening there was much to see and hear – a gigantic cinema, radio, concerts and fireworks. . . . Workers from Goznak came forward. Among them was a group of workers in disguise leading 'NEP' by the reins. Workers of the Red Rubber plant came out with an airship and other products from their factory. The Artomonov's new tram moved forward proudly. This was their present to the revolutionary workers. Proletarian students from the workers faculty named after Comrade Pokrovsky gave a whole range of sketches revealing the wiles of capitalism.

The columns of demonstrators marched to the rostrums on Devichy Field where meetings took place. The All-Russian leader, Comrade Kalinin, spoke from one of the rostrums.

In the evening there was a splendid fair on Devichy Field. . . . A 'living newspaper' was performed and this enjoyed great success with the workers.

Workers' clubs addressed the people from the rostrums. Despite the bad weather there were large numbers of workers present. There were rockets, films and radio-concerts – everything to accompany the festivities. . . .

Rabochaya Moskva (Workers' Moscow), no. 94, 3 May 1923

PETROGRAD

All documentation indicates that arrangements for the 1923 May Day festivities in Petrograd were very similar to
140 **those in Moscow, likewise using elements of both carnival**
141 **and the symbolism of production. Several scenes of the**
142 **political carnival coincided almost exactly with the subjects used in Moscow's celebrations described above.**

Sixth Anniversary of the October Revolution

MOSCOW

52 *Symphony of factory sirens*

An appeal from Moscow's Proletkult to the Factory Committees of Moscow on the subject of the Symphony of Sirens during the Celebration of the Sixth Anniversary of the October Revolution

23 October 1923

On the initiative of Moscow Prolekult it has been decided to mark the sixth anniversary of the revolution by performing a Symphony in A during the demonstration. The symphony will be played on the steam central heating pipes and by sirens from factories in the Transriver district and from the railway stations. The MOGES power stations, Armatrest factory and Trubosoedinenie Pipe Works have taken on the responsibility for setting up and constructing the pipes. The People's Commissariat for Railway Transport and the 'train cemeteries' of the Moscow-Kursk line will give most of the hoots. The Communist cell of the Moscow Conservatory will perform the work as requested by Moscow Proletkult. The concept and the music of the symphony are the work of A. M. Avramov.

Sixty steam hooters will be positioned on the roof of the Central Electrical Power Station on the Raushskaya Embankment. The headquarters of RVSR [the Revolutionary Armed Forces of the Republic] is giving a group of 'percussion' instruments (cannons, machine-guns, motor transport and gun volleys). The Moscow Committee of the Russian Communist (Bolshevik) Party has sanctioned the organization of this event and has given the means with which to put it into practice. On the programme are the 'Marseillaise', the 'Internationale', the Young Guard march, the 'Varshavyanka' and the funeral march.

It has only been possible to realize such a complex

scheme so quickly thanks to the energetic, comradely support of the Union of Metalworkers who have shown great interest in the project.

It is possible that a similar symphony may be organized in a number of other major towns of the USSR: St Petersburg, Kharkov, Rostov-on-Don and Baku have all received instructions from the organizers.

The first major attempt at such a scheme was made in Baku for the fifth anniversary when the whole fleet and all the different regions of the city took part in the symphony. Even earlier (in 1920) there was a more modest attempt in Nizhny Novgorod.

Moscow Proletkult appeals:

1   that factory committees from the Transriver district which have steam sirens at their enterprises should pass on information about their suitability for participation in the symphony
2   that factory committees from other districts should offer their sirens for temporary use
3   to the Russian Union of Young Communists, that its active members should be drawn into organizational work and into performance
4   to professional musicians, that they should take part in the musical part of the work.

GAMO, f.880, op. 1, d.5, l.81.

numerous and lively as they were in, say, 1918 or 1919. But their character is different. Now they have become somehow more confident, more peaceful, merrier. In 1918 or '19 there was a kind of tense, almost ominous, atmosphere. The demonstration then was not only a festive anniversary, it was a show of strength. The spirit of struggle permeated the demonstration and the streets seemed to blaze with passion. Demonstrators could feel the hate-filled eyes of the residents of Nevsky Prospekt on them and they were at that time engaged in a moral and political fight against their enemies.

. . . Now all the enemies have been beaten. We are no longer fighting with them in the demonstration, we are merely laughing at them and mocking them. That is why the posters proclaiming 'Death to Capital' and 'Down with Capitalism' have been replaced this time by a simple penal carriage on a lorry bearing the sign 'Rest-home for the Bourgoisie'.

Previously the worker was fighting, now he is simply celebrating.

Petrogradskaya Pravda (Petrograd Pravda), no. 254, 9 November 1923

PETROGRAD

53 *Enemies have been beaten*

Extract from a report about the October Revolution celebrations in Petrograd, published in the newspaper *Petrograd Pravda*

9 November 1923

There is now more noise and gaiety and more festive mischief. The columns of demonstrators are just as

May Day Celebrations 1924

MOSCOW

54 *Proletkult projects*

Description of the Proletkult painting studios and their models for Red Square decorations on 1 May, from the magazine *The Furnace*

August 1923

The studio has worked out a wide range of badges, stamps and posters. One of its most significant recent pieces of work, however, has been the preparation of models for the decor of Red Square during the May festivities. The sketches have been approved by the Central May Commission attached to the Moscow Party Committee and have been accepted for use in 1924.

In accordance with the design put forward, the Place of Execution on Red Square will be transformed into a three-dimensional banner of the Russian Communist Party; the monument to Minin and Pozharsky will be disguised by the May Day rostrum and by the Kremlin wall there will be a 'Hammer and Sickle' rostrum. The idea of the Studio is that these three structures should be joined both with each other and with the Kremlin by radio wires and electric letters saying 'Workers of the world, unite'. It is proposed to have decorations on the GUM building and on the Kremlin walls which are linked by colour and form with the basic structures on the Square. As a dynamic element two lorries are to be introduced onto the Square; one is to hold workers and the other peasants and the lorries are to be designed so that they characterize production in the town and in the country.

Workshops are carrying out theatre-related work at the moment in that they are trying to design a universal portable stage.

During the October celebrations in 1924 it is intended to organize the first street exhibition; this will . . . honour the work of the Art Studio of Moscow Proletkult.

Some of the members of the painting workshops are currently working in the districts as instructors.

Gorn (The Furnace), 8th book, August 1923

55 *May Day without Lenin*

Extract from a report about the 1924 May Day celebrations in Moscow, published in *Izvestiya*

4 May 1924

On Red Square
We have become accustomed to seeing extravagant decorations in Red Square on the First of May; we have become used to the gay spectacle of sunlight, general staff officers, moving forests of posts with red flags, rumbling weapons, decorated vehicles, allegorical processions and winged flotillas hovering in the sky. But this year, the first May Day since Lenin's death, there has been neither the traditional military parade nor the official speeches nor the merry, noisy carnival. . . . The May Day demonstration in Red Square, in front of the Lenin Mausoleum with its fresh tomb, has been very modest in character; it has been very much a peaceful festival of the people. Unfortunately the sun, usually blessing Soviet festivals, was absent this year. Betraying us, it hid behind the clouds. The captivatingly bright mosaic colours of Red Square were concealed in a tearful funereal curtain of rain and the demonstration itself had a somewhat funereal character, thus harmonizing with the general appearance of the square and with the mood in view of our recent priceless loss.

The decoration of the square was similarly modest. The motto was: keep the expense as low as possible. The square was decorated by Proletkult in accordance with the tasks set by the district political education department. It is a difficult artistic task to decorate such a colossal and unique square as Red Square especially when means are limited. In general it was well thought out and well executed; a broad piece of cloth stretched from the Kremlin wall over the memorial stone. It bore in large letters the slogan of the Russian Communist Party: 'Our banner is Lenin. Our weapon is Leninism. Our task is world revolution'.

Funeral banners were leaning on each side of the Mausoleum. They carried the slogans of the USSR and of Comintern in different languages: 'We shall do your bidding', 'We shall carry our banner throughout the world' and 'Workers of the world, unite'. But in the plans the banners looked much finer and more impressive. They were somehow lost and hardly noticeable in the depths of the immense square alongside the heavy, gloomy Mausoleum. In themselves they were beautiful enough but they were lost in the square and they should have been made much bigger. However, it would have been much more expensive.

It was rainy, damp and grey. Nevertheless the demonstration was large. The columns of demonstrators went on and on and on. The Transriver, Khamovniki and many other districts took three hours to process across the square. For the first time Red Army soldiers from different divisions took part in the demonstration, joining the ranks of demonstrators and mixing with them. In friendly united ranks, firmly holding each other's hands, marched students from the military academies in grey greatcoats reaching to their feet, female workers in their indigo and blue skirts, with leather jackets and scarlet silk bands, young workers in red shirts – the new thing this May Day and so on and so forth. Family workers pushed prams and infants and young children in them. Young students were especially numerous. All the Latvian quarter from the Khamovniki district was out in strength. There were many members of the intelligentsia, lots of students and plenty of office workers. But the members of the intelligentsia who took part in the demonstration were on absolutely the same level as the workers, joining with them so that it was difficult to differentiate the two. The colours that dominated in the May Day crowd of demonstrators were indigo and scarlet, in calico and cotton. . . .

The banners, as they moved past, bowed to the Mausoleum. There were few new or original posters. The districts also observed the rule of economy. Just one allegorical poster attracted attention; this depicted Poincaré trying to extinguish a world conflagration with a

hose. . . . The rain became heavier but the human avalanche kept on coming. . . .

Izvestiya TsIK, no. 100, 4 May 1924. (On 23 July 1923 the newspaper *Izvestiya* became the organ ('news') of the Central Executive Committee of the USSR, TsIK, not of the All-Union Executive Committee, VTsIK.)

56 *Lenin Mausoleum*

Pravda **describes the newly completed first building for the Lenin Mausoleum on Red Square, a wooden structure by A. V. Shchusev**

4 May 1924

Just completed, in dark brown with black edgings, the Mausoleum immediately catches your eye when you enter the square. Round the Mausoleum a little brick-paved park has been made; this has black rectangles of earth with asphalt paths enclosed by iron railings. . . . A little further from the Mausoleum there are rostrums on both sides for greeting the parades. The banner of the Moscow Committee of the Russian Communist Party is fixed to the side of the Mausoleum itself.

Pravda, no. 99, 4 May 1924

Seventh Anniversary of the October Revolution

LENINGRAD

57 *Displays of industry*

Extract from a report on the celebrations for the Seventh Anniversary of the Revolution in Leningrad, from *The Red Newspaper*

8 November 1924

Since 1917 Leningrad has not seen such a magnificent demonstration, one so colossal in terms of its scale and the number of participants. Even the 1918 demonstration, if you please, could not compete in power and profound content with yesterday's. . . . Yesterday was a great economic show, a brilliant display of all our achievements over the last seven years. . . .

And yesterday there were very few Macdonalds, Curzons and Herriots. When the working class is concerned with more serious, deeper tasks then Macdonald loses his pungency. Macdonald is an entertainment. Macdonald is suitable for May Day. October is a great economic display.

At yesterday's demonstration there was a string of figures but in these figures there was more content than in the most scathing political slogan. We have ceased making promises. We have ceased protesting and threatening. We can boast about our achievements. Here we could see the growth of Leningrad's industry as if on the palm of our hand. . . .

Our boast is supported by millions of pairs of galoshes turned out by the Krasny Triugolnik (Red Triangle) Factory and by our production figures – 'the best answer to the capitalists is the rise in our labour productivity'. On the enormous turning swing of the Skorokhod (Fastrunner) footwear factory were these impressive gold letters. '1923 – 1.4 pairs of boots per worker. 1924 – 2.8 pairs of boots per worker. We have already overtaken the pre-war figure. 1914 – 2.4 pairs of boots per worker.'

Each factory shows its achievements. This is its greatest pride. That is the most important thing, the biggest, the most significant. This is the essence of the October Revolution. In the face of this, the Macdonalds, the Curzons, the Poincarés pale – yesterday's figures are a better slap in the face for them than thousands of satirical sketches.

The demonstration was not only a matter of figures. Factories brought what they were proud of to the demonstration – they brought new things that have never been seen in Russia before. It is not long since the ODVF (Voluntary Air Force Society) put forward the slogan 'Give it a Motor'. Now the aero-engine 'Bolshevik' – a new, clean, shining 400 horse-power version of the 'Liberty' – is already proudly standing there.

The town was beautifully decorated with flags, greenery, banners, portraits and busts of our leaders. Large red banners with slogans and flags had been stretched across the central streets.

In the evening the streets were lit with millions of lights. The stations and the main post office and telegraph office were beautifully illuminated by garlands of electric light bulbs thrown across the streets. The vessels at anchor on the Neva were illuminated by electric bulbs whose light poured over their sides and masts, outlining their contours in the darkness. The streets were filled with a moving throng of people.

Krasnaya gazeta (The Red Newspaper), no. 256, 8 November 1924

May Day Celebrations 1925

LENINGRAD

58 *Production and politics*

**Extract from a report on the May Day celebrations in
Leningrad from *The Red Newspaper***

2 May 1925

The whole city is in red flags as if it were wearing beads.
Thee are many busts and portraits of Lenin – on walls, in
shop windows, on balconies. . . . The propellors of white
birds with red stars on their wings seem almost to touch
the roofs of the buildings. A white snowstorm of leaflets
flutters down onto the heads of the crowd and a whole
forest of hands reaches up to seize them. Some, however,
are taken by the wind and they fly into the distance like
doves. . . .

The demonstration moves to Uritsky Square where the
rostrum is decorated by an inscription which can be seen
from afar. It says 'Lift the banner of Lenin higher, it will
bring victory'. . . . It is a carnival to production. Factories
demonstrate examples of their products as well as tables,
charts and diagrams explaining what they make. . . . From
a long way off one can see a model of a rolling mill. . . . The
workshop of the North-Western Railway has brought two
carriages, a passenger one and a freight one. From little
windows peep out the happy faces of children – they are
young Leninists, passengers who are being steadily
transported to a bright future. . . .

A dairy farm has built a trough on a lorry and some
peaceful and contented cows are looking down at the
crowds. Beside them an enormous churn – large enough to
hold all the milk from the cows of a good-sized village –
sways with the movement of the lorry. Above the heads of
the crowd swim cranes, a steam engine from the Institute
of Individual Upbringing, factory chimneys with smoke
coming from them, machines, enormous bobbins and a
hammer.

A troika of huge cart-horses is pulling a cottage reading-
room. This is not a troika like Gogol's hastening he knew
not whither; it is a troika from a strong and harmonious
economy and its path is clear.

Goodness, what a telephone! The telephone receiver is
bigger than a tree trunk, the mouthpiece is like a barrel.

There are interesting and occasionally very witty
performances, dramatizations and caricatures which are
presented from plaforms on the lorries. These are of two
types. Some are linked with production; others have a
political content.

An entire tragic scene calls us to the aid of MOPR [an
international workers' organization]. A prisoner is waving
a red handkerchief from behind iron bars. Nearby a fascist
is crucifying a blood-stained worker. Further on a huge
worker's fist is ceaselessly cudgelling a spineless bourgeois.
A living Wilhelm is humbly hiding behind a vast guy of
Hindenburg. Very effective in its brevity was the
inscription on a cage where a repulsive beast was lying.
The inscription read 'Tsankov-hyena'. Workers, bourgeois,
peasants, fascists in top-hats, old time officers in colourful
uniforms, appeasers in checked tail-coats, Orthodox
priests, Catholic priests, masks and disguises – all these
people appear on the squares and platforms, calling to the
crowd, singing and declaiming. The carnival spatters the
crowd with healthy and strong laughter and evokes a
sympathetic response.

And on the embankment beyond the Winter Palace
cannons thunder over the broad open space of the River
Neva. They may be the same cannon which sounded to call
people to fight for the right to this festival which is
becoming more and more deeply a part of our lives.

Krasnaya gazeta (The Red Newspaper), no. 103, 2 May 1925

59 *Colourful state goods*

Extract from the article by V. Ya. Brodsky, 'The external appearance of the mass celebration', published in 1926 in the book *Mass Festivals*

. . . The colourfulness of the festive days in comparison with ordinary days is undoubtedly the strongest element which forces us to take on the mood appropriate to the celebration of a particular event.

One of the officials taking stock of the overall picture of the May Day celebrations on Uritsky Square in 1925 wrote at the beginning of his report: 'From all the festivities there remains with me an impression of a colourful sea of posters, women's red kerchiefs, Pioneers' red scarves, red flowers, ribbons and badges. . . .' The colourful aspect of the festival goes through his whole report. 'The rostrum was decorated with fir trees and a huge red poster . . . leaflets were thrown from a balcony to fly like the first white birds in the air . . . and there were red posters with white and black letters moving like the waves of a stormy sea.' Red balloons flashed through the air. . . .

Shop windows were decorated, gratefully combining the tasks of festive decoration with those of advertisement. In the window of the Leningrad State Publishing House (Lengiz) there was a model of the Lengiz building, from whose door a stream of books printed by Lengiz was flowing. In the windows of the State Weights and Measures Department (Gosmetr) there were stars made out of rulers and an inscription written in weights. In the windows of the North-West State Trade Office (Sevzapgostorg) a moving machine was displayed. Inside it there were flames depicted by red ribbons which were illuminated from within and which moved in air provided by a fan. Cars from various publishing houses were used for publicity purposes and these travelled the streets of the city until late at night. In the evening, apart from the illumination of decorations and banners, there were two additional features: street film shows and fireworks.

If we add to this the illuminations and searchlights on the vessels standing on the Neva, then we have exhausted all the different types of decorations used in the city apart from the triumphal arches, which were formerly frequently used but have now almost disappeared, at least in Leningrad.

Since those days, the colourfulness of ordinary days has increased. There are more posters, more illuminated advertisements, more banners and more highly decorated shop windows. All this forces the coming festival to become still brighter.

Massovoye prazdnestva. Sbornik Komiteta sotsiologicheskogo izucheniya iskusstv (Mass Festivals. A Collection of Papers from the Committee for the Sociological Study of the Arts), Leningrad, 1926, pp. 98–9, 101–2, 104.

This book represented the results of a survey of the revolutionary festivals of 1924 and 1925, made on the initiative of the Department for the History and Theory of Theatre at the State Institute for the History of the Arts. The survey was carried out by the Department's Theatrical Laboratory and by the bureau dealing with figures and records on club work and the mass festivals. Documents 60, 63 and 64 also derive from this collection of material.

FIFTH ANNIVERSARY, 1922

Fifth Anniversary of the Revolution, 1922, Moscow

136 Agitational floats in the form of ships, manned by sailors, passing through Red Square.

137 Float in the form of a steam engine passing through Moscow streets.

MAY DAY, 1923

May Day, 1923, Moscow
138   (*right*) Float from the Transriver District.
139   (*below*) Crowds by the rostrum in Red
Square.

Petrograd (facing page)
140   (*above left*) Crowds and the new Red
Army hat: 'The Red Army is the terror of the
world's Bourgeoisie'.
141   (*above right*) Factory float, 'The Entente
in Galoshes'.
142   (*below*) Red Army on the Field of
Victims of the Revolution (Field of Mars), with
arch dedicated 'to those who died in the
business of liberating all workers'.

MAY DAY, 1924

May Day, 1924, Leningrad

143 (*right*) A band from the Kirov Spinning Factory proceeds through Uritsky Square in front of the Winter Palace.

144 (*below left*) A group of participants bearing two masks on poles; the left-hand one, inscribed 'I buy from private traders', was described in the newspaper report as 'a green, exhausted-looking face', while the right-hand one, reading 'I buy from co-operative shops', was described as 'cheerful, fat and rosy'.

145 (*below right*) A float bearing a bust of Lenin, who had died on 21 January that year.

SEVENTH ANNIVERSARY, 1924

Seventh Anniversary of the Revolution, 1924, Leningrad

146   Float from the Bolshevik Factory, displaying some of the engineering components which it produced. This was a typical interpretation of the 'production' theme of that year's parade.

147   Float bearing a chimney and 'working models' representing one of the city's factories, with a very dirty and battered looking Winter Palace behind.

MAY DAY, 1925

May Day, 1925, Leningrad

148, 149   (*far left*) Float with model telephone, 'Face to the countryside is your slogan for 1st May' and (*left*) float with crude mock-up of Tatlin's model for his 1919 Monument to the III International.

150   (*below*) Float representing the Red Triangle factory enters Uritsky Square.

151, 152   (*above right*) Float from the New Village publishing house with a miniature 'cottage reading-room' as created in the villages to give peasants access to newspapers and books and (*below right*) float, 'Down with the White Terror'.

EIGHTH ANNIVERSARY, 1925

Eighth Anniversary of the Revolution, 1925, Leningrad

153 (*right*) Rostrum constructed around the base of the Alexander Column in Uritsky Square, decorated to represent 'The ship of the Boshevik Party'.

154 Float passing over Anichkov Bridge on Nevsky Prospect.

60 *Analysing the new genre*

From an article by N. P. Izvenkov entitled 'The First of May 1925', published in 1926 in the book *Mass Festivals*

The materials used for the festival parades [of May Day 1925] varied widely. Iron, wood, living greenery, tin, leather, shavings: in a word, everything that could somehow help the designer to realize his ideas. . . . Everything was used in the most varied forms, from the simplest greenery-decked wagons with Young Pioneers in them to dynamic arrangements and moving figures.

It is interesting to note the proportion of two- as opposed to three-dimensional decorations. Of the total number of displays, 88.5% were three-dimensional and 11.5% were two-dimensional.

The use of actual objects in the May Day celebrations can be broken down into the following four categories.

The first category consists of objects having an independent significance of their own. They provided the centre of attention for the organizations displaying them. All exhibits from factories and workplaces were of this type, when they used stands on vehicles, etc. Thus the Red Putilov factory showed its tractor, and another showed an engine with the inscription 'Give it a Soviet engine!' . . .

The second type consisted of products and objects, but used as a background for some demonstration or action to be staged. . . .

The next, third category consisted of objects used as props in a theatrical action. Such for example was the invariable use of a sledge-hammer or ordinary hammer for beating the head or the back of the bourgeois or the appeaser; such were the ink-well and bast-shoe hung on a string and used as a priest's censer; also the black coffin carried by Red Army soldiers and bearing the inscription 'Here lies the last illiterate Red Army soldier', and so on.

The fourth category consisted of things of a mixed character. On the one hand they were products of the workplace, but at the same time they were used in a special way. Such were the majority of production diagrams: those from the cork factory were made of cork, for instance, or from the Sputskaya Textile factory of ribbon. The Sev cable factory used wire for its decorations and the timber works used shavings, and so on.

Here arises yet another of the principles behind the arrangements for the May Day demonstrations – their close relationship to professional and production traits. As we shall see below, this principle runs like a thread through the entire May Day celebrations and thus serves as one of the major determinants of its character.

The theatre arrived at the morning demonstrations in the most varied of forms, ranging from complete plays to separate fragments of performances. Of course, we are not talking here about traditional theatre and performances, such as we are accustomed to seeing in stone buildings, although these did have some part to play in the demonstrations, albeit a small one. We are in general talking about some kind of theatrical action with which the whole May Day carnival was permeated. There was theatre not only in those groups which dramatized some subject on the platform of a lorry or in the middle of a crowd of demonstrators. Theatre could also be seen occasionally in different installations, from mechanized figures and even exhibits. . . .

One of the factories at the May Day demonstration built, for example, a wooden cottage with a thatched roof on a lorry. A red cock sat on the roof. The scene also demonstrated fire-extinguishers and hosepipes. On the lorry there were about fifteen men and women dressed in a peasant style. All this was constructed on the principle of a 'living picture': one man was standing with a fireman's hook, another with a hose and so on; but two or three comments from the lorry to the crowd were enough for the 'living picture' to turn into a most genuine piece of theatre.

Let us take another example from a different demonstration. Among the columns, not far apart from each other, walked two costumed figures – a Catholic priest and a bourgeois with their arms linked by iron chains. Behind them was a tall, thickset worker, without any make-up and in an ordinary modern three-piece suit with a cap on his head and a heavy mock hammer in his hand with which he occasionally hit the heads of the priest and the bourgeois. All three moved silently, they simply walked in the midst of the marching columns, but the costumes, the make-up, the hammer and its blows all did their bit. This was a complete theatrical act. . . .

Together with this, factories use their products at the demonstration for purely theatrical purposes. Thus one factory took on stage an enormous model of the kind of frying pan it makes. In the huge pan, a Polish bourgeois was being fried (political satire). . . .

Political satire, which has worked out a number of contemporary masks, has also, of course, created distinctive costumes to accompany each of them. The bourgeois and the appeaser are unthinkable without their tail-coats and top-hats or bowlers just as the white officer is always in his greenish-blue uniform, epaulettes and sabre. Determining such costumes went along the lines of taking the most characteristic details. These details were particularly strongly marked in the 'Living Newspapers' where a top-hat on the head (even if the person was otherwise in ordinary working clothes) was enough to signify a 'bourgeois', a 'minister' or an 'appeaser', in a word the person required from the White Front. In clubs' performances the top-hat played a most significant role and from there it moved also to dramatization at mass festivals. In contrast to the top-hat (worn by the bourgeois and the appeaser) the worker usually wears a cap.

In general we can note the following approximate categories of costume used in dramatizations: . . . (1) ordinary city dress, (2) national and local everyday dress (genuine), (3) theatrical costume, (4) sports clothes, (5) work clothes and (6) ordinary clothes with characteristic details added to them. . . .

It is also necessary to note that make-up was used in the main only for negative and comic characters. All the positive characters in the dramatizations – workers, Red Army soldiers and so on – were merely dressed in an appropriate costume and did not wear make-up.

Massovoye prazdnestva. Sbornik Komiteta sotsiologicheskogo izucheniya iskusstv (Mass Festivals. A Collection of Papers from the Committee for the Sociological Study of the Arts), Leningrad, 1926, pp. 114–16, 120, 124, 126.

Eighth Anniversary of the October Revolution

MOSCOW

61 *One million workers*

Report in *Pravda* on celebrations for the Eighth Anniversary of the Revolution in Moscow

10 November 1925

After a short ceremonial transfer of banners, the procession of columns of demonstrators started. This procession of the Moscow proletariat showing its strength and achievements for the eighth anniversary of the Revolution made an exceptional spectacle not only because of the uplifting mood among the demonstrators but also because of their extraordinary numbers. About one million organized workers took part in the demonstration. In the columns of demonstrators there are flags, numerous slogans on banners, political caricatures, dramatizations and so on. . . .

Among the banners and posters fluttering over the demonstrators with slogans dedicated to the eighth anniversary of the October Revolution, there were satirical scenes and notices. In one you could see a rubbish cart driven by a Red Army soldier; inside it, in the uniforms of different western European armies, there were several seated figures, all defenders of the capitalist system; on this rubbish cart was the caption 'To the rubbish tip with the bourgeoisie of Western Europe'.

Pravda, no. 256, 10 November 1925

LENINGRAD

62 *National and international*

Extract from an article by B. Brodyansky, 'The steps of thousands', on the Eighth Anniversary celebrations in Leningrad, from the newspaper *Leningrad Pravda*

10 November 1925

Against the background of many thousands of demonstrators, rectangles of banners and placards stood out. Lenin and the Party echoed from poster to poster in all tones and combinations. Entire rivers flowed into the human sea on Uritsky Square. . . . And the decorated
153 rostrum [representing 'The Bolshevik Party ship'] swam past in an unchecked wave, seemingly overwhelmed in its ardent embrace. Looking into the passing rows of demonstrators could be seen workers' delegations, now Czech, now Danish. Beside the fur jackets of delegates there were strong tall figures of our dear peasant guests brushing the snow from their beards.

Lord Curzon and you, noble Mr Chamberlain, you have the complete right to receive a performance payment. In
154 tens of different combinations you have been dragged out onto the street and placed on a carnival lorry to be the butt of a strong Komsomol October joke.

And you, lay 'specialists', you have not been forgotten either. Workers who make Chernigov refrigerators brought an ice coffin to the demonstration with a frozen 'Second International' in it and a worthy crown to the Second International in the form of a dirty broom. . . .

Gaily coloured cars from each enterprise and factory were headed by distinctive festive banners. Electric Power Station No. 4 sparkled with an entire little tram park, shining with signal lights and railway points, with a slogan above them saying 'All this was previously imported from France but now it is totally Soviet production'. On an enormous galvanometer shaped like a hammer and sickle, large arrows were moving up to a red mark, the level of 1913: 'We shall press on and on', it said. Over a tractor was the joyful greeting 'The first tractor for the Demyanov district from the workers of Petrograd'. 'Triangle' tyres, 'Putilovets' and 'Bolshevik' – these names are living pages

from the course of the history of the class struggle.

Leningradskaya Pravda (Leningrad Pravda), no. 257, 10 November 1925

63 *Themes and genres*

Extract from the article by N. A. Lastochkin, 'Artistic designs for the festivities', written sometime after November 1925 and published in 1926 in the book *Mass Festivals*

. . . Simple industrial items were displayed without any decorations. Such exhibits as tractors, machines, industrial products took up approximately 45% of the overall quantity of three-dimensional displays contributed to the demonstration. The remainder consisted of models made to look exactly like their real counterparts. . . .

A particular place amongst the displays was given to illustrating the process of work and everyday conditions of life of the proletariat. You could see one of the servicing points from the October Railway, as several railway workers on a lorry demonstrated changing rails, fixing sleepers, and strengthening the embankment. Another lorry showed a proletarian cottage equipped with electricity, and so on. . . .

The next type of display could be called politico-satirical. This genre changes little from one festival to the next, as they mock the League of Nations, Locarno Mill, the attempts of the world's bourgeoisie to preserve their domination by various diplomatic means. They show Germany's acceptance into the League of Nations by means of a 'baptism', where Chamberlain, Briand and Stresemann lower a doll representing Germany into a real church font labelled 'League of Nations'. Then the 'godparents' join hands and dance around the font singing specially composed verse. . . .

The themes of MOPR and the White Terror were similarly not infrequently used, and allegorical figures representing the triumph of socialism and the independence of the USSR were used with particular wit. Scales depicted socialism outweighing capitalists; in the other a figure of a worker on a pedestal was giving a decisive gesture indicating 'no chance' to a bourgeois who is proposing a loan. The theme of the linking of the town and the country was also usually expressed in a similarly allegoric way. Co-operative enterprises did not simply display their products, they also threw products and leaflets into the crowd of spectators. It was interesting to see the historical and revolutionary display where an armed car was decorated with the slogans of 1917 and filled with armed people dressed in the 'style' of the times. A comparatively large number of displays illustrated the power of the Red Army and the Soviet people. . . .

The organizational and artistic initiatives arose from the lower cultural groups – from artistic clubs and circles and from culture committees attached to different enterprises. All the dramatizations put on by factories, institutions, clubs and higher education colleges were staged almost exclusively by amateurs, regular members of clubs from the above institutions. . . .

The theatrical presentations were concise and constructed according to already tried and tested patterns of so-called 'dramatizations'. These have either a total absence of plot or else a very minor one. Their aim is to show simply one moment from international or internal political life and to portray it with the utmost brightness and conviction. The content is schematic, the characters too are presented as types. Quite different, however, is the style of acting used by the most popular characters, who are not types in the same way. Sometimes these may be factory workers – phrase-mongers, wits in their 'special' costumes – but more usually it is a priest, blessing the crowd, or sometimes it is 'Lord Chamberlain', a 'fascist' and so on. They are equivalent to those people who, in popular theatre in all countries throughout history, have won the largest popularity bouquets from the public. It is the Russian Petrushka, the Italian Zanni, Harlequin, the German Hanswurst. Their strength is their contact with the audience, the way they draw the observer to participate in the action. Hanging from the edge of the float an impassioned and merry fellow is shouting verses and jokes which he or his collective have composed to the crowd. He pokes fun at the characters in the dramatizations, ridicules the audience with caustic but still benevolent remarks, and constantly interrupts the action. These fascists, priests and lords, however crude they may be, still move, listen to the audience, call out something amusing or witty. The 'positive characters', the worker, the Red Army soldier, the peasant, are in general more static.

Mobile exhibitions for a festival are very numerous and usually well composed in the demonstration. Libraries display copies of new books and diagrams of their work; factories fix products they have made to plywood screens (for example, there might be an exhibition to show the various stages in the production of some instrument or other); clubs present diagrams showing the rise in the cultural level of their membership; social organizations illustrate the growth of their influence on the masses and so on and so forth.

Lighting effects during the daytime are generally extremely poor. Only a few cases were noted: torches for example, in the armed car from the dramatization of 1917; the lorry with the demonstration of autogenous welding, whose bright beam cut through the daylight, and a number of other demonstrations of a production process. More frequently electricity was used to make illuminated displays: there were brightly lit trams with their edges and monograms made of different coloured electric bulbs.

The November evenings, however, took on a fairy-tale character. Each building in the centre of the town was decorated with figures or slogans in lights. . . . The building of the Stock Exchange was particularly splendidly and artistically lit on these evenings.

Massovoye prazdnestva. Sbornik Komiteta sotsiologicheskogo izucheniya iskusstv (Mass festivals. A Collection of Papers from the Committee for Sociological Study of the Arts), Leningrad 1926, pp. 168, 171, 178, 180.

64 *Theatrical techniques*

Extract from the article by N. P. Izvenkov, 'Mass festivities in Leningrad 1924–25', published in 1926 in the book *Mass Festivals*

Dramatizations at a mass festival have all sorts of purely technical limitations which have to be overcome by the performers and any specific 'theatrical' technique cannot, of course, be all that much help to the participant in the demonstration. He has to 'play' in front of an audience which is on all four sides of him. The audience may be below him (when he is on a lorry) or it may be in a tight ring round him (when he plays to those accompanying him as he marches) or it may be a long way above him (on a rostrum). He may have to 'speak' on a wide open square and then immediately afterwards on a narrow street. In other words he has constantly changing acoustic conditions. There are a large number of most capricious variations for the performer. I am not here even talking about the fact that ninety per cent of what happens is pure improvisation, from which the performer emerges the victor thanks to the firm basis which his improvisation has – class consciousness. The improvisation is further complicated by the fact that the 'spectators' are constantly heckling and even taking on a part themselves. As an example of such 'acting' I should like to quote the following example: on a stage erected on a lorry there were a number of characters including a priest who waved a censer to left and right as the lorry moved along the line of spectators. Then suddenly one of his swings of the censer almost hit a mounted militiaman. Smiling benevolently the militiaman pulled his sword from its scabbard and began swinging it in front of the priest. All around there were jokes, laughter and comments from the lorry and the 'spectators'. The priest, of course, did not take all this in silence; while the militiaman was putting his sword back in its place, he showered him with humorous curses. All this happened at a very fast tempo and lasted only thirty or forty seconds. The surrounding spectators were very closely involved in what happened. Although these moments could be called 'theatricalized', they are not the kind of 'theatre' which we are used to imagining when we·hear the word. Here we are, on the one hand, meeting a large number of concepts and acting techniques for playing in an open square or on a mobile stage which have been lost during the history of the theatre; on the other hand, we are coming face to face with some completely new sources and impulses for creation which are being born through the social dynamic and are thus organically linked with the present day.

Massovoye prazdnestva. Sbornik Komiteta sotsiologicheskogo izucheniya iskusstv (Mass festivals. A Collection of Papers from the Committee for Sociological Study of the Arts), Leningrad 1926, pp. 90–91.

PART 3
1927-33

Celebrating the Industrial Dream

IN 1925 THE Soviet Union's economy was almost back up to pre-1914 levels of output. Total industrial output for that year reached 75% of pre-War levels. Agricultural output was even better, at 87%. More than that, the desired structural shift from private and co-operative enterprises to publicly owned concerns was being achieved: in 1925 76% of industrial output came from the various branches of the state or 'socialized' sector. In retail trade, the proportion was only 47% though rising. The nature of the battle which had achieved this success for the state retail sector has been discussed by Elena Chernevich, and illustrated through the relevant advertising material by Mikhail Anikst, in their recent book, *Soviet Commercial Design of the Twenties*.

The progress had been achieved essentially by repairing existing plant and getting inherited factories back into production where they stood. The next year, 1926, represented the conscious turning-point from this process of 'restoration' to a quite different one officially termed 'reconstruction'. Henceforth the focus was on expansion, executed and located in a manner that would simultaneously restructure the national economic machine and co-ordinate its parts into something susceptible to central planning. This meant constructing entirely new production centres on virgin sites in regions rich in resources but hitherto underdeveloped. It meant a parallel programme of building new towns to house the workers.

The documents of Part 3 show this activity graphically, as industrial growth and the campaigns for greater efficiency became the dominant subject-matter of both festivals. The explicitness of the international political propaganda which accompanied reconstruction in the late twenties and early thirties had a dual aim. It would rouse the energies of the home population by a constant reminder of the essential precariousness of their revolutionary achievement. It also displayed the country's unbending political line to two important sections of foreign opinion: to the potential enemy, and the fraternal socialist parties within those capitalist countries which the Soviet Union aspired to lead.

The need for urgent industrial growth was considerable. The Soviet Union's industrial muscle was trivial compared with the size of her body.

Smaller states in Europe had far larger outputs of iron, steel, coal, oil and electricity. Chemical industries were very underdeveloped and likewise the production of the heavy-industrial machine tools on which other expansion depended. There was no home production of cars or tractors, far less of aeroplanes. Agriculture still represented two-thirds of national output and was worked with medieval manual equipment. In the Communist Party's view, survival depended on turning this backward agrarian country into an advanced industrial power.

During 1926, the first new power stations of Lenin's GOELRO electrification plan came on stream. The project for a hydro-electric dam on the Dniepr river got government approval in October that year. Construction began on the new north-south railway from Siberia to Turkestan in 1927. Private capital was rapidly being squeezed out of the economy, so that by 1928, 82% of the total industrial output derived from the state sector, and the percentage in retail trade was 76%. Even the festivals were by now something of an industry in their own right, and Documents 65, 68, 69, 70, 71 and 73 describe the increasingly institutionalized and bureaucratic procedures for design submissions, budgets and decision making. Celebrations for the tenth anniversary of the Revolution in 1927, in particular, were accompanied by a whole industry of what Document 72 calls 'jubilee products'. A positively capitalist concern for their quality (Documents 71 and 74) and the aspiration to 'overall unity' (Document 71) reflect a new consciousness of their image in front of 'fraternal' foreign delegations.

The special mention of the British and Chinese delegations in Document 66 and the particular pillorying of British politicians are direct reflections of two major diplomatic events of spring 1927. With the consent of the British government under Baldwin and Chamberlain, the headquarters of ARCOS, the Soviet trading company in London, had been raided in May that year, and the British had broken off diplomatic relations with the USSR two weeks later. As Britain had been the first country to establish relations, this affair offered plenty of propaganda points about 'unreliability' now: hence the laughter of the English socialists' delegation in Red Square, as well as the Soviet crowds, at the Macdonald and Baldwin puppets paraded in November. Soon after the London incident, there had been attacks on the Soviet government's new embassy in Peking, and its consulates in Shanghai and Tiensin, with similar results for diplomacy and entertainment.

In central government circles within the USSR, the nation's economic future was shaped in 1927 by more fundamental events than these. In April, the Fourth Congress of Soviets voted to establish a Five Year Plan. Campaigns for 'rationalization' and 'economy' launched these words into the slogans. An October Plenary of the Party adopted a specific set of goals for that Plan, and in December the Fifteenth Party Congress adopted its proposals for collectivizing agriculture. The die was thus cast, in an atmosphere of cultivated scepticism as to the real motives underlying such Western solidarity enterprises as the League of Nations. At the next May Day celebrations in 1928, *Pravda*'s report in Document 75 observes how the festivities reflected 'these tasks of the moment' in the same slogans for 'socialist rationalization' and against the 'lethargy' that 'working Moscow is experiencing' in its everyday life.

From a special Moscow spring carnival of 1929 we have particularly lively accounts of both the staging process and the public reaction to such an event, through reminiscences of students of the famous VKhUTEMAS art school who took part. In one telling incident the Foreign Minister Maxim Litvinov came down to Gorky Park in person to advise the students on how to 'adjust' their satirical figures of Churchill, Macdonald and other foreign leaders in order 'to avoid diplomatic problems'.

As the economic pace quickened, festivals were seen as inappropriately slow. 'The tempo of the demonstrations should correspond to the tempo of industrialization' declares Document 80, from 1929. In a country attempting to complete its Five Year Plan in four years, there could be no more 'waits at street corners' for marching groups to catch up. Likewise the relationship of spontaneous local effort and co-ordinated city-wide plan was again under scrutiny as the decade closed.

In the festivals of the early thirties there were successes from earlier industrial campaigns to display. In November 1930, pilots somersaulted their by now Soviet-made planes over Red Square 'like tumbler-pigeons' (Document 85). Engineering achievements out on the new construction sites, and the way their drama was communicated to the capital and visitors, are vividly described in reminiscences by the contributing artists (Documents 87 and 90), and the corresponding photographs show poignant juxtapositions of the old city and the new Soviet world.

Equally poignant is the encounter with such great names from the early avant-garde as the Stenberg brothers, regularly employed as co-ordinating designers for Red Square (Documents 95, 96, 98 and 99) and their former fellow Constructivists Lavinsky (Document 93) and Klutsis (Documents 96 and 100), amidst ever firmer political orchestration of the festivals' content. Thus Toot remarks in Document 88 that 'for the first time a political editor worked side by side with the artist on the designs' in planning the November celebration of 1931, and a year later these 'editors' have become 'qualified political consultants' (Document 91). With the creation of 'a permanent commission' of the Moscow City Soviet for the staging of these festivals (Document 91), their routinization into the familiar formal parades of the later thirties and today was under way.

After Kaganovich's speech of 1931 on the future plans for Moscow, the city became the subject of its displays, and it celebrated its own achievements as Petrograd had done in the early years, but now through highly trained engineers rather than illiterate factory labourers. Still the proper nature of the new genre was under debate, and the political emphases shifted. The last document, however, reminds us that what actually produced such events, then as now, was a combination of 'ceaseless telephone calls' and 'innumerable pots of paint'.

Tenth Anniversary of the October Revolution

MOSCOW

65 Plans

Extract from a report on the preparations for the Tenth Anniversary celebrations in Moscow, published in *Pravda*

30 October 1927

Decorations for the squares and the demonstration:
Two huge banners emblazoned with the dates 1917 and 1927 will be unfurled on Red Square along both sides of the Mausoleum. A slogan to be floodlit at night will stretch in the air on cables from Spassky Tower to the Place of Execution and the Building of the All-Union Central Executive Committee (VTsIK). On the site of the Place of Execution a model of an armoured car will be set up with captions summarizing the military work of the Red Army.

157   Similarly illuminated and decorated will be Sverdlov Square, Soviet Square, Revolution Square, Strastnaya Square, Timiryazev Square and Arbat Square as well as Krymsky, Kamenny and Moskvoretsky Bridges.

155   Satirical masks for the demonstrations have been prepared by an artistic sub-committee. Material has also been prepared for the verbal element of the demonstration (slogans, verses, greetings, songs and so on). . . .

Pravda, no. 249, 30 October 1927

Documentation in State archives indicates that Proletkult craftsmen and artists collaborated in this work on the squares and bridges. Their own records state:

The Decorative Arts studio of Moscow Proletkult prepared designs for the decoration of several squares and bridges and some other sketches for posters and diagrams to be published by the Moscow Soviet.

The Arts Section of the October Commission of the Moscow Soviet announced that there would be a competition for the decorations for the squares and bridges. The following were accepted by the Commission: a design for the decoration of Red Square, the Kremlin Wall, GUM and the History Museum proposed by Comrade Letkar, a sketch for the decoration of Arbat Square done by Comrades Ageev and Serov, a sketch for Timiryazev Square done by Comrades Makarychev and Balkov, a design for the decoration of Kamenny Bridge by Comrade Borovkov and one for Krymsky Bridge by Comrades Filimonov and Kaloshin. The design for the poster on the theme of the uprising, 'All Power to the Soviets', was made by Comrade Letkar, the poster dedicated to the women's movement was designed by Comrade Makarychev, the one dealing with construction was done by Comrade Ageev and the one concerned with information by Comrade Borovkov.

GAMO, f.880, op.1, d.5, l.183–4.

66 Laughing foreigners

Extract from an article in *Pravda* by Nikolai Pogodin, 'About what is great', on the Tenth Anniversary celebrations in Moscow

10 November 1927

On Red Square
156   The different districts have gone past. Then some workers dragged across the square a coffin with the Second International in it and behind that there was another coffin with Russian capitalism in it, deceased in accordance with all the laws of nature and buried with candles.

Loud laughter from the foreign stands greeted the Macdonalds and Chamberlains carried above the columns of demonstrators. The English really enjoyed two figures. Macdonald was applauding Baldwin and behind them was a model of a hemisphere showing the USSR. A worker-blacksmith was standing on the red earth and from the other side of the sea a top-hatted head would pop up. It would no sooner appear than the smith would strike with his hammer and the head would disappear.

'Wonderful', shouted the Germans, 'wonderful!'

At the head of the Chinese group moved a number of giants disguised to represent all sorts of counter-revolutionary scarecrows. They were walking on stilts and could be seen from a long way off. Members of the government laughed, they laughed on all the rostrums, the entire square laughed. A huge dragon crawled along above the Chinese demonstrators. It was so vivid that it seemed alive. It crawled along over the heads of people to the middle of the square and then it seemed to feel ill. It twitched, sighed, wriggled in spasms, stretched out and died.

An amazing number of flowers, colours, amusing inventions and profound Bolshevik slogans crossed Red Square.

Pravda, no. 257, 10 November 1927

67 Capitalists in chains

From a description of the Tenth Anniversary celebrations in Moscow in *Our Newspaper*

10 November 1927

Here are some different images of the carnival. The Kauchuk [Rubber] factory carried an air balloon symbolizing the world fettered with chains. . . . In one part of the procession a chain of champions was carried on poles: there was Mussolini, champion of hoolganism; there was Chamberlain, champion of false promises; there was Vandervelde, the Belgian court socialist, champion of toadies. The group of workers and colleagues from the newspaper *Izvestiya* carried a pack of snarling dogs, symbolizing eight foreign newspapers, headed by the Paris *Le Matin*.

Nasha gazeta (Our Newspaper), 10 November 1927

A further description preserved in the State Archives tells how:

Workers from the Sokolniki District came to the demonstration with a gigantic hydra made of scraps of material – the two heads of the hydra were Chamberlain and Mussolini.

TsGALI SSSR, f.645, op.1, d.489, l.36.

LENINGRAD

68 An October Commission

Extract from the Bulletin of the Leningrad Regional Commission for celebrating the Tenth Anniversary of the Revolution (The October Commission), dealing with its composition

Not earlier than 4 December 1926

In accordance with the resolution of the Leningrad Regional (Guberniya) Executive Committee of the Party dated 4 December 1926 (transaction no. 80) a Regional Commission has been established to deal with preparations for the celebrations of the tenth anniversary of the October Revolution. The Commission consists of the following comrades: N. Komarov (Chairman), Stetsky (Deputy Chairman), I. I. Kondratyev, Veynberg, Shitkina, Edelson, Fedorov, Osipov, Irklis, Romanov, Rzhanov, Maletsky, Rafail, Chagin, Sergeev, Geft, Saakov, Smirnov, Yefimov, Kudelli, the presidents of all the district Soviets and of the Leningrad District Executive Committee. . . .

TsGALI SSSR, f.645, op.1, doc.480, l.82.

69 *A working group*

Extract from the minutes of a five-member working group of the October Commission

26 August 1927

Present were Comrades Stetsky, Kondratyev, Shitkina, Romanov (from GPP), Volf (from LGSPS), Maletsky (finance subcommission), Podolsky (the exhibitions subcommission), Roslavlev (the artistic-decorations subcommission), Vinogradsky and Nikitin (from APO).

Agenda:
1   Report from the finance subcommission on the financial situation.
2   Report from the artistic-decorations subcommission.
3   Report from the exhibitions subcommission.
4   Plan for the participation of the female-workers' section in the celebrations.
5   Current matters.

1   The report from the finance subcommission on the financial situation was given by Comrade Maletsky.
It was decided to: (a) take Comrade Maletsky's report into account. The minutes of the finance subcommission's meeting of 17 August were accepted; (b) allow the Academy of Arts 6350 roubles to spend on designs for the decoration of the town; (c) allow regional commissions a one-off payment of 500 roubles for preparatory work.
2   The report from the artistic-decorations subcommission was given by Comrade Roslavlev.
It was decided to: (a) accept the proposals concerning which places in the city should be especially decorated; (b) ask the artistic commission to review the list of posters to be prepared with a view to reducing their number; (c) create another artistic subcommission to be attached to the Academy of Arts. This should consider designs for decorations for the city and should consist of Professors of the Academy – Ivan (I. A.) Fomin, M. I. Roslavlev and P. S. Naumov – as well as representatives from Proletkult and the Art-Workers Union and Comrade Vinogradsky from APO; (d) complete the preparation of all plans by 1 October, after which the Regional Department of Municipal Services should immediately start work on

executing the designs; (e) finish the originals for posters by 15 September; (f) organize an art exhibition in association with the Academy of Arts with the aim of helping organizations to acquire artistic works and designs; (g) erect a monument to Comrade Lenin by the Smolny according to the design by the sculptor Kozlov. Academician Shchuko should be asked to devise a pedestal for this monument and, as soon as this is completed, the Regional Department of Municipal Services should without delay proceed to erect the monument.

TsGAOR Leningrad, f.1000, op.11, d.249, l.55.

70 *The decorations subcommission*

Minutes of the artistic-decorations subcommission of the Leningrad Regional Commission for the October celebrations, to discuss designs

10 September 1927

1   We listened to consideration of a plan for decorating the square beside the Technological Institute proposed by the architect B. A. Smirnov.
It was decided to approve the idea and to ask the author to work things out in pencil and to present it on 14 September.
2   We listened to a plan for decorating Uritsky Square proposed by the architect Udalenky.
It was decided to ask Comrade Vinogradsky to clarify all the possibilities in connection with the proposal regarding development of the decorations for the square and to ask the author, after the facts have been clarified, to make a proposal in pencil for 14 September.
3   We listened to a plan for decorating the square in front of the Smolny proposed by the architect Almedingen.
It was decided to ask the author to work on a new version and to present it in pencil for 14 September.
4   We listened to a plan for decorating the Moscow Gates, proposed by the architect A. E. Belogrud.

It was decided to accept the idea for the decorations and to ask the author to work towards Wednesday 14 September of this year, taking into account the wishes of the artists' conference and clarifying the real possibilities vis-à-vis the use of military tents and the order in which the procession will move.

5   We listened to a plan for decorating Lieutenant Schmidt's Bridge proposed by the architect Vaks.

It was decided to accept the plan. The author should be asked to work on the central part of the design for the lighthouse-tower for 14 September 1927.

6   We listened to a proposal for an armlet to be worn on the days of the October celebrations which the Maternity and Child Protection Department from the Regional Health Office can distribute round the region.

It was decided to ask the proposer to agree on a slogan with Comrade Vinogradsky and to rework the central part of the drawing.

7   We listened to a plan for decorating the embankment between the Academy of Arts and the Academy of Sciences proposed by the architect Taleporovsky.

It was decided to ask Comrade Taleporovsky to clarify with the municipal services department the question of the use of tram posts for decorating in the character of the proposal.

8   We looked at a sketch for a wallpaper frieze to be produced by a wallpaper trust and to be distributed on a mass scale.

It was decided to ask the proposer to rework his design with a view to making the parts of the drawing larger.

9   We looked at the model of a lamp post presented by an authorized agency of the Moscow Workers' Bureau for Patronage of the Countryside.

It was decided not to object to the distribution of such lamp posts although, as they were noted to be unsatisfactory in form, they should be modified in accordance with models provided by the meeting.

10   We listened to a plan for decorating the tombs and the Square of the Victims of the Revolution proposed by the architect Rudnev.

159   It was decided to accept the plan and to ask the proposer
160   to present a completed sketch, agreed with the public services department, for 19 September.

11   We looked at a sketch of a design for the former residence of Kshesinskaya, proposed by the architect Trotsky.

It was decided to approve the design and to ask the proposer to work it out for 14 September agreeing an estimate of costs with the public services department.

12   We looked at a sketch for a design for decorating the square in front of the Stock Exchange, proposed by the architect Igor (I. I.) Fomin.

It was decided to accept the basic idea for the design but pay attention to defining the theme more precisely.

13   We looked at a sketch for a design for decorating Liteiny Bridge, proposed by the architect Rachmanina.

It was decided to accept the basic design but to suggest that agreement must be sought with the Orsk Railway Transport Department regarding the attachment of banners to posts.

164   14   We looked at a sketch for a design for decorating the Narva Gates proposed by the architect Buryshkin.

It was decided to ask the architect to work further on the theme.

15   We looked at a sketch for a design to decorate the square by the Volodarsky Monument, proposed by the architect Tversky.

It was decided to accept the basic design and to ask for the pediment to be the basis for a banner theme 'The press in Volodarsky's epoch'.

161   16   We looked at a sketch for a design decorating Finland Station Square proposed by the architect Duplitsky.

It was decided to accept the basic plan but to ask for the centre to be reworked with a view to a greater unity of style.

17   We looked at: a sketch for a mask of Chamberlain to be made for mass production in papier mâché or other materials.

It was decided to raise no objections.

18   We looked at a sketch for a design for emblems and coats of arms to be made for mass production out of papier mâché. The proposal was submitted by the sculptor Malakhin.

It was decided to accept the proposal using the following colouring: the X in bronze, the hammer and sickle in dark silver on a red background.

158   19   We looked at a sketch for a design for decorating Uprising Square, proposed by the architect Ivan Fomin.

It was decided to approve the idea and to ask the proposer to consolidate his idea paying attention to how it would actually be realized. At the same time the question of additional allocations should be raised.

20   We looked at a sketch for a poster 'Worker and Peasant Woman' prepared by the artist A. N. Samokhvalov.

It was decided to approve the idea of the preliminary sketch and to ask the artist to present a detailed proposal on a large sheet of paper on Wednesday 14 September.

Chairman: Roslavlev.
Secretary: Naumov.

TsGAOR Leningrad, f.1000, op.11, d.249, l.110–11.

71   *Achieving unity*

Extract from the Bulletin of the October Commission about the Tenth Anniversary decorative arrangements for Leningrad

Not later than *30 September 1927*

The October Commission, bearing in mind how much work is involved in organizing the decorative arrangements for the city and being conscious of how responsible this work is not only from an ideological point of view but also because of the need for artistic consistency, has established a special artistic-decorations subcommission affiliated to the Academy of Arts. The chairman of the subcommission is the head of the design department, M. I. Roslavlev, and members of the subcommissions are Comrade Vinogradsky, the chairman of the Regional October Commission, Ivan Fomin, an academician of architecture, Professor Naumov from the Academy of Arts, Comrade Andreev as the Prolekult representative, a representative from the regional department of the All-Russian Union of Art Workers and a representative from the Chief Science Department, the architect and artist A. P. Udalenkov.

It is the subcommission's responsibility to organize the basic decorative work and to have a preliminary look at sketches for jubilee posters and designs for decorating major points in the city as commissioned by and under the direct leadership of the Regional October Commission.

The subcommission has also been charged with the task of having a look at the preliminary sketches for all major district decorations, for the main city streets and for all mass-produced anniversary products. This has the aim of achieving an overall unity in the general decorations in the town and of ensuring a fittingly high standard of quality for mass artistic products manufactured by various organizations for the tenth anniversary of the October Revolution.

A   Jubilee posters. Seven posters are being issued to mark the tenth anniversary of the October Revolution in Leningrad in accordance with the brief given by the October Commission.
1   Uprising (October 1917)
2   Strengthen the defence of the USSR
3   Industrialization – the path to socialism
4   The way for the countryside – through co-operation to socialism
5   Woman worker and woman peasant protect the achievements of the October Revolution
6   Our well-wishers (satirical)
7   The stages of the October Revolution (a photomontage)
The originals of these posters have already been passed by the October Commission and delivered for publication by 10–15 October. The posters have been designed by the best craftsmen from Proletkult and the Academy of Arts.

B   Basic places in the city to be decorated by the Regional October Commission and the themes for their decorations.
163   1   The former Kshesinskaya Palace. Theme: 1917–1918, from imperialism to civil war. Designed by Professor N.A. Trotsky.
159   2   The Field of Victims of the Revolution. Theme:
160   Remembering those who fell fighting for the Revolution. Their work is being continued by the working class of the USSR as it builds socialism and fights in the ranks of Comintern for the worldwide October Revolution. Artist L. V. Rudnev.
3   Uritsky Square. Theme: Remembering the storming of the Winter Palace (to be complemented by a mass cinema screening of the film 'October' on the Square). Designed by the architect and artist A. P. Udalenkov.
158   4   Uprising Square. Theme: Overthrowing the autocracy.

Artist Academician of Architecture, Ivan Fomin.

5   Equality Bridge. Decorations here are part of the plan of the Commission for Visual Spectacles. Designed by the architect and artist O. L. Lyalin.

6   Republic Bridge. Decorations also under the Commission for Visual Spectacles. Designed by the architect and artist N. V. Olenev.

7   Lieutenant Schmidt's Bridge. Theme: The Red Fleet. Designed by the architect and artist I. A. Vaks.

8   Liteiny Bridge. Linked with the decorations for Finland Station Square (The Apotheosis of October). Designed by the architect and artist E. N. Rakhmanina.

9   The Stock Exchange. Theme: Industrialization. Designed by the architect and artist Igor Fomin.

10   Technology Institute Square. Theme: From the first Soviet to the USSR and from the USSR to the worldwide October Revolution. Designed by the architect and artist V. A. Smirnov.

164   11   Narva Gates. Theme: The Red Guard. Designed by the architect and artist D. P. Buryshkin.

12   Moscow Gates. Theme: The Red Army. Artist Professor A. E. Belogrud.

13   Volodarsky Monument. Decorations of the square to be done by the architect and artist L. M. Tversky.

14   Smolny Square. Theme: the headquarters of the October Revolution. Slogan 'All Power to the Soviets'. Designed by the architect and artist B. A. Almedingen.

15   University Embankment. Theme: The union of labour and science. Artist Professor V. N. Taleporovsky.

161   16   Finland Station Square. Theme: The Apotheosis of October. Designed by the architect and artist P. S. Duplitsky.

Sketches for the decorations, already generally approved by the October Commission, are to be submitted by 1 October to the public services sub-department of the Regional Municipal Services Department for their execution. In accordance with a resolution of the Regional Commission, the work should be carried out by members of the Union of Art Workers.

C   All the other more or less significant places in the city are to be decorated by district commissions, which must submit all sketches for approval to the artistic subcommission of the Regional October Commission. Sketches of decorations for the main city streets must similarly be submitted.

D   In accordance with a resolution of the Regional Commission all mass-produced artistic jubilee articles made either by particular organizations and enterprises or by private people in Leningrad must be presented for approval to the decorations subcommission. The same applies to similar goods imported into Leningrad for distribution from other parts of the USSR except for such things as have already been passed by the Central Commission dealing with celebrations for the tenth anniversary of the October Revolution.

Organizations and institutions dealing with decorations: if other decorations are proposed to you for the tenth anniversary of the Revolution, then you must require from the people or organizations presenting these decorations a written verification that the aforesaid decorations have already been passed for production.

E   In accordance with a resolution of the Regional October Commission the right to produce and distribute jubilee armlets to mark the tenth anniversary of the Revolution has been awarded to only two organizations: in the city of Leningrad to the society, the Children's Friend, and in Leningrad Region to the society of Maternity and Child Protection. The preparation and distribution of banners to decorate buildings, . . . institutions and homes is allowed only to Posredrabis.

A number of other objects for mass artistic production were considered.

TsGALI SSSR, f.645, op.1, d.489, ll.85, 86.

TENTH ANNIVERSARY, 1927

Tenth Anniversary of the Revolution, 1927, Moscow

155 (*right*) Floats from *Izvestiya*, with circulation figures and slogans praising 'the Soviet press'.

156 (*below*) Group of paraders in Red Square with slogans about food and domestic hygiene.

157 (*bottom*) The riverside building of MOGES, the Moscow State Electric Power Station, lit up to designs by Vladimir and Georgii Stenberg.

Tenth Anniversary of the Revolution, 1927, Leningrad

158 (*facing page, above*) Uprising Square decorated by the architect Ivan A. Fomin on the theme of the 'Overthrow of autocracy', with the Alexander III monument 'imprisoned', rather than screened.

159, 160 (*facing page, below*) Drawing and built structure on the Field of Mars by Lev Rudnev, in memory of Revolutionary heroes.

161 (*right*) 'The Apotheosis of October' on the square outside Finland Station, by P. S. Duplitsky.

162 (*below*) Figure of 'Capital' for river procession.

163 (*below right*) Structure by Natan Trotsky on the gazebo of the ballerina Kshesinskaya's mansion.

164 (*below far right*) Arch at the Narva Gates decorated by David Buryshkin for 'The Red Guard'.

165 (*next page, above*) M. P. Bobishov, sketch for carnival floats to represent the Maly Theatre.

166 (*next page, below*) Sketch for an agitational vehicle 'welcoming the Bolshevik Party as the leader of the Revolution'.

MAY DAY, 1929

May Day, 1929, Moscow

167 (*right*) Performance of *Petrushka* by a puppet theatre in the streets.

168 (*below*) *May Day, 1929*, by V. V. Kuptsov.

SPRING CARNIVAL, 1929, MOSCOW

169 (*above far left*) Vast figures of 'British Imperialists', from 'The ship of Imperialism'.

170 (*above left*) A. S. Magidson's designs for 'The marriage of Mussolini with the Pope'.

171 (*below far left*) Group by L. I. Khokhlova, 'Capitalist France and the countries of the Lesser Entente'.

172 (*below left*) E. I. Kheifets's float depicting 'The elephant as a symbol of the colonialization of India'.

173 (*right*) The whole parade, totalling fifty-four vehicles, on Red Square.

174 (*below*) A group of the young art students and teachers who took part in making the carnival floats, at the VKhUTEIN workshops in Gorky Park.

Spring Carnival, 1929, Moscow

175 (*right*) Composition by N. S. Starodub and Ya. F. Kozlovskaya for a float showing 'The ship of Imperialism'.

176 (*below left*) A. S. Magidson, design for a composition called 'The yellow press'.

177 (*below right*) Magidson's composition 'The yellow press' standing in the studio before the carnival.

72 *Exhibiting the designs*

From a report in the State Archives on an exhibition of the design proposals

In the first days of October the Regional Commission opened a city exhibition in the Palace of Labour. This was to display the mass jubilee artistic products issued by various organizations and different people for the tenth anniversary of the Revolution (sculptures, bas-reliefs, posters, banners, flags, jubilee products from trusts and so forth) and also model sketches for the decoration of houses for Housing Departments. The subcommission on the artistic arrangements for the demonstration also displayed here sketches showing designs for the columns in the October demonstration.

TsGALI SSSR, f.645, op.1, d.489, l.106.

73 *Examining the sketches*

Minutes of the artistic-decorations subcommission of the Leningrad Regional Commission for the October celebrations, to discuss artists' sketches

26 October 1927

The following members were present:
From the October Commission – absent; From the Academy of Arts – Professor Ivan Fomin, P. S. Naumov and M. I. Roslavlev; From the Chief Department of Science – A. P. Udalenkov; From Proletkult – A. Andreev; From the Union of Art Workers – Comrade Rutkovskaya. With the right to speak at the meeting:
From Posredrabis – absent; From GET – absent.

1 We listened to a statement from Professor Rudnev and his consideration of the design for decorating the Palace of Labour.

It was decided to approve the plan with some corrections to the pylons at the entrance and, in two cases, raising the numerals for the '10' one storey higher.

2 We listened to a statement from the artist Kibrik, about the following sketches (a) Amsterdam, (b) The Capitalist, (c) The United Front, (d) Target shooting, (e) Co-operation, (f) Devastation, (g) The Industrialization of the Country, (h) Recognition of the USSR, (i) The Air Force, (j) The Defence of the USSR, (k) The Planned Economy, (l) The Rationalization of Production, (m) The Red Army and the Mobilization of Trade Union Members, and the following sketches by Comrade Landberg (n) The Union of the Town and the Country, (o) The Monopoly of Foreign Trade, (p) Construction, and (q) Monetary Reform.

It was decided that (a) the theme 'Amsterdam' was not expressive enough, (b) that the theme 'Capitalist' was basically acceptable but that it needed some more work, (c) The United Front was acceptable, (d) there were no objections to Target Shooting, (e) the theme of Co-operation was acceptable but corrections should be made by an artists' meeting, (f) no objections, (g) no objections, (h) no objections but with some corrections to the Kremlin wall, (i) the theme deserved attention but it had not been satisfactorily worked out from a technical point of view, (j) it should be re-done in accordance with comments from artists' meeting, (k) it would be rejected as it was not suitable for large-scale use, (l) there were no objections, (m) there were no objections, (n) there were no objections, (o) there were no objections, (p) it should be rejected because it was unsatisfactory with regard to scale, and (q) it should be rejected.

3 We listened to a statement from the artist, Popov-Voronezhsky, presenting his own sketches of (a) a decoration for the Regional Finance Department building on the side facing the Street of the Third of July and (b) a decoration for the side facing the Catherine Canal.

It was decided to accept (a) on condition that coins depicted on the railings should be omitted and the slogan should be lifted to the height of the frieze of the side pylons, and not to object to (b) although it was felt that a star and also a hammer and sickle should be placed at the sides of 'USSR'.

4 We listened to a note from minute no. 8 from the meeting of the Petrograd District October Commission of 26 October 1927 with its resolutions relating to the decorations for Leo Tolstoy Square.

It was decided to accept the proposals and to ask the artist to take the comments of Petrograd District October Commission into account. It was, moreover, proposed by the artists' meeting that a large panel on the theme of the Defence of the USSR should be introduced into the design.

5   We listened to a statement by the artist Malaga presenting his sketches: (a) decorations for the Moscow Narva Building and (b) decorations for the rear side of the same building.

It was decided to accept (a) but to ask that the slogans should be placed at a lower level, replacing the upper linking part with a garland. The sloping slogans should be removed, (b) was accepted.

6   We listened to a statement from A. A. Ivensen with a sketch of a banner to be used during the October festivities.

It was decided not to object.

7   We listened to a statement from the architect N. V. Golubev presenting three sketches.

It was decided to accept one of the sketches with some simplifications.

8   We listened to a statement from the theatre-artist G. S. Tolmachev, presenting sketches for the carnival procession: (a) Geneva, (b) Lowering of Prices, (c) Co-operation and the Private Trader, (d) Chamberlain's Little Birds, (e) The Ambassador's Murder and (f) The Struggle against Bureaucratism.

It was decided to accept (a), not to object to (b), to reject (c) on the grounds that the idea had not been worked through sufficiently artistically, to reject (d), to re-do (e) and not to object to (f).

Chairman: Roslavlev
Secretary: Naumov

TsGAOR Leningrad, f.1000, op.11, d.249, ll.247–48.

Plan by the Leningrad Proletkult for the October celebrations, detailing intentions and themes

Sometime before *7 November 1927*

Outline of the plan for the celebrations to mark the tenth anniversary of the Revolution (in Leningrad)

Arrangements

1   The general theme of the celebrations will be a grand, mass report and demonstration of the achievements of the ten years since the Revolution.

a   Throughout all the reports will dominate the idea of the transition from the rebuilding period (immediately after the war) to the time of the socialist reconstruction in both the economy and culture of the USSR.

b   Every organization has to give an account of itself to everyone and everyone has to give an account of him or herself to each organization.

c   A show of our achievements. The demonstration of our growth.

d   A summary of achievements through the prism of today.

e   Isolation of particularly significant moments of current reality.

2   Included in the reports will be:

a   The results of economic construction. A report on production.

b   The defence of the USSR.

c   The results of the struggle of the working class of the USSR on the front of the International Revolution – Komintern [Communist International], Profintern [Trades Union International], Krestintern [Peasant International].

d   Cultural achievements and the building of a new daily life.

3   Arrangements for the mounting of the celebrations.

a   These should take into account the mass nature of the celebrations and the need for consideration of maximizing its visual impact.

b   The staging should make use of our ten years' experience of mass street dramatizations and should mobilize all the strengths of professional and amateur art.

c   Real things instead of props and models.

d   The mass diagrams using things and people should be expressive.

e   There should be as much economy as possible in the means of expression used (there is a danger of overload).

4   The celebrations will have a planned character.

a   Mass initiatives and amateur presentations should be in line with the unified plan for festivities.

b   The plan gives a pivot to mass amateur activity and unites unco-ordinated performances into a united, collective whole.

c   The celebrations will last for three days.

1st day: during the day – a mass demonstration (reports), in the evening – ceremonial meetings dedicated to the October Revolution. These will take place both in the centre and in clubs in the districts.

2nd day: during the day – a display of military strength, in the evening – mass stage presentations in both the centre and the districts.

3rd day: day and evening – mass popular fairs in the districts.

1st day of the festivities

A   *Decoration of the city*

1   This should be on a magnificent scale. The decorations should be large in size.

2   There should be sanctioning of decorations of buildings by commissions (decorations that are trivial or cheap in their content should not be permitted). Included should be:

a   Accounting diagrams for institutions and organizations on buildings.

b   Arrows regulating the movement of the columns of demonstrators (every ten buildings and to be the size of the buildings on which they are placed).

c   Work and production posters with slogans corresponding to the character of the particular institution or enterprise.

3   Arrangements for the rostrum and the approach to it.

a   The rostrum should be the culminating point for the procession. There should be an intensification of organizational and artistic factors corresponding to the heightened emotions as the masses move towards the rostrum.

b   Thus, the intervals between arcs, banners, standards and flags should get smaller as one gets closer to the rostrum.

c   There should be fewer decorations by the rostrum. The rostrum should be expressively presented. The leaders. A complex variety of influences. Slogans from loudspeakers. Leaflets dropped from aeroplanes. A choir over the loudspeakers.

4   The evening illuminations. Lit-up posters dedicated to themes connected with the October Revolution should dominate on buildings throughout the city. There should be slogans in lights, film shows and radio performances.

B   *The daytime demonstration*

1   The forms used in the daytime demonstration sum up our experience of celebrating the anniversaries of the revolution:

a   The basic structure of the day demonstration remains as before (a procession of columns from the suburbs to Uritsky Square).

b   The basic task of the demonstration is to show the achievements of the ten years since the Revolution. The procession should be as carefully organized as possible.

2   Arrangements for the columns. Principles behind the alternation of military and civil sections:

a   The district grouping of columns be divided into the following sections: workers, military divisions, students, physical culturists and Soviet officials.

166   b   Each of the groups indicated should appear with their material 'production' reports. Use should be made of theatricalized living diagrams.

162   c   There should be a visual unmasking of enemies and saboteurs in the different productive groups of socialist construction and a display of our achievements in our struggle against them in the ten years since October.

d   There should be a broad demonstration of the patronage and increasing links between the town and the country (the attraction of the peasantry to the town).

e   The procession should alternate in a planned and balanced way with each type of transport taking its turn.

f   Tanks, armoured divisions, artillery, trams, lorries, buses, draymen, motorcycles, cyclists and fire brigades should take their turn in the procession in an ordered way.

g   The professional characteristics of each participating group should be clearly defined (as far as is possible). Production organizations and workshops should join the procession in their work clothes.

h   Means of transport (lorries and other vehicles) which accompany groups of workers on foot should proceed at a professionally consistent speed.

i   There should be a mass participation of lorries with pioneers.

3   Examples of forms for the mass diagram.

a   The numbers of the Red Army during three periods of Revolution (1918, 1920, 1926).

b   The uniforms of the Red Army in the three periods of its existence.

c   The starting and finishing points of the Soviet military defence (the Red Guard, the Red Army).

d   The growth in the numbers of workers employed on production over the period 1920 to 1926.

e   Growth in wages (illustrated in a material way).

f   Growth of industrialization (diagram showing this in material terms).

g   Growth of the peasant economy (laden carts should process carrying diagrams of yields and so on as well as examples of particular crops).

h   Medical care (a demonstration of the first aid service) at the beginning and end of the decade (stretchers, ambulances, health teams in their uniforms and so on).

i   Education (the growth in the demand for books, the growth of literacy and so on).

4   Principles behind the contrasting presentation of the first and final stage of the first decade since the October Revolution.

5   Amateur activity in the columns during their stops. Masters of ceremonies, moving sports and physical culture performances, competitions and the distribution of prizes, Swiss wrestling, dances and games – these have the aim of eliminating tiresome waiting on one spot.

6   Badges and numbers for each column. The demonstration should proceed according to the numbers. Loud-speakers should regulate the procession.

7   Solemn processing of the Regional Committee, the Petrograd Soviet, the Executive Committee, the Regional Trade Union Council and other organizations – from the Smolny to the rostrum on Uritsky Square.

8   Attraction of foreign delegations to take part in the celebrations marking the tenth anniversary. Mass welcome for the foreigners as representatives of the Western proletariat.

9   Loud-speaker: military slogans for the day. High moments in reports from around the Union. Radio transmission of the Moscow demonstration.

C   *Evening celebrations*

1   Ceremonial meetings dedicated to the Revolution in the regions and in the centre.

2   Ceremonial meetings in clubs. Evenings of reminiscences about the Revolution. Shows of film reels connected with the Revolution. Concerts and theatrical performances. Mobile theatre-trams with performances by professional and amateur troupes. Radio broadcasts of ceremonial meetings in Leningrad, Moscow and other cities.

2nd day of the festivities
Daytime: a display of the armed forces. . . .
In the evening: mass performances.

1   Dramatizations should have a mass character. They should not be just a spectacle but they should be a mass performance. The public should be drawn into the action.

2   The subject of the performances should be particularly significant moments in the class struggle of our citizens.

3   Links with the historical experience of the particular district.

4   Points for the development of mass evening performances:

a   The Peter and Paul Fortress, the Winter Palace (Central, Petrograd and Vasily Island districts).

b   The Finland Station (the Lenin Monument) – (Vyborgsky district).

c   The Smolny (Volodarsky district).

d   The Narva Gates (Moscow-Narva district).

5   Suggestions of subjects for mass performances:

a   The storming of the capitalist stronghold (the taking of the Peter and Paul Fortress).

b   The arrival of Ilyich (the monument can play its part in the dramatization).

c   Key moments in the October Revolution (the Smolny plays a leading part here).

d   The founding of the Red Guard (at the Narva Gates).

6   Mass performance at the Peter and Paul Fortress. Storming of the stronghold of capitalism. Scene – the Neva, the canal surrounding the Peter and Paul Fortress. The audience will be on the Embankment of January the 9th and on the three bridges. The Peter and Paul Fortress as the support of world capital. Characteristics of the white terror. In front of the Fortress is the silhouette of a capitalist battleship (made out of cardboard or plywood and standing on two barges). The movement of the Red Fleet. Marches of red divisions meeting at the Fortress. The Air Force. Sea and air battles. Salvos from both sides.

Departure of the armed train (a disguised steam engine and tram freight platforms). On Republic Bridge – rocket shooting at the Fortress. Salvos and cannonade in response. Floodlighting effects. Shafts of red and white light. Slogans on the clouds. The capitalist battleship explodes and is burnt. Landing. The taking of the Peter and Paul Fortress. Red flag on the spire of the Peter and Paul Cathedral. Shaft of floodlighting. Red star over the Fortress. Fireworks. Over the Peter and Paul Fortress a splendid poster in lights of Lenin. Loudspeakers play the 'Internationale' throughout the town. Choir of sirens and hooters. The crowd sings.

7   The action is played according to the planned scenario.

The 3rd day
1   Arrangements for a mass popular fair. A wide range of spontaneous activity.
2   Mobile performances of physical culture. Sports games. Physical culture competitions. Pioneer groups to be driven on lorries all round the town. Mobile theatres. Political satire. Burning of guys (the tsar, a priest, a kulak, a bourgeois, a policeman). 'Living newspapers'. Stalls. Carts selling sweets. Sales of badges and toys dedicated to the festivities; carnival entertainments. Advertisement for co-operatives and state enterprises.
3   In the evening on the streets there will be film shows . . . fireworks, posters in lights, bonfires, radio concerts, mobile performances. The whole city will be alive.

Organizational details
1   Attracting the Red Academicians from the General Headquarters to take part in the mass spectacle at the Peter and Paul Fortress.
2   Mobilizing all cars and motorcycles for the festivities.
3   Mobilizing the Young Communist League and activists from clubs and circles to help in organizing and preparing for the festivities.
4   Mobilizing ciné cameras to film the festivities.
5   Campaign to inform people about the festivities. Preliminary information about the programme of the celebrations to be broadcast on the radio. Special leaflets to be produced. Posters with the route. Timetables and programmes for the festivities. Campaign in the periodical press. Publication of a series of posters to embellish the celebrations.

TsGALI SSSR, f.1230, op.1, d.1453, ll.1–8.

May Day Celebrations 1928

MOSCOW AND LENINGRAD

75 *Current campaigns reflected*

Extract from a report on the First of May celebrations in Moscow and Leningrad, from *Pravda*

4 May 1928

May Day Moscow
. . . Columns of demonstrators slowly moved along Tverskaya Street, filling its whole width. Banners, posters and caricature figures floated above their heads – the response of these organized proletarians to the tasks of the moment, to the political anger of the occasion.

The columns moved. Look and read and you will realize what working Moscow is experiencing at this moment.

'Socialist rationalization is the basis of the material and cultural rise of the working class!'

'A merciless war on lethargy, carelessness and thoughtlessness in the socialist workplace!'

'All achievements and failings to be subjected to inspection by and criticism from the masses.'

The posters appealed and castigated; evil that deserved ridicule was ridiculed. Moreover, the slogans were not only on the posters. Here there was a 'green snake' crawling out of a huge bottle and winding itself round a group of workers with its annulated body . . . 'The industrialization of the country is not possible without raising the cultural level of workers'.

There was a living illustration of a poster about military danger. The columns were interspersed with divisions of armed working lads carefully keeping in step with a march played by the factory orchestra. . . . There was a shaft which turned constantly and had speared some long-tongued gentlemen in top-hats. Its caption was 'Beating around the bush over the question of disarmament. The League of Nations'.

The column of demonstrators moves forward. There are

now more workers' bands. There are larger numbers of choirs and musical circles in our clubs and each of them was putting their achievements on show on the street today. . . . The demonstration was powerful and impressive. It finished at five o'clock in the evening but that does not mean that the festivities finished then.

In the evening May Day Moscow was illuminated by varicoloured lights and the decorated buildings shone with elegance. People were drawn onto the streets and squares, to loudspeaker points and to watch films projected onto the sides of buildings.

The First of May in Leningrad
. . . The demonstrators moved in a solid multi-coloured mass. Thousands of posters with slogans and banners fluttered over this sea of heads. Hundreds of bands filled the square. Outwardly the demonstration differed from previous ones in that it was managed with a greater economy of resources. There were none of the cumbersome vans, giant galoshes, ships, wheels, cars and entire workshops with which factories used to demonstrate in previous years. The productive element, however, was as strongly stressed as before. The chief slogans of the demonstration were 'For the Cultural Revolution' and 'Down with Bureaucratism and Thriftlessness'. The demonstration went on until five o'clock in the evening. No less than seven hundred thousand workers passed in front of the rostrum. Leningrad was crowded with festive groups of people until late at night.

Mass popular fairs took place in all districts of the town on 1 and 2 May. Entertainers performed and there were 'living newspapers' and dances to the music of workers' bands. Mass games were organized at thirty different places in Leningrad. There were eighteen 'living newspapers', about twenty itinerant cinemas and many other events.

According to preliminary figures, more than one hundred thousand people attended workers' clubs over these two days. Peasants and workers of sixteen different nationalities came to the city to celebrate the holiday with its workers.

Pravda, no. 102, 4 May 1928

Moscow Street Carnival May 1929

76 *Students experiment*

Former VKhUTEIN student N. S. Starodub recalls from her youth the students' work for the street carnival in late May, 1929

In 1929 a large carnival of fifty-four decorated lorries was organized in the Central Park of Culture and Rest [Gorky Park] to mark the opening of the summer season. It was the first Moscow spectacle on such a large scale. . . .

The designs for the artistic side of the carnival were carried out by students from the theatrical design department of the painting faculty of VKhUTEIN under the leadership of Professor I. M. Rabinovich and it was part of the course work. After the designs had been approved students from different faculties within VKhUTEIN brought all the designs to life, working in the Park, and thoroughly enjoyed it. Rabinovich allowed great freedom to everyone's ideas. The subjects were dealt with in a politically sharp way and showed great inventiveness. At one point we had to consult the People's Commissariat of Foreign Affairs on international questions for some satirical bits and I remember the special visit of People's Commissar M. M. Litvinov who, having looked at the satirical figures, gave the young artists advice about how to adjust their work as necessary to avoid diplomatic problems. . . .

Muscovites remembered that carnival for a long time afterwards.

From the personal archives of N. S. Starodub

174

170
171
172

77 *British Imperialism*

N. S. Starodub recalls in detail the float she designed with Ya. F. Kozlovskaya on the theme 'The Ship of British Imperialism'

175   The ship was mounted on three lorries disguised within the composition but joined together and forming the hull of an enormous aluminium warship sailing along the streets of Moscow.

On the first lorry was mounted the bows of the ship representing the three-dimensional head of the old British lion with wide open jaws in which could be seen the remnants of predatory fangs. The lion's mane consisted of separate three-dimensional snake-like locks which were winding themselves around the heads of a negro, an Indian and a Malaysian and strangling them. On the lion's head there were two figures of social-democrats dressed as lackeys with napkins across their arms. They were supporting the golden crown of the British Empire on the head of a miniature figure of a woman in royal robes.

On the second lorry was the middle part of the ship. A three-dimensional mast rose up from its centre. Cannon of different calibres were mounted here. They were in three layers becoming smaller in size as they went up. There were also wires stretched out with flapping signal flags. The central part of the ship was in two layers. The lower level took the form of a darkened hole lit from underneath and it represented a mine in which the bent figures of miners worked with picks. The miners were real entertainers from sideshows in the Park of Culture and Rest.

The upper level was a deck with three-dimensional figures on it. These were twice the size of real people. The comparison between the living figures below and the huge decorative characters up above emphasized very

169   effectively the difference in scale. There was one group of two figures representing British imperialists playing golf. One of these two figures playing golf was Macdonald, and instead of a golf ball they were using a worker's head of papier mâché.

On the third lorry there was the ship's stern. This was crowned by the muzzle of a cannon on which Churchill was sitting holding the ship's wheel and looking through a telescope. Along the entire hull of the ship on both sides

were heads of the oppressed peoples from British colonies.

The heads of the particularly large three-dimensional figures like the golfers and Churchill had wire frameworks with cloth stretched over them. This was then painted and finished off. Plywood was used for a number of details such as the telescope, their hands, headwear and so on. We executed all this ourselves, with the help of five other students.

From the personal archives of N. S. Starodub

78 *Enjoyable work*

Reminiscences of former VKhUTEIN student A. S. Magidson

The theatrical design department of the painting faculty at VKhUTEIN prepared artists for work in the theatre, which included not only arrangements for traditional theatrical performances but also designs for events in Parks of Culture, stadiums, book markets, streets, squares, workers' demonstrations, mass fairs and carnivals, for public festivals and so on.

One of these tasks on which our course worked in 1929 was a large carnival organized on the Moscow Soviet's initiative for 'Anti-Imperialist Day'. We had the task of finding the gaudiest, the most grotesque and most accessible forms for our ideas so that they would be easily understood as the carnival passed, evoking a string of associations in relation to the current political life of

172   imperialist countries. For example, colonial India was

171   depicted as a huge enchained elephant, imperialist France surrounded by her serving dogs – the countries of the Petite Entente – was portrayed as a dandy dancing on the backs of black slaves with an umbrella, showing a map of France's colonies. There were compositions on the themes 'Imperialism and its colonies', 'Fascism', 'The Ku Klux

170 Klan', 'The marriage of Mussolini and the Pope' and many
other subjects.

We prepared our plans in the classrooms of VKhUTEIN
but we carried out our full-size work in the Central Park of
Culture and Rest. Junior classes from the Theatrical
Department as well as students from other faculties were
176 invited to help us make the masks and figures out of papier
177 mâché and all kinds of other, sometimes rather unlikely,
materials (tin, wire, matting, rags, etc.). We did all this
unusual and enjoyable work in a mood of creative
enthusiasm and gaiety.

Each theatrical carnival group was mounted on an
individual lorry or a separate cart and united by
accompanying banners with texts. This long string of
colourful carnival groups aroused tumultuous laughter
from the spectators.

From the personal archives of A. S. Magidson

Critique:
September–October 1929

79 *New scale?*

**Extract from an article by L. Roshchin, 'Raising
enthusiasm to the nth degree', published in the magazine
*Art to the Masses***

September – October 1929

. . . On the face of it we have all the elements of
exceptional mass celebrations which are quite outstanding:
tens and hundreds of thousands of participants,
enthusiasms, slogans of struggle and construction, a huge
variety of impressions, joy, music, colour. But we have not
yet found a new form for the new content, a form which
would fuse all the elements of the festivities together and
would unify them into one immense artistic production, . . .
and hold each and every participant in a state of joyful
tension.

All the art forms should be represented as live
participants in this mass celebration, but for the mass
spectator and listener they must be enlarged to
monumental scale. It is this aspect of the mass festivals
which indicates the particular path they should follow
within the artistic revolution. They create the need for
super-powerful musical instruments, super-powerful
cinema, super-sized sculpture and painting. Here the
revolutionary epoch is posing massive tasks for our
inventors, engineers and architects.

It is essential to repeat and expand the experiment of
'monumental propaganda' (which was Lenin's concept),
throughout the streets and spaces of Moscow. In huge
posters and three-dimensional charts we must express the
scale of the Five Year Plan, our enthusiasm for
industrialization and the all-embracing scale of socialist
construction! In the city's squares we propose
'monumental propaganda' pavilions with illuminated
charts and diagrams instead of walls; in the public gardens
we will have three-dimensional diagrams in wood with
sculptural decorations. Along the processional route there

should be vast, multi-coloured posters with agitation for the new way of life and for work discipline. Prominent surfaces should be exploited for hard-hitting and uncompromising cartoons on political and social themes. At a time like this it is vital that we should hit out at drunkards, idlers and hooligans.

In shop windows the corsets, stockings and mannequins should be replaced by pictures, which a special jury will select from workers' clubs and self-taught artists.

Once again we assert the necessity for a mass festival to be conceived and organized as a magnificent and integrated work of art, as the very embodiment of the proletarian revolution in art, and therefore as something entirely new and unprecedented.

Iskusstvo v massy (Art to the Masses), no. 5–6, 1929, pp. 28–30.

80 *New scale, ancient techniques?*

Extract from an article, 'We appeal', published in the magazine *Art to the Masses*

September – October 1929

The October Revolution has given birth to a new phenomenon: the demonstration-festival. There are three elements to this festival: protest, propaganda and entertainment. For eleven years we have seen the Soviet proletariat and labouring peasantry parade on the streets to challenge the bourgeoisie which surrounds us. Floats have reflected all the horrors and frauds they perpetrated in order to focus and organize the rage and contempt of participants, and to prepare them for battle in the class struggle both within the country and without. . . . Our revolutionary festivals reflect both anger and triumph: they are an organization of the will for the final victory. . . . This means that they cannot be made to fit some boring canon . . . but participants deserve festivals which are

powerfully gripping and are active expressions of their enthusiasm.

It is time we mastered the art of these demonstrations. For a start, their tempo should correspond to the tempo of industrialization. Down with long futile waits on street corners and three hours to walk the hundred meters from Lubyanka Square to Theatre Square! Any pause should be used for a meeting or a performance.

Actors! Your place is out on the streets these days in mass spectacles! Acting methods from the dawn of theatre in ancient Greece and Rome should be reborn here in a new form. We need the street actor of old, the actor on a pedestal, with an unnaturally large body and a character mask on his face. The thundering voices of old can be reproduced by loudspeakers, but masks and vast forms are essential. Our mass spectacles have shown clearly that the normal chamber actor cannot be seen or heard in the street, that his gestures are ineffectual and incomprehensible!

We also need specially written plays. Our authors should carefully study the comedies of Aristophanes to re-educate themselves. What astonishing wit those plays have, taking the burning issues of their day by the throat. Despite the passage of time they have lost none of their significance for today.

A short, fast-moving bit of grotesque with some eccentricity, some clowning, some dances and some verse: that's what we need at the street corner. A kaleidoscope of mummified social-democratic opportunists, capitalist monsters, the dregs of our social life: this will fill ten to fifteen minutes during a stop at a street corner. A lorry will drive up and give the performance. Actors should emphasize their movements in a clear and precise way; each should be enlarged in height and volume and should use changeable masks, each representing one state of the soul, be it grief, joy, laughter, meanness, villainy or whatever. Such an actor is comprehensible to the masses!
. . . Compare even the clown's traditional striving for political satire with the petty bourgeois triviality of our versifiers. We need couplets that expose society's cancers, not couplets based on obscene innuendo! . . .

The spring carnival at the Park of Culture and Rest gave us a lot of experience in this respect. Papier mâché figures are expressive, but they are silent and immobile like a diagram: those who already understand will recognize them, but others will simply walk away. . . .

That carnival was an example of another interesting fact: amazingly, it was done without any authors or scenario-writers. The artists themselves created the play.

It is typical that at present the only people active in creating our street festivals are the fine artists. Actors, writers, musicians: they are all silent!

All our talented people with witty tongues: bring your talents out onto the streets! Smirnov-Sokolsky, Zoshchenko, Lazarenko: can you hear? We are appealing to you! . . . Dramatists and scenario writers have scarcely touched the question of mass performances. Only some theatrical people, such as Meyerkhold, have made some attempt, but nothing systematic.

Fine artists have generally taken on work for demonstrations as a kind of hobby. Only VKhUTEIN and MGSPS have tried to organize exhibitions of designs for the October celebrations. But MGSPS's exhibition was dismally poor and VKhUTEIN's was imposed on the school at a time of heavy academic commitments.

VKhUTEIN must be given its due, however: their's was the first voice to raise the issue. But henceforth it must be dealt with by graduates of the school through artistic organizations outside the confines of higher education. . . . Otherwise, as before, no classes will begin until the celebrations are over.

Iskusstvo v massy (Art to the Masses), 1929, no. 5–6, pp. 22–3.

Twelfth Anniversary of the October Revolution

MOSCOW

81   *Events on Red Square*

Extract from a report on the celebrations to mark the Twelfth Anniversary of the October Revolution in Moscow, published in Workers' Moscow

10 November 1929

178   . . . When the chimes from the Spassky Tower had sounded eleven and the last weary parade of soldiers had crossed Red Square, a dense wall of people appeared from the direction of the History Museum. This human wall moved quickly forward, colourful with hundreds of banners and posters, and soon it filled all the remainder of the square. The six different districts of the city came forward simultaneously.

The majority of the posters and slogans were proclaiming the successes of the Five Year Plan, of non-stop production, of socialist competition, with concrete achievements – the facts and figures of socialist construction. The general slogan of the demonstration is: 'We shall complete the Five Year Plan in four years.'

A wittily produced dramatization answers those moaners and idlers and those right-wing opportunist elements who are afraid of our decisive attack on capitalism: a worthless mare, caught up in the traces of an anti-diluvian plough, has reared up and, by raising its meagre tail, is trying to halt the progress of a column of tractors. This tableau drew ecstatic comments from the demonstrators. Next comes a funeral cortège: Sunday is

179   being buried. Priests of all nationalities accompany the coffin. Bringing up the rear of the cortège is a poster saying 'Introduce non-stop production'. Idlers, drunkards, absentees, bureaucrats and other scum received their due in caricatures. The demonstration did not finish until dusk, and by then about one million people had passed through the Square.

On that day Moscow resembled a gigantic photograph reflecting, with perfect accuracy, the twelfth year since the Revolution as the year of great change. Moscow was full of life and festively decorated, breathing with the Party's slogans and reflecting the great turning-point from which socialism will make a more concerted attack. The rapid tempo of industrialization, the Five Year Plan and collectivization of agriculture – the masses marched to these slogans, following these stars to guide them to socialism. In this mighty demonstration proletarian Moscow once more showed its unity with the Party and its determination to struggle for the Party's general line.

Rabochaya Moskva (Workers' Moscow), no. 259, 10 November 1929

LENINGRAD

82 *The Five Year Plan*

Extract from an article, 'Towards the twelfth anniversary of the October Revolution: a conversation with S. E. Radlov', published in the magazine *Life of Art*

6 October 1929

After the Theatrical Arts College's staging of an anti-Easter spectacle last spring, they have now received another commission from the Regional Department of Education, Oblono, to organize a mass performance on the scale of the entire city to mark the celebrations of the twelfth anniversary of the Revolution on 7 November. Links have been established between the College and the Cultural Department of the Leningrad Regional Trade Union Council which has taken responsibility for realizing their ideas.

The theme of the scenario, proposed by S. E. Radlov, is The Factory Roll Call. It has been worked out collectively with representatives from the Cultural Department, from factories and enterprises and from the Directing Department of the College. Arrangements for the performance are also being decided upon collectively: the main organizer responsible is Comrade Serebryakov, the head of the artistic section of the Cultural Department, the chief director is S. E. Radlov, other directors are a group of club workers and students from the Directing Department of the College are acting as lab assistants. Artistic aspects are under the leadership of V. M. Khodasevich; this work has, moreover, attracted a number of students from the theatrical department of the painting faculty of the former Academy of Arts, now VKhUTEIN. Music is under the leadership of I. V. Nemtsev.

Underlying the whole performance is the principle of giving the initiative to people on the spot – to the factories and enterprises which will work out the scenes allocated to them independently. The necessary dimension of Socialist competition is generated by theatrical competitions between factories.

The performance will be given on Uritsky Square, and the backcloth will be the semi-circle of the buildings of the General Staff Headquarters; the audience will thus have their backs to the Winter Palace.

Forty-five Leningrad enterprises are taking part in the performance and they have presented more than fifty lorries to the spectacle. Up to four thousand people in all are involved.

The presentation is dedicated to the Five Year Plan and particularly the achievements of its first year. It falls into six parts: (1) a dramatized parade of up to forty lorries from different enterprises, bearing the emblems of each; (2) a factory roll-call dealing with questions of production, the lowering of costs, the growth of production, improvements in labour discipline and so on – technically this will be done by posing questions over loudspeakers and by each factory giving dramatized answers; (3) an interlude in the form of an enlarged puppet theatre in which saboteurs participate – also drunkards, bureaucrats, hooligans, kulaks and so on, each of whom do a particular dance number and are then chased off by workers; (4) a Symphony of Labour, showing the growth in the numbers of workers in our new period of construction and the industrialization of the countryside; (5) the defence of our country and the Red Army and all workers' readiness in this area; (6) a solemn promise to fulfil the Five Year Plan. In conclusion there will be a finale with fireworks, radio and so on.

Zhizn iskusstva (Life of Art), no. 40, 6 October 1929, p. 12.

180

Thirteenth Anniversary of the October Revolution

MOSCOW

83 *Concept of demonstration*

Extract from the directives of the Central Regional Headquarters of the Moscow Executive Committee, dealing with arrangements for the Thirteenth Anniversary

Sometime before 7 November 1930

Now to deal with the very content of the concept of 'demonstration'. This is not some specific type of mass action – it is the whole complex of mass events. This complex consists of the following separate elements: (a) an agitational procession; (b) an agitational meeting; (c) the October parade (mass procession); (d) the demonstration itself.

These elements do not simply follow one after the other. They happen simultaneously at different points within the demonstration (as will be shown below). It is the combination of these elements and a skilful distribution of material elements and of slogans which gives the demonstration its colourful and at the same time balanced diversity.

The masses of people who take part in the demonstration are grouped according to a production plan. People from the same place of work form one column together. Where a place of work is small then several places join together.

A large column subdivides into smaller battalions of about three hundred people. In each small column the people stand so that they form a slogan (theme). Each small column or battalion divides into three parts:
1   The introduction (head). Banners, flags, badges, a band.
2   The centre. A cart or lorry with a display (something to correspond with the basic theme).
3   The concluding part (a choir, flags, badges). . . .

Colour scheme:
After the actual ordering of the procession, the factor that makes the strongest impression is the colour scheme, i.e., the use of all the colours. Red must be given a particularly honoured place, so it is not appropriate to use it everywhere. Red should be used only when it looks genuinely red, when it is highlighted by other equally bright colours, in competition with which red looks more effective.

Material elements:
Flags (cloth – 50 by 90 cm, post – 2 m long and 3 cm in diameter) are carried on a band across the shoulder with a leather holder at the front in the flag-bearer's belt. Apart from flags and standards, material elements and props consist of:
1   banners – vertically stretched out pieces of material with slogans.
2   slogans written on pieces of linen stretched horizontally – these should be fixed into frames.
3   badges and emblems; material for badges and emblems is preferably not linen but rather tin, glass, wood, paper, straw and in general any material that comes to hand which can be used in an interesting style or painted.

Badges depicting real subjects (people, instruments, animals) should be of the realistic size. Surfaces cut out of plywood are not worth using – they are unconvincing.
4   Structures on lorries and carts are the most effective parts of the demonstration and they give their displays a scenic character.

In such constructions one particular theme should be clearly expressed. Moreover, the display should be a parade arrangement of the theme. It should not be just drily presented facts: the facts should be demonstratively emphasized in a triumphal procession. From this it follows that satire evoking mockery is completely inappropriate. Moments of living, healthy humour evoked by the central constructions are transferred to the choir (which is declamatory rather than vocal) for the singing technique of choirs is rarely perfect.

Materials for the structures, as for badges and emblems, are various. To these large constructions may be added such materials as fluttering ribbons, flags, pennants and banners. . . .

Massovoye deistvo-oformlenie Oktyabrskoi demonstratsii (Mass action decoration for the October demonstration), Moscow, 1930, pp. 4, 8–9, 11–13.

84 *Banners for Kirov Street*

85 *Aeroplanes somersault*

Extract from the manuscript memoirs of the Moscow artist N. A. Musatov, who worked on various celebrations of the late twenties and early thirties

The year 1930 arrived. A more organized approach to the arrangements for revolutionary celebrations was required. To this end the Moscow Soviet formed a Central Artistic Subcommission under the leadership of Comrade Malkin.

We artists had already joined into creative unions and so it was easy for the Moscow Soviet to choose us and to draw us into work on arrangements for the decoration of the city. I was entrusted with Kirov Street (formerly Myasnitskaya) leading to Dzerzhinsky Square. I proposed to Boris Afanasyevich Rodionov that we should work together. It would have been difficult for one person to do such a job alone as a considerable amount of time had to be spent on organizational aspects and it was impossible to leave the decorations to be worked on without supervision. At that time you could only get to the Moscow Soviet headquarters by tram and there were few tram lines operating.

We looked at our area, and the street was narrow. This meant that our design should be something 'continuous' all down the street. It was fortunate that many buildings facing each other were more or less of the same height. Having contemplated the buildings, we threw ropes from the roof of one building to the roof of the one opposite. We were anxious to keep the rhythm of our design. On the ropes we hung large calico banners several storeys long.

Taking the strength of the wind into account we sewed them like sails with strong twine. On both sides they had government slogans; thus the street was decorated. These banners, fixed in the space above the central part of the street, would hit the passers-by in the eyes. So that the wind should not blow them about too much, we sewed iron pipes to their lower edges and because of this the banners merely swayed majestically.

From the personal archives of N. A. Musatov

Extract from a report on the celebrations of the Thirteenth Anniversary of the Revolution in Moscow, from *Izvestiya*

10 November 1930

The Seventh of November on Red Square
Moscow greeted the thirteenth anniversary of the Revolution noisily and festively. Early in the morning, long before the beginning of the demonstration, the streets were filled with crowds of people, banners, slogans and posters. Hundreds and thousands of proletarians processed to Red Square in columns. . . . First went the schoolchildren and pioneers. After them came groups from the various factories. . . . Shock-workers marched with rifles in a horizontal position. On their bayonets guys were impaled, representing saboteurs, bureaucrats, absentees and opportunists. . . .

There was a large tram car with the sign 'Stop for the commune' and decorating the tram posts were the numbers '5–4' (the Five Year Plan completed in four years). . . .

The Khamovniki district – the area with many higher education institutions – demonstrated a 'cadre factory'. Students promised to prepare new regiments of red specialists for their country. From the rostrums, delegates from England, America and Germany greeted one placard held on high by demonstrators with particular applause. The slogan on the placard was 'We are completing the Five Year Plan for the benefit of the proletariat of the whole world'.

Above people's heads there were hundreds of tough, witty caricatures as well as figures showing the fulfilment of industrial and financial plans. . . . In the air, aeroplanes turned somersaults like tumbler-pigeons . . . and a team of five pilots did a 'collective dance' showing the power and art of our best Soviet aviators.

Izvestiya TsIK, no. 309, 10 November 1930

185

Fourteenth Anniversary of the October Revolution

MOSCOW

86 *Stenberg's scheme*

Extract from an article by E. Zagorskaya, 'The artistic decoration of Moscow', published in the magazine *For Proletarian Art*

August 1931

Moscow Soviet has attracted a number of artists and architects to participate in the artistic transformation of the city's streets and squares. The streets which have been designated to be dealt with first are: Sretenka, Arbat, Tverskaya Street, Kuznetsky Bridge, Dzerzhinsky Street, the main road joining Sverdlov Square to Mokhovaya and Volkhonka, the B ring-road and the Bolshaya Dmitrovka.

It is proposed to decorate the Arbat in accordance with the Stenberg brothers' design and Tverskaya Street, Kuznetsky Bridge, Dzerzhinsky Street and Sretenka according to the designs of the German architect Leistikov. The main road from Sverdlov Square to Volkhonka is being decorated to the design of the artists and monument-designers Odintsov and Ivanov. The B ring-road and the Bolshaya Dmitrovka will be decorated to designs by the team of artists attached to the Park of Culture and Rest. Hangings and shop-windows will be dealt with first and then the buildings will be painted. . . .

In the decorated streets everyday trade or advertising hangings will be replaced by standard slogans and shop windows will be turned into three-dimensional posters. On Kuznetsky Bridge the shop windows should be used not for pens, rubbers, ink and other objects like that but solely for displays of socialist construction. The chief radial streets – Lubyanka, Sretenka, Tverskaya, Myasnitskaya – should each have their own range of typical characteristics. It is proposed to have street lighting of the Western or American type using what is called 'new lighting'. To strengthen the street lighting it is proposed to put

floodlighting and moving, illuminated advertisements on the remaining churches and bell-towers.

According to the design of the Stenberg brothers the basic principle of designs for the street should be in line with the lighting arrangements. Thus they propose that all the houses on the Arbat should be painted grey and all the windows, frames and doors should be black.

Za proletarskoe iskusstvo (For Proletarian Art), no. 8, August 1931, p. 31

87 *Kuznetsk to Moscow*

Manuscript reminiscences of the artist A. S. Magidson describe her contribution to decorations for the Fourteenth Anniversary of the Revolution in Moscow

In the summer of 1931 my fellow artist N. F. Korotkova and I set off for a creative mission to the construction site of the Kuznetsk Metallurgical Combine, one of the most significant sites of the first Five Year Plan.

When we arrived we were immediately flung into the whirlpool of the site. Our impressions were overwhelming: ditches, cranes, blast furnaces in the forest, the carcases of gigantic workshops, mountains of overturned earth, and everywhere people, like ants, determinedly and purposefully scurrying about in this apparent chaos. The most modern technology of our times was all mixed up with primitive, age-old hand tools like wheelbarrows, spades and crowbars.

The contours of the most modern socialist town were already delineated with the gloomy, squat barracks and dugouts beside it, and at the same time the comfortable village set up for the foreign specialists. But the most interesting thing of all was the extraordinary diversity and multi-national character of the army of workers. There were people with all sorts of specialisms and qualifications – from navvies with their spades and wheelbarrows to welders and fitters, all equally necessary and each one finding his or her own niche.

A fair number of artists had gathered there. Besides N. Korotkova and myself, there were other Muscovites including A. Bubnov, M. Gurevich (a future Hero of the Soviet Union), Igumnov, I. Murzaev. All of us were literally dazzled by the multitude of impressions to be gained. Everything was of interest, from the vast panorama of the construction site and its separate parts, the portraits of people at work and in breaks between shifts. We wanted to capture all these images and to engrave them on our memories. We found ourselves drawn into the communal life of the site, into its voluntary Saturdays, the *subbotniki*; into arrangements for such special meetings as when K. E. Voroshilov came to the site, and into many other such events. Thus we returned to Moscow bursting with impressions and laden with heaps of sketches, longing to pass on our experiences and impressions.

Still imbued with all this, I joined a team of people organizing the decorations of Sverdlov Square for the 1931 October Revolution celebrations. I was to be the designer. The designs done for this square in the years immediately after the Revolution already had their history, with a variety of solutions produced by numerous different artists. All, however, had merely created a festive atmosphere through decorative means, whereas our designs had to express a specific theme in a precise way. I do not recall now whether our theme was 'Industrialization' or 'Construction sites of the first Five Year Plan', only that my summer journey to Kuznetsk had provided me with the richest possible material for creating a decorative composition on our given theme. I had to find a resounding and intense image which would set the tone for the whole idea. The memory arose of a silhouette of a blast furnace under construction: at Kuznetskstroi this had been the centre of attention and the focus of all efforts. Strict account was kept of the days remaining until the furnace could be set in motion and everyone on the site carefully followed the progress of work there. Hence a

193 blast furnace under construction took the place of honour on the square and became a symbol of the construction of heavy industry, with portraits in a gallery alongside showing leading personnel from construction sites all over the Soviet Union.

The decorative blast furnace was constructed on a fountain opposite the side wall of the Metropole Hotel. Because of its size, construction and colour, the furnace was striking enough to form one of the two visual centres of the whole square. The other centre was in the public garden opposite the Bolshoi Theatre. Here we set up a decoration consisting of three cranes, each of which was carrying products from one of the major car and tractor factories (AMO, ChTZ, KhTZ). This construction was painted silver which, in combination with the red paint, created a feeling of the severity of metal combined with the magnificence of the festival.

194 The illumination plan was very important, and both these key thematic features were carefully picked out in lights. All buildings around the square – the Maly Theatre, Second Arts Theatre, the Metropole Hotel and the Vostok cinema – were hung with large paintings on industrial themes and these were brightly lit in the evenings.

The 1931 designs marked the first of a series of thematic, three-dimensional solutions to the problem of handling urban spaces on these occasions. In subsequent years Sverdlov Square would be treated with such themes as 'The Dam of the Dniepr Hydro-Electric Power Station', 'Ball-bearings', 'Bloomery mills' and the like.

From the personal archives of A. S. Magidson

88 *Using a political editor*

Extract from the article 'Artistic decoration of October festivals' by V. S. Toot, published in *For Proletarian Art*

November – December 1931

Undoubtedly the decorations for the fourteenth anniversary of the October Revolution surpassed anything done in previous years and they were even better than what was done for May this year.

The form was both politically sharper and artistically better quality. We made fewer political mistakes and were subjected to fewer ideologically hostile influences. The character of different enterprises was more brightly displayed. Displays showing the achievement of the industrial-financial plan at different factories were more sharply done. The town was more smoothly divided into thematic areas. To some degree there was specialization of decoration for different parts and districts of the town.

These successes were in large part due to the fact that the artistic arrangements for the celebrations attracted the attention of the party and of community and professional organizations. For the first time a political editor worked side by side with the artist on the designs. . . .

The fourteenth anniversary of the Revolution for the first time applied the principle that arrangements should be divided between districts according to the production profile of the particular area. Thus, for example, on Nogin Square where the USSR's VSNKh [the Supreme Economic Soviet], the headquarters of our industry, is situated there was an exhibition of Soviet machinery and the achievements of Soviet technology were on display. This exhibition, attracting many visitors as it did, had one weakness; it did not pay enough attention to the question of graphics. There was an absence of artistic shape to the exhibition and so the true face of our construction was not reflected. The machinery emphasized only our technical achievements. The same mistake was repeated on Arbat Square too where an exhibition was organized by the Ministry of Road Transport.

A very interesting new feature of the arrangements was the Alley of Caricatures done by Moor's brigade of artists; these were a series of precise, politically sharp caricatures in the form of three-dimensional figures. Significant achievements could also be noted in relation to shop-window decorations. It is true, however, that the short time available for the decoration of windows meant that photographic material was the main content of most windows.

Despite a greater political sharpness and a higher artistic quality too, artistic arrangements for the October anniversary celebrations still suffer from a number of weaknesses. There is still too much constructivism, formalism and abstractness.

In some instances, on the other hand, arrangements suffer from an overloading of images.

In certain squares one could see a division between the decorative arrangements, and the monumental art, sculpture and so on. This marred the unity of the effect. Thus, on Red Square, for example, the wooden sculptured group on the Place of Execution had nothing to link it with the rest of the decorations on the Square.

In order to avoid such disharmonies between different art forms in the future, it is imperative that there should be collective planning of the arrangements for any given square or part of the city; a political editor, an easel artist, a decorative artist, a sculptor, an architect and so on should all be working together.

Za proletarskoe iskusstvo (For Proletarian Art), no. 11–12, November – December 1931, p. 17

TWELFTH ANNIVERSARY, 1929

Twelfth Anniversary of the Revolution, 1929, Moscow

178 (*right*) The Anniversary parade on Red Square.

179 (*below right*) Part of the procession on the theme of 'The funeral of religious festivals' passing through Red Square.

Leningrad

180 (*below left*) Agitational wagon with a sculptural group created by students of the Academy of Arts, on Uritsky Square.

MAY DAY, 1930

May Day, 1930, Moscow

181 (*above right*) Decorative composition on the theme of the Promfinplan, 'The State Industrial and Financial Plan', erected in Red Square.

182 (*right*) Agitational tram with a group of theatrical artistes passing through Taganka Square. Dressed apparently as old-style rich peasants, the banner above them reads somewhat incongruously 'Through Socialist emulation and shock brigades we shall fulfil and over-fulfil the State Industrial and Financial Plan'.

Leningrad

183 (*below right*) A decorative composition of political cartoon figures forming the background to the rostrum on Uritsky Square, executed by students of the VKhUTEMAS.

184 (*below left*) V. A. Raevskaya, decorative structure on the theme of 'The Red Front', erected on the Field of Victims of the Revolution.

THIRTEENTH ANNIVERSARY, 1930

Thirteenth Anniversary of the Revolution, 1930, Moscow

185 Political tableau on a wagon passes through the streets.

Leningrad

186 Agitational wagon made by students of the Academy of Arts with a sculptural caricature where 'Trotsky rides in the chariot of world imperialism'.

MAY DAY, 1931

May Day, 1931, Leningrad

187   (*right*) Design for decorations in
Volodarsky District, by a team from the Fine
Arts Organization for Working Youth,
IZORAM.

188   (*below left*) Grandiose installations
behind the tribune on Uritsky Square, created
by a team from IZORAM led by M. S. Brodsky
and L. I. Karataev.

189   (*below right*) Decorative installation on
Leningrad's Red Square, celebrating 'the
victory of the building of socialism in the
USSR'.

190   (*facing page, above left*) Sketch for an
agitational vehicle for the street parades.

191   (*facing page, above right*) Installation
representing the role of the 'cultural front' in
transforming 'the old lifestyle', with its
traditional Easter foods and its primitive
primus stoves, to 'the new way of life' housed
in modern architecture, through the work of
collective farms and factories. The structure
was erected on International Prospect.

192   (*facing page, below*) Design by P. I.
Akishkin and a team from the City Committee
of the Party (GORKOM), for decorating the
arch at the city's Moscow Gates.

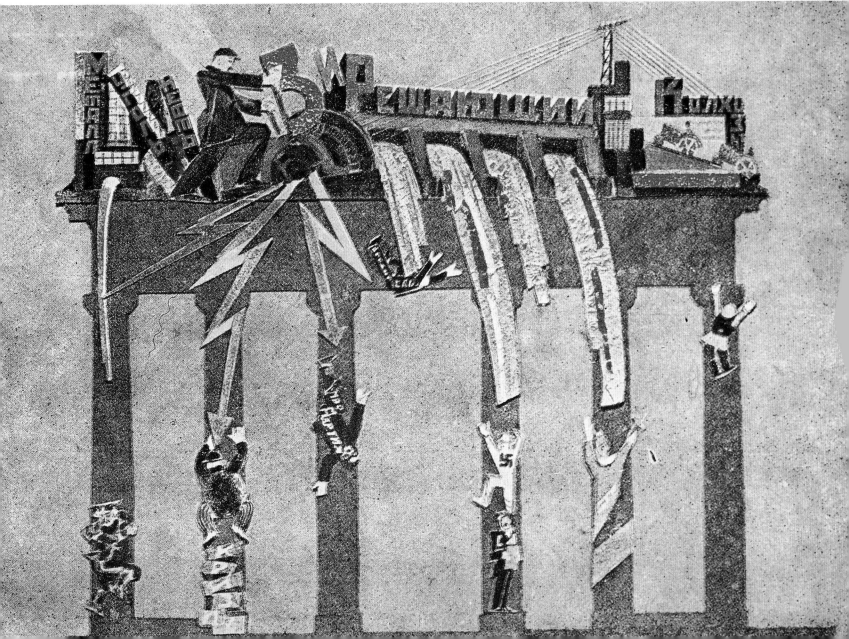

FOURTEENTH ANNIVERSARY, 1931

Fourteenth Anniversary of the Revolution, 1931, Moscow

193 (*far left above*) Decorations on industrial and technological themes for Sverdlov and Revolution Squares by a team from the Russian Association of Proletarian Artists, RAPKh, comprising Ya. P. Shchukin, Ya. D. Romas, A. S. Magidson and A. D. Kuznetsova.

194 (*far left below*) The same, illuminated at night.

195 (*above left*) A procession of workers carrying models of the new housing being erected for them in Moscow under the Soviet regime.

196 (*below left*) N. S. Starodub, F. T. Sevortian, Ya. F. Kozlovskaya, designs for the procession of Power Station workers.

Leningrad

197 (*above right*) One of the city's bridges decorated with panels on an anti-imperialist theme.

198 (*below right*) Photograph of the far right-hand portion of the vast installation against the Winter Palace facade in Uritsky Square.

Fourteenth Anniversary of the Revolution, 1931, Leningrad

199   Central portion of the installation standing in front of the Winter Palace.

200   Design for the entire central composition.

LENINGRAD

89 *Exhibitions in the clubs*

Extract from a report on celebrations for the Fourteenth Anniversary of the Revolution in Leningrad, from *The Red Newspaper*

10 November 1931

October in the city
For three days Leningrad's streets were filled with crowds of people. It seemed as if the whole city had gone out onto the streets to celebrate the fourteenth victorious year since the Revolution.

197
200

  Mobile cinemas were in operation in the squares on the night of 7 November. Mass fires were organized in almost all houses of culture and clubs. In several areas, carnivals and mass theatrical performances took place. Museums and houses of culture showed exhibitions relating to all the major issues of contemporary life. The radio centre had a magnificent musical exchange with Moscow, Kharkov and other towns.

  In workers' clubs, you could see the amateur artistic work of Leningrad trade unions. The work displayed covered all areas: agitational propaganda, musical collectives, literary circles, artistic and photographic film teams, entertainers' circles and so on.

Krasnaya gazeta (The Red Newspaper), no. 265, 10 November 1931

May Day Celebrations 1932

MOSCOW

90 *Socialist sites*

Extracts from manuscript reminiscences of the artists G. S. Zamsky and N. A. Musatov on their work for the May Day celebrations of 1932 in Moscow

Zamsky writes:
It was spring of 1932. The whole country was moving forward, was full of enthusiasm for the major construction sites of the first Five Year Plan. Moscow was preparing to mark the international proletarian festival of workers – the first of May.

  There was a planning headquarters for all aspects of the event in the Moscow Soviet lead by Boris Fyodorovich Malkin. All around him were artists, editors, electricians and builders, all young, fervent, full of ideas and creative plans.

  My colleague N. G. Borov and I, still being young, were delighted to get the job of designing the festive decorations for Sverdlov Square. Our theme was the building of socialism in our country, showing the new construction sites of the first Five Year Plan.

  We had the difficult but attractive task of trying to reflect in a decorative form the spirit and experiences of life out on the major sites of socialist industry and energy. At our disposal was the central square of the capital and we had to decorate it in a manner that was both ideological and artistic, using its space effectively and three-dimensionally. The task was further complicated by the fact that the artists had very little time or materials at their disposal. There were pine boards, plywood, red calico, photos and electric light bulbs, and that was all.

  We chose to feature the Dniepr Hydro-Electric Power Station, Magnitostroi and the First Ball-bearing Factory (in Moscow), as these three major sites were the most inspiring and significant of that period.

  To exploit the space fully we decided to set up our

decorative set pieces in such a way that they would 'seize' the whole of Sverdlov Square and would be on the same scale as the buildings surrounding the square: the Bolshoi Theatre, the Maly Theatre, the Central Children's Theatre, the Metropole Hotel and the Vostok Cinema.

Our decorative images had to avoid being lost in the square beside such buildings; but at the same time had to preserve some human scale with respect to the spectators. Magnitostroi and the Dniepr H. E. P. station each had their own distinctive profile and characteristic architecture. The Ball-bearing Factory, on the other hand, had no particular distinguishing characteristics and we decided to use its product, the ball-bearing, as the basic feature in our decorations.

201   A model of a ball-bearing, magnified hundreds of times to a diameter of around ten metres, was placed on a cylindrical pedestal in the public garden outside the Bolshoi Theatre (on the site previously occupied by a fountain), and was a most impressive decorative construction. It did not obstruct the view of the Theatre and could be seen from all parts of the square. The trees in the garden were still without leaves and so did not obscure it. In the evening it was lit in a highly dynamic way with the balls turning in one direction and the outer rings in the other. This attracted thousands of spectators. Through the inner ring of the ball-bearing, the portico and facade of the Bolshoi Theatre could be seen, which was unexpected and interesting.

We decided to use the other part of the public garden, which still had its fountain standing, as the place for our display of Magnitostroi and the Dniepr H. E. P. Station. Along the lengthwise axis were placed three-dimensional decorations representing a blast furnace and four other machines, joined by a narrow horizontal surface with a slogan. The height of the model blast furnace was approximately sixteen metres and the other machines were up to twelve metres. These decorations and all the arrangements for the square were completed by an enormous model of part of the Dniepr H. E. P. Station and by two gigantic portraits of Lenin and Stalin on either side of this model.

The decoration for the Dniepr H. E. P. Station was in the form of an arc with the white piers of the dam. Between the piers there was a large photographic display showing many new construction sites of the first Five Year Plan.

The full-length portraits of Lenin and Stalin were twenty-five metres high and ten metres wide. They were as tall as the Metropole Hotel.

In solving the problem of how to decorate such an enormous square the designers restrained themselves from introducing even one distracting element to the decorations. The facades of the buildings surrounding the square had already been planned with decorative elements, inscriptions and slogans of their own, and they had to take account of this. They did Magnitostroi in red and the models of the Ball-bearing Factory and the Dniepr H. E. P. Station in white. All three decorations were lit by dynamic electric lights.

Musatov writes:

204   The artist Troshin and I were entrusted with the decorations for Hunter's Row for the 1932 May Day celebrations. At that time all the buildings on the street had been demolished and foundation work was under way for the Hotel Moskva, separated from the street by a two-hundred metre long fence. Our theme was to be: 'The Reconstruction of Urban Transport'.

This theme was broken down into a number of sub-themes. The tasks being tackled by the Party in the interests of the people were highlighted on boards and poles raised above the fence.

This produced what was effectively an exhibition stand on the scale of the square. For colours we used red with white. We also had to deal with the decorations for Tverskaya Street (now Gorky Street), from Hunter's Row to the Moscow Soviet building.

A good decorative treatment for the lamp posts along the pavements suggested itself immediately, then it was proposed to stretch banners across the street from building to building. In the end we only succeeded in having one such banner at the south end of the street adjoining Hunter's Row. There were simply not the technical resources for more at that time: the city could only make available to us one fireman's ladder.

But the great significance of this street as a place for people to stroll also dictated that there should be some less casual decorations than these. We had thought of turning the shop windows into picture galleries. We looked through the stock of pictures at the central co-operative gallery Vsekokhudozhnik but were convinced that the idea would not work for technical reasons. At that time windows were not made of one sheet of glass but were broken up into smaller panes. Moreover, the subjects of the paintings we saw were not up-to-date enough.

Then the idea arose of filling the shop windows with architectural designs for the reconstruction of Moscow. This exactly fitted the bill. People strolled around, looking at the plans carefully. Everyone was interested to see how far the reconstruction plans would affect their own lives. Such an exhibition was repeated in future years too.

From the personal archives of G. S. Zamsky and N. A. Musatov

Fifteenth Anniversary of the October Revolution

MOSCOW

91 *Regulations and instructions*

Extract from a resolution of the Central Committee of Art Workers on decorations for the Fifteenth Anniversary of the Revolution in Moscow, 1932, from the Decoration Commission's *Bulletin*

22 October 1932

The Presidium of the Central Committee of Art Workers has highlighted the need to give great importance to the artistic decoration of the city. It has told Moscow organizations working on the artistic front of the need to facilitate the participation of as many artistic workers as possible.

In accordance with this the Central Committee of Art Workers has decreed that:

1 Theatrical stage-designers should be drawn into work on decorations for the anniversary celebrations; they should take part in consultations both in the centre and in the districts and they should, in particular, organize special consultations to deal with lighting effects, greenery and so on.

2 Work on artistic arrangements should be strengthened by organizing qualified political consultants (in the centre, in the districts and at enterprises). Co-operative work between artists and consultants should be facilitated.

3 Along with the central squares and main roads, some ten to fifteen major enterprises should be selected. Designs for these should be under the direct guidance of the general city commission which should at the same time raise the general level of attention given to arrangements in the districts (selection of qualified artists, consultancy, provision of instruction).

4 Help and qualified artistic advice should be provided for the mass art clubs at enterprises and the appropriate sector of the Central Organization [literally: House] for

Workers in the Arts should be drawn into this work.

5 Work on the decorations should be supplied with all necessary materials and people should be appointed to be responsible for the provision of general labouring assistance, thus freeing artists from routine tasks.

6 Artistic guidance and checks should be provided for mass production of objects for the festivities by cottage industries (such as armbands, flags, badges, etc.). New artistic ideas should be sought for any earlier items that were not up to standard.

7 Artistic checks should be carried out over the decoration of shop windows especially in the districts far from the centre. This work should be given to one of the members of the district artistic commission.

8 As many artist-sculptors should be involved as possible in such aspects of the anniversary celebrations as decorative sculpture.

9 There should be widespread socialist competition between different artists, teams and regions. Prizes should be given for the best work done by artist-designers and co-designers as well for that done by those who put the designs into practice. The best work by amateur arts clubs should also receive prizes. To this end special funds should be set up in the districts and at enterprises following the example of the All-Moscow Commission.

10 Measures should be taken to preserve all these artistic works being created to decorate buildings and columns for the fifteenth anniversary of the Revolution (panels, emblems and portraits of shock-workers etc.), which should then be presented to workers' clubs.

11 The Moscow Regional Committee of Art Workers should be entrusted to:

a ensure the fulfilment of the decisions of the Central Committee listed above, with one member of the Presidium of the Moscow Regional Committee of Art Workers being selected for permanent work in the Moscow Soviet commission;

b to pay artists according to the tariffs of the Central Committee of the Art Workers and at the end of the year to provide a proposal for a more precise definition of the tariff for 1933;

c to provide appraisals of what has been done in the current campaign for the decoration of Moscow and, in particular, to study the experiment of displaying major easel paintings representing Soviet art, in shop windows. After the anniversary is over to organize an evening in the

artists' club when results of the anniversary arrangements will be presented and to attract to this evening representatives of the Communist Academy as well as art critics and amateur artists;

d in connection with the fact that arrangements for the revolutionary celebrations are now reaching the state where they have to be put into practice, to call a general meeting of the artists and designers under the general co-ordination of the City Fine Arts Committee.

12 In connection with the increasing scope of such work it is essential for cadres of artists to be provided by the Moscow Regional Union of Soviet Artists. In the name of the Central Committee of Art Workers, Moscow artists are urged to involve themselves at once in arrangements for the decoration of the proletarian capital.

13 The question should be raised with the Moscow Soviet as to creation in Moscow of an organizational and economic centre for the staging of mass political campaigns; in particular a permanent commission dealing with arrangements for the city should be set up.

14 The question of training for special cadres of artists to deal with arrangements for the staging of mass political campaigns should be raised with the People's Commissariat of Education.

15 Moscow Regional Art Workers Central Management, as well as district and regional Art Workers' committees should be encouraged to pay maximum attention to participation in this work.

Byulleten Tsentralnoi khudozhestvennoi komissii pri Mossovete po oformleniyu Moskvy k 15-letiyu Oktyabrskoi revolyutsii (Bulletin of the Central Artistic Commission of the Moscow Soviet for the decoration of Moscow for the 15th anniversary of the October Revolution), no. 1, 22 October 1932, pp. 6–7.

Page 15 of the same issue of the *Bulletin* records the formation under the Moscow Soviet of a Central Artistic Commission for decorating the city for the Fifteenth Anniversary celebrations, which comprised the following:

The chairman of the committee was B. F. Malkin. The organization sector was headed by Ganapolsky. The sector for artistic arrangements was headed by Toot; the sector for the organization of transport by D. Osipov; the shop window sector by Sinaysky; the sector dealing with lighting in the squares by Belkind; the sector dealing with lighting inventions and technical arrangements by Lazarev; the sector for sculpture arrangements by C. D. Tavasyev; the sector of cadres by Kiberdin; the supply sector by Filippov; the sector for the realization of designs by A. K. Burykin. The commission for amateur art was headed by V. F. Tochilkin.

October celebrations committees were also formed in the districts and were headed by the following artists: Dzerzhinsky district – V. M. Firsov; Oktyabrsky district – Kirichko; Frunzensky district – M. S. Bogman; Sokolniki district – G. A. Sorochkin; Stalin district – Markin; Proletarsky district – Konovalov; Lenin district – Ivanov; Krasnopresnya district – I. V. Petrovsky; Bauman district – Matveev.

92 *Artists describe*

Various artists' descriptions of their work on decorating Moscow for the Fifteenth Anniversary of the Revolution in 1932, from the Decoration Commission's *Bulletin*

October 1932

Vladimir and Georgii Stenberg on their work for Red Square

'Unique amongst all other squares, Red Square greets the parade; Moscow's proletarian masses in their millions pass through it along with republican representatives and foreign guests. It is the most active square.

This determines the nature of its decorations, and the theme for the coming celebration will be: "Three cheers for the fifteenth anniversary of the October Revolution! Three cheers for the world revolution!"

When planning how to develop this theme we decided that no additional architectural elements should be introduced into the square. They would overload it and would also prevent the parade from turning round.

In putting our plans into practice we are laying a strong emphasis on quality. . . .

The centre-piece of the design will be the GUM building. In the middle will be stretched a general slogan some 115 metres long. On each side of it will hang the same words in foreign languages, and above it will be a huge panel bearing a portrait of Lenin.'

B. Rodionov, N. Troshin and N. Musatov on their decorations for Hunter's Row

'The theme which we have been given for decorating Hunter's Row, Gorky Street and Soviet Square is "Moscow's Urban Economy".

We have decided to divide this theme into sub-themes for particular areas. On the square of the former Hunter's Row we have decided to develop the theme, "The Volga Canal". . . . We are preparing an enormous electrified plan of the Volga Canal which will be 230 metres long and 80 metres high. . . .

Along the fence around the site where the Hotel Moskva is being built there will be a longitudinal cross-section of the canal with all its locks depicted on different panels. Models of ships will move along this cross-section.'

Ya. D. Romas on his designs for Comintern and Revolution Squares

'The theme of the arrangements (for Comintern Square) is the world communist revolution. Our brigade has decided to develop the theme in the following way. On the centre of the facade of the Comintern building, on a tower of a light metallic construction, there will be a turning sphere emanating millions of sparks which will give the square unusually effective lighting. Below there will be a saluting rostrum from which the demonstration will be reviewed. Along the building, in the reflected light, there will be slogans in five languages. To the left on the tower there will be three huge neon portraits: (1) Marx and Engels (2) Lenin and (3) Stalin.

On the Manège Building there will be a picture representing the world revolution: in the centre of its pediment there will be the gigantic figure of a proletarian with a capitalist town in the background. He is breaking his chains and is appealing to the proletariat of all countries to throw off the yoke of capitalism. . . .

On the sides of the Manège Building there will be paintings on the related theme of "The revolutionary

202

struggle of the proletariat in capitalist countries'', which will be done by the famous foreign artists F. Ellis, Bela Uits, Griffel, Kupka-Ilesh and Comrade Pavlenko.'

Byulleten Tsentralnoi khudozhestvennoi komissii pri Mossovete po oformleniyu Moskvy k 15-letiyu Oktyabrskoi revolyutsii (Bulletin of the Central Artistic Commission of the Moscow Soviet for the decoration of Moscow for the 15th anniversary of the October Revolution), no. 1, p. 8 (Stenbergs); no. 2, p. 8 (Rodionov, Troshin and Musatov); no. 2, p. 9 (Romas).

93 *Decorating transport*

Extract from an article by D. Osipov on 'Decoration of the public transport in Moscow for the fifteenth anniversary of the Revolution', 1932, from the Decoration Commission's *Bulletin*

26 October 1932

Artistic decoration for Moscow transport first took place in an organized fashion in the re-election campaign for the Soviets in 1930, when not only city transport was decorated but also the railways. . . .

Artists have tried to find new methods and ideas for an expressive interpretation of themes and slogans as each year transport has been decorated in preparation for external campaigns and celebrations. Particularly many methods and possibilities were revealed in the preparations for 1 May 1931. . . .

Instead of the previous approach which treated a moving unit as a static surface on which the artist developed his themes regardless of its own special properties, in 1931 artist and technical consultant worked together to develop a theme which took the special characteristics of transport into account.

Thus in 1931, for the first time, we used the artist L. A. Labas's interesting and light-weight constructions on buses. These not only managed to avoid scratching the

vehicles, they did not impede their movement, nor did they cover the windows or disturb the passengers.

In the same year an interesting form was used for trams too – this was a contour drawing by the artist Lavinsky, which avoided burdening the tram with large plywood surfaces.

In its work preparing for the fifteenth anniversary of the Revolution, the transport section of the October Artistic Commission is not only making use of the successful experience of the past but is also providing much that is new. . . .

A further distinguishing characteristic in the theme of current arrangements for the celebrations is the considerable attention paid to aspects of the reconstruction of Moscow such as the Metro, increased parks and greenery in the city, the Volga–Moscow link and so on. . . . Also significant this year is the use of three-dimensional objects and figures, the replacement of stationary, static panels with moving objects and figures, the widespread use of lighting arrangements, greenery, flowers and so on.

From the sketches which have already been presented to the transport section as proposals for the decoration of the trams, particularly striking are 'Long live the worldwide October Revolution', 'The Dniepr Hydro-Electric Power Station', 'The Moscow Metro', and 'The Air Force' by the artists Barshch and Cherkas.

Lavinsky, using the form of the tram itself, gives a most witty interpretation of the theme, 'The Volga–Moscow Link'. The artists from the satirical magazine *Crocodile*, Ganf, Belsky and Rotov, have done some interesting and profound interpretations of a number of important political themes: 'The Crisis of Capitalism', 'The Red Front', 'Disarm' and others.

This group of talented artists is the first to have brought political caricature out onto the trams and they have created bright things, very different from last year's transport decorations.

Road transport will be no less expressively decorated in this year's celebrations. . . . The lightness and mobility of the proposed constructions and the fixtures for them have greatly eased all work on the artistic decorations for the buses.

In the future it is imperative to preserve the valuable material which we have already amassed on this type of decorations in order to subject it to deeper study. As this kind of work is new and little researched, the opportunities

208

for developing artistic and political propaganda in this field are immense.

Byulleten Tsentralnoi khudozhestvennoi komissii pri Mossovete po oformleniyu Moskvy k 15-letiyu Oktyabrskoi revolyutsii (Bulletin of the Central Artistic Commission of the Moscow Soviet for the decoration of Moscow for the 15th anniversary of the October Revolution), no. 2, 26 October 1932, pp. 3–4.

94 *Workers' suggestions*

Extract from a report on suggestions received from workers for the Fifteenth Anniversary decorations in the districts and individual economic enterprises of Moscow, from the Decoration Commission's *Bulletin*

26 October 1932

In all the districts of Moscow lively discussions are continuing on how best to organize the October celebrations; a number of most interesting proposals have been put forward by workers suggesting how to turn the magnificent Revolution demonstrations into a powerful display of production – to make it into a set of living statistics of our victories and achievements.

Each enterprise will come out with a brightly coloured poster indicating the nature of the enterprise and its success at fulfilling its industrial and financial plans. The posters and reports and their artistic presentation will be discussed and voted on at a general meeting. They will then be produced by artists and art clubs.

There have been a mass of suggestions about enlivening the columns of the procession themselves – there should be musical stations at points where the procession concentrates, balconies should be decorated and turned into stages with the help of sports enthusiasts and others. Involved in all this would be mass organizers, variety performers, comics, musicians. There should be

caricatures, witty inventions, flowers, and coloured balloons. However, all these elements should tie in with the overall design for the demonstration. The progress of the demonstration must become a bright processional event and all the squares, streets, houses and shop windows on its route should be decorated in an artistic and political way.

The celebrations for the evenings of 6 and 7 November are being discussed separately – it is proposed to organize a number of mass fairs in Moscow.

The very fact that all these questions concerning arrangements in the city for the fifteenth anniversary demonstration have undergone mass discussion in our largest enterprises – as well as the large number of workers' proposals that have been received – makes it clear that the fifteenth anniversary in Moscow will truly be a splendid mass proletarian display of our prospects and achievements.

Byulleten Tsentralnoi khudozhestvennoi komissii pri Mossovete po oformleniyu Moskvy k 15-letiyu Oktyabrskoi revolyutsii (Bulletin of the Central Artistic Commission of the Moscow Soviet for the decoration of Moscow for the 15th anniversary of the October Revolution), no. 2, 26 October 1932, pp. 10–11.

207

The History of Decorating Gorky Park

MOSCOW

95

Description of the development of activities in Moscow's Central Park of Culture and Rest (Gorky Park), from the periodical *Park of Culture and Rest*

4 November 1932

On 12 August 1928 powerful tides of people literally drowned the square, the avenues and all the pavilions of the park. It was on this day that the Park of Culture and Rest, created by the will of the Moscow proletariat, joined the ranks of the cultural achievements of the revolution.

Tensely we waited for comments and opinions as the workers of Moscow took the park that had been opened for them.

Our victory was complete.

A child of the Revolution, the Park of Culture and Rest, has become a favourite place of rest for workers. . . .

The magnificent carnival at the opening of the 1929 season not only in the park itself but also in the streets of Moscow, spoke for the park's success and was an event that reached beyond the bounds of Moscow. . . .

In the field of the arts the Park has become an All-Union base for the display of achievements, the exchange of experience and exhibitions of the amateur artistic activity of the masses. . . .

The artistic arrangements of the park are being raised to a higher level. Its own arts factory is being created and the best artists are being attracted to work there.

After 1929, a number of those who had contributed to the carnival of that year whilst students in VKhUTEIN's theatrical design department continued to work on decorations for the Park itself. The year 1932 saw some very interesting compositions created there on political and social themes of the day, amongst them N. S. Starodub's

213
215

214 'Avenue of the Enemies', F. T. Sevortyan's 'Avenue of
212 Trash', and 'The Black Savings Bank' and 'Hooligans' by Ya. F. Kozlovskaya. Amongst the well-known theatre designers and artists who worked in the Park in this period were the former Constructivists Vladimir and Georgii Stenberg.

Park kultura i otdykha (Park of Culture and Rest), no. 25, 4 November 1932

MAY DAY, 1932

May Day, 1932, Moscow

201   Installation depicting a vast ball-bearing erected on the main elevation of the Bolshoi Theatre, to designs by a team from the Society of Workers for the Revolutionary Poster, ORRP, comprising G. S. Zamsky and N. G. Borovoi.

202   Banners on the GUM building in Red Square, forming part of the decorative scheme designed by Vladimir and Georgii Stenberg for the central area of the city.

May Day, 1932, Moscow

203 (*above left*) D. M. Moor, figure of 'a capitalist' erected on Malaya Dmitrovka street.

204 (*below left*) Decorative installation celebrating the new programme for building a Metro system, with a map of its proposed lines and exhortations to achieve it 'at a Bolshevik tempo', erected on Hunter's Row to designs of N. S. Troshin, B. A. Rodionov and N. A. Musatov.

Leningrad

205 (*above right*) Installation and decorations on Uritsky Square, photographed during what appears to be a mass parade with semaphore flags.

206 (*below right*) Floating decorative sculpture on Obvodny Canal by E. I. Liskovich, entitled 'Capitalism in the grip of a crisis'.

FIFTEENTH ANNIVERSARY, 1932

Fifteenth Anniversary of the Revolution, 1932, Moscow

207 (*above left*) The House of Unions decorated with slogans declaring 'Under the banner of the Bolshevik Party and its Leninist path we shall go forward to new victories'.

208 (*below left*) The Ilich Gates, decorated for the festival with industrial models.

209 (*below*) Yaroslavl Station decorated with a map of the railway route from Moscow to the Kuzbass coal fields.

Leningrad

210 (*above right*) Ships of the Baltic Fleet, lit up on the River Neva. To the right is the cruiser *Aurora*, heroic base for the shots that launched the Revolution, and still preserved near this position.

211 (*below right*) House of Culture of the Vyborgsky District lit up at night.

GORKY PARK PARADES, 1931–32

Agitational parades in Gorky Park, Moscow, 1931–32

212 (*right*) Caricature figures in Gorky Park, 1931, by Ya. F. Kozlovskaya. A group of three-dimensional caricatures representing 'Hooligans' (in Soviet parlance, this means trouble-making layabouts), with the slogan 'Let us eradicate uncouthness'.

213 (*below left*) Carnival caricature figures of 'a capitalist' and 'a priest', made by members of the Workers Club of Communal Emloyees, being paraded through Gorky Park on 25 May 1931.

214 (*below centre*) Three-dimensional caricatures from an 'Avenue of Trash' made by Ya. F. Kozlovskaya to stand in Gorky Park, 1932.

215 (*below right*) N. S. Starodub, three-dimensional caricatures from an 'Avenue of the Enemies' created in Gorky Park, 1932. This one represents the Polish Catholic priest Ksendz.

MAY DAY, 1933

May Day, 1933, Moscow, Sverdlov Square

216, 217 (*right*) Installation by N. A. Musatov propagandizing the Machine-Tractor Station, MTS, and (*below*) Musatov's design sketch for the installation.

218 (*bottom*) A view from the Metropole Hotel. The MTS display is left and in front of the Bolshoi Theatre is the model of a bloomery mill.

SIXTEENTH ANNIVERSARY, 1933

Sixteenth Anniversary of the Revolution, 1933, Moscow

219   Long street-hoarding panels decorated in celebration of the project for constructing a metro in Moscow, painted by Ya. D. Romas and Z. M. Vilensky

220   Street corner installation in Trubnaya Square celebrating the Anniversary, and the increase in aerial sowing planes within Soviet agriculture over the First Five Year Plan period from 4000 in 1928 to 58,000 in 1933.

May Day Celebrations 1933

MOSCOW

96 *Harmoniously blended themes*

Extract from an article by A. A. Andreev, 'Light, colour and movement', from the magazine *Soviet Art*

8 May 1933

Every year the headquarters dealing with arrangements for May Day used to call artists together. Hundreds of designs flooded into the White Hall of the Moscow Soviet. The arrangements for every street and square were worked out carefully. Themes were divided into sub-themes and slogans and diagrams looked colourful laid out on wooden constructions.

At one time there were attempts to regulate strictly the lighting, the sizes of materials used, of emblems and of the decorations used on buildings' facades. The streets were marked out like constructivist textbooks and they had to be read like books.

And every time the decorations for the First of May brought disappointment. It seemed as if all slogans and themes had been used, all points had been decorated with numbers, paints and photo-documentation and as if all the squares had been saturated with real cars and with models of products and yet somehow all this work did not give a unified artistic and political effect.

It is only this year, despite much more modest work on the part of the First of May headquarters, that Moscow has achieved a truly festive decor. A picturesque brightness, an artistic expressiveness and a clear political statement all blended together harmoniously.

What is the secret of the success of the 1933 May Day decorations which have been so admired by the masses themselves who have stood for hours in front of different subjects attentively looking at the details of the festive decor of the city?

When, in the first years after the Revolution, 'leftist' artists covered the city in futurist posters and shocked its architecture with colourful abstract surfaces, this was to some degree a vindication of the very presence of such decorations despite the formalism and ideological clumsiness of their means of expression. The artist was struggling with the private houses of merchants and with the stagnant art nouveau style of Moscow buildings. On days of revolutionary festivities he would cover over the old city. Moreover, at that time, red calico, plywood and paints were his only materials. Later any attempt to return to these canons of cubo-futurist decorations only obscured the political purpose of the May Day artistic propaganda. Moscow has been rebuilt by the proletariat. Moscow in its architectural appearance too has become the red capital of the world proletariat. Any attempt to cover the facades of the town with decorative panels or constructions or with seven-mile long extravagant slogans is in basic contradiction to the underlying task of the festive decorations – which is to demonstrate the victory and achievements of the Soviet proletariat as the owner and creator of the new Moscow. The clean lines of the streets, the new buildings, even the scaffolding have become landmarks in his decorations.

However, up till last year, the artist has always been trying to compete with the city. With his quickly assembled structures and monumental bits of plywood he juxtaposed his ideas to the character of the city, rather than learning to love and understand it. He chaotically overloaded the streets with slogans, photographs, workbenches, cars and examples of industrial products, and as ever with the attempt to achieve a purely quantitative fulfilment of every possible point, the qualitative effect left much to be desired.

This year the First of May headquarters chose a different method – a more miserly disposal of decorative emphases. More attention was paid to the central squares and streets at which the districts meet on the First of May. Light, colour and movement became the basic means of expression. Crudely painted decorative panels and vast abstract wooden structures with diagrams and photographs occupied a much less important position than before.

As in previous years, the Stenberg brothers submitted a well-thought out model for the strict and expressive decoration of Red Square. Kuznetsov's sculpture on the Place of Execution, the huge illuminated slogans in five lánguages, portraits of Lenin and Stalin, completed the square. It must be pointed out that the Stenbergs were exceptionally successful in their application of spotlights for illuminating the red panels of material. The same kind of lighting was used at many other places in the city too but in most cases the slovenliness of the technical execution spoiled the potential effect.

216   Extraordinarily successful were the giant models of a
217 bloomery mill and a Machine-Tractor Station on Sverdlov
218 Square made by the artists Musatov, Troshin and Rodionov. Here they used a new and complex method of artistic and agitational display by exploiting light, musical arrangements, radio and the decorative arts. The stationary plywood constructions of previous years were replaced by mobile designs pierced by blue beams from projectors. Rejection of the previous solid plywood imitations of real structures made for greater decorative beauty and a more dynamic treatment of the city. This year's experience has shown that the best material for all models is light cloth on a slender timber frame, which can play beautifully in light.

Also outstanding were decorations on the buildings of Moscow Soviet and *Izvestiya*. On the Moscow Soviet building the artist Romas successfully managed to combine red materials arranged at an angle to the facade with green spotlighting. On the *Izvestiya* building the enormous silk banners, the neon slogan and the real flowers on all the balconies could serve as a model for the decoration of the new architecture.

Also interesting were the decorations on the scaffolding round the hotel currently being built on what used to be called Hunter's Row. An enlarged poster by Klutsis with portraits of Marx, Engels, Lenin and Stalin here covered only the lower part of the scaffolding. From the lace of posts and beams projectors picked out the red point of a banner crowning the scaffolding and also separate parts of the construction, thus making itself seem to participate in the May decorations.

This year shop windows were widely used for purposes of artistic campaigning. Kuznetsky Bridge was turned into a 'street of satire'. The artists from the satirical magazine *Crocodile* here gave shining examples of how to do political caricatures given plenty of space. Particularly splendid was the use of the closed gates of the State Publishing House behind which characters representing fascist bestiality were raving.

Also interesting was the 'parade' of the Moscow theatres. Unfortunately the exhibition of pictures in the windows on Gorky Street must be admitted to have been unsuccessful. The pictures had been randomly selected and were generally weak in their execution; they could only undermine the aim of showing Soviet art's achievements.

This was the only failure in the decorations for the May festival. Artists this year have shown that, with the most modest of means, it is possible to achieve great artistic effect; it is necessary only to distribute resources carefully, to use materials rationally and to subordinate all designs to the larger ends of creating both an artistic image and a politically sound decoration for the city.

Sovetskoe iskusstvo (Soviet Art), no. 210, 8 May 1933

97 *Bloomery mill on Sverdlov Square*

Extract from the personal reminiscences of the artist N. Troshin, written in March 1977, on his participation in the decoration of Sverdlov Square, Moscow, for the May Day celebrations of 1933

There were three of us, Musatov, Troshin, Rodionov, a team of artists: at that time there was a fashion for 'teams' an idea taken, apparently, from factories. We were given very serious and responsible areas for decoration, mainly for the October and May celebrations. Thus in 1933 the Central Commission dealing with arrangements for May decorations in Moscow entrusted us with the decoration of
218 Theatre Square [now Sverdlov Square]: our theme was to be 'The Bloomery Mill', the results of the first Five Year Plan.

Our task was not straightforward. From the artistic point of view we had to make a design and then execute it so powerfully and colourfully that it would not get lost in its environment of huge theatre buildings, vast space, immense sky and bright sun. The bloomery had to be seen first and to look brighter than everything else as a symbol of the success of Soviet industry and as a monument to the victory of the first Five Year Plan.

We decided to make a gigantic model of the bloomery in the gardens in front of the Bolshoi Theatre and then to develop the theme of 'The Success of Soviet Industrialization' around that, using illuminated, embossed panels showing the growth of industry over the period of the Five Year Plan. The bloomery would be shown in action by means of light and pyrotechnics (sparks, steam, a red-hot piece of metal, movement).

We had to work out the scale for our design, to calculate the area of the park, to determine how to colour our decorations using a minimum of different shades. Colour and light – those were to be our main sources of effect. Bright patches of colour should attract the viewer's attention, should make him stop and should be memorable for him. Everything should be utterly simple and laconic, understandable and expressive. The red bloomery dominated everything. Both in its own right and as a symbol.

As well as the bloomery we made another arrangement in the second square on the theme 'Machine-Tractor Stations and the collective farms'. Gigantic tractors assaulted the earth and electrified panels developed the theme of construction and the role of Machine-Tractor Stations and, in a satirical way (through drawings), showed examples of the class struggle from the countryside. As a whole the volume of work was enormous.

The bloomery theme was revealed in a complex theatricalized spectacle which included elements of music, words (through loudspeakers), pyrotechnics and light dynamics. We even wrote a special light and sound scenario, as if it were the score of an oratorio dedicated to the first Five Year Plan. In this we introduced sound into the decorations for the first time. Our dream was that the appearance of the red bloomery should remain in the viewers' memories and we even wanted everyone to have a bloomery badge on their lapel as a souvenir of the festival.

Despite the emergency nature of the work, the decorations were done on time. And people were pleased by them. We ourselves witnessed an extraordinary crowd of people.

Our brief to achieve maximal decorativeness helped us and created a true Soviet people's festival.

Personal archives of N. Troshin.

216
217
219

Sixteenth Anniversary of the October Revolution

MOSCOW

98 *Bold preparations*

'The square on the table: a model of designs for the October Revolution anniversary celebrations', from the newspaper *Evening Moscow*

11 October 1933

Twice a year the White Hall of the Moscow Soviet changes its appearance. This happens on the eves of 1 May and 7 November.

Less than a month remains till the sixteenth anniversary of the Revolution and, true to established traditions, the White Hall of the Moscow Soviet has started to bustle with preparations for the great holiday. Moscow artists and sculptors and architects and engineers come and go. Already standing on long tables in the White Hall are miniature but elegant little squares.

Here you can see Sverdlov Square on one table. A group of comrades are looking at the details of the design. . . .

And here's the Metro. Muscovites can see it opposite the Metropole building. They can see an entire cross-section of the underground, starting from the surface and going down to the tunnels and trains.

Above, there is a large net and on this a plan of the metro. Under the net there is the way down below ground. The entrance hall of the metro. There is the complete impression of marble. A special screen creates the impression of moving escalators. Lower still, there is the cross-section of a tunnel and the metro tracks. . . .

Red Square hangs on the walls. It is the work of the Stenbergs. In contrast with previous years they have introduced the colonnade along the GUM building. The columns are supporting a slogan more than 120 metres long. According to the design, all the lower part of the GUM building should be bathed in light. In the middle there are large portraits of Lenin and Stalin.

Beside that, on the next table, you have Revolution Square with an 11-metre figure of a Red Army border guard.

The designs for these models are being heatedly discussed. Moscow wants to meet the Revolution holiday in a colourful and festive way.

Vechernaya Moskva (Evening Moscow), no. 234, 11 October 1933

99 *Stenberg and the Park*

The younger Stenberg brother, Georgii, died in a road accident on 15 October 1933, aged 33. Two weeks later, his colleagues at the Central Park of Culture and Rest (Gorky Park), where he had been chief artist for decorations, published the following 'Memoir on Georgii Stenberg' in the publication *Park of Culture and Rest*

27 October 1933

Stenberg was a rare artist, who fully understood the particular characteristics governing the development of the Park which had to cater for the leisure of millions. Their unusual feeling for colour and space and the wide scope of their graphic imagination enabled the Stenbergs to give great help to the Park in the development of its architecture, flower-gardens and decorations.

Park kultura i otdykha (Park of Culture and Rest), no. 31, 27 October 1933

100 *The buzz of preparation*

Extract from the article by D. Kalm, 'Rehearsal of the squares', from the magazine *Soviet Art*

2 November 1933

In five days' time Moscow's streets and squares will become unrecognizable. They will be blooming with scarlet banners and will be aflame with flags; grandiose constructions will be erected on the smooth asphalt. The avenues and cross-roads, boulevards and embankments, preparing to welcome many thousands of demonstrators, will themselves become festive participants in the revolutionary celebrations. The White Hall of the Moscow Soviet is the centre of all the Moscow squares both literally and figuratively.

It has the atmosphere of a military headquarters: the telephone rings ceaselessly and people, not bothering to take their coats off, hurry in and out again.

Behind a long table is the leadership of operations: the central commission for the arrangements for the October Revolution celebrations. From Dzerzhinsky district someone is requesting canvas. In Krasnaya Presnya artists are not being allowed the premises they need. It is essential to have permission from management of the Arbat market. . . .

Spread out on the tables are models of the prospective arrangements. There is a miniature Red Square with a modestly decorated GUM building. A toy-like ship is sailing across Sverdlov Square from the Bolshoi Theatre. There is a small-scale underground railway hardening on a cardboard background. . . .

The rehearsal of the squares is taking place. . . .

The 'rehearsal' premises are varied and spread all over Moscow. Somewhere deep in the bowels of the Metropole Hotel office number four cannot be found. Architects with their jackets removed, are hurriedly finishing off their sketches of the White Sea Lock. On the square in front of the Bolshoi Theatre is growing a model of a ship passing through a lock on the White Sea–Baltic Canal. The gates of the lock are the same height as an eight-storey building. On two open screens films will be shown. On both sides lit-up relief maps show the route leading from the Baltic to the White Sea, the famous Povenchanskaya locks and Lake

220

Vyg. The design has been done by the artists Musatov, Rodionov and Troshin. On the deck of the ship a band will be playing.

Strastnaya Square is 'rehearsing' in the church of Dmitry Solunsky. The artists Baev, Gavrilov and S. Ivanov are drawing enormous panels under the vaulted roof. The familiar Ford advertising the Roadways Lottery gaily winking at night from the heights of the Spassky Tower is now hidden from view. Its place has been taken by three huge panels: the silver gondola of the stratosphere, indefatigable Soviet cars in the red, shifting sands of the Kara-Kum, the blue ice of the Arctic being sliced by a Soviet ice-cutter. Above the 'Palace' Cinema will appear a Soviet trolley-bus – a hybrid of a bus and a tram as yet unseen by Muscovites.

An old woman wandering into the church retreats in horror from a painter's brush. . . .

Hunter's Row is being prepared in the Gymnastics Hall of the stadium of the Iskra (Spark) printers. Here the artists Konnov, Gaponenko, Nevezhin, Nemov and Tsirelson are drawing portraits of the members of the Politburo following the photomontage made by Klutsis.

It is lucky that the printers have given them their Gymnastics Hall. Their work takes up an area of 1328 square metres. The photograph is being magnified four-and-a-half thousand times. If the artist had to buy gouache in the usual-sized little pots, they would need over a thousand of them.

But even in the Gymnastics Hall it is not possible to unroll completely any one of the sixteen portraits for the poster. It will go right to the top of the ten-storey Moscow Soviet Hotel in Hunter's Row.

The squares are urgently rehearsing. The make-up and wardrobe people – the artists of Moscow – are preparing them for their performance.

In the White Hall of the Moscow Soviet the ceaselessly buzzing telephone bell jingles again.

Sovetskoe iskusstvo (Soviet Art), no. 50, 2 November 1933

List of Abbreviations

AMO	Machinery Building Joint Stock Company
APO	Agitational Propaganda Department (of the Communist Party Central Committee)
ChTZ	Chelyabinsk Tractor Factory
GAMO	State Archive of the Moscow Region
GET	State Electro-technical Trust
GOELRO	State Commission for the Electrification of Russia
Gosmetr	Trust for the Manufacture and Sale of Metric Weights and Measures
Goznak	Organization of Factories Producing State Signs (an organization in the NEP period, for state advertising, etc.)
GPP	Politico-Educational Department of the Leningrad Gubernia Department of Popular Education
GUM	Sate Department Store
IZO	Fine Arts Department of Narkompros (q.v.)
KhTZ	Kharkov Tractor Factory
LEF	Left Front of Art
Lengiz	Leningrad State Publishing House
LGSPS	Leningrad City Council of Trade Unions
MGSPS	Moscow City Council of Trade Unions
MOGES	Moscow State Electric Power Station
MONO	Moscow Department of Public Education
MOPR	International Organization for the Aid of Fighters for Revolution
Narkompros	People's Commissariat for Public Education (literally, for Enlightenment)
NBA AKh SSSR	Scientific Library of the Academy of Arts of the USSR
Oblono	Regional Department of Education
ODVF	Society of Friends of the Air Force
Posredrabis	Labour Exchange for Arts Workers, attached to the Leningrad Department of Labour
Proletkult	Proletarian Culture (cultural and educational organization under Narkompros, q.v.)
RAPKh	Russian Association of Proletarian Artists
Rosta	Russian Telegraph Agency
RSFSR	Russian Soviet Federative Socialist Republic
RVSR	Revolutionary Armed Forces of the Republic
Sevzapgostorg	North-West State Trade Office
Sovnarkom	Council of People's Commissars
SU	Collection of Decrees and Government Directives
TsGALI SSSR	Central State Archive of Literature and Art of the USSR
TsGAOR Leningrad	Central State Archive of the October Revolution, Leningrad
TsGAORSS Moscow	Central State Archive of the October Revolution, Moscow
TsIK	Central Executive Committee of the Council of Workers' Deputies, i.e. of the Bolshevik Party. After January 1918, this became VTsIK, the All-Russian, and later All-Union, Central Executive Committee (but TsIK is still sometimes found as a short form after that date), of The USSR, i.e. of the Communist Party of the Soviet Union
VKhUTEIN	Higher Artistic and Technical Institute, Moscow
VKhUTEMAS	Higher Artistic and Technical Studios (became an Institute, above, in 1928)
VTsIK	All-Russian, later All-Union, Central Executive Committee of the Communist Party of the Soviet Union (Bolshevik Party). Before the Revolution, and up to January 1918, this was simply the Party Executive Committee, TsIK (q.v.)

Bibliography

BOOKS *1917 to the present*

Agitatsionno-massovoye iskusstvo pervykh let Oktyabrya. Materialy i issledovaniya (Mass Agitational Art of the First Years after October. Materials and Investigations), Moscow, 1971

Agitatsionno-massovoye iskusstvo pervykh let Oktyabrskoi revolyutsii. Katalog vystavki (Mass Agitational Art of the First Years after the October Revolution), exh. cat., Moscow, 1967

Andreeva, Mariya F., *Perepiska, vospominaniya, stati, dokumenty* (Correspondence, Reminiscences, Articles and Documents), Moscow, 1968

Bakhtin, M. M., *Tvorchestvo Fransua Rable i narodnaya kultura srednevekovya i Renessansa* (The Work of François Rabelais and the Popular Culture of the Middle Ages and Renaissance), Moscow, 1965

Bibikova, Irina M., and Levchenko, N. I., compilers; Tolstoy, Vladimir P., ed., *Agitatsionno massovoye iskusstvo. Oformleniye prazdnestv 1917–1932* (Mass Agitational Art. The Design of Festivals, 1917–1932), Moscow, 1984. See Editor's note below

Bonch-Bruevich, V. D., 'Vospominaniya o V. I. Lenine 1917–1924gg' ('Reminiscences of V. I. Lenin during 1917–1924'), *Izbrannye sochineniya v 3–x tomakh* (Selected Works in 3 Volumes), vol. 3, Moscow, 1963

Borba za realizm v izobrazitelnom iskusstve 20–x godov. Materialy, dokumenty, vospominaniya (The Battle for Realism in the Fine Arts in the Twenties. Materials, Documents, Reminiscences), Moscow, 1964

Chicherov, V. I., *Zimnyi period russkogo zemledelcheskogo kalendarya* (The Winter Period in the Russian Farming Calendar), Moscow, 1957

Gan, Alexei, *Konstruktivizm* (Constructivism), Tver, 1922

Gavrilov, A., *Organizatsiya, Stsenarii prazdnika. Oborudovanie* (Organization. The Staging of the Festival. Equipment and Props), Moscow, 1928

German, M. G., *Serdtsem slushaya revolyutsiyu* (Listening to the Revolution with our Hearts), Leningrad, 1980

Gershuni, E. P., *Massovye zrelishcha i narodnye predstavleniya* (Mass Spectacles and Popular Productions), Moscow, 1962

Glan, B. N., *Udarno rabotat – kulturno otdykhat* (To Work Hard and to Have Civilized Relaxation), Moscow, 1933

Glyazer, S. V., *Karnaval* (The Carnival), Moscow, 1935

Gushchin, A. S., *Izoiskusstvo v massovykh prazdnestvakh i demonstratsiyakh* (Fine Art in Mass Festivals and Demonstrations), Moscow–Leningrad, 1930

—, *Opyt organizatsii massovogo prazdnestva* (The Experience of Organizing Mass Festivals), Moscow–Leningrad, 1931

—, *Samodeyatelnoe izoiskusstvo* (Amateur Art), Moscow–Leningrad, 1931

—, *Oformlenie massovikh prazdnestv za 15 let diktatury proletariata. Fotoalbom* (Design of Mass Festivals during Fifteen Years of the Dictatorship of the Proletariat. Collection of Photographs), Moscow, 1932

Iskusstvo rabochikh. Kruzhki IZO rabochikh klubov Leningrada i masterskikh IZO Oblpolitprosveta pri DPP im. Gertsena (Art of the Workers. Fine Art Hobby Groups in the Leningrad Workers' Clubs and the Fine Art Studios of the Oblast Organization for Political Education under the Hertsen Building for Political Education), Leningrad, 1928

Istoriya sovetskogo teatra (A History of Soviet Theatre), vol. 1, Leningrad, 1933

Iz istorii stroitelstva sovetskoi kultury, Moskva, 1917–1918. Dokumenty i vospominaniya (From the History of the Building of Soviet Culture in Moscow during 1917–1918. Documents and Reminiscences), Moscow, 1964

Kak prazdnovat Oktyabr (How to Celebrate October), Moscow–Leningrad, 1925

Kerzhentsev, P. M., *Revolyutsiya i teatr* (Revolution and Theatre), Moscow, 1918

—, *Tvorchesky teatr. Puti sotsialisticheskogo teatra* (Creative Theatre. Paths to a Socialist Theatre), Petrograd, 1919

Khazin, E., *Otdykh millionov. Moskovsky park kultury i otdykha im. M Gorkogo* (The Leisure of Millions. The Gorky Park of Culture and Rest in Moscow), Moscow, 1932

Khudozhnik–oformitel. Sbornik statei (The Artist-Designer. Collected Articles), Leningrad, 1962

Kinofotodokumenty po istorii Velikogo Oktyabrya (Cinema Documentaries on the History of the Great October Revolution), Moscow, 1958

Kogan, P. S., *V preddverii gryadushchego teatra* (On the Threshold of the Future Theatre), Moscow, 1921

Krupskaya, N. K., *Iz ateisticheskogo naslediya* (From the Atheist Heritage) Moscow, 1964

Kuznetsova, A. D.; Magidson, A. S., and Shchukin, Yu. P., *Oformlenie goroda v dni revolyutsionnykh prazdnestv* (Designing the City for the Days of Revolutionary Festivals), Moscow–Leningrad, 1932

Lebedev, P. I., *Sovetskoe iskusstvo v period inostrannoi voennoi interventsii i grazhdanskoi voiny* (Soviet Art of the Period of the Foreign Intervention and Civil War), Moscow–Leningrad, 1949

Lenin i Lunacharsky, Perepiska, doklady, dokumenty. Literaturnoe nasledstvo (Lenin and Lunacharsky, Correspondence, Lectures, Documents. Literary Legacy), vol. 80, Moscow, 1971

Lenin, V. I., *O literature i iskusstve. Sbornik.*

Vstup. stat. B. Ryurikova (On Literature and Art. A collection with an Introductory Essay by B. Ryurikov), Moscow, 1967

Leningradskaya oblastnaya komissiya po provedeniyu prazdnovaniya 14-letiya Oktyabrskoi revolyutsii (Leningrad Oblast Commission for Carrying out the Festival of the 14th Anniversary of the October Revolution). *Sbornik materialov po khudozhestvenno-zrelishchnoi rabote. XIV godovshchina Oktyabrya* (Collection of Materials on the Artistic Work for the Spectacles. XIV Anniversary of October), Leningrad, 1931

Lobanov, V. M., *Khudozhestvennye gruppirovki za poslednie 25 let* (Artistic Groupings of the Last 25 Years), Moscow, 1930

Lukyanov, A., *Massovye kulturno–politicheskie zrelischa 8 tys.* (A Mass Cultural and Political Spectacle of Eight Thousand People), Moscow, 1930

Lunacharsky, A. V., *Rech, proiznesennaya na otkrytii Petrogradskikh gosudarstvennykh svobodnykh khudozhestvenno-uchebnykh masterskikh 10–go oktyabrya 1918* (Speech delivered at the Opening of the Petrograd State Free Art–Study Studios, 10 October 1918), Petrograd, 1918

—, *Teatr i revolyutsiya* (Theatre and Revolution), Moscow, 1924

—, *Stati o teatre i dramaturgii* (Articles on Theatre and Drama), Moscow–Leningrad, 1938

—, *Stati ob iskusstve* (Articles on Art), Moscow–Leningrad, 1941

—, *Vospominaniya i vpechatleniya* (Reminiscences and Impressions), Moscow, 1968

Lvov, N. M., *Postroenie agitzrelishcha* (The Structure of the Agitational Spectacle), Moscow, 1930

Malkov, P. D., *Zapiski komendanta Moskovskogo Kremlya. Lit. zapis. A. Ya. Sverdlova* (Notebooks of the Commandant of the Moscow Kremlin. Literary Notes of A. Ya. Sverdlov), Moscow, 1961

Mardzhanashvili, K. A., *Tvorcheskoe nasledie, v 2–x tomakh* (His Creative Legacy, in Two Volumes), vol. 1, Tbilisi, 1958

Massovoye deistvo. Oformlenie Oktyabrskoi demonstratsii (Mass Action. The Design of the October Demonstration), Moscow, 1930

Massovoye deistvo. Pervomaisky prazdnik 1932 goda (Mass Action. The Festival of 1 May, 1932), Moscow–Leningrad, 1932

Massovoye deistvo. Rukovodstvo k organizatsii i provedeniyu prazdnovaniya desyatiletiya Oktyabrya i drugikh revolyutsionnykh prazdnikov (Mass Action. Guidance for the Organization and Execution of Festivals for the Tenth Anniversary of October and other Revolutionary Festivals), Moscow–Leningrad, 1927

Massovoye deistvo. Stsenicheskie igry. Vsemirny Oktyabr, postavlennyi na 1–i Vsesoyuznoi

spartakiade, i drugie stsenicheskie igry (Mass Action. Scenographic Pieces. 'October Worldwide', performed at the 1st All-Union Spartakiad, and other Scenographic Pieces), N. I. Podvoiskogo, ed., Moscow, 1929

Massovye prazdnestva. Sbornik Komiteta sotsiologicheskogo izucheniya iskusstv (Mass Festivals. A Collection of Papers from the Committee for the Sociological Study of the Arts), Leningrad, 1926

Massovye prazdnestva. Vstup. statya A. V. Lunacharskogo (Mass Festivals. Introductory Essay by A. V. Lunacharsky), Moscow, 1921

Massovye prazdniki i zrelishcha (Mass Festivals and Spectacles), Moscow, 1961

Massovye teatralizovannye predstavleniya i prazdniki (Mass Theatrical Productions and Festivals), Moscow, 1963

Matsa, I., *Leningradskii IZORAM* (The Leningrad Organization for Fine Art among Working Youth), Moscow–Leningrad, 1932

Matsa, I.; Reingard, L., and Rempel, L., compilers, *Sovetskoe iskusstvo za 15 let. Materialy i dokumentatsiya* (Soviet Art of the Last 15 Years. Materials and Documentation), Moscow–Leningrad, 1933

Mazaev, A. I., *Prazdnik kak sotsialno-khudozhestvennoe yavlenie. Opyt istoriko-teoreticheskogo issledovaniya* (The Festival as a Socio-cultural Phenomenon. An Attempt at a Historico-theoretical Investigation), Moscow, 1978

Mgberov, A. A., *Zhizn v teatre* (Life in the Theatre) vol. 2, Leningrad, 1932

Nekrylova, A. F., *Russkiye narodnye gorodskiye prazdniki, uveseleniya i zrelishcha, konets XVIII–nachalo XX veka* (Russian Popular Urban Festivals, Amusements and Spectacles of the late XVIII to the early XX centuries), Leningrad, 1988

Nemiro, O. V., *V gorod prishel praznik. Iz istorii khudozhestvennogo oformleniya sovetskikh massovykh prazdnestv* (A Festival has come to Town. From the History of the Design of Soviet Mass Festivals), Leningrad, 1973

—, *Prazdnichnyi gorod. Iskusstvo oformleniya prazdnikov. Istoriya i sovremennost* (The Festive City. The Art of Festival Design in History and Today), Leningrad, 1987

Nasha glavnaya ploshchad (Our Main Square), Moscow, 1966

Obzor deyatelnosti otdela izobrazitelnykh iskusstv. Narodnyi komissariat prosveshcheniya (A Survey of the Activity of the Department of Fine Arts of the People's Commissariat for Public Education), Petrograd, 1920

Olbrakht, Ivan, *Puteshestvie za poznaniem. Strana Sovetov 1920 goda* (A Trip for Getting Acquainted. The Land of the Soviets in 1920), Moscow, 1967

Opyt organizatsii massovogo prazdnestva. Brigada sotrudnikov LOGAIS v sostave: A. S.

Gushchina, S. S. Danilova, R. B. Konskogo, M. A. Shuvalovoi (The Experience of Organizing Mass Festivals, by a Team from LOGAIS: A. S. Gushchin, S. S. Danilov, R. B. Konsky, M. A. Shuvalova), Moscow–Leningrad, 1931

Piotrovsky, A., *Teatr. Kino. Zhizn* (Theatre, Cinema, Life), Leningrad, 1969

Piotrovsky, A. I., *Za sovetsky teatr. Sbornik statei* (For Soviet Theatre. A Collection of Articles), Leningrad, 1925

Pisarevsky, D. S., *Parki kultury i otdykha* (Parks of Culture and Rest), Moscow, 1940

Polevoi, V. M., 'Izobrazitelnoye iskusstvo Moskvy v gody grazhdanskoi voiny' ('Fine Art in Moscow during the Years of the Civil War'), *Istoriya Moskvy v 6-ti tomakh* (A History of Moscow in 6 Volumes), vol. 6, book 2, Moscow, 1959

Pomerantseva, A. V., *Kalendar revolyutsionnykh prazdnikov i velikikh godovshchin* (Calendar of Revolutionary Festivals and Anniversaries), Moscow–Leningrad, 1927

Radlov, S. E., *Stati o teatre, 1918–1922* (Articles on Theatre, 1918–1922), Petrograd, 1923

—, *Desyat let v teatre* (Ten Years in the Theatre), Leningrad, 1929

Rezhissura massovykh zrelischch. Sbornik statei (The Producer of Mass Spectacles. A Collection of Articles), Moscow, 1964

Rid, Dzh. (John Reed), *10 dnei, kotorye potryasli mir* (Ten Days that Shook the World), Moscow 1958

Rollan, Roman, *Narodnyi teatr, Predisl. Vyach. Ivanova* (Popular Theatre, with a Preface by Viacheslav Ivanov), Petrograd–Moscow, 1919

Russky sovetsky teatr. Sovetsky teatr. Dokumenty i materialy 1917–1921 (Soviet Russian Theatre. Soviet Theatre. Documents and Materials, 1917–1921), Leningrad, 1968

Ryumin, E., *Massovye prazdnestva* (Mass Festivals), Moscow–Leningrad, 1927

Shchukin, Yu. P., and Magidson, A. S., *Oformlenie massovykh prazdnestv i demonstratsii* (The Design of Mass Festivals and Demonstrations), Moscow–Leningrad, 1932

Shelavin, K., *Pervoe Maya v Rossii. Ot pervogo prazdnovaniya po 1925g* (The First of May in Russia. From the First Celebration to 1925), Leningrad, 1926

Shklovsky, V., *Tetiva. O neskhodstve skhodnovo* (The Bow-String. On the Incompatibility of the Compatible), Moscow, 1970

Sidorov, A. A., 'Khudozhestvennaya Moskva, 1917–1920' ('Artistic Moscow'), *Krasnaya Moskva* (Red Moscow), Moscow, 1920

Stepanov, Z V., *Kulturnaya zhizn Leningrada 20–x – nachala 30–x godov,* (The Cultural Life of Leningrad in the Twenties and Early Thirties), Leningrad, 1976

Stifel, B., *Prazdnichnoe oformlenie russkogo goroda* (Festival Decorations of the Russian City), author's summary of 'kandidat'

dissertation in architecture, Leningrad, 1949

Strigalev, A. A., 'K voprosu o vozniknovenii leninskogo plana monumentalnoi propagandy' ('On the Question of the Origins of the Lenin Plan of Monumental Propaganda'), *Voprosy sovetskogo izobrazitelnogo iskusstva i arkhitektury* (Questions of Soviet Fine Art and Architecture), Moscow, 1976

—, 'M. V. Dobuzhinsky v revolyutsionnye gody' ('M. V. Dobuzhinsky in the Revolutionary Years'), *Sovetskoe monumentalnoe iskusstvo* (Soviet Monumental Art), nos 75–77, Moscow, 1979

Tairov, A. Ya., *Zapiski rezhissera* (Notes of a Producer), Moscow, 1921

Tamashin, L. G., *Sovetskaya dramaturgiya v gody grazhdanskoi voiny* (Soviet Drama during the Years of the Civil War), Moscow, 1961

Teatr i zhizn (Theatre and Life), Moscow–Leningrad, 1957

Terso, Zh., *Prazdnestva i pesni Frantsuzskoi revolyutsii* (Festivals and Songs of the French Revolution), Petrograd, 1917; Moscow, 1933

Tolstoy, V. P., 'Materialy k istorii agitatsionnogo iskusstva perioda grazhdanskoi viony' ('Materials for a History of Agitational Art in the Period of the Civil War'), *Soobshcheniya Instituta istorii iskusstv Akademii nauki SSSR,* (Papers of the Institute for the History of the Arts of the Academy of Sciences of the USSR), no. 3, Moscow, 1953

—, *Sovetskaya monumentalnaya zhivopis* (Soviet Monumental Painting), Moscow, 1958

Tsekhnovitser, O. V., *Demonstratsii i karnival. K desyotoi godovshchine Oktyabrskoi revolyutsii* (Demonstrations and Carnivals. For the Tenth Anniversary of the October Revolution), Moscow, 1927

—, *Prazdnestva revolyutsii* (Festivals of the Revolution), Leningrad, 1931

Tugenkhold, Ya. A., *Iskusstvo oktyabrskoi epokhi. Propaganda i agitatsiya v resheniyakh i dokumentakh VKP(b)* (Art of the October Epoch. Propaganda and Agitation in the Decisions and Documents of the Bolshevik Party), Moscow, 1947

Tumanov, I. M., *Rezhissura massovogo prazdnika i teatralizovannogo kontserta,* (The Producer of the Mass Festival and Theatricalized Concert), Leningrad, 1974

Vasilev-Vyazmin, I. I., *Iskusstvo lyudnykh ploshchadei* (Art of the People's Squares), Moscow 1977

Veprinsky, M. Ya., *Khudozhestvennye kruzhki i krasnyi kalendar* (Art Hobby Groups and the Red Calendar), Moscow–Leningrad, 1926

Vtoroi kongress III kommunisticheskogo Internatsionala. Albom (Second Congress of the III Communist International. Album), Moscow, 1920

Vulis, A., *Metamorforzy komicheskogo* (Metamorphoses of the Comic), Moscow, 1976

Vystavka proizvedenii khudozhnikov dekorativno-oformitelskogo iskusstva, Katalog (Exhibition of Work by Artists working in the Field of Designing Decorations. Catalogue), Moscow, 1962

Yudin, N. S., *Rezhisser o karnavale* (A Producer on the Carnival), Moscow, 1957

Zhemchuzhnyi, V., *Kak organizovat oktyabrskuyu demonstratsiyu. Posobie dlya oktyabrskikh komissii, politprosvetov, profsoyuzov, klubov* (How to Organize an October Demonstration. Handbook for October Commissions, for Workers in Political Education, Trades Unions and Workers' Clubs), Moscow–Leningrad, 1927

ARTICLES IN RUSSIAN   *1957 to the present*

Alyansky, S. M., 'Vstrechi c Blokom' ('Encounters with Blok'), *Novyi mir* (New World), 1967, no. 6, p. 183

Annenkov, Yu. P., 'Shtrikhi vospominanii' ('Touches of Reminiscence'), *Nedeliya* (The Week), 1966, 10–14 April, p. 4

Bibikova, Irina M., 'Kak prazdnovali desyatiletie Oktyabrya' ('How they celebrated the Tenth Anniversary of the October Revolution'), *Dekorativnoye iskusstvo SSSR* (Decorative Art of the USSR), 1966, no. 11, pp. 4–8

Bibikova, Irina M., and Raikhenstein, A., 'Moskva v 1918 godu' ('Moscow in the Year 1918'), *Dekorativnoye iskusstvo SSSR* (Decorative Art of the USSR), 1965, no. 11, pp. 39–43

Efimov, A., 'Prizvannoye revolyutsiei' ('Called by the Revolution'), *Yuzhnyi khudozhnik* (The Southern Artist), 1980, no. 4, pp. 6–9

Gerasimov, S. V., 'Pervoye prazdnestvo Oktyabrskoi revolyutsii' ('The First Festival of the October Revolution'), *Iskusstvo* (Art), 1957, no. 7, pp. 44–45

'Gorod i prazdnik' ('The City and the Festival'), accounts from artists and designers themselves, *Dekorativnoye iskusstvo SSSR* (Decorative Art of the USSR), 1976, no. 2, pp. 6–11

Kamensky, A. A., 'Prazdnik – teatr ideala' ('The Festival as the Theatre of the Ideal'), *Dekorativnoye iskusstvo SSSR* (Decorative Art of the USSR), 1978, no. 11, pp. 29–34

—, 'Russkiye prazdniki Borisa Kustodiyeva' ('The Russian Festivals of Boris Kustodiev'), *Dekorativnoye iskusstvo SSSR* (Decorative Art of the USSR), 1980, no. 6, pp. 39–45

Khodasevich, V. M., 'Massovye deistva, zrelishcha i prazdniki' ('Mass Actions, Spectacles and Festivals'), *Teatr* (Theatre), 1967, no. 4, pp. 12–13

—, 'Gorod-teatr, narod-akter' ('The City as a Theatre, the Masses as the Actor'), *Dekorativnoye iskusstvo SSSR* (Decorative Art of the USSR), 1979, no. 11, pp. 44–47

Lunacharsky, A. V., 'Ob otdele IZO' ('Concerning the IZO Section'), with a commentary by A. Ermakov, *Novyi mir* (New World),

1966, no. 9, pp. 247–48

Matveeva, V., 'Pervye sovetskie znamena' ('The First Soviet Banners'), *Dekorativnoye iskusstvo SSSR* (Decorative Art of the USSR), 1977, no. 11, pp. 46–47

Mazaev, A. I., 'Massovye revolyutsionnye prazdnestva 20–x godov' ('Mass Revolutionary Festivals of the Twenties'), *Dekorativnoye iskusstvo SSSR* (Decorative Art of the USSR), 1966, no. 11, pp. 2–4

—, 'Khudozhestvennaya sreda revolyutsionnoi epokhi' ('The Artistic Environment of the Revolutionary Epoch'), *Dekorativnoye iskusstvo SSSR* (Decorative Art of the USSR), 1977, no. 11, pp. 18–29

Mezhuev, V., 'Rozhdenie novoi kultury' ('The Birth of the New Culture'), *Dekorativnoye iskusstvo SSSR* (Decorative Art of the USSR), 1977, no. 11, pp. 1–17

Nemiro, O. V., 'Oformlenie Petrograda k pervoi godovshchine Oktyabrya' ('The Decoration of Petrograd for the First Anniversary of the October Revolution'), *Iskusstvo* (Art), 1964, no. 11, pp. 41–46

—, 'Khudozhestvennoe oformlenie massovykh prazdnikov' ('Artistic Design of the Mass Festivals'), *Iskusstvo* (Art), 1965, no. 11, pp. 43–51

—, 'Khudozhniki Petrograda – revolyutsionnym prazdnikam' ('Artists of Petrograd – to the Revolutionary Festivals'), *Iskusstvo* (Art), 1967, no. 10, pp. 52–56

—, 'Lenin i revolyutsionniye prazdniki' ('Lenin and the Revolutionary Festivals'), *Iskusstvo* (Art), 1969, no. 10, pp. 2–6

—, 'Vospitanniki i pedagogi Akademii khudoshestv – oformiteli revolyutsionnykh prazdnestv' ('Educators and Teachers of the Academy of Arts as Designers of Revolutionary Festivals'), *Iskusstvo* (Art), 1976, no. 11, pp. 39–42

—, 'Dekorativnoye iskusstvo i prazdnichnyi gorod' ('Decorative Art and the Festive City'), *Iskusstvo* (Art), 1978, no. 8, pp. 63–69

Okhlopkov, N., 'O stsenicheskikh ploshchadkakh' ('On Stage Areas'), *Teatr* (Theatre), 1959, no. 10, pp. 36–58

Raikhenshtein, A., 'Pervyi prazdnik Oktyabrya v Moskve' ('The First Festival of the Revolution in Moscow'), *Iskusstvo*, (Art), 1967, no. 12, pp. 50–57

Rozhdeistvensky, K. I., 'Zadachi sovetskogo oformitelskogo iskusstva' ('The Tasks of the Soviet Art of Design', *Dekorativnoye iskusstvo SSSR* (Decorative Art of the USSR), 1974, no. 8, pp. 12–14

Shishlo, B., 'Ulitsy revolyutsii' ('The Streets of the Revolution'), *Dekorativnoye iskusstvo SSSR* (Decorative Art of the USSR), 1970, no. 3, pp. 4–13

Sidorov, A. A., 'Pervye shagi sovetskogo iskusstvovendeniya' ('First Steps of Soviet Art History'), *Iskusstvo* (Art), 1976, no. 1, pp. 44–47

—, 'Iskusstvo 20–x godov i ego mastera' ('The Art of the Twenties and its Masters'), *Iskusstvo* (Art), 1977, no. 11, pp. 66–67

Stifel, B., 'Romantika pervykh let' ('The Romanticism of the First Years'), *Dekorativnoye iskusstvo SSSR* (Decorative Art of the USSR), 1959, no. 11, p. 6

Strigalev, A. A., 'Beseda Lenina c Lunacharskom o monumentalnoi propagande' ('Lenin's Conversations with Lunacharsky on Monumental Propaganda'), *Iskusstvo* (Art), 1968, no. 4, pp. 29–30

—, 'Proizvedeniya agitatsionnogo iskusstva 20–x godov' ('Products of Agitational Art of the Twenties'), *Iskusstvo* (Art), 1968, no. 5, pp. 43–48

—, 'Oformlenie prazdnikov i monumentalnaya propaganda v revolyutsionnom Petrograde' ('The Design of Festivals and Monumental Propaganda in Revolutionary Petrograd'), *Iskusstvo* (Art), 1978, no. 4, pp. 44–48

—, 'Svyaz vremen', ('Link of the Times'), *Dekorativnoye iskusstvo SSSR* (Decorative Art of the USSR), 1978, no. 4, pp. 1–2

Editor's note: Russian-speaking readers pursuing research in this field are recommended to refer to the two-volume Soviet publication from which the present book derives, *Agitatsionno-massovoye iskusstvo. Oformleniye prazdnestv, 1917–1932* (sic), compiled by Irina M. Bibikova and N. I. Levchenko, ed. Vladimir P. Tolstoy, published by Iskusstvo, Moscow, 1984. This contains numerous supplementary documents and a further bibliography of 85 articles of the period from 1917 to the early 1930s.

BOOKS AND ARTICLES IN ENGLISH ON REVOLUTIONARY FESTIVALS AND RELATED TOPICS

Anikst, M., and Chernevich, E., *Soviet Commercial Design of the Twenties*, London and New York, 1987

Bojko, Szymon, 'Agit-prop Art: The Streets were their Theater' in S. Barron and M. Tuchman, eds, *The Avant-garde in Russia 1910–1930: New Perspectives*, Cambridge, Mass., 1980, p. 72–77

Elliott, David, *New Worlds: Russian Art and Society, 1900–1937*, London and New York, 1986

Fitzpatrick, Sheila, *The Commissariat of Enlightenment: Soviet Organization of Education and the Arts under Lunacharsky*, Cambridge, 1970

Fueloep-Miller, René, *The Mind and Face of Bolshevism*, London and New York, 1927

Guerman, Mikhail, *Art of the October Revolution*, Leningrad, 1981

Lane, Christel, *The Rites of Rulers: Ritual in Industrial Society – The Soviet Case*, Cambridge, 1981

White, Stephen, *The Bolshevik Poster*, New Haven and London, 1988

List of Illustrations

Index

Index